D0990216

A gift has been made by:

Jean & Rob Robinson

In memory of

Nathan Gray

The Routes Not Taken

The Routes Not Taken

A *trip through* NEW YORK CITY'S UNBUILT SUBWAY SYSTEM

JOSEPH B. RASKIN

ESE

EMPIRE STATE EDITIONS
AN IMPRINT OF FORDHAM UNIVERSITY PRESS
NEW YORK 2014

Copyright © 2014 Fordham University Press

All rights reserved. No part of this publication may be reproduced, stored in a retrieval system, or transmitted in any form or by any means—electronic, mechanical, photocopy, recording, or any other—except for brief quotations in printed reviews, without the prior permission of the publisher.

Fordham University Press has no responsibility for the persistence or accuracy of URLs for external or third-party Internet websites referred to in this publication and does not guarantee that any content on such websites is, or will remain, accurate or appropriate.

Fordham University Press also publishes its books in a variety of electronic formats. Some content that appears in print may not be available in electronic books.

Library of Congress Cataloging-in-Publication Data

Raskin, Joseph B.
    The routes not taken : a trip through New York City's unbuilt subway system / Joseph B. Raskin.
        pages cm
    Summary: "A history of unrealized plans to expand New York City's rapid transit and commuter rail systems"—Provided by publisher.
    Includes bibliographical references and index.
    ISBN 978-0-8232-5369-2 (hardback)
  1. Subways—New York (State)—New York—Design and construction—History.
  2. Subways—New York (State)—New York—History.   I. Title.
    TF847.N5R37 2014
    388.4'2097471—dc23   2013018741

Printed in the United States of America

16   15   14   5   4   3   2   1

First edition

For Nicholas and Natalie, who never fail to fill me with pride,
my parents, who have never owned a car,
and Karli, who has had to put up with a lot while I was writing this book.

CENTRAL ARKANSAS LIBRARY SYSTEM
ADOLPHINE FLETCHER TERRY BRANCH
LITTLE ROCK, ARKANSAS

Contents

Preface

"This is the D train to Curtiss Airport. Next stop, Gun Hill Road."

My desire to tell the story of the New York City's unbuilt subway lines and the efforts to bring subway service to the areas not now served by rapid transit began by accident more than twenty years ago.

At that time, I was working in the Queens borough president's office, handling transit issues. The Archer Avenue line was opening, and would use old track ramps running from the Queens Boulevard line east of the Van Wyck Boulevard station.

Those ramps had always been there and I had no clue as to why. There had been a few articles in the *Long Island Press* and other newspapers about a third platform that had been built above the Roosevelt Avenue–Jackson Heights station on the Queens Boulevard line for a line that was going to be built to the Rockaways, but I had never seen anything written about the ramps.

This was intriguing. I read through the collection of New York Board of Transportation plans in the borough president's map room. These materials concerned the subway lines and stations that were built in Queens and the other four boroughs of New York City.

There was also an envelope containing a map. It looked like an old subway map, except that it included much more than the subway lines that were in operation at the time and the elevated lines that had been demolished over the years. The map also showed other lines, stretching across the entire width of Queens, as well as parts of Manhattan, the Bronx, and Brooklyn, that were never served by subways.

It was a copy of the 1929 plan for the expansion of the subway system, known today as the "Second System." This was even more intriguing. I made a copy of the map and showed it to my dad. One of the lines on the map was an extension of the Concourse line that crossed Bronx Park, and traveled along Burke Avenue and Boston Road into the Northeast Bronx. He grew up on Adee Avenue, a block to the south of Burke Avenue.

He remembered the plans for the Burke Avenue line and told a story about seeing work being done there in advance of its construction. During the 1930s, when he was a teenager, he saw people working for the Board of Transportation doing preliminary engineering work along Burke Avenue (see Chapter 8). He followed them as they did their work, asking many questions (knowing him, he undoubtedly had a lot of serious questions, but also a lot of wise guy comments).

We lived in the Rochdale Village housing development in southeastern Queens. The Metropolitan Transportation Authority had been planning to build an extension of the

Queens Boulevard line past Rochdale as part of the 1969 "New Routes" program, a further extension of the Archer Avenue line. The Southeast Queens line, as that route had been designated, would have turned south from Archer Avenue, gone under the future home of my alma mater, York College, and along or adjacent to the Long Island Rail Road's Far Rockaway branch, past Rochdale, to its terminal stop at Springfield Boulevard, by Springfield Gardens High School, my old school. There would have been four stops on the line; one of them would have been at Baisley Boulevard, two blocks from my building.

The MTA built the Archer Avenue segment of the line and opened it on December 11, 1988. They also built the part of the line that ran under York College's campus (which is now used to store trains). The tunnel ran toward South Road, a block below the campus and right across the street from the LIRR.

That's where the construction stopped. The Southeast Queens line went the way of most lines proposed in previous decades, a victim of the financial crisis that crippled the economy of New York City and State in the 1970s.

Preliminary engineering work had been done for the entire length of the Southeast Queens line. I found this out on a visit to the Archives of the New York Transit Museum, where I discovered preconstruction photographs, including a number of images of a large field on the other side of the LIRR tracks from Rochdale Village.

This was completely engrossing and led to my obsession with doing research on the plans to expand the New York City subway system. The most famous of these lines is the (until now) unbuilt 2nd Avenue subway, but that's just one part of a much larger story. Other lines had equally long and colorful stories. I visited the various libraries in the New York metropolitan area to find microfilm editions of old newspapers to look for articles on the old plans and documents pertaining to those lines, and learned about a part of the history of the New York transit system that I had never known of before.

The year 2004 marked the centennial of the opening of New York's first subway line, the inaugural route of the Interborough Rapid Transit Company. In the following century, that one line, running from City Hall to Harlem, expanded into one of the largest and most heavily traveled rapid transit systems in the world. Its development spurred the expansion of New York City's population from concentrated areas adjacent to downtown to its farthest reaches. On a number of occasions it could have taken on different and more substantial forms.

There were demands to expand the subway system even before the first lines opened. This resulted in a series of proposals for construction of new lines or expansion of existing ones. The city and state governments, the various agencies and authorities that administered operation of the transit system, and civic, business, and transit-oriented organizations put these plans forth.

Some plans never got beyond the planning, preliminary design, or engineering phases before being halted. Others proceeded further. There are tunnel and station segments throughout the New York City subway system built for lines that were never completed. A platform under the IRT's Nevins Street station has remained unused for over a century. Other proposals underwent radical changes before they were actually built.

No proposal for a line enjoyed an easy path from inception to implementation. In most cases, my question actually was how lines have ever *been* built, rather than why they *weren't*. This was due to a range of political, economic, and logistical concerns that beset every project. How the government and governing agencies responded to these concerns led to the subway system taking on its present form.

Economic conditions affected proposals to expand the system. One plan, the second phase of the IND system, was made public in 1929, six weeks before the stock market crashed (this plan contained the original proposal for the 2nd Avenue line, long the symbol of dashed dreams for an expanded subway system). Plans released in the late 1960s were starting to move forward when the city and state were hit by the financial crisis of the 1970s, forcing cessation of the work.

Long-term plans for the system were deferred in the interest of meeting urgent short-term needs. Plans for the construction of the 1940s and 1950s versions of the 2nd Avenue line were sacrificed to carry out necessary work to upgrade existing subway lines and rolling stock, even though voters approved a transportation bond issue in 1951 that was specifically meant to finance construction of new lines. Several plans failed to proceed due to heavy political opposition over such wide-ranging issues as who would operate the new lines, or whether some would be built as elevated lines.

An example is the Brooklyn–Queens Crosstown line, today's G train. The line as we know it was proposed in 1924 and built in the 1930s. It had first been proposed as an elevated line in the 1870s but didn't proceed, due to opposition from the business and residential communities along the route. Similar proposals met a similar fate through the early 1920s, although a very small section of the elevated line was built away from the Queensboro Plaza station in the Long Island City section of Queens. Even after the Crosstown line was proposed as a subway, it was a still source of controversy, but in a different way, as communities in Brooklyn fought to have the line built through their neighborhoods.

Some plans disappeared as they evolved into other plans that were superior to what had been proposed, enjoyed greater political support, or triggered less opposition. In other cases, elected officials and civic and business groups had the vision to see that an expanding subway system would further the economic growth of their communities.

Another unbuilt line that had particular resonance was the one planned along Utica Avenue in Brooklyn. In 1910, real estate interests in the Rugby section attempted to sell properties along Utica Avenue, using a never-built subway line as the key selling point for buying those properties. One real estate company that had made a significant investment in Rugby made a similar effort on Staten Island in anticipation of a subway tunnel from Brooklyn that was never built.

That same hope for a subway line along Utica Avenue led other property owners to attempt to create a special assessment district to finance construction of a subway line. Similar consideration was given to the creation of an assessment district to finance construction of a subway line along Nostrand Avenue in Brooklyn well to the south of its current terminal.

In the 1960s and 1970s, properties along 2nd Avenue were developed around the locations of where subway stations were planned. Zoning variances were granted for developers who would build station entrance areas into their properties. Plans for other lines proposed at that time discussed how their service areas would develop as a result of the opening of the new lines.

A number of years ago, I went into the New York Public Library at 5th Avenue and 42nd Street on a summer day and started to scan through the daily editions of the *Bronx Home News*. I was rewarded by finding a wealth of information on the efforts to build the Concourse line extension along Burke Avenue not available elsewhere. By using other libraries and resources, I was able to read newspapers like the *Brooklyn Daily Eagle* and the *Long Island Daily Press* and find how transit issues evolved on a daily basis. For most of its existence *The Brooklyn Eagle* called itself the *Brooklyn Daily Eagle*. Similarly the *New York Post* has also been called the *New York Evening Post* and the *New York Post and Home News*. The different names are used where appropriate.

As my research went on about the unbuilt lines, I learned about the passionate battles that were fought to get a subway line built, those between communities over where and how it would be built, and, ultimately, what form it would take. Familiar names would show up, albeit in a new context—Fiorello H. La Guardia, Robert Moses—but also names I had been completely unfamiliar with, such as James J. Lyons, George A. McAneny, John Purroy Mitchel, William E. Harmon, George W. Pople and Nathan Straus, Jr. I learned who Major Edward Deegan and Henry Bruckner were. Going through all these newspapers provided a much deeper understanding of everyday life in New York City decades ago.

Through my research, I was able to learn about other places and other issues that broadened my understanding of why the unbuilt lines were so important to the areas they would have served. This book is not a comprehensive study of every proposal. There have been far too many of these plans to fully recount here. What I want to do is give you a picture of some of the major proposals, the people behind them, and the times in which these initiatives were issued.

I hope all of this comes out in my telling of an earlier, less remembered time in the history of New York City.

1

Building (and Not Building) New York City's Subway System

Robert A. Van Wyck, the first mayor of the Greater City of New York, broke ground for the first subway line, near City Hall, on March 24, 1900. George B. McClellan, the third mayor of the five boroughs, officiated at its opening on October 27, 1904. It took four years, seven months, and three days to build the line from City Hall to West 145th Street in Harlem.

Things rarely went that quickly again. The *New York Times* article about the groundbreaking spoke of building extensions to areas like Staten Island "before this town is very much older."[1] It wasn't the first time, and definitely not the last, that a promise to expand the subway system went unfulfilled. More than a century later, Staten Island still awaits subway service.

For as long as there have been plans for a subway system, people have wanted to build it farther—to the city's limits and beyond. In some cases, their efforts have resulted in lines being built; other ambitions went unfulfilled. Some plans will soon achieve a degree of success after decades of failure.

A series of agencies were responsible for planning the growth and development of the subway system in the first three decades of the twentieth century.

The first was the Board of Rapid Transit Railroad Commissioners (RTC), created in 1894. As work on the first subway line was underway, the RTC considered the next steps to expand the system. On May 9, 1902, RTC President Alexander E. Orr wrote to Chief Engineer William Barclay Parsons, instructing him to begin "the preparation of a general and far-reaching system of rapid transit covering the whole City of New York in all its five boroughs."[2] Parsons developed proposals for expanding the system into Brooklyn, the Bronx, and Queens during 1903 and 1904. Parsons resigned on December 31, 1904; an overall plan was released on March 30, 1905. His successor, George S. Rice, prepared a second plan, which was released on May 12.

The RTC was responsible only for planning the lines. The responsibility for operation rested with another agency, the State Board of Railroad Commissioners. Governor Charles Evans Hughes[3] wanted one agency to regulate public transit, railroads, and all other public utilities. Despite protests that local authority was being abrogated, Hughes signed a law sponsored by State Senator Alfred R. Page and Assembly Member

Edwin A. Merritt on June 7, 1907, creating the New York State Public Service Commission (PSC). The legislation split the state into two PSC districts: the first consisted of New York City's five boroughs, and the second the rest of the state. The RTC's last act was approving construction of Brooklyn's 4th Avenue line from downtown Brooklyn to Sunset Park on June 27.

There were doubts about the PSC. "The public has heard so much of the Utilities Commission that it expects the impossible," the *New York Times* quoted an unidentified expert on transit issues saying a few weeks after they came into existence. "I believe that the new board will come in for quite a good deal of criticism before it accomplishes anything, but this does not mean that the Commissioners are at fault. If in two years the commission has improved the rush hour service on the various lines to any marked extent, it will have accomplished a great deal. The best it can do in the next few months will be to improve the midday, Theatre hour, and early morning service."[4]

The 4th Avenue line was included in a proposal made to the RTC by Brooklyn Borough President Bird S. Coler in 1906. He called for a line to be built from Pelham Bay Park to Fort Hamilton and Coney Island, running along Westchester Avenue, Southern Boulevard, and 138th Street in the Bronx, 3rd Avenue and the Bowery in Manhattan, and Flatbush Avenue and 4th Avenue in Brooklyn after crossing the Manhattan Bridge. A branch would run to Coney Island via 40th Street, New Utrecht Avenue, 86th Street, and Stillwell Avenue.[5] The New York Board of Transportation would use this concept four decades later in plans for the 2nd Avenue Trunk Line. In 1906 this was the start of what would eventually become the first major expansion of the subway system.

Rice expanded on Coler's proposal, proposing that ten new subway lines be built to serve Manhattan, the Bronx, and Brooklyn by 1916. Rice thought that Queens would be well served by trolley service through the Belmont Tunnel, then approaching completion (but not put into service for eight years as a subway tunnel, used by the Flushing line), and over the Blackwell Island's Bridge, which would open in 1909 as the Queensboro Bridge.[6] This led to the release of the PSC's first major plan, the Tri-Borough Plan.

The heart of that plan was the Broadway–Lexington Avenue line, running from the Battery to Woodlawn and Pelham Bay Park in the Bronx. The Tri-Borough Plan would begin to build toward subsequent plans, containing elements of the Lexington Avenue, Broadway, Jerome Avenue, Pelham, 4th Avenue, West End, and Brooklyn–Queens Crosstown lines.

The Tri-Borough Plan was not well received. The Flatbush Taxpayers Association protested the lack of a Nostrand Avenue line.[7] The Queens Borough Transit Conference protested that its borough had been ignored. "We will resort to the courts if necessary if Mayor [William Jay] Gaynor and the Board of Estimate and the Public Service Commission insist on developing the outlying sections of Brooklyn and the Bronx at the expense of Queens," said the Conference Chairman, James J. O'Brien.[8]

Figure 1-1. The routes of the Tri-Borough Plan. (Queens Borough Chamber of Commerce)

Mayor Gaynor had qualms. The PSC wanted the Tri-Borough Plan lines built as a system independent of the IRT (Interborough Rapid Transit Company) and the BRT (Brooklyn Rapid Transit Company). Gaynor wanted to base the subway system's expansion on extensions of existing lines. This difference in philosophy lasted for years and affected the Tri-Borough Plan. When the time came to open bids for constructing and operating its lines, the PSC found that no one submitted offers. Moreover, the IRT and BRT appeared to be dragging their heels on extending their lines.

It wasn't until William Gibbs McAdoo sought to link the Tri-Borough routes with his Hudson and Manhattan Railroad system and further expand them[9] that the IRT and BRT considered expansion. In January 1911, a committee from the Board of Estimate consisting of Manhattan Borough President George A. McAneny, Bronx Borough President Cyrus C. Miller, and Staten Island Borough President George Cromwell met with the PSC and began the process that led to the issuance of the Dual Systems Contracts in 1913.

The IRT and BRT maneuvered back and forth to gain authorization to operate the lines that the Committee and the PSC were considering, offering to operate all or many of the new lines. Both companies staged PR campaigns to gain favor with both the general public and elected officials.

When the PSC approved the Dual Systems Contracts in March 1913, plans to extend service to northeast Queens, Staten Island, and along Utica Avenue in Brooklyn were deferred—permanently, as events turned out. Construction of the Crosstown line, a north–south route between Brooklyn and Queens proposed by the BRT was postponed for more than a decade; when work began, it was part of a transit system operated by the Independent City-Owned Subway System (IND). Lower-level platforms and connecting tunnels that had been built at the IRT's Nevins Street station in anticipation of that company being awarded the franchise for 4th Avenue line (along with the tracks running over the Manhattan Bridge and along Lafayette Avenue in Brooklyn) have sat unused by trains for more than a century.

Nonetheless, the lines built under the Dual Systems Contracts represented the single biggest extension of the subway system to that point. The IRT would stretch farther out into the Bronx and well into Queens and Brooklyn. The BRT (later to become the BMT) would rebuild the lines they were operating in Brooklyn, expand farther into that borough and Manhattan, and extend into Queens.

However, the PSC was still viewed as slow and cumbersome, as it had functions and responsibilities beyond the transit system. In 1919, the doubts that had been expressed when the PSC took control over the transit system were still being discussed. Questions were raised as to how their operations could be streamlined. One person who thought he had an answer was New York's new governor, Alfred E. Smith. In his inaugural message Smith called for change:

There is widespread dissatisfaction, particularly in New York City, with the Public Service Commission.

In the First District, a radical change should be made in the structure of the commission itself if it is to accomplish results. At the time of its formation in [1907] there was expressed grave doubt as to whether or not it would work out well. There were many who believed that the function of constructing rapid transit railroads for the City of New York should be divorced from the function of regulating public utility corporations generally. In my opinion experience has demonstrated that they were right.

For years the trend in New York City, as well as in the state, has been towards single headed commissions to the end that the responsibility may be fixed upon one man. During the recent war the Federal Government taught us the lesson that results may be best obtained by a single executive clothed with proper power when any great work is to be carried out successfully.[10]

Smith signed the legislation creating the position of transit construction commissioner on May 3, 1919, offering the post to William Barclay Parsons, then serving with

Figure 1-2. John H. Delaney in 1928. (Photo courtesy of the Queens Borough Public Library, Long Island Division, Chamber of Commerce of the Borough of Queens Records)

the army in France; Parsons declined. Smith turned to New York City's commissioner of plants and structures, John Hanlon Delaney.

Delaney is not well remembered today, but he was the dominant figure in the New York City transit system for twenty-five years. He grew up in North Adams, Massachusetts, working in the printing trades, and came to New York in 1892. In less than a decade, Delaney became the president of the Printers' Union and then moved into management. In 1913, Governor William Sulzer asked him to serve in the New York State government as an efficiency expert. Mayor John F. Hylan appointed Delaney commissioner of plants and structures in 1918. A year later, he became transit construction commissioner, supervising the construction of the subway system, with Smith promising a more hands-on approach to advancing transit capital programs.

John Delaney was a political insider who developed a strong knowledge of transit issues. More than two decades before the consolidation of the subway system, he saw the virtues of unification.[11] In 1921, the *New York Times* wrote that Delaney "worked in accord with the Board of Estimate and with all of the influential Democrats in the city. Much of his time in office was occupied in studying the transit problem, and he was soon recognized as an expert on the subject. He gets along famously with the traction [subway] officials as well as with the city officials, and it was understood that his plan for solving the traction problem was the practical solution of the matter."[12]

Delaney appointed Daniel Lawrence Turner, another major figure in the history of the subway system, to the position of chief engineer. He had worked for the Board of Rapid Transit Commissioners and the PSC as the original parts of the subway system were being built. He followed Delaney to the Board of Transportation and would later work with the New York State Transit Commission, the North Jersey Transit Commission, and the Suburban Transit Engineering Board. He would also play a major role in the development of the Regional Plan Association's *Plan for New York and Its Environs* in 1927.

Turner had the task of developing plans to expand the subway system. He knew the need to start planning. "Since the Dual System contracts have been under construction, the attention of the Public Service Commission and of the Transit Construction Commissioner necessarily has been devoted to the completion of these contracts," Turner wrote. "But it has been recognized that a new transit program was imperatively necessary. Therefore, in the Fall of 1919, which was as early as the commissioners permitted, I undertook to formulate a comprehensive transit plan. . . . The time has now arrived when we must look ahead again and provide plans for and begin the work of construction on the enlargement of the rapid transit system."[13]

The plan Turner drew up, released in September 1920, would be ambitious at any time in the history of the transit system. He laid the foundation for the subsequent plans to expand the system, envisioning the development of the outer regions of all five

Figure 1-3. Daniel L. Turner in 1929. (*Brooklyn Daily Eagle*)

boroughs. His belief was that transit should be built ahead of development, anticipating growth, rather than reacting to it.

Turner called for five new trunk lines and nine new crosstown lines in Manhattan, eight new lines or extensions in the Bronx, thirteen new lines or extensions in Queens, fifteen new lines or branches in Brooklyn, and five new lines to serve Staten Island over a twenty-five-year period. Over 830 miles of new routes would be built in the city, carrying five billion riders over the course of a year, more than double the number of route miles in today's subway system. By comparison, the 1929 plan for the second phase of the IND, the most famous of the unrealized plans, would have added just over one hundred miles in new and extended lines, and lines "recaptured" from the IRT and BMT.

Delaney thought Turner's plan was needed, because "in about another ten years the whole dual system will have been saturated with traffic."[14] Even in 1920 street congestion was a concern: "The growth of traffic per annum has been consistently greater than the per capita growth of the city per annum . . . the new transit plan takes into consideration the fact that vehicular and pedestrian traffic on the street surface is increasing to such an extent that it will soon be regarded as inadvisable to continue surface passenger traffic, either on the main arteries of travel or on the main cross streets, and that surface passenger transportation must be replaced by elevated or subway, with more cross-town 'tie-lines' operated on a platform device or by shuttle car service."[15]

Delaney and Turner's efforts were sidetracked after the 1920 elections, in which Nathan C. Miller defeated Governor Smith. Miller had a different idea for running the transit system. Citing the close links that Delaney and Lewis Nixon, Smith's appointee as commissioner for utility regulatory issues, had with Tammany Hall, Miller wanted to establish a new state agency to oversee transit issues. He proposed the New York State Transit Commission.

Mayor Hylan led the opposition to the proposal, characterizing Miller's plan as attacking home rule: "The creation and the power of the proposed new transit board is opposed to the best interests of the city and to sound public policy, in that it would mean the revising and the rewriting of franchises without giving the city any voice in the matter."[16]

The State Senate passed legislation creating the Transit Commission on March 16, 1921; the State Assembly approved it on March 22. George A. McAneny, who had played a significant role in drawing up the Dual Systems Contracts as Manhattan borough president and president of the Board of Aldermen, was appointed to serve as chairman.

Mayor Hylan and the city government never fully accepted the Transit Commission's authority, beginning three controversial years that stopped transit planning and construction cold. John P. O'Brien, the city's corporation counsel (who would serve as mayor in 1932), wrote to Delaney on April 22, ordering him to stay in office and maintain his papers. The city sought an injunction in court. O'Brien contended that the Transit Commission had no legal standing to take over the city's franchises.

Justice John W. McAvoy of the State Supreme Court denied O'Brien's request, stating that there was no legal basis to prevent the Transit Commission from operating. (This was not the last time that McAvoy would be embroiled in the fight between the city government and the Transit Commission. In 1924 and 1925, he led an investigation of that issue that led to the downfall of the Hylan administration.) After managing the mayor's reelection campaign in 1921, Delaney returned to the city government when Hylan appointed him docks commissioner that December. He also became Hylan's unofficial transit adviser.

Turner became the Transit Commission's consulting engineer and prepared several plans for the expansion of the rapid transit and commuter rail system. Not to be outdone, Hylan and the city government issued a plan in 1923 that built on the lines proposed in the Transit Construction Commission plan and began work on a controversial mixed passenger and rail freight tunnel connecting Brooklyn and Staten Island, which was opposed by the Transit Commission and later stopped by state legislative mandate in 1925.

CITY'S GROWTH DISCOUNTED IN PLANS FOR ADDING 830 MILES OF TRACK TO RAPID TRANSIT SYSTEMS

Work to Cover Period of Twenty-five Years and Cost $350,000,000—New Lines and Extensions Would Provide for a Population of Nine Millions and Carry Five Billion Passengers

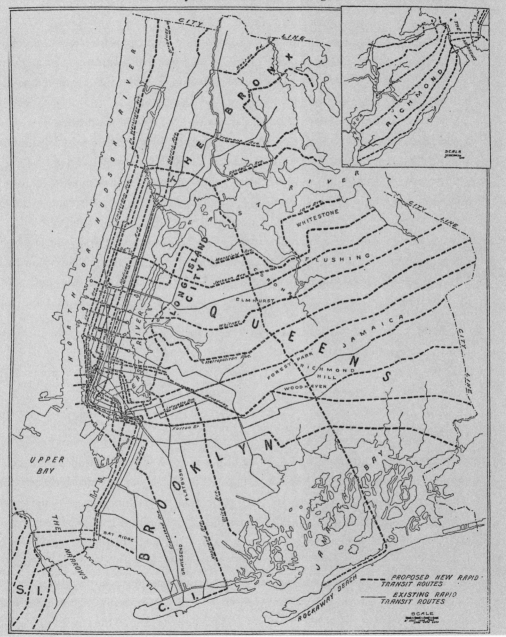

Figure 1-4. The *New York Times* published this map of the Transit Construction Commission's plan on October 6, 1920.

In 1922 Alfred E. Smith returned to the governor's office and the Democrats won control of the State Senate. A day after Smith was sworn in, Mayor Hylan called for the establishment of a city commission to replace the state's Transit Commission. John Delaney was rumored to be slated to chair the city commission; he was also reported as being the author of the bill calling for it.[17] It was sponsored in the State Senate by the majority leader, James J. Walker, who later succeeded Hylan as mayor, and the Assembly's minority leader, Charles D. Donahue.

The Republicans in the Assembly resisted, opposing municipal ownership of the subway and surface lines. Hylan was often quoted as saying that he would not build any new lines for the IRT or the BRT.[18] This deadlocked consideration of the Walker–Donahue bill and prevented completion of the Flushing, Nassau Street, and 14th Street–Canarsie lines and the planning of new subway lines. Assembly Republicans drafted their own legislation, sponsored by George N. Jesse of Manhattan, giving the Board of Estimate authority over subway construction, but not regulatory control over the system.[19]

Debate over the two bills continued through 1923 and into 1924. Assembly Republicans offered a compromise bill on February 6, 1924. It offered the city the control Hylan wanted, with the condition that the city-owned lines eventually become self-sustaining.

At a Senate–Assembly conference attended by Governor Smith and John Delaney, ostensibly representing Mayor Hylan, an agreement was reached on legislation that greatly resembled the Assembly's bill. Asked if Hylan would support this agreement, Delaney replied:

I do not know. I will have not been in conference with the Mayor since the compromise was reached. If the Mayor takes my advice, he will accept the bill.

His approval is not necessary. It becomes binding on the city the moment it is signed by the Governor. In passing upon this agreement I was acting not for the Mayor, but as a technical umpire at the request of Senator Walker and Assemblyman Bloch, Democratic leader of the Assembly.[20]

Hylan accepted the agreed-on legislation, which made the city responsible for completing the remainder of the Dual Systems Contracts lines, but not without objections. He complained that while it gave the city the right to build new subways it didn't allow city voters to authorize raising $275 million above the city's debt limit to do so (an issue that would repeatedly affect later mayors). Hylan was asked if he had authorized Delaney to accept the deal, and he replied, "I didn't authorize anyone to accept anything. But no doubt he accepted he best possible deal they could get, which means practically nothing."[21]

The Assembly passed the bill on April 11. Assembly Member Victor R. Kaufman took the occasion to fire back at Hylan: "It will be a great pleasure to bring Mayor Hylan out from his cover of darkness and make him do something for the people of New York City instead of continuing to make a political issue out of it. The people of New York are wise to everything the Mayor has done over the last five years."[22]

After the State Senate approved the legislation Governor Smith signed it into law on May 2. Mayor Hylan announced that John Delaney would be chairman of the Board of Transportation on May 6. He served in that role for the next twenty-one years, overseeing the completion of the Dual Contracts, the construction of most of the IND, and the unification of the subway system.

Although Delaney had close ties to the Democratic Party's power structure in Tammany Hall, he worked closely with Fiorello H. La Guardia. Delaney served in five consecutive mayoral administrations. He survived changes in four separate Democratic administrations controlled by Tammany Hall and the scandals that engulfed the New York City government in the early 1930s, and served through La Guardia's three terms.

The Board of Transportation officially began operations on June 1. Hylan warned them to be cautious of the civic and business groups and newspapers that were increasingly critical of him. They began from scratch with planning new subway lines, ignoring the Transit Commission's proposals, and released the initial plans for the first phase of the Independent Subway System on December 9, 1924.

The IND's first phase was the start of a long series of plans released by the New York Board of Transportation (BOT) over twenty-eight years to expand the rapid transit system. The IND's second-phase plan, issued in 1929, was the first to include the 2nd Avenue Trunk Line. Other lines reflected Daniel L. Turner's view that rapid transit should expand ahead of population growth.

One route proposed in 1929 was the South 4th Street / South Queens Trunk Line. It was clearly intended to have the same impact in Brooklyn and Queens that the 2nd Avenue Trunk Line would have had in Manhattan and the Bronx. In fact, it may have been more ambitious than the 2nd Avenue plan.

The trunk line began in Manhattan as an extension of the 6th Avenue–Houston Street line, using its two middle tracks east of the 2nd Avenue station and a spur of the 8th Avenue line, running from the Canal Street station and across Worth Street and East Broadway. These routes formed the trunk line in Williamsburg at a station connected with the Brooklyn–Queens Crosstown line's Broadway station. Running eastward across Brooklyn and Queens, three spur lines would branch off: the Utica Avenue–Crosstown line to Sheepshead Bay; the Fresh Pond Road / Winfield line, running north to connect with the Queens Boulevard line at the Roosevelt Avenue–Jackson Heights station; and the Rockaway line, creating new lines running to Far Rockaway and Riis Park. The BOT proposed a fourth branch in October 1930, connecting with the Crosstown line at the Bedford–Nostrand station.[23]

The trunk line would cross southern Queens, meeting the Van Wyck Boulevard branch of the Queens Boulevard line as it ran along 120th Avenue, terminating in Cambria Heights at Springfield and Foch Boulevards (now Linden Boulevard). Many of the streets the trunk line would operate along were narrow. It is possible they would

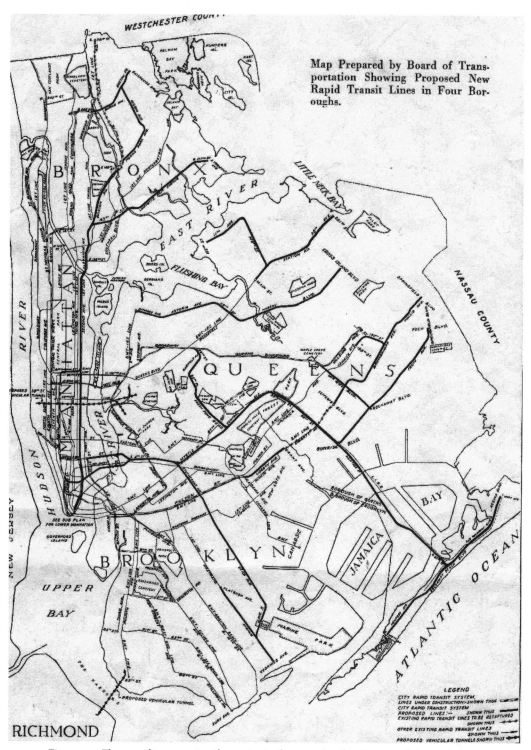

Figure 1-5. The map diagramming the routes in the 1929 plan for the second phase of the Independent Subway System. (*Queensborough Magazine*)

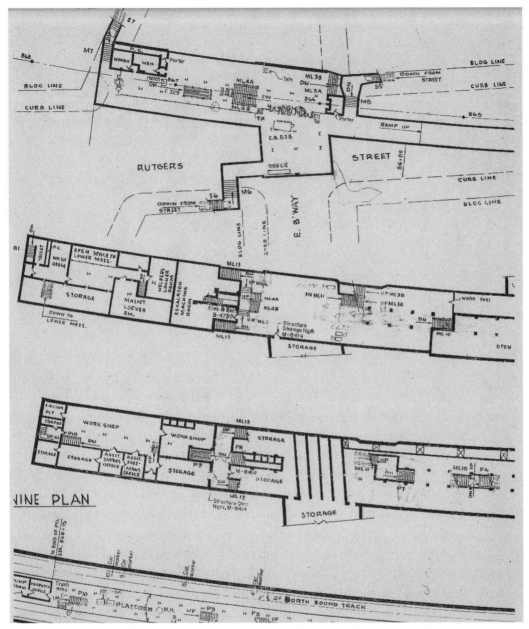

Figure 1-6. A diagram of the East Broadway station on the 6th Avenue–Houston Street line showing the space left for the Worth Street line to pass through. (Courtesy of the New York Transit Museum Archives)

have been widened, turning into thoroughfares similar to the Grand Concourse or Queens Boulevard, thereby affecting the development of those areas.

The plan to elevate sections of proposed lines in the Bronx, Brooklyn, and Queens elicited storms of opposition; the proposal to build the South Queens Trunk Line as a *subway* along Myrtle Avenue in Ridgewood and Glendale did the same. "Myrtle Avenue

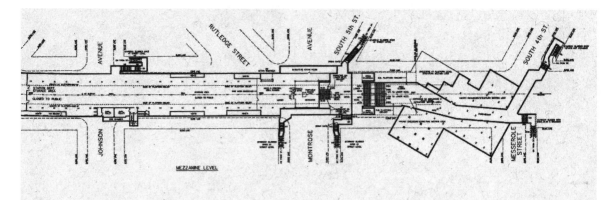

Figure 1-7. The mezzanine of the Broadway station on the Brooklyn–Queens Crosstown line in Williamsburg was built to allow for transfers to the unbuilt South Queens Trunk Line. (Courtesy of the New York Transit Museum Archives)

means to Ridgewood what Fulton Street means to Brooklyn," Martin Gehringer of the Manufacturers Trust Company said at a BOT hearing on February 17, 1930. "It would mean financial ruin to the merchants if a subway were to be constructed along Myrtle Avenue. The erection of the Fourteenth Street–Eastern District subway line along Wyckoff Avenue resulted in many failures of merchants on that avenue. With the present high rents and the loss of business, due to necessary obstructions in building[,] the subway conditions on Myrtle Avenue would be even more disastrous than those on Wyckoff Avenue."[24] Another speaker, Herman Gohlinghorst, opposed the line because construction would interfere with sewer trunk lines on that street.[25]

The 1929 plan was the only time that the BOT proposed building the full South 4th Street / South Queens Trunk Line. Components of the plan were included in BOT capital plans from 1938 and 1945. The Fresh Pond Road / Winfield line and the Crosstown line connection were never again proposed. The Houston Street and Worth Street lines continued to be proposed to connect with the Utica Avenue–Crosstown line. The South Queens segment would become part of the plans for the Fulton Street subway, which was slated to be connected with the Fulton Street El in the 1929 plan.

This was also the only time extensions of the Jamaica Avenue and Fulton Street Els were contemplated by the BOT, instead of the Queens Boulevard line, something done in all their later plans through 1945. The Board proposed to extend and link the lines along two narrow streets, Hollis and Brinkerhoff Avenues, in eastern Queens. Beginning with its 1932 plan, the BOT proposed to extend the Queens Boulevard line along Hillside Avenue to Springfield Boulevard, and later proposed further extending it to Little Neck Road (now Parkway), a short distance from the city line.

The Board proposed building an entirely new line to the Rockaway Peninsula in 1929, serving more of that area than did the Long Island Rail Road's Rockaway Beach branch.

The LIRR had made overtures to sell its line; the BOT and the Board made its interest in buying the line known a day after releasing its plan.[26] Discussions between the BOT and LIRR continued while the Board tried implementing the second-phase plan. There was very strong interest on the Rockaway Peninsula for buying the LIRR line. Most of the two hundred speakers at the Board's hearing on the Rockaway proposal on February 17, 1930, supported the purchase, so much so that Commissioner Daniel L. Ryan asked one of the speakers if he was speaking for the LIRR.[27]

People in the Rockaways believed it would take less time and money to purchase the LIRR and connect it with the subway system than it would to build a new line. Their strong response may have affected the BOT. Commissioner Francis X. Sullivan told *The Wave*, the Rockaways' weekly paper:

> You have the evidence that the Board is trying to give you relief. We have proposed a definite route; that was the first step. Next we held a hearing, which was the second step. Now the third step was taken by the injection of the Long Island Railroad purchase.
>
> We certainly shall investigate to determine the cost of this acquisition. That cost will be compared with the cost of paralleling the route as shown in our plan.[28]

The BOT made acquisition of the Rockaway Beach line part of the capital plan that superseded the 1929 plan in February 1932. They filed plans to purchase the line with the Board of Estimate that December. The Board of Estimate voted to "put it on the rapid transit map for consideration,"[29] but didn't formally approve the purchase. This vote was taken in the waning days of the short-lived mayoralty of John P. O'Brien, elected to fill out the remainder of James J. Walker's second term (a corruption scandal forced his resignation). It was intended to leave formal approval to the incoming mayor, Fiorello H. La Guardia.

Planning was underway for the subway line connecting with the Rockaway Beach branch, designated Route 119-F. A spur line would connect it with the Queens Boulevard line's local tracks in Rego Park, built with tunnel portals east of the 63rd Drive–Rego Park station. This rendered irrelevant some work that had already been done at the Roosevelt Avenue–Jackson Heights station for the line connecting with the South Queens Trunk Line, including construction of a third platform on the mezzanine level.[30] The LIRR spent $500,000 to facilitate that connection from its end;[31] the BOT would charge a fifteen-cent fare in the Rockaways to pay for the purchase of the Rockaway Beach branch and construction of the connection.

Mayor La Guardia wanted the matter reconsidered. It was referred back to the BOT on March 23, 1934, just when it seemed that progress was being made. The financial burden was too great. Depression-era economics had affected the BOT's ability to build anything.

"For Rockaway transit, the city would have to spend $32,000,000 to buy the Rockaway Branch of the Long Island Railroad," City Comptroller W. Arthur Cunningham told the Queens Borough Chamber of Commerce. "It would require an expenditure of an additional $15,000,000 for equipment for rapid transit operation of this line. I see no way for carrying out this project this year or next. It would not be practical for the city to own and operate this line under present conditions."[32] The BOT would continue to discuss purchasing the Rockaway Beach branch again, but more than twenty years would pass before it actually became part of a subway line, with a different link to the system than what initially had been discussed.

The Board issued smaller capital plans in 1932 and 1937, reflecting the economy and reacting to the 1929 plan. Elevated lines weren't discussed. Beginning in 1938 and continuing through 1952, when the New York City Transit Authority replaced it as the agency operating the transit system, the Board released a series of ambitious plans on an almost yearly basis—in three cases, twice in a year.

The plans changed yearly, reflecting changes in priorities and political pressure. A route would be highly ranked, rise, fall, or disappear. The 1932 plan marked the start of when the BOT began active consideration of acquiring commuter rail lines for use as subway lines, which would have a major impact on the Northeast Bronx and the Rockaways. Because the Board experienced major difficulty in finding money for the IND's first phase, little was done beyond planning work.

With the first phase of the Queens Boulevard line apparently nearing its expected completion in 1936 (it actually had fifteen years to go), the La Guardia administration and the BOT considered what to do, particularly in Queens. The mayor issued proposals calling for the purchase of the Rockaway Beach line, express service on the Flushing line, extending that line to Bayside, extending the Queens Boulevard line to eastern Queens, and constructing the Van Wyck Boulevard extension of the Queens Boulevard line (with track ramps used a half-century later for the Archer Avenue line).[33] La Guardia wanted the BOT to acquire the BMT's Culver line in Brooklyn to connect with the IND's Smith Street line, to connect the BMT's Fulton Street elevated line in Queens with the Fulton Street subway, and to acquire the Rockaway Beach line from the LIRR.[34]

This was a step toward the BOT's later capital programs. It issued a new plan in 1937 and began to prioritize its proposals a year later. Its first priority in 1938 was finding a new home, taking advantage of properties where there had been demolition work in order to facilitate construction of the 6th and 8th Avenue subway lines. Chairman Delaney concluded a letter to the Board of Estimate introducing the 1938 list with caveats about financing these projects, points that would be repeated in similar form each year. He hedged the Board's bets:

This board is aware that the present financial resources of the City are not sufficient to permit the adoption at this time of any considerable part of this future program,

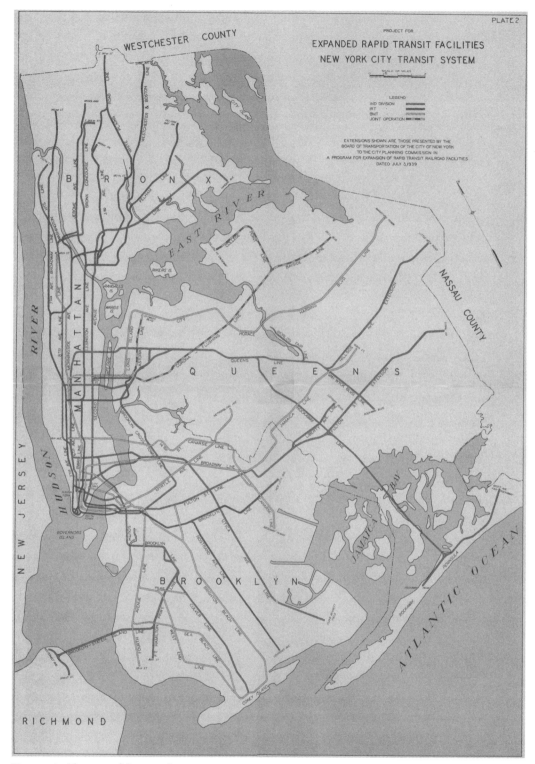

Figure 1-8. The map of the 1939 plan.

but it is of the opinion that the City Planning Commission and the Board of Estimate should have before them a comprehensive outline of what this Board deems to be the most useful development of transit facilities during the coming years.

These proposed projects are arranged generally in order of priority and upon the assumption that rapid transit unification will be effected in the near future. Changes in the City's financial condition or in the volume of rapid transit travel, or delay in the consummation of unification, may cause this program to be amended during succeeding years, and therefore it should not be regarded as rigid and inflexible.[35]

The BOT submitted plans without providing a financial strategy or expressing much desire to fight for them. It was a self-fulfilling prophesy of failure. In the years to come, Robert Moses would always have a plan for funding his proposals in place and was ready to do battle to achieve his goals, representing a major difference in mind-set.

Between 1938 and 1945, the Board proposed building a line between Staten Island and Brooklyn. The 1938 and 1939 proposals differed sharply from previous plans, featuring a link with the 4th Avenue line south of the 59th Street station. A line was planned to meet with the IND's Smith Street line near the Church Avenue station. This would allow trains to travel to Staten Island from the northern parts of the Bronx or eastern Queens via the 2nd, 6th, or 8th Avenue or Crosstown lines.

This would bring subway service to Staten Island, but it's questionable if riders would be happy. Trains would follow an indirect route requiring a much longer trip than would a connection with the 4th Avenue line. That concern may have occurred to the BOT, since the route they proposed from 1940 through 1945 restored the link with 4th Avenue.

A second component of the Smith Street line extension remained after the Board returned to planning for a 4th Avenue–Staten Island connection. This was the 10th Avenue line, a route sought by groups in southwest Brooklyn for over a decade. As the 1929 plan evolved, the Allied Subway Campaign, representing a coalition of groups from that area, sought the construction of a line to fill the gap between the West End and 4th Avenue lines.

The 10th Avenue line wasn't a component of the 1929 plan, but the Allied Subway Campaign continued its efforts and the line was included in the BOT's 1938 capital plan. Initially planned to branch away from the Staten Island line at Fort Hamilton Parkway and 65th Street and continue to 86th Street in Bay Ridge, it remained as a separate line from 1939 to 1945. One reason why was that it had a champion on the City Council, Edward Vogel, who represented southern Brooklyn on the Council from 1940 to 1960.

Vogel and the Allied Subway Campaign wanted to break their subway service away from the bottleneck at the BMT's DeKalb Avenue station. They wanted a connection with the IND, which was expanding into Brooklyn. One way was to connect the Smith Street and Culver lines. The Culver line, then a branch of the BMT's West End line, couldn't provide adequate service to his constituents (and it limited the number of trains that could run along the West End line). The other way to do that was building the 10th Avenue line. Vogel tried to accomplish both.

He staged rallies in support of his cause and held a City Council hearing on October 15, 1940, to ask why the line wasn't higher on the BOT's priority list. In 1942, he put a motion before the Council to make scrap metal available to the City Council in exchange for prioritizing construction of the Culver–Smith Street line connection, which had slowed to a stop after ground had been broken for it on June 10, 1941.[36]

Vogel's efforts brought him into conflict with Bronx City Council Member Joseph Kinsley, who was advocating for an extension of the IND's Concourse line into the Northeast Bronx via Burke Avenue. In 1940 Vogel proposed a resolution calling on the BOT to extend the Smith Street line to Coney Island via the Culver line. Kinsley accused him of having a "selfish attitude" and offered an amendment that would have given the Bronx "proper provision to meet its unification needs before Brooklyn could get a new subway." The vote on Kinsley's amendment, which was expanded to include Queens, produced a tie; City Council President A. Newbold Morris broke it, supporting Vogel.[37]

Kinsley and Vogel clashed again in 1942 over a resolution calling for a scrap metal exchange benefitting the Culver line. While claiming to be one of Brooklyn's "best friends," Kinsley said the Council had given Brooklyn enough and the Bronx had been "short changed on transit lines in favor of other boroughs. I am unable to understand why the resolution should specify Brooklyn alone."[38] "Heaven help our good borough from our Bronx friends," Vogel responded. He eventually got improved subway service for his area, but it wouldn't happen until the 1950s, when the Smith Street and Culver lines were connected.

Two capital plans were issued in 1942. The first, released on June 30, followed up on work that was underway or required immediate action. The second, sent to the City Planning Commission on July 28, was the 1944–48 Postwar Plan, establishing long-term goals for subway system expansion.

While efforts to expand the subway system went on, other parts were contracting. Elevated lines ceased operation and were demolished in the eleven-year period between the extension of the Queens Boulevard line from the Union Turnpike–Kew Gardens station to the 169th Street station in 1937, and the Fulton Street subway between the Broadway–East New York (now Broadway Junction) and Euclid Avenue stations in 1948.

In Manhattan, the 2nd Avenue and 6th Avenue Els were gone as was most of the 9th Avenue El. All that remained were the 3rd Avenue El and the section of the 9th Avenue El needed to link the Jerome Avenue line with the Polo Grounds in Manhattan and the New York Central Railroad's Putnam branch in the Bronx. The BOT wanted a ten-block extension to link the Jerome and Lenox Avenue lines, but that never happened.

In Brooklyn, the Fulton Street and 5th Avenue Els were gone; the Lexington Avenue El remained in service, but only until 1950. The elevated tracks that ran over the Brooklyn Bridge, connecting Lower Manhattan and the BMT's network of lines, were removed. The tracks on the Queensboro Bridge connecting the Flushing and Astoria lines and the 2nd Avenue El service were gone.

Some lines were redundant due to subway construction, but the els provided services that weren't replaced. The remaining lines needed rehabilitation, but the BOT didn't act. The lines deteriorated, leading to the conditions justifying demolition of the 3rd, Myrtle, and Lexington Avenue Els and the remainder of the 9th Avenue El. One of the reasons given for not building a connection between the 9th Avenue El and the Lenox Avenue line in the late 1950s, requiring the construction of a ten-block-long line, was that it cost too much to upgrade that small stretch of line to justify the work.[39]

Two plans were again released in 1945. The first contained the BOT's yearly priorities. The second, made public in August, the 1944–48 Postwar Plan's successor, was as ambitious as the original. However, as postwar economic realities set in, the BOT's plans were scaled back.

As the Second World War drew to a close, the tenures of Fiorello La Guardia and John Delaney ended. La Guardia chose not to run for a fourth term in office. He expected the Republican, American Labor, and Fusion Parties, the coalition that elected him, to support Newbold Morris as his successor. The Republicans, joined by the Fusion and Liberal Parties, endorsed Jacob Goldstein, a judge with Democratic ties. The American Labor Party supported Brooklyn District Attorney William O'Dwyer, the Democratic candidate (O'Dwyer was the Democratic candidate against La Guardia in 1941). Morris refused to accept this, and with La Guardia's support he formed the "No Deal" Party to continue his run. O'Dwyer won in a landslide.

Delaney retired as BOT chairman on October 21, and La Guardia named Major General Charles P. Gross to replace him. Gross (1889–1975), a Brooklyn native, served in World War I with the U.S. Army Corps of Engineers, won a Purple Heart, and was chief of the Army Transportation Corps during World War II. At the same time, La Guardia also appointed City Collector William Reid to the Board.

La Guardia expressed concerns about the transit system's financial needs. The five-cent fare remained sacred, and the BOT's debt load was growing. The mayor pointed out that a choice would have to be made—raise the fare or further overload the city's

Figure 1-9. Major General Charles P. Gross in 1943. (*Brooklyn Eagle*)

budget. This would, in turn, affect the BOT's abilities to finance the operation and further growth of the system.[40]

When La Guardia swore Gross in on December 1, he said, "If you think war is hell, then you have something waiting for you on this job."[41] Gross knew that. Upon his appointment, Gross remarked, "New Yorkers will have to decide sooner or later the kind of subway that they want. I'll do my best to give it to them."[42]

Sound to Shore

2

THE UNBUILT BROOKLYN–QUEENS CROSSTOWN LINE

The Brooklyn–Queens Crosstown line was part of the IND's first phase. Its first segment, between the Queens Plaza and Nassau Avenue stations, opened on August 19, 1933; the second, connecting with the Smith Street line at the Bergen Street station, opened on July 1, 1937.

A much different route was originally planned. The Crosstown line was first proposed in 1878, after Brooklyn Mayor James Howell appointed a Rapid Transit Commission. Howell, the other elected officials, and advocates for the development of a transit system, such as the *Brooklyn Daily Eagle*, saw how the first elevated rail line, the 9th Avenue El, would affect New York City.[1] An *Eagle* editorial discussed Brooklyn's needs:

> Rapid transit is no longer a speculative matter in New York City. It is now a fact accomplished. The first train over the Gilbert Elevated Railroad was run yesterday. The time occupied in going from Trinity Church to Fifty-eighth street was seventeen minutes. It is not necessary to dwell upon the value of this enterprise to people engaged in business down town, and forced by the pressure of commerce upon the city to find homes in the vicinity of Central Park and beyond it. Apart from the accession of manifest comfort which the new road brings to travelers between the extraction of the city, the saving in time to thousands of people will be about two hours daily. In other words, the gain to the home life of those persons amounts to a full day every week. This immense contribution to the means of movement in our sister city must tend to reawaken interest in rapid transit in Brooklyn.[2]

The Commission, chaired by Felix Campbell, reported to Howell on June 1, 1878. Much of what they proposed became the lines operated by the Brooklyn Rapid Transit Company at the start of the twentieth century. They saw the need for a rapid transit system in Brooklyn:

> That rapid transit of some kind in Brooklyn has become even now necessary, admits of no doubt. The outlying districts of Brooklyn can by the scheme of transit, which we shall bring to your notice in a future communication, be brought nearer, in point of time, economy of transportation and convenience to the business part of New York City, by way of the bridge, than can the upper part of the island on Manhattan

by the steam transit road now being inaugurated there [the 9th Avenue Elevated]. But to effect this there should be a feeling on the part of our authorities that this consummation is most desirable, and toward which, in the material interest of their constituencies and the prosperity of the whole city, they should labor.[3]

The Commission proposed a route running from Myrtle Avenue to Newtown Creek along Franklin, Wythe, and Manhattan Avenues and Commercial Street and Avenue in Williamsburg and Greenpoint. The *Eagle* called this route the Crosstown line, most likely giving the line its name.[4] Another line running through this area was planned to operate between Fulton Street and Broadway via Nostrand and Lexington Avenues. The Fulton Street Elevated was the main component of the 1878 plan, running from East New York to the Brooklyn Bridge, then five years away from opening.

There was opposition from Brooklyn's business community. "There is such a thing as the defacement of a city," said W. C. DeWitt, a representative of Fulton Street property owners:

It would occur if an elevated railroad were put on the Strand, London, or the chief boulevard in Paris, or Broadway and Fifth Avenue, New York or Fulton Street, Brooklyn . . .

. . . The business of the [Fulton Street] stores is not distant, but in the vicinage. It is not transported, it is local. New York [Manhattan] lies upon a long tongue of land and with remote commercial relations, the customers of her stores demand rapid transit to overcome long distances. Brooklyn is spread out like a fan, and the home customers of her stores do not need the appliances of elevated railroads. Hence, the leading merchants in Brooklyn oppose elevated railroads on Fulton Street. The entire business of elevated railroads in Brooklyn will consist in transporting people to and from New York; such railways will, therefore be an unmitigated evil to the abuttor.[5]

The Kings County Elevated Railway and Brooklyn and Long Island City Railway Companies were among those making proposals to operate lines. Commissions appointed by Howell and his successors, Seth Low, Daniel D. Whitney, and Alfred C. Chapin, evaluated routes. The Fulton Street and Myrtle Avenue lines were approved on December 26, 1885.

Travel patterns in and out of Brooklyn forever changed when the Brooklyn Bridge opened in 1883. The bridge did make it easier to get to New York City, but what DeWitt didn't foresee was how easy it became to get to Brooklyn, resulting in a major change and expansion of that city's residential and business communities.

The Fifth Rapid Transit Commission identified more routes in March 1886, including the Crosstown line and the 5th Avenue and Broadway–Brooklyn elevated lines. These lines were adopted on April 13; the Brooklyn Board of Aldermen gave approval for the Brooklyn Union Elevated Railroad Company, one of the BRT's predecessors, to begin construction work on the lines on July 7.

Protests stopped the Crosstown line. Greenpoint business owners and Rev. Patrick O'Hare, the pastor of St. Anthony's Roman Catholic Church, met with Mayor Whitney on August 3. They claimed that Greenpoint's main street, Manhattan Avenue, was too narrow for an elevated line and that the construction of such a line would harm businesses and private properties.[6] These objections were echoed at a meeting of Franklin, Wythe, and Division Avenues property owners on September 17. The New York State Supreme Court did allow a commission to be established to condemn land along Franklin and Wythe Avenues for construction work.

A hearing was held on October 12. Several people spoke in opposition, claiming that the noise and smoke from the trains would depreciate the value of the adjoining land.[7] They felt that surface lines provided enough service. Rev. O'Hare said trains passing his church would interrupt services and prevent clergymen from resting after night calls. George Palmer, a real estate agent, spoke against moving the line closer to the waterfront on Kent Avenue; he thought it would interfere with the operation of the manufacturing plants in the area.[8]

The hearing continued on October 20. General George W. Wingate,[9] representing the railroad, presented its organizational papers. A reporter, Timothy J. Dyson of the *Brooklyn Union*, spoke for the line, stating that it would improve property values in the surrounding area and keep businesses from leaving Brooklyn. There was little support provided beyond this testimony.[10]

The Rapid Transit Commission approved the 5th Avenue El in January 1887. This route would run from Fulton Ferry to Sunset Park. It would later be extended to Manhattan over the Brooklyn Bridge and south to Bay Ridge along 3rd Avenue.[11] The Commission and the railroad had no enthusiasm for building the Crosstown line due to the opposition it attracted.[12]

The Kings County Elevated Railway appealed the awarding of the Fulton Street El's franchise to the Court of Appeals, winning the rights on March 23, 1887. Brooklyn Union wanted to build the Crosstown line, but given the opposition they experienced, they wouldn't specify the exact route. Kings County had no interest.[13]

The Brooklyn Union Elevated Railroad Company conceded nothing. "The Court holds as to the other routes substantially to build on Fulton Street, according to the papers that were laid before the Court," Wingate said. "So without desiring to commit myself to any positive action, I should say that the decision has taken away from us the right to built on Fulton Street. I am not prepared to say just what our company will do, except that we shall build wherever we can."[14]

Francis Kernan, a referee appointed by the State Supreme Court on June 15, supported Wingate. Brooklyn Union retained the right to build the remaining routes. At the end of his term, Whitney was asked to appoint another Rapid Transit Commission;

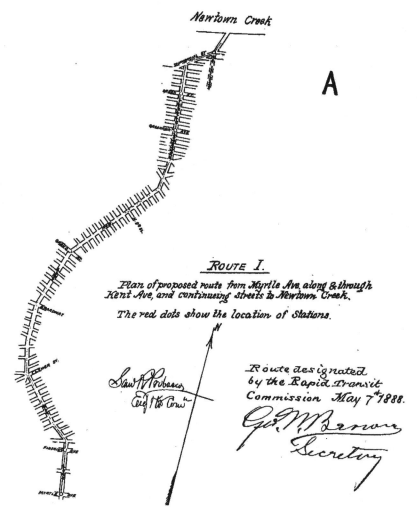

Figure 2-1. The 1888 plan for the Crosstown Elevated.

he deferred to his successor, Alfred C. Chapin, who appointed the members on February 4, 1888. This commission wanted to focus on the Fulton Street, Myrtle Avenue, and Crosstown lines. In view of the earlier opposition, it stepped back from building the Crosstown line on Wythe Avenue, beginning a process to determine a more acceptable route.[15]

The route of the Crosstown line changed, with a significant part running on Kent Avenue, one block to the west of Wythe Avenue, closer to the industrial part of Williamsburg and Greenpoint. Nostrand Avenue was considered for the route's southern leg, but this plan experienced opposition from area residents and businesspeople.

The Myrtle Avenue line began service on April 10, 1888. The Commission supported building both the Crosstown line, operating between Myrtle Avenue and Newtown Creek on Kent Avenue and Franklin and Commercial Streets, and the Broadway–Brooklyn line.

The Fulton Elevated Railroad Company filed incorporation papers on July 7 identifying station locations. Brooklyn Union maintained interest in the Crosstown line, still wanting to use Wythe Avenue as the main part of the route. They also wanted to use Franklin Avenue, a significant part of most proposals for the next three decades, as part of the route.

The Board of Aldermen's Railroad Committee issued a report on December 11 that favored granting the franchise for the two routes under study to Fulton Elevated. The route appeared set, but it still experienced opposition. Opponents of the plan testified at a hearing of the Commission on January 10, 1890, set up by the State Supreme Court to evaluate Fulton Elevated's proposal. William Jay Gaynor, later mayor of New York City,[16] objected because the Crosstown and Myrtle Avenue lines would be run by two different companies, not allowing for connections between the lines. He presented a petition from property owners on Kent Avenue and Franklin Street and a statement from both the DeCastro and Donner and the F. W. Wurster sugar refining companies.[17]

A week later, representatives of the sugar refining plants along the East River discussed the difficulty their companies would experience in shipping and receiving goods if an elevated line was built along Kent Avenue.[18] At a third hearing, on January 25, Gaynor presented petitions and a copy of the original Brooklyn Union plan to show that there was little difference between the current one and what was so strongly rejected three years earlier. No one spoke for the plan.[19]

The Supreme Court's Commission ruled against the Fulton Elevated plans on February 8. The arguments about the lack of connections with other lines and the impact the Crosstown line would have had on the operation of the manufacturing district were telling.

There was little interest in the Crosstown line for many years. The Ninth Rapid Transit Commission's report in March 1890 created the network of elevated lines extending from the Brooklyn Bridge that would be operating when the first subway lines opened. More parts of Brooklyn were now open for development, setting an example for communities in other parts of New York City of how rapid transit could influence their own development.

Brooklyn was one of New York City's five boroughs in a new century when the Crosstown line was again considered. In May 1902, the Board of Rapid Transit Commissioners authorized Chief Engineer William Barclay Parsons to prepare plans for new lines. Writing to Seth Low, once Brooklyn's mayor, now mayor of Greater New York, Commission President Alexander E. Orr noted:

> It was not the intention that the plan should be prepared for immediate execution; but it was the expectation that if a general scheme was wisely prepared, rapid transit construction would proceed upon the lines so laid down as rapidly as the needs of the city and the amount of private capital ready for such investments would permit . . .

. . . The necessity for undertaking this general study of the rapid transit situation in the city was made all the more evident by the fact of the enormous increase in passenger travel on all existing lines in the year 1903. The statistics clearly indicate that when the present subway system now under construction from Brooklyn to the Bronx is completed, it will almost be immediately congested, so that no great amount of permanent relief can be counted on from that source. In order to meet the growing and immediate demands for increased facilities it is evident to the Board that new lines should be laid out and put under construction as soon as possible.[20]

Parsons and George S. Rice, his successor, both proposed new versions of the Crosstown line as part of a network of lines covering Williamsburg, Greenpoint, Bushwick, and Bedford–Stuyvesant that led to the creation of the 14th Street–Canarsie line.

Parsons's plan extended the Crosstown line into Queens as an elevated spur of the Brighton Beach line from its connection with the Fulton Street El at Franklin Avenue,[21] operating along Franklin Avenue, Wallabout, Gwinnett, and Lorimer Streets, and Manhattan Avenue in Brooklyn, and Vernon and Jackson Avenues in Queens to the Blackwell's Island Bridge. A northern extension would run along Debevoise Street (now 31st Street) to the Long Island Sound.[22] Rice didn't include the Franklin Avenue connection—running from the Williamsburg Bridge Plaza to the Blackwell's Island Bridge via Driggs and Manhattan Avenues in Brooklyn and Jackson Avenue in Queens—as a subway.

Rice incorporated the lower section of Parsons's route into a line with a component of the Crosstown line built in the 1930s. The Brooklyn and Manhattan Loop line would run on Centre and William Streets in Manhattan, and Cranberry, Pineapple, or Montague Streets to Willoughby Street, then Flatbush Avenue to Lafayette Avenue in Brooklyn. Rice wanted to use Lafayette Avenue in Fort Greene and Bedford–Stuyvesant as a trunk route running to Bushwick, with lines branching out in either direction. The line would use Lafayette Avenue to reach Bedford Avenue, turn toward Broadway, and connect with the elevated line there for the return trip to Manhattan over the Williamsburg Bridge.

Area property owners wouldn't consent to the northern extension of the route to Queens, as required by the New York State Rapid Transit Law. The New York State Public Service Commission, which succeeded the RTC as the governing body for transit planning and construction, won a court order to allow work to proceed in March 1907

The Crosstown line wasn't in the PSC's Tri-Borough Plan, but that plan did incorporate the part of Rice's planned line that ran along Lafayette Avenue from Flatbush Avenue[23] to Broadway. When planning began for the Dual Systems Contracts, it included the Crosstown line as a BRT elevated route from Fulton Street to Queensboro Plaza, connecting with the BRT's Brighton Beach line on the south and the IRT and BRT at the Queensboro Plaza station.

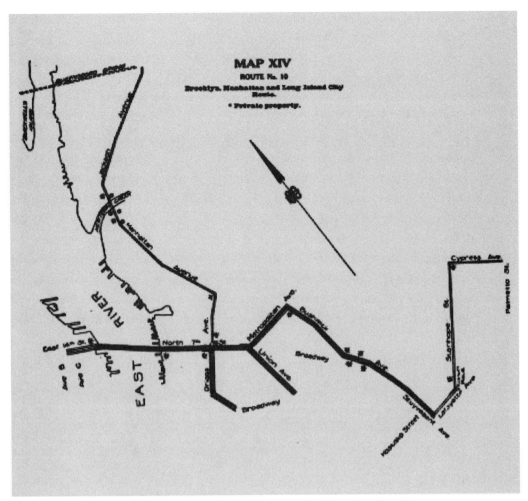

Figure 2-2. A plan for the extension of subway service to central and northern Brooklyn.

The BRT would build the Crosstown line with their own money; they had support in Brooklyn and Queens. The Crosstown Rapid Transit Committee of Brooklyn and Queens, with members representing civic and business groups, had been formed. The Queens Borough Chamber of Commerce advocated for the line. Mayor William Jay Gaynor supported it, as did the Board of Estimate's Subway Committee, chaired by Manhattan Borough President George A. McAneny.[24]

Opposition to an elevated line from community and religious groups along the route was as strong and vocal in 1913 as it was decades earlier. Despite the BRT's and PSC's claim that there was no money to build a subway, to these community groups it would be a subway or nothing. Brooklyn's newspapers were filled with articles and advertisements about the efforts of supporters and opponents of the Crosstown line throughout 1912 and into 1913. The BRT ran an extensive advertising campaign to show the benefits of building an elevated.

The BRT gave the Crosstown line lyrical names like "The Sound to Ocean Line" or "The Sound to Shore Line." One advertisement showed how Brooklyn would benefit by the rapid transit network that would develop with the Crosstown line's connections with existing lines and those in the Dual Contracts. Another countered the argument that elevated lines lowered property values by showing the positive impact of el construction in Manhattan, Brooklyn, and the Bronx. They sponsored a poll showing support for an elevated line, although the *Brooklyn Daily Times* ran a different poll to elicit support for a subway instead of an el.

The opposing groups weren't buying. The language became stronger as the Dual Contracts approached approval by the PSC and the Board of Estimate, and a series of rallies and meetings took place.

Rev. O'Hare was a strong part of the opposition to the Crosstown line in 1886. The leaders of the churches along the route played a similar role in 1913. At a meeting at the Central Congregational Church in Bedford[25] on March 22, 1912, its pastor, Rev. S. Parkes Cadman,[26] said, "We are by no means so provincial as to stand in the way of rapid transit. We want something in the nature of an up-to-date method, such as a tunnel properly built and equipped and not an archaic structure which has long ago been criticized by the public in general."[27]

Colonel Timothy S. Williams of the BRT responded:

Of the value of the line projected there is no doubt whatsoever. It seems to me that it would be a good thing for Dr. Cadman's church [located by Franklin Avenue] inasmuch as it would make it much more easier living on the general parallel from the river

Figure 2-3. Rev. S. Parkes Cadman. (*Brooklyn Daily Eagle*, July 13, 1936)

to get there. Against the complaint that there should be no more elevated roads all I can say is that the traffic would not warrant the building of a subway at $5,000,000[28] a mile, for that is what it would cost, and furthermore, would not support it if built. We think a line of some sort very necessary, and an elevated appeals to us as the sensible plan.[29]

The area's elected officials joined the pastors. State Senator Eugene M. Travis protested the BRT's advertising:

The advertisement is the result of a vivid imagination and deliberate attempt to mislead the public. The BRT wants only a connection between the Lexington Avenue and Fulton Street roads, and, through Franklin Avenue, so as to carry the crowds to the new ball grounds and to Coney Island, and is indifferent of the ruin that it will bring to my constituents . . .

. . . People are advocating beautiful Brooklyn, and committees are appointed to bring it about. Meanwhile, we are told by the Public Service Commission that we may expect a lovely, pretty elevated line through built-up parts of the borough. Consistent, aren't we?[30]

Senator Travis was not the only one to refer to Ebbets Field, then under construction. At a rally at the Bedford branch of the YMCA on May 27, its chairman, Brooklyn Young Republican Club President Darwin R. James, Jr., said, "Some time ago we were

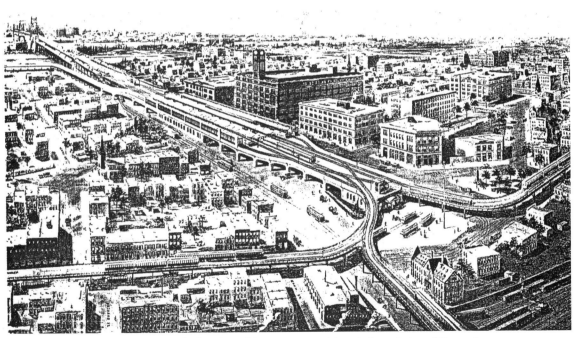

Figure 2-4. The Queens Borough Chamber of Commerce ran this artist's rendering of Queensboro Plaza in its January 1913 publication *Queens Borough*.

surprised to hear that the baseball interests had bought quite a strip of property near [Prospect Park]. That led to the inquiry as to how they were to get people to the baseball field. Those on the inside gave out the tip that there was to be a connecting line between the Lexington Avenue line and the Brighton Beach. There was not much attention paid, because it was generally shown that this was not contemplated, yet it shows what was clearly in the minds of those in favor of an elevated structure."[31]

Charles Ebbets, president of the Brooklyn Superbas, supported the Crosstown line. He went to Albany on March 26 to testify for legislation sponsored by State Senator Robert F. Wagner[32] enabling construction of the line.[33] Ebbets Field was being built in an area already served by public transit, within walking distance of two BRT stations, Prospect Park and Consumers Park (now the Botanic Gardens station). Once the Eastern Parkway line opened, it would be even more accessible. The ballpark was well served by the trolley lines crisscrossing Brooklyn, giving residents of Brooklyn the nickname "Trolley Dodgers" and his team one of its names (and the one it keeps to this day, though the franchise has moved to Los Angeles).[34] Ebbets apparently did nothing more than lobby for a transit service that would allow easier access to his ballpark; he never issued a statement in response to James's statement.

Rev. John L. Belford of the Church of the Nativity struck a theme that recurs even now:

In Manhattan they feel their cast off clothes are good enough for us; like the little fellow who has to have his clothes made over from his father's. They don't care how they feed us as long as they keep us clothed.

But the minute you cross the river you find yourself in a different atmosphere. We feel in Brooklyn as part of a first class city—and Brooklyn was a first class city before it became affiliated with New York—that we are entitled to something other than to the method of rapid transit which is provided in the present subway scheme. Elevated railroads are not only unsightly and unsanitary, but a confounded nuisance as well.[35]

The PSC held marathon hearings on the Dual Contract proposals in January 1913, giving the opportunity to many to speak for and against the overall plan and individual lines.

One of them was New York City Magistrate John F. Hylan, five years away from being elected mayor. Hylan bore a grudge against the BRT, its successor (the BMT), and other rail lines. He worked his way through law school as a BRT engineer and was involved in an accident in 1897. Hylan was fired, despite protests that he had done nothing wrong ("They should have given me an award," he complained to the *New York Times* in 1924).[36] For the rest of his career, Hylan wanted to get even. It seems incredible today that a standing judge would speak in such a forum, but he had the chance to go after the BRT: "We are not going to stand supinely by and see these contracts rushed through to protect the interests of the BRT at the expense of the people of the city and particularly of the Borough of Brooklyn,"[37] he said on January 14.

Figure 2-5. The BRT ran this ad in support of the Crosstown line on March 24, 1912.

Well over a thousand people attended the hearing on January 18 about the Crosstown line and the extensions of the Broadway–Brooklyn and Fulton Street Els into Queens. Most wanted to talk about the Crosstown line. The majority, led by Travis and Hylan, opposed the line being built as an elevated. Anyone favoring the BRT plan was

Figure 2-6. Mayor John F. Hylan.
(Wikimedia Commons)

subjected to boos and threats. PSC Chairman William R. Willcox summoned police officers to maintain order.

Hylan complained about both the overcrowding of the hearing room, doubting that everyone who wanted to speak would be heard, and the BRT's outreach efforts: "These advertisements that we have seen in the newspapers and the car advertisements are nothing but frauds . . . it is going to be used by the advocates of the elevated line and that is important. I ask that that vote be taken again. It was a fraud, nothing else."[38]

Rev. W. W. W. Wilson of the DeKalb Avenue Methodist Episcopal Church spoke: "To run this road that has been planned would be to knock out five or six churches. Our property would be seriously damaged, if not ruined. I am for the city beautiful and even if this matter did not effect our parish in any way, I would be opposed to it."[39]

Rev. Cadman supported the Dual Contracts but opposed els: "This monstrous scheme would be a degradation to the community. This does not belong to the general scheme, and should not be allowed to disfigure it and disgrace it. [The BRT] needs to be watched. . . . Reject this plan and the great majority of all residents of Brooklyn will applaud your decision."[40]

The PSC was overwhelmed by the reaction to the proposal. The State Legislature was considering legislation filed by State Senator William B. Carswell and Assembly Member Harry B. Kornobis forbidding construction of elevated lines in Fort Greene and Bedford. The PSC removed the Crosstown line from the Dual Contracts on January 29. Colonel Williams accepted their decision without protest; he thought it was more important to get the BRT's other lines built.[41] A compromise would be sought.

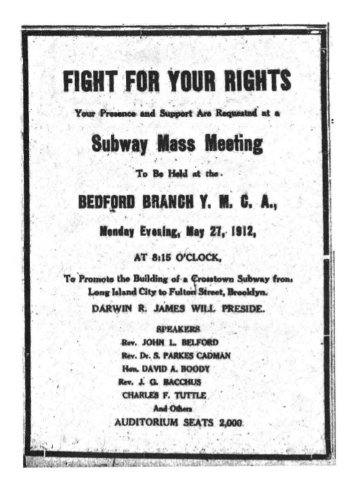

FIGHT FOR YOUR RIGHTS

Your Presence and Support Are Requested at a

Subway Mass Meeting

To Be Held at the

BEDFORD BRANCH Y. M. C. A.,

Monday Evening, May 27, 1912,

AT 8:15 O'CLOCK,

To Promote the Building of a Crosstown Subway from Long Island City to Fulton Street, Brooklyn.

DARWIN R. JAMES WILL PRESIDE.

SPEAKERS
Rev. JOHN L. BELFORD
Rev. Dr. S. PARKES CADMAN
Hon. DAVID A. BOODY
Rev. J. G. BACCHUS
CHARLES F. TUTTLE
And Others
AUDITORIUM SEATS 2,000

Figure 2-7. On May 25, 1912, the *Brooklyn Daily Eagle* ran this ad for the May 27 rally.

The Carswell / Kornobis legislation was passed on February 25 with virtually no opposition. With Mayor Gaynor's support, Governor Sulzer signed the bill into law on March 25.[42]

The Crosstown Subway League held a banquet at the 23rd Regiment Armory on March 4 to honor the pastors who had led the fight. Dr. J. Richard Kevin addressed the feelings in the affected communities:

> Not long ago, the peace and serenity of this neighborhood was stirred by the attempted invasion of [the BRT] to destroy our homes, to desecrate our churches, to sever the ties of friendship, which were welded by the chains of years to disorganize a neighborhood which was built on the solid foundation of civic pride and loyalty.
>
> This naturally aroused a protest so strong and loud that its echo reverberated to every section of the city, and our state and city officials listened patiently to our demands and came to our rescue.[43]

All the speakers promised to apply the energy given to opposing els to build a subway; planning began anew.

A new route was announced early in 1914. It would run underground from the existing Franklin Avenue line through Bedford, as an elevated through Williamsburg, and underground through Greenpoint, becoming elevated again to cross Newtown Creek and Long Island City to connect with the Astoria and Flushing lines at Queensboro Plaza. The elevated structure at Queensboro Plaza would be built to allow for the connection.[44]

PSC Chairman Edward McCall knew financing was a problem. "The financial condition of the city is the only barrier to immediate action on this crosstown route," he said at a PSC hearing at City Hall on October 8, 1913. "Can we find an honorable way immediately to put this project in course of construction[?] That is the only issue that confronts us."[45] Similar statements came from the Board of Estimate's Subway Committee. "Your committee is prepared to approve this plan," George A. McAneny, now the Aldermanic president, told his colleagues on June 30, 1914. "But we wish to make it clear that the approval carries with it no promise of construction. It simply places the line on the map. Neither your committee nor the Public Service Commission is in a position to state when this line will be built."[46]

Despite McCall's concerns, the PSC approved the line the next day without indicating when the line would be built or when the money needed to build it would be made available.

There was a plan to build the line, and a will to build it. But there was no money. A plan was advanced to build the line by assessment, taxing the property owners along the route to finance construction, but that approach encountered opposition.[47] The PSC wouldn't divert funds from building the Nassau Street line in Manhattan. The BRT, once willing to build the elevated Crosstown line with its own funds, now gave greater priority to building an express track along the Fulton Street El and linking it with the 4th Avenue and Brighton Beach lines near the DeKalb Avenue station.[48]

Building the Crosstown line became more difficult in 1917. Supported by Tammany Hall and William Randolph Hearst's newspapers, John F. Hylan defeated Mayor John Purroy Mitchel. Despite support for building the line, Hylan opposed any BRT effort to build new subways beyond the Dual Contract lines then under construction.

The subway under Flatbush Avenue connecting the Brighton Beach line and 4th Avenue lines at DeKalb Avenue opened in 1920. The section of the Brighton line between Prospect Park and Fulton Street, planned to become part of the Crosstown line, remained in service as the Franklin Avenue Shuttle.

Nothing was done beyond planning the lines that would follow the Dual Contracts. The Transit Construction Commission issued a plan during its short existence. The New York State Transit Commission, which succeeded them, came up with four sepa-

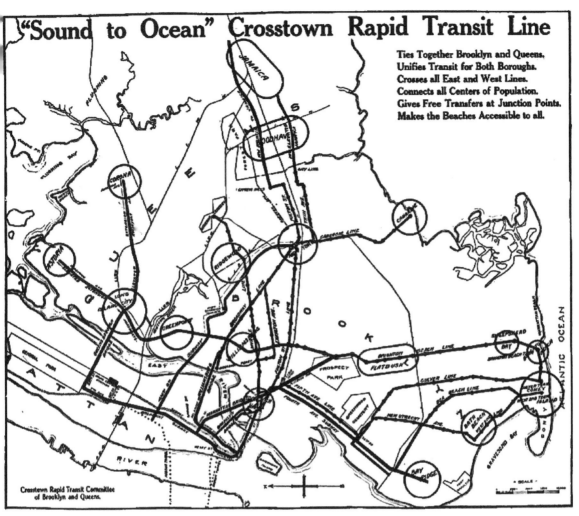

Figure 2-8. The Queens Borough Chamber of Commerce published this map in its 1920 publication *Queens Borough, New York City, 1910–1920*, showing the communities that could be reached were the Crosstown line built.

rate proposals for the Crosstown line between May 1922 and August 1923. Mayor Hylan issued a proposal in August 1923.

Hylan wasn't in a hurry to build IRT and BRT subways. He wanted a city-owned system. When the *New York Times* editorialized that New Yorkers wouldn't care who built the subways as long as they were built quickly, the mayor responded with a letter to the editor: "If the *New York Times* and the traction interests [the IRT and BRT] think that they can force me into the 'don't care' attitude, as they have done with other public officials, into spending millions of dollars of the people's money and burdening them with more millions to be put into the budget every year for a continuance of the abominable transit service given to the people every day, they are barking up the wrong tree."[49]

The Transit Commission viewed Hylan as a hindrance to building subways. George McAneny, who became Transit Commission chairman, stated in 1922, "The Mayor's plan for a new grouping of lines under municipal operation is built around his idea of recapturing the city owned sections of the dual subway. No decision could be made about the recapturable parts of the Interborough system until 1925, nor about the B.R.T. lines until 1926, in each case upon a year's notice to the operating company. That means no real decision can be made until the city administration has gone out of office, and another takes its place."[50]

The Board of Estimate approved the initial plans for the Crosstown line and the 8th Avenue–Washington Heights line on August 3, 1923. No specific connection at either end of the line was discussed, just that it would run along Manhattan and Bedford Avenues in Brooklyn.

While no BRT / BMT line was linked with the IND for three decades, the construction delay lived up to McAneny's prediction. Groundbreaking for the 8th Avenue–Washington Heights line, the first IND line, didn't take place until March 14, 1925, shortly before Mayor Hylan was defeated in the Democratic primary by James J. Walker. The line needed to survive further controversy before it was finally approved and construction would start.

Hylan adamantly opposed the BMT (the reorganized BRT) operating any line. "A connection will tie up a $44,000,000 subway proposition with the Brooklyn–Manhattan Transit corporation (formerly the B.R.T.) to be operated by that company," he wrote to the members of the Board of Estimate. "Such a connection will provide nothing but deficits to be made up by the taxpayers, in the yearly budget, in addition to the $10,000,000 which the taxpayers are now forced to provide in the budget under the present subway contracts."[51]

Figure 2-9. George A. McAneny.
(Wikimedia Commons)

Hylan wanted the Crosstown line to be a "self-sustaining"[52] spur of the 8th Avenue–Washington Heights or 6th Avenue lines across 23rd Street in Manhattan to Brooklyn, where it would run from Greenpoint to Coney Island. Shortly after the letter went out, the State Legislature enacted legislation creating the Board of Transportation, giving Hylan control over the transit process by appointing its members.

The mayor wrote to BOT Chairman John H. Delaney opposing private operation of the Crosstown line:

> The transit lines and their professional propagandists [Hylan referred to the *Brooklyn Eagle*, the *New York World*, the Brooklyn Chamber of Commerce, and other groups critical of city-operated transit lines] know that you are working on a subway line in the neighborhood of Sixth Avenue, New York, connecting there with the new Washington Heights–Sixth Avenue line, running to and through Greenpoint and across town in Brooklyn to the Flatbush and Coney Island sections of Brooklyn. They know that this line will be laid out to give the maximum of service to the people and not merely to continue the monopoly control of the present grasping traction operators.
>
> The *Brooklyn Eagle* and Chamber of Commerce headed by [Arthur S.] Somers, who is a director of the B.M.T., are continually harping on a crosstown line and endeavoring to lead the people to believe that without them that they would never get any improvement in transit, whereas their suggestions, if carried out, would result in nothing more that the perpetuation of the present private transit monopoly in the City of New York.[53]

Somers responded: "Mayor Hylan, now in his seventh year as Mayor, won his election to give more and better subways to Brooklyn and Manhattan. He has significantly failed to keep his campaign promises. . . . Now another year has passed and the action promised by the Board of Estimate last August has been nullified. Mayor Hylan, in a recent letter, announced new subway plans which will mean a continuing delay."[54]

The BOT announced its Crosstown line plan in January 1925. Eschewing Hylan's call for a connection with the 6th Avenue line at 23rd Street, it wanted a link with the Queens Boulevard line and the 53rd Street Tunnel at Van Alst Avenue (now 21st Street) and Nott Avenue (now 44th Drive) in Long Island City, which would run along Manhattan, Union, Throop and Gates Avenues in Brooklyn to connect with the planned Fulton Street subway. It wouldn't run south of Fulton Street.

Brooklyn Borough President Joseph A. Guider and Queens Borough President Maurice E. Connolly opposed the plan at the Board of Estimate in June. Guider wanted to revive the BRT's Sound to Shore plan and the Tri-Borough Plan's Lafayette Avenue line. Connolly didn't think Queens benefited sufficiently. "The routes which your Board of Transportation proposes for Brooklyn will not do at all," Guider said. "We in Brooklyn feel that the Board of Transportation has not given us the needed relief. I have alternate proposals and must insist that they be thoroughly considered. . . . Look at what Mr. Delaney suggests for Brooklyn. He shows that he does not know his territory very well. His plan does not meet the plan of my borough and is impractical."[55]

"The Brooklyn Borough President is misinformed if he thinks I do not know my Brooklyn," Delaney responded. "I have lived there for twenty-seven years and we have selected the best possible route for the borough. . . . Let me tell you men that if you want subways you've got to get busy and take some action. You can't procrastinate forever."[56]

The Board of Estimate discussed the IND on July 1. Hylan surprised Delaney by supporting Guider. Plans for other IND lines were approved; Hylan moved that the Crosstown line "be disapproved and sent back to the Board of Transportation with suggestions by the Borough President of Brooklyn for the purpose of further study and consideration."[57] The BOT was almost back to square one. When the Crosstown line was again discussed, a new mayor, James J. Walker, was in office.

The Board of Estimate met to consider the 53rd Street line on February 5, 1926, connecting the 8th and 6th Avenue and Queens Boulevard lines in Manhattan. The northern leg of the Crosstown line would link with it in Long Island City. When Lawson H. Brown of the Brooklyn Chamber of Commerce protested that his borough was shortchanged in the IND planning process, Guider reassured him: "I am satisfied with the way things are going. We will get our share. No one need worry about that."[58] Mayor Walker promised the same thing.

Borough President Guider died on September 22 from a peritonitis infection resulting from a burst appendix. His successor, James J. Byrne, sought accord with the BOT. Delaney outlined the compromise route, the Crosstown line we now know, on April 6, 1927, in the *Brooklyn Eagle*:

[The Crosstown line] will start from the heart of Queens and run across Greenpoint, Williamsburg and Central Brooklyn to Boro Hall [the Hoyt–Schermerhorn Street station, a few blocks from Borough Hall], where it will connect up with the South Brooklyn line along Smith Street. This in turn, eventually will run into and absorb the recapturable Culver line to Coney Island.

On this line there will be transfer points established at L.I. City for the 53rd Street tube, at the intersection of the 14th Street line [at the Metropolitan Avenue–Grand Street station] and at Borough Hall for trains bound to Manhattan.[59]

Delaney was asked what happened to the BOT's original plans, to which he responded, "This plan was opposed by the late Borough President Guider and rejected by the Board of Estimate which compelled me to revise the plans. . . . The present plan, which we have finally approved—will connect the Crosstown line with the local service in Queens Boulevard so that it will run to Long Island City. It will be actually a

Brooklyn–Queens line."[60] The BOT announced its plans on July 16, 1927, acknowledging the impact of the Guider's plan:

> Lafayette Avenue was the street indicated by the borough authorities as being the more desirable thoroughfare in effecting more rapid transit service by the shorter route to the Borough Hall section of Brooklyn and giving greater convenience to the territory intended to be served. While the Board of Transportation does not depart from the reasons which originally controlled in the presentation to the Board of Estimate and Apportionment, viz. Union, Throop and Gates avenues, it believes that the use of Lafayette Avenue is now proper in view of the fact that there is presented simultaneously the proposed route and general plan for the Fulton Street line to East New York.[61]

The Board of Estimate approved the plan on July 28. "We are all delighted. It is the best thing that ever happened to Brooklyn," Edward Ward McMahon of the Committee of 100, a Brooklyn civic group, commented. "The new plan meets with the satisfaction of every member of the committee and of the entire borough. All we want is to get the work started immediately, and every man who has been working on this will press this now."[62]

After close to half a century of proposals and controversy, work would begin on the Crosstown line. The long sought north–south line would be built, though differently than first envisioned.

The BOT tried to retool the Crosstown line after work started. On October 12, 1930, it announced a plan to connect the route with the South 4th Street/South Queens Trunk Line planned to extend east from Manhattan as part of the second phase of the IND. The connection would run from the Bedford–Nostrand Avenue station and swing north to merge with the trunk line in Williamsburg. It would have created a second route to southern Brooklyn and the Queens Boulevard line. This route went as far as the other second-phase lines, but the Bedford–Nostrand station was built to accommodate a connection with an eastbound line, with an extra track, two platforms, and track ramps leading away from the Crosstown line east of the station.

When service began on the full length of the Crosstown line in 1937 the BOT saw the need to extend it. It was the Queens Boulevard line's only local and there was more demand for service between Queens and Manhattan than between Queens and Brooklyn. The BOT knew the communities in central Queens would develop and that demand for service to Manhattan would only increase.

The BOT proposed a new connection between the Queens Boulevard line and the BMT's 60th Street Tunnel in 1940.[63] The Queens Boulevard–60th Street connection became one of the most important links in the subway system after it opened on December 1, 1955, so much so that the Crosstown line was cut back to the Court Square station in 2001 on weekdays and eliminated in 2010. This made room for more service from Manhattan via the connection with the 63rd Street Tunnel, which opened in 2001.

Figure 2-10. The Bedford–Nostrand station on the Crosstown line was built to allow for linkage with an unbuilt line. (Photo by the author)

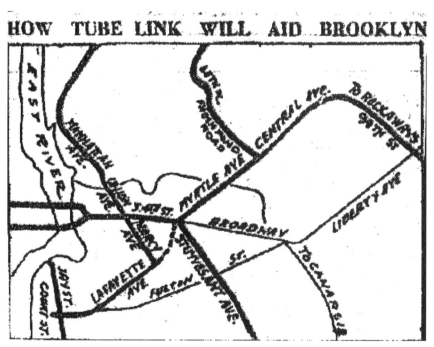

Figure 2-11. The *Brooklyn Eagle* showed the proposed Crosstown / South 4th Street Trunk Line connection on October 12, 1930.

The BOT also wanted to extend the Crosstown and Smith Street lines southward, proposing extensions to Staten Island and Bay Ridge between 1938 and 1945. Neither connection had the financing to proceed, and it was not until 1954 that a southern connection was established when the original plan for the Smith Street line, the connection with the BMT's Culver line, began service.

The "Sound to Shore" concept was revived during the 1930s and 1940s. The BOT proposed building a route from the Franklin Avenue line north to connect with the Crosstown line by the Bedford–Nostrand station. Another proposal called for building a line along 21st Street in Long Island City, meeting an extension of the BMT's Broadway line at 34th Avenue in Astoria, and then running across Queens to Horace Harding Boulevard (now the Long Island Expressway) and Marathon Parkway in Douglaston. Neither proposal had the funding to proceed.

One northern extension was actually put into service and operated for a short time. The BOT ran a spur line from the Queens Boulevard line to serve the 1939–40 World's Fair. Crosstown line trains ran from the Jamaica Yards and north to a terminal near the intersection of Horace Harding and College Point Boulevards. This was a temporary routing. The BOT asked the Board of Estimate to allow the removal of the tracks and terminal after the Fair closed.

Queens Borough President George U. Harvey objected, wanting to make the line permanent and extend it to Flushing. The borough president saw an extended line as a way to further Flushing's growth as a residential community.[64]

The BOT opposed making the World's Fair spur a permanent route. At a meeting of the Board of Estimate's World's Fair Committee at the Summer City Hall in College Point in 1937, Delaney stated, "We recommended a temporary spur from our yards between Kew Gardens and Forest Hills [New York City Transit's Jamaica Yards] because a permanent line would be useless after two years."[65]

Delaney was adamant that the spur wasn't a feasible route after the World's Fair closed in 1940:

> The only thing planned for there is a stadium, which would seat a maximum of 8,000 persons, where an occasional track meet or concert could be held during the summer months. That would mean maintaining a permanent line all year for traffic, which would be slight. As it is, the Queens Boulevard line's Woodhaven Boulevard station is only a short distance from the main portal of the World's Fair.[66] If we didn't have a lead-in from Queens Boulevard to our yards, construction of even a temporary spur would be out of the question.[67]

Delaney stated that the New York State Rapid Transit Law required that a permanent subway be built as an underground line rather than as a grade-level line. This would drastically increase construction costs.

Queens elected officials tried to keep the line operating. City Council Member Hugh Quinn discussed the issue with Delaney at a Council Finance Committee hearing. Quinn wanted to extend it to serve College Point and Whitestone. "To me it seems a waste of money to demolish this line if there is any possibility of converting it and building extensions to carry it through these two committees," Quinn said.

Delaney retorted, "The spur to the World's Fair will be utterly useless when the Fair is over next year." He continued:

> It is not suitably located for extension to Whitestone and College Point. It was built very superficially and wouldn't stand up. It is only a temporary railroad constructed at the lowest possible cost . . .
>
> . . . Rapid transit ought to be built out to Bayside and then through to College Point and Whitestone. That's been our plan for seven or eight years and I am all for it if anyone can get us the money to do it with . . .

Figure 2-12. Looking north at the tracks of the Franklin Avenue line from Eastern Parkway in 2011. (Photo by the author)

. . . It would be utterly useless and a waste of money to convert the World [*sic*] Fair into a rapid transit facility for Whitestone and College Point.[68]

The BOT, supported by Parks Commissioner Robert Moses, didn't change their opinion. Significant upgrading was needed; Moses wanted the land to build Flushing Meadows Corona Park and the Van Wyck Expressway's northern extension. The Board didn't share Harvey's enthusiasm for the area's potential. He stated that the construction work needed to make the line permanent would cost $6 million ($78.2 million in 2011 dollars, according to the inflation calculator on MeasuringWorth.com), which they felt was "an improvident waste of public funds."[69]

Harvey was correct. The neighborhoods east of the World's Fair grew. Queens College, near the terminal, opened in 1937 and would have benefited from an extended line. A second station could have been built between the World's Fair Terminal and the next stop south, Forest Hills–71st Avenue. This would have provided access to the neighborhoods that developed there. Despite the support both of community groups across northern and central Queens and of Queens College President Paul Klapper, the view of the BOT and Commissioner Moses won out, and the Board of Estimate authorized the removal of the line on December 19, 1940.

The plans drawn up in the 1930s and 1940s didn't deal with the Crosstown line's biggest problem—the need for a direct connection to Manhattan. The demand for Manhattan-bound trains has exceeded the demand for north–south service between Brooklyn and Queens. The way the line was built after adoption of the compromise plan made it impossible for Manhattan-bound track connections to be built in either borough.

Construction of the Crosstown line was a victory for the community, business groups, and elected officials who had fought for it over the course of a half century. However, what they wanted wasn't what they necessarily needed.

Why the No. 7 Line Stops in Flushing

3

The neighborhoods in Queens served by the Flushing line show the impact that rapid transit can have on residential, commercial, and industrial development. Bracketed by Hunters Point and Flushing, two of the oldest neighborhoods in Queens, the Flushing line, known to most riders as the No. 7 line,[1] went through largely undeveloped land when its first segment was built to 103rd Street and Roosevelt Avenue in Corona in 1917. When the Public Service Commission planned the route in 1911, they referred to the street that it would run along as "the proposed Roosevelt Avenue."[2]

With the Dual Systems Contracts, the PSC followed the thinking of planners like Daniel Lawrence Turner by extending the subways into the outer reaches of the boroughs instead of greater development in the interior sections of the city. William Barclay Parsons and George S. Rice hadn't seen the need for much service to Queens in the Rapid Transit Commissioners' plans in 1905. In 1900, 152,999 people lived in Queens, less than 25 percent of Brooklyn's population and less than 10 percent of Manhattan's population. They proposed construction of the Brooklyn–Queens Crosstown line into Queens only on the northern side of the borough and the extension of the Jamaica Avenue and Fulton Street lines on the south side.

The PSC's Tri-Borough Plan neglected to call for service to Queens, which didn't sit well with borough officials and business and community groups. They shared Turner's view that rapid transit should extend into less-developed areas of the city to stimulate their growth.

As the line extended along Queens Boulevard and Roosevelt Avenue, the adjoining neighborhoods—Long Island City, Sunnyside, Winfield, Woodside, Jackson Heights, Elmhurst, Corona, and East Elmhurst—experienced massive growth. What were empty expanses of land—called "cornfields" by Mayor William Jay Gaynor—became major residential communities. When the line reached Main Street and Roosevelt Avenue in Flushing in 1928, a tree-lined village dating back to the Dutch settlers in the seventeenth century became a major commercial district, the hub of the northeast Queens transit network. The 7 line's Main Street station is the biggest single interchange between local bus and subway lines in North America. However, Main Street was meant to be another stop on a line running well to the east of Flushing—a very important stop, to be sure—but not the terminal point.

Queens representatives felt they were slighted in the planning process. They wanted subways, seeing the impact that the new subway and elevated lines were having elsewhere. A group of civic leaders from the north shore of Queens met with PSC Chairman Edward M. Bassett on October 2, 1907. They were advocating for the construction of a subway line that would run from the already-constructed Steinway Tunnels[3] to Douglaston, in the northeastern part of the borough. They felt that the fare charged by the Long Island Rail Road to travel between Whitestone and the LIRR's ferries in Hunters Point[4]—thirty-three cents[5]—was too high.

One civic leader, Samuel F. Sandborn of Flushing, said the Queens population would increase by tenfold if subways were built. Clarence A. Drew talked about how Queens real estate values would benefit from subway construction. He felt that it would be cheaper to build in Queens, taking advantage of open land, than it would in Manhattan or Brooklyn.

Bassett wasn't encouraging, saying that the construction costs would be too high. The PSC's priority was building subways where congestion was greatest. He promised that the Commission would do its upmost to benefit Queens with service from the Steinway Tunnels.[6]

At a civic conference at Schuetzen Park in Astoria on November 29, 1909, Bassett discussed the borough's potential:

> The reason Queens Borough is so intensely interested in transit problems is because it is so near the City Hall in Manhattan and yet its accommodations are so limited. Within a radius of ten miles of City Hall, Manhattan has a population of 260 to the acre, while Queens has but 11 in the same area. The bridges and tunnels under the rivers at both sides of Manhattan Island tend to distribute Manhattan's congested population. These people are going into Kings County [Brooklyn] and New Jersey. Few are coming to Queens because of its poor transit facilities. But when Queens gets what it deserves it will surpass all the other boroughs. It is here that people can live in separated units, and the more its population live in units smaller than the tenement houses of Manhattan, the better will be the city.[7]

Borough President Lawrence Gresser and groups such as the Rapid Transit Committee of Queens, the Real Estate Exchange of Long Island, the Flushing Association, and the Queens Borough Chamber of Commerce campaigned to extend subways into Queens. A group of public officials including Gresser, Bassett, and Bronx Borough President Cyrus C. Miller toured Queens on April 1, 1911. From that came a plan for an elevated line connecting the previously built Steinway Tunnels, which connected between Queens and Manhattan, with Queensboro Plaza, Astoria, and Flushing.[8]

Complications ensured as planning for the Flushing line and the other Dual Systems Contracts lines continued through 1912. The biggest problem was the PSC's plan to build an elevated line into Flushing.

Figure 3-1. One of the "cornfields" Mayor Gaynor may have been talking about. This is looking east on what will be Roosevelt Avenue toward Junction Boulevard in 1913. (Photo courtesy of the New York Transit Museum Archives)

Figure 3-2. The same view today. (Photo by the author)

Downtown Flushing was a quiet place in 1912. What is now a crowded commercial district was an almost rural village. Only a few buildings from that era remain. The prospect of an elevated line was alarming.

Amity Street,[9] along which the elevated line would run, needed to be widened to accommodate the structure. The cost concerned home and property owners alike. They

Figure 3-3. New York City's five borough presidents in 1910. Bottom row (*left to right*): Alfred E. Steers of Brooklyn, Cyrus C. Miller of the Bronx, and Lawrence Gresser of Queens. Top row (*left to right*): George A. McAneny of Manhattan and George Cromwell of Staten Island. (*Wikimedia Commons*)

wanted to wait until the entire length of Roosevelt Avenue was laid out so as to share the cost of the work with the communities to the west.[10] The Flushing Business Men's Association suggested that the line swing north to Broadway (now Northern Boulevard) and Main Street. They thought the Flushing line could go farther east. Using Broadway, even then a wide street, would lower the project's cost as it wouldn't require widening Amity Street.[11]

The PSC approved the route of the Flushing line as far to the east as Wateredge Avenue[12] on December 17, 1912. It would be one of the IRT's lines under the Dual Systems Contracts. The plan was supported by the Flushing Association, a civic group. John W. Paris, chairman of its Transportation Committee (and president of the Real Estate Exchange of Long Island), said Flushing couldn't expect rapid transit service to Main Street unless the people in that community supported one specific plan. Building along Amity Street to Main Street created the most convenient route to downtown Flushing and the communities to the east of Flushing. He also foresaw that area trolley lines could be extended to Amity Street, creating a transit hub.[13] Hearings would be held in early 1913.

It seemed as if the groups in Flushing had put their qualms aside about an elevated line on Amity Street. The Flushing Business Men's Association and the Flushing Association met on December 27 about the route. George W. Pople, the president of the

Business Men's Association, noted the efforts to obtain rapid transit service going on elsewhere in the city. Given the city's resources, Pople felt that if the people of Flushing didn't articulate their needs it would take at least a decade for a line to be built.[14]

Both groups preferred a subway through their area but would accept an el. The route they wanted ran along Amity Street to Boerum Avenue (now 150th Street), south to Madison Avenue (now 41st Avenue), east to 16th Street (now 156th Street), and north to either Mathews Place (now Depot Road) or Lucerne Place (now Station Road) to 22nd Street (now 162nd Street).[15]

The two groups knew that Amity Street, fifty feet wide to the west of Main Street, needed to be widened to allow either an elevated line or subway to be built through. Borough President Maurice E. Connolly was asked to meet with Amity Street property owners to gain permission for this work. Since the project needed to be funded through assessment, they asked that the assessment area be expanded over the entire Third Ward of Queens[16] to lessen the financial burden.[17]

Representatives of the Flushing groups met with PSC Commissioner William R. Willcox on January 6 to discuss their recommendations. They claimed the Third Ward had been discriminated against. Willcox took exception, saying that some lines could be added on at one point, and others later on. He went on to say, "The Sycamore Avenue [now 104th Street] terminal is within two miles of Flushing and it should be a very easy matter later on in bringing it to your village. In fact, I intend introducing a resolution before my commission at an early date which will legalize this extension to Flushing."[18]

Pople asked Willcox if the line could be built as a subway. He said that if the people of that area wanted rapid transit in the near future they should ask for an el. While acknowledging the advantages of an underground line, Willcox acknowledged that such a line required more time and money to build.[19]

Not everyone shared that attitude. One person who disagreed was a major Amity Street property holder, Magistrate Joseph Fitch:

Amity Street is a residential thoroughfare and will remain so for at least twenty-five years to come. Look at Myrtle Avenue, Brooklyn, now that the elevated line is running there. This line has changed this street from one of the best residential sections in Brooklyn to one of the poorest tenement sections in Brooklyn. Do we want Amity Street like that thoroughfare in a few years? Thirty years from now if a man suggests an elevated line he will be laughed at.

In my opinion this line is being advocated by real estate developers who don't care what happens to Queens after they sell their land. They act like the steamship companies who bring immigrants over to America. They get their little $30 per passenger and what do they care if the men and women they bring to America fill our prisons? I am progressive in a reasonable way and I am not standing in the way of healthy progress, but I can't understand why our civic workers are advocating an elevated line through Amity Street.[20]

"Amity Street up to Union Street and beyond Central Avenue [now 149th Street] out is now mainly a business thoroughfare," countered Maynard H. Spear of the Flushing Association. "There are just four blocks between Union Street and Central Avenue that may be said to be exclusively a residential street. That, of course, is where Judge Fitch lives and owns considerable property. The judge's remark that an elevated structure would materially reduce the value of his or other property along the street is to my mind erroneous. On the contrary, I am sure it would greatly increase property values. This has been proved in numerous cases throughout the city."

"I think the judge is wrong in saying that the elevated structure through Myrtle Avenue, Brooklyn,[21] has spoiled that street," he continued. "While it may have spoiled it as an exclusive residential street, it has without a doubt greatly increased property values along the avenue and today Myrtle Avenue is one of the busiest business thoroughfares in the Borough of Brooklyn."[22]

Other property owners attended a joint committee meeting on January 9 to voice opposition. Judge Harrison S. Moore said, "The city will have to pay for changes to the property necessary for the widening of West Amity Street if an 'L' structure is to be built. Take the money necessary for these condemnation procedures, add it to the cost of an 'L' structure and you will find a subway to be cheaper. An elevated structure will do untold harm to residents of West Amity Street, who have toiled year after year to acquire their homes only to have them destroyed by an unnecessary elevated structure if this goes through."[23]

Ira Terry, the meeting's chairman, read a letter from Daniel Carter Beard,[24] who lived at Amity Street and Bowne Avenue (now Bowne Street):

[An el] would necessitate the chopping down of every tree along Amity Street, denude the whole street of foliage and then, if the elevated structure were erected it would practically occupy the whole street space level with the second stories of the buildings, making all below that level dark, dingy and disagreeable . . .

. . . With an elevated road running along Amity Street the properties would be valueless except for policy shops, chop suey restaurants or tall gloomy tenement houses tall enough to reach above the elevated tracks with rents cheap enough to induce people to endure the racket and noise of the trains in front of their windows.[25]

Judge Moore suggested that protesting property owners form their own committee. The joint committee subsequently voted to await a decision by the PSC before acting,[26] but one group began to change. Three days later, the Flushing Business Men's Association met, reelected Pople as its president, and debated a motion from Judge Fitch opposing the construction of the elevated line and calling for the construction of a subway line.

Noting that a meeting would be held with a PSC representative the next day about the line, Pople spoke about the need to proceed regardless of what would be built, using the South Bronx as an example:

> Thanks to the increase in rapid transit facilities, the price of lots at 149th Street and Third Avenue has increased from 300 to 900 percent within the past four or five years. Today that part of the city is the most densely populated part of the city and the reason for that it has both a subway [the extension of the original IRT line, now the route of the 7th Avenue line] and elevated system [the 2nd and 3rd Avenue Els], giving a five cent fare . . . Thanks to rapid transit, the assessed valuation at 149th street and Third avenue is from $6,000 to $60,000[27] a lot, 25×100 feet . . .
>
> . . . I favor a subway on Amity Street. I talked to Public Service Commissioner Willcox and he has assured me that it is perfectly feasible to have a subway out Amity Street. I am not, however, in favor of any drastic resolution as to prohibit the erection of an elevated structure on this side of Flushing Creek.[28]

James H. Quinlan supported Judge Fitch's resolution: "There is nothing at all impossible about a subway to Flushing. They are going to build a subway nine miles to the Bronx[29] to accommodate a population of 24,000. Why should it not be possible to continue a subway to Flushing from Sycamore Avenue, Corona, two and one-half miles to accommodate a population of 40,000?"[30] After further discussion, the Business Men's Association passed a resolution calling for the construction of a subway through Flushing and that a committee be appointed to meet with the PSC on this issue.[31]

Pople, Terry, and Spear led a group from the joint committee that toured Flushing with Daniel L. Turner, representing the PSC, and Charles U. Powell of the Borough President's Topographical Bureau. They inspected the streets that had been recommended for the route of either the elevated or the subway line.

Other Third Ward groups wanted to extend rapid transit service to their communities. Frank E. Knab of the Whitestone Improvement Association, one of those who met with Commissioner Bassett in 1907, said his group would oppose extending the route through Flushing if an effort were not taken to bring rapid transit to College Point, Whitestone, and Bayside, supporting the construction of elevated lines: "I cannot see why the people of Flushing oppose a 'L' when two miles of elevated road can be built for what one mile of subway would cost."[32]

The objections raised in Flushing influenced the PSC. "The people in Flushing themselves have changed the situation," a commissioner said. "They might as well understand right now that transit facilities are not going to be thrust down the throat of any community. From every section of the city we are receiving demands for transit and within a short time after the present [Dual Systems Contracts] are signed we propose to

Figure 3-4. Frank E. Knab. (*Brooklyn Daily Eagle*, April 4, 1918)

take up the matter of extensions. The strongest and the most united demands are about to be made by the Bronx, Staten Island and Brooklyn. Naturally, the Commission will give the most favorable consideration to those sections from which the demand is most united," he continued. "The situation settles itself right down to this proposition: If the people of Flushing desire to continue to pay for transit extensions to other sections of the city and get none of the benefits themselves they may do so, for all the commission cares."[33]

A *Long Island Daily Star* editorial on January 20 supported an elevated line:

The attitude taken by the opponents of elevated railroads through Flushing is an injury to the development and progress of that entire locality embracing also College Point, Whitestone and other sections that are all contiguous to the old village.

We honestly believe, therefore, that the Public Service Commissioners would do well to entirely ignore the demonstrative opposition of certain Flushingites to the elevated railroad.[34]

That editorial had no impact. The Flushing Association voted that evening to call for a subway. The opposition expressed by the property owners affected them. A. E. Sholes said, "It seems to me that what this town wants is united effort. The thing we want is a subway and under Amity Street as a direct line."[35]

The Whitestone Improvement Association met on January 22. Knab also wanted unity:

> Now is the time to stop bickering and stand unitedly for some form of transit. You have seen what united effort has done for the Bronx and for Manhattan. Never mind whether we get an elevated or subway, let us get something. What we want is transit, and we want it just as soon as we can secure it.
>
> If the current policy of protesting every plan or route proposed by the Commission be continued we will never get transit. The Public Service Commission is tired of receiving protests from Queens. If the residents of Whitestone, College Point and Bayside and Flushing will unite in some definite plan it will go through.[36]

Groups representing communities south of Flushing bore out Knab's call on January 24. They supported building an elevated line through their neighborhoods, using the right-of-way of the Stewart Railroad, a spur from the LIRR's Port Washington line that ran to eastern Queens.[37]

Gaynor and Willcox spoke at the Flushing Business Men's Association dinner on January 27. Gaynor wanted to extend rapid transit to Flushing, but said that "we cannot put a subway out to the doorway of every one of you. We can only do what the City's credit will allow us to do."[38] Willcox praised Pople for his efforts.[39] He spoke at the dinner of the Queens Borough Chamber of Commerce the next night. While he admitted the need for subways in Queens, Willcox kept as his priority the approval for the Dual Systems Contracts.[40]

On January 28 the Flushing Association discussed what should be built. A resolution was again made calling for the construction of a subway. Frank E. Andrews moved

Figure 3-5. Mayor William Jay Gaynor. (*Wikimedia Commons*)

to delete the language, saying, "Let us get away from the narrow-minded view that an elevated line will bring all the bad people out here. This is a nice town to live in; we have good schools and churches and the residences, but why build a wall around Flushing and keep the other people out?"[41] The amended resolution was passed.

A rally supporting the Dual Systems Contracts was held on January 30 at Hettinger's Hall in Astoria. PSC Commissioner George V. S. Williams stated that the elevated line would be extended "clear out to Little Neck Bay,"[42] well to the east of Flushing. This was a surprise, and the PSC tried to backtrack. Travis Whitney, the PSC's secretary (and future commissioner), told the *Flushing Daily Times* the next day that Williams hadn't meant to say what he said, but rather that the line would be extended as far as Main Street.[43] Williams tried to amend his prior claim, saying the line would be built to Main Street, but the Commission's intent was to continue the line to Little Neck Bay.[44] This was the first time there was any indication that the PSC had a plan to build the line east of Flushing.

Williams again tried to clarify his comments on February 1 to the *Flushing Evening Journal*. The PSC would send the plan for the initial extension of the line to the Board of Estimate. This was the section to be built from Corona to Flushing. "Nothing is to be done at present as to the second section of the proposed route from Main Street, Flushing to Bayside," said Williams. "We will lay out the second section from Flushing to Bayside and hope to carry rapid transit ultimately to that section. At this time, however, it is our desire to have the Board of Estimate approve the elevated structure to Main Street so the Public Service Commission can legalize it."[45]

Williams outraged those opposing an el by stating that the PSC was pushing the one to Flushing to move the plan ahead. "You can say for me that I will fight the construction of an elevated structure through Flushing and will do all that I can to have the Board of Estimate approve a subway east of Lawrence Street," said Ira Terry.[46] "We will carry this fight to the bitter end. We will not have an 'L' through our street either above or below Main Street," insisted Daniel Beard. "As we have said time and again it would ruin our property. They can't get our consent and the only way that they can get our property is by condemnation procedure."[47]

The extended route would run past Flushing and along Warburton Avenue (now 38th Avenue) to Bayside Boulevard (now 221st Street) near Little Neck Bay. For much of this distance, the Flushing line would closely parallel the LIRR's Port Washington line.

The Bayside Civic Association rallied for the line on February 11. There were calls in the community to swing the line farther to the south of the LIRR, providing access to an area that didn't have rail service.

With the plan going to the Board of Estimate on February 13, Borough President Connolly announced his support for a subway: "I want to say to the residents of Flushing that I favor a subway through Amity Street and I will be with them in their fight for

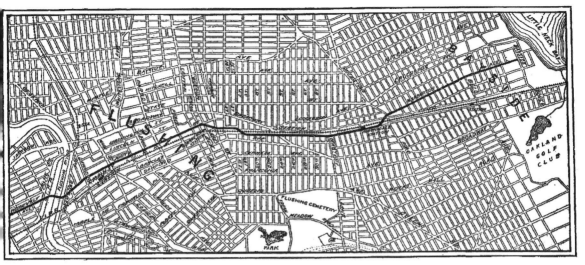

Figure 3-6. The *New York Times* ran this map on February 9, 1913, showing the Flushing line extension in the Third Ward.

the subway when the proper time comes, as aggressively as I know how and I see no reason why a subway cannot be secured for this portion of this route."[48]

Pople came to the meeting with a petition signed by five thousand people who supported a subway. James W. Treadwell, an attorney who lived and owned property on Amity Street, opposed the construction of *any* transit line on Amity Street. Treadwell said the LIRR and the trolley lines in the area provided sufficient service.[49] He called on the PSC to hold a hearing before the Board of Estimate proceeded with its deliberations.

Manhattan Borough President George McAneny asked Treadwell if there were objections to rapid transit service through Flushing. Treadwell hesitated and said no. "Would it not be better to approve the laying on of the route through Flushing and leave the question of subway or elevated construction until the matter of construction comes up?" McAneny said. "Then in all probability, subway construction will be adopted, since this will not add more than $100,000[50] to the cost."

"But we have no hearing before the Public Service Commission, and we demand one," Treadwell responded. "There are others here to be heard," Connolly said. Gaynor interrupted, saying, "We cannot require the Public Service Commission to give a hearing. We can give a hearing here." Treadwell started to speak, but Gaynor stopped him: "Don't talk so much."[51]

Pople defended the PSC: "The Public Service Commission has gone into this matter thoroughly. We have been before members of the Board on several occasions, and in company with a Flushing Committee, the engineer of the Public Service Commission has been over this and all other proposed routes in Flushing, with the result that he recommended this Amity Street route."

"Would not a subway be satisfactory to all citizens of Flushing?" Connolly asked. "It certainly would," Pople answered. Treadwell said that while a subway was satisfactory there was no assurance one would be built.

"If we lay out the route today as proposed, you may be sure that everything will be done in the best interest of Flushing," Gaynor responded. "If [the] route were approved today with the understanding that the character of construction would be considered later, it would meet all conditions," Connolly said.[52] Gaynor then closed the hearing, deferring action for two weeks in order to give the PSC an opportunity to further consider the plan.

The PSC didn't act on the Flushing line in those two weeks, and the matter returned to the Board of Estimate. When it came up for discussion, Treadwell approached the podium with other members of his group. Gaynor stopped him and said, "Gentlemen. The Board has decided to return this matter to the [Board of Estimate] Transit Committee as it believes that the committee can handle it better than the entire Board. Your application to the Public Service Commission for a public hearing was refused, was it not?"

"It has not been refused, your honor," Treadwell answered. "Our application for a hearing is still on file and we have been given no decision."

"Well, I think our Transit Committee can take the question up with your people with great advantage to all concerned," Gaynor said. "Will that be satisfactory?"

Treadwell's group conferred. "Your honor, to refer this matter to the Transit Committee of the Board will be very satisfactory to the people who favor the Amity Street route as it is," Pople said. "Well, this seems to be satisfactory to everybody," Gaynor said.[53] The full Board of Estimate then referred the matter to the Transit Committee.

Discussion continued of how the line would be built. Connolly, McAneny, Brooklyn Borough President Alfred E. Steers, and Clifford Moore and Charles U. Powell of the Queens Topographical Bureau toured Flushing in early March to determine the best means of tunneling. They determined that the most feasible way of doing this was "open-cut" construction—digging a trench, building the tunnel, and then filling it in.[54]

Third Ward groups continued their efforts to extend the line. The Bayside Civic Association passed a resolution on March 11 supporting an extension. Another rally was held the next night at the Zion Parish House in Douglaston for residents of both that community and Little Neck. A week later, Jacob Graeser of the College Point Taxpayers Association told the *Flushing Evening Journal* that his community wanted consideration as well.[55] These efforts didn't affect the Board of Estimate. It laid over the Flushing line at its March 13 meeting after Treadwell reported that the PSC hadn't acted on their request for a hearing.[56]

Connolly spoke the next day of the need to proceed: "The question is now one of expediency. The routes are first adopted in the Public Service Commission, after which they must again be approved by the Board of Estimate. This route has already been approved by the Public Service Commission. The Board of Estimate cannot change it or reject it and the process must, if rejected, be started over again in the Public Service Commission. If the route is rejected, there may be possibly some difficulty in starting it again."[57]

Some saw ulterior motives behind those opposing the extension. "It is a well-known fact that real estate interests are [in] back of this proposed route as a means of booming certain real estate propositions in Bayside and the eastern part of Flushing," Knab said. "I feel certain that the men who are [in] back of this proposed route do not really care whether or not the line is even built. All they want is to have the line approved, and have a handsome map of it in their respective offices. To the prospective buyer they can say: 'Here is where the elevated line (or subway) is coming and it will give you a five-cent fare to any part of the greater city' and their lots will then sell for high prices."

"On the other hand," he continued, "we of Whitestone, as well as the people of College Point, have consistently asked for extensions, but have not been even considered in the laying out of the routes. Neither we nor the residents of Amity Street, who are chiefly affected by the route laid down have been given a hearing by the Public Service Commission, although we have time and time again asked for one through the various civic associations."[58] The Douglaston Civic Association voted on April 1 to call for the line to continue through Bayside to Douglaston and Little Neck.

City Comptroller William A. Prendergast and Borough Presidents Connolly and McAneny toured Flushing on March 29 to again evaluate the type of line to build. The property owners on Amity Street continued their efforts to block the construction of an el. A delegation of Amity Street property owners met with Gaynor, Aldermanic President John Purroy Mitchel, Prendergast, Connolly, and McAneny on April 2. Connolly suggested that the proposal be returned to the PSC to reconsider building a subway. McAneny agreed: "We cannot build this line for three or four years. Why not wait a few weeks until we can work the thing out satisfactorily?"[59]

The question arose of approving the route of the line and then changing the type of line that would be built. Gaynor and McAneny said doing that affected property values.[60] Gaynor urged the delegation to meet with the PSC. Accompanied by Connolly, they did just that, and met with PSC Chairman Edward E. McCall and the other members.

McCall promised that the PSC would reassess the plan for the Flushing line. On April 3, the Board of Estimate acted on a motion made by Connolly to return the proposal for the line to the PSC for reconsideration. Connolly spoke to approximately three hundred people from the Third Ward who attended:

Gentlemen, Wednesday the Public Service Commission assembled in extraordinary session told a large representative body of citizens from the territory affected by this proposed elevated line that if they, the citizens would appear before you to-day and ask you to refer this matter back to the commission, the commission would change the proposed line and issue a certificate authorizing the construction of a subway through Amity Street, Flushing, instead of the elevated railroad that has caused so much objection from the citizens of that section.

This great representative body of citizens that has come here to-day to ask you to refer this matter back to the Public Service Commission with the recommendation that a subway line be laid down from Lawrence Street to Murray Hill instead of the elevated line now laid down.[61]

McAneny interrupted with correcting language: "No. We will not do that. We will not go on record as having any recommendations. We will simply refer this matter to the Public Service Commission and let them do as they like with it."[62]

"Mr. McAneny is right, Mr. Connolly," Prendergast said. "It would not be wise for us to make any such recommendation. Let us simply send this matter back to the Public Service Commission for whatever action they might want to take upon it. If they desire to change the route from an 'L' to a subway, all well and good, and when they send the proposition back to us again, we can take it up again as an entirely new matter."[63] The matter was referred back to the PSC.

There were differing reactions in the Third Ward. Treadwell and Fitch took a wait-and-see attitude. Knab led a delegation from Whitestone and College Point to meet with the Commission members to discuss bringing a subway to their area.[64] The Third Ward Farmers and Taxpayers Association discussed the proposal to use the Stewart Railroad to enter eastern Queens.[65] The Upper Flushing Improvement Association, representing Murray Hill and Auburndale, the neighborhoods beyond where the line would again become elevated, insisted that were the line built through Flushing as a subway, they wanted it built that way through their area as well.[66]

When the PSC met on April 23, they voted to change the line, officially designated as Route 52, from an el to a subway through Flushing. It would become elevated again near the intersection of Matthew Place (now Depot Road) and Eagles Street (now 157th Street), and continue on to Warburton Avenue and Bayside Boulevard.

The line went back to the Board of Estimate. Its advocates were in for a shock. The Board deferred action, questioning how much a subway would cost. It was thought the line would cost an additional $200,000 to build as a subway ($8.91 million in 2011 dollars, according to MeasuringWorth.com). To the Board's apparent horror, they now found it would cost $1.2 million more ($20.8 million in 2011 dollars). "This estimate puts a new light on this matter," McAneny said. "When I tentatively approved this subway proposition some weeks ago, it was my understanding that the extra cost over an 'L' structure would not be more than $200,000. Now, however, I do not see how the city can afford to spend this much extra for one mile of subway in Flushing, desirable as such a route would be for that residential section."[67]

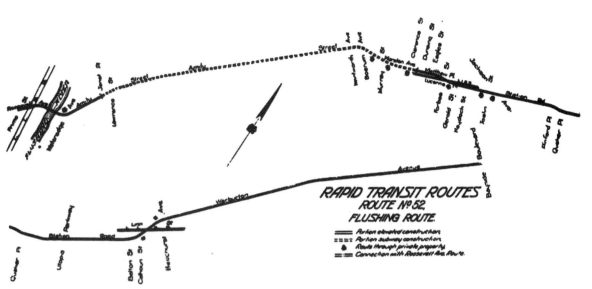

Figure 3-7. The PSC's map of Route 52 from its 1913 *Annual Report.*

This situation was further complicated by the interest that College Point and Whitestone groups had in transit service.[68] The Third Ward Transit League, noting reports of the additional cost of building a subway, suggested that the Flushing line be built as a two-track line through the area to reduce costs.[69]

The issue wasn't resolved when the Board of Estimate met on May 29; the matter was postponed until June 5. McAneny gave a report in favor of the construction of a subway, but only as far as Main Street. Given the costs, he didn't endorse a further extension.

The next day, Commissioner Williams raised a point that McAneny brought up at the Board of Estimate: "The remainder of the route may be laid out by us, but that does not necessarily mean it will ever be built. When the time comes for building the road beyond Main Street, the Public Service Commission and the Board of Estimate may entirely change the plan. By that time, the personnel of the Commission and Board may be considerably changed."[70]

The Board of Estimate approved McAneny's plan on June 12, calling for the line to be built with three tracks to Main Street. As a second phase, two tracks would be built to Bayside. The Board began to look at widening Amity Street. The only portion of the street to be widened would be west of College Point Boulevard to accommodate the portal for the subway tunnel.

Mayor Gaynor died on September 12. Aldermanic President Mitchel was elected to replace him in November.[71] Before the election, there was concern in the Third Ward as to what would happen to the subway. Mitchel sought to dispel those worries: "I am heartily in favor of the immediate construction of every rapid transit line that has been laid out in the Borough of Queens and when I am elected Mayor I shall take whatever

Figure 3-8. John Purroy Mitchel in 1912. He was president of the Board of Aldermen at the time; a year later, at age thirty-four, he would become mayor of New York City. (*Wood-Harmon Magazine*)

steps may be necessary to compel prompt action for the letting of construction contracts for the building of the Bayside Extension and every Queens route included in the so-called Dual Systems Contracts."[72]

"I may assure you that I am in favor of building this line to Bayside as soon as the city can provide the funds," said McAneny, now the Aldermanic president. "There is no reason why the extension from Corona to Main Street, Flushing, should not be started within the next few months."[73] PSC Chairman McCall and Commissioner Williams made commitments to the Bayside Extension at the Flushing Business Men's Association dinner on February 2, 1914.

The PSC awarded the contracts for the construction of the Flushing line from the Steinway Tunnels to Corona on February 5. The Third Ward Rapid Transit League had fears for the rest of the line. They saw how the cost of constructing the Jerome Avenue and Pelham lines in the Bronx had exceeded cost estimates. They were concerned that a similar situation would affect the construction of the line east of Corona.

There was also a literal roadblock to extending the Flushing line to Bayside—the Long Island Rail Road. The LIRR and the subways would be part of one regional transit agency more than half a century later; in 1914, however, the LIRR viewed the subways, and the Flushing line in particular, as competition. In order for the Flushing line to be extended to Bayside, it needed to cross the LIRR's tracks and property, near its Broadway and Auburndale stations. The LIRR wouldn't allow this to happen.

On February 23, 1915, T. Gardiner Ellsworth of the United Civic Association called on the city and the PSC to connect the Flushing line with the Port Washington line in Corona. Not only would this enable the establishment of the Bayside Extension at reduced costs, but it would expand on what had been proposed.

The LIRR operated a branch route from the Port Washington line at the west bank of the Flushing River that ran through College Point, Malba, and Whitestone to the Whitestone ferry landing.[74] Ellsworth sent his proposal to LIRR President Ralph Peters, who took it to his Board of Directors. The PSC considered it,[75] waiting to see what the LIRR would do with its tracks and land near the Broadway station or with Ellsworth's proposal. Connolly supported the new plan as a short-term action. He wanted the original Bayside Extension[76] but saw the value of Ellsworth's plan: "It seems to me that if we can get transit for Whitestone and College Point and the sections to the east of Flushing under an arrangement of this kind, it will be of great advantage to these sections."[77]

McCall met with the Whitestone Improvement Association on March 3 and told them of the Commission's interest. He instructed the PSC's staff to work on a lease agreement with the LIRR.[78] There were issues to be resolved. The LIRR would operate Port Washington line freight and passenger service; these services needed to be coordinated. But this was nothing new: BRT trains ran from a spur of the Broadway–Brooklyn onto the tracks of the LIRR's Atlantic Division in the summer to provide subway service to the Rockaways.

The PSC received the required number of consents from property owners in Flushing to build the subway. On March 10, they authorized action to proceed with construction, but first needed to achieve resolution with the LIRR situation.

PSC engineers made an interesting discovery while resurveying the area near the LIRR's Broadway station: the land needed for the Bayside Extension was six feet to the south of the railroad's property.[79] They wouldn't need the LIRR's permission. While the PSC was hopeful about the lease agreement, they also voted to proceed with work on the Flushing–Bayside line on March 11. It would take another two years for the Flushing line to be built out as far as Corona, and more years after that to extend the line out to Main Street, so there was time to determine the next step. It probably wasn't a coincidence, but Peters then sent a letter to the PSC offering to lease track space on the Port Washington and Whitestone lines for rapid transit service.

The response in Queens was muted. The Third Ward Rapid Transit League supported negotiations on a lease but wanted the PSC to proceed with the Bayside Extension, suspicious that the LIRR's proposal came right after the PSC decided to proceed with its original plan. In 1915 parlance, they thought there was a joker hidden in the LIRR's proposal.[80]

The PSC liked the idea of the lease. McCall told a delegation of representatives from the Third Ward community groups that he had instructed the PSC's counsel to go ahead with seeking a lease.

There was debate over where to build the connection. The United Civic Association suggested that the line continue to run from its terminal at Alburtis Avenue (now the 103rd Street–Corona Plaza station) to Corona's Myrtle Avenue (now 111th Street).[81] Pople wanted to build the connection from a point east of Main Street.[82] Still another

Figure 3-9. Queens Borough President Maurice E. Connolly. (Photo courtesy of the Office of the Borough President of Queens)

plan called for the connection to be built just to the west of the junction between the Port Washington and Whitestone lines in Flushing Meadows.[83]

Connolly's idea of what to do was in line with Pople's, and he knew that where the connection would be built was less important than getting one built at all. "The one thing that is likely to kill this project is disputes among ourselves," he told a meeting of the Whitestone Improvement Association on March 24. "Everyone interested should get together on the merits of the plan and on the method of doing it. A committee should be appointed from this meeting to confer with other committees and see that the people really want."[84] The one group not in support of the lease agreement was the Flushing Association, whose members preferred to stay with the PSC's original plan.[85]

Peters told the Third Ward Transit League that Connolly and Pople's plans were unacceptable. The LIRR wanted a connection built between Corona and Flushing Meadows. He thought it could be done for a cost of about $500,000 ($23.1 million in 2011 dollars, according to MeasuringWorth.com).[86]

The LIRR wasn't the only company causing suspicion in Queens. William Randolph Hearst's *New York American* charged that IRT Chairman August Belmont and the Degnon Construction Company (who had also been involved with building the Steinway Tunnels) had obtained land in the Flushing Meadows to fill it in and build the subway toward Flushing. The *American* implied that the IRT was delaying action on the lease agreement.[87] Colonel William Hayward, a new PSC member, promised action.

Support was growing for the lease. Knab presented to the PSC a nine-foot-long petition supporting the plan. He then presented a second petition signed by the leaders of the Third Ward's major civic groups.[88]

The LIRR made a formal proposal to the PSC on April 5 for a ten-year lease, with an option for ten more. The annual cost would be $250,000 ($5.77 million in 2011 dollars, according to MeasuringWorth.com), with additional charges covering maintenance and electrical costs. While the civic groups thought the price was high, they still supported the plan.

State Senator Bernard M. Patten introduced an amendment to the Rapid Transit Law to facilitate subway service along the LIRR's tracks. It was passed by the State Senate on April 16 and the State Assembly on April 20. Mitchel gave his approval on April 29; Governor Charles S. Whitman signed it into law on May 10. The PSC was free to actively negotiate with the LIRR; Chairman McCall, President Peters, and representatives of both organizations toured the Port Washington and Whitestone lines on May 13.

This would turn out to be the high point in the efforts to build the connection. Work on the lease agreement proceeded slowly, making it impossible for the Board of Estimate to act. With all the work going on to build the Dual Systems Contracts lines, the PSC's staff couldn't devote much attention to working on the second phase of rapid transit expansion before finishing the first.

There was consternation throughout the Third Ward. Knab criticized the PSC at the Whitestone Improvement Association meeting on July 16:

> It is suicidal to think of swapping horses and advocating a new plan at this juncture. We all know that the commission has a report from its engineers for several weeks; some of us have been given to understand what this report contains. The question is "why has not the report been made public by the commission?" What is the influence or influences keeping that report from coming out? We have a mighty good notion as to what that is, and before long there may be some rather interesting facts brought to light regarding it.
>
> If the commission does not get its report within a very short time we are going to know why. Delay can serve no legitimate ends.[89]

Mistrusting the LIRR, the Flushing Business Men's Association called for building the subway along Amity Street. This viewpoint started to alienate some of the groups in the Third Ward that benefited more from the lease than from a subway to Flushing. "There are 70,000 persons now in the Third Ward that must be served by this transit and the railroad proposition is the only sound one that we have heard," said Charles Posthauer of the College Point Committee. "A line terminating in Flushing will never meet the needs of the community. If it ends there, there is no hope for the other sections getting transit for years; there is too little money now."[90]

The talks between the LIRR and the PSC were delayed throughout the summer of 1915. The PSC did offer $150,000 per year for the lease ($3.45 million in 2011 dollars, according to MeasuringWorth.com); the LIRR said it was amenable to reduce its original demand,[91] but nothing was put on paper. It wasn't until August 11 that a meeting took place at McAneny's apartment at the Ritz-Carlton Hotel in Manhattan. Progress was reported, but no agreement was imminent.

A second meeting took place in September. McAneny told the LIRR that the proposed rent of $250,000 per year ($5.77 million in 2011) was unacceptable. He forced a reduction to $125,000 ($2.89 million in 2011) for the first year, with an increase of 8 percent for each year of the contract. Third Ward civic group representatives met and drafted a letter to Mitchel, McAneny, and McCall endorsing the new proposal. McAneny and McCall responded positively, but nothing was heard from the LIRR or IRT until October, when Peters wrote to McCall to say the rental fees were acceptable.

That was where everything stood for more than a year. It seemed as if the PSC and LIRR wanted to proceed. The communities along the Port Washington and Whitestone lines certainly wanted subways, even with a second fare paid by those who lived east or north of Flushing. The elected officials wanted to take the next step. But problems remained. The IRT and BRT appeared to be unwilling to use the LIRR's tracks, and New York City's Corporation Counsel had advised Mitchel and the Board of Estimate that they couldn't compel either company to do so.[92] The year 1916 wound up being one of stalemate, and the Third Ward grew impatient. The Whitestone Improvement Association was so frustrated that they approved a resolution asking the PSC to build the subway to Amity and Main Streets, even though their community wouldn't directly benefit from it.[93]

PSC Chief Engineer Alfred Craven prepared a report justifying the connection with the LIRR. He estimated that 20,600 passengers per day would ride the subway along the Port Washington and Whitestone lines in each direction in 1920, a number that would rise to 34,000 by 1927 (by comparison, close to three times as many riders now board the No. 7 line at Main Street alone). The report called for elimination of all grade crossings over the Port Washington and Whitestone lines, although Craven thought this could be done over time.[94] He noted that the extension of subway service to and beyond Flushing would significantly increase the assessed valuation of land in the entire Third Ward, providing the funds needed to offset any operating deficits. This allowed him to convince the IRT and BRT to provide service:

> We understand that Counsel to the Commission and the [New York City] Corporation Counsel agree that the operating companies cannot be forced to operate over the L.I.R.R. tracks as an extension under the operating contracts. If, however, the companies would agree to such operation as an extension and if the City is willing to assume the probable operating deficit of about $200,000 [$4.23 million in 2011, according to MeasuringWorth.com] and particularly in view of the fact that the City has only about $1 million at present time available for rapid transit development in the Third Ward of Queens the Long Island Railroad Company's proposal to lease its tracks to Whitestone Landing and to Little Neck for rapid transit operation seems desirable and if such arrangement is consummated advantage should be taken of the Degnon proposal for the construction of the connection between the current

City line at Alburtis and Roosevelt Avenues and the Long Island Railroad Company's tracks to insure the cost of this work not exceeding $410,000.[95]

The Third Ward Rapid Transit Association endorsed a two-fare zone beyond Flushing to induce the IRT and BRT to use the LIRR's tracks. "We have a good reason to believe that with a ten-cent fare to all stations east of Main and Bridge Streets[96] it will be a paying proposition and that the operating companies will consent to run their trains,"[97] said Clinton T. Roe of the Third Ward group.

Frustration grew at the lack of progress. The Third Ward Rapid Transit Association prepared a report showing how much work they had done over the past decade with little to show for it on the part of the city, the PSC, and the operating companies.[98] James H. Quinlan of the Flushing Business Men's Association questioned the LIRR's motives:

It still seems to me as it did long months ago that President Peters simply suggested this leasing so as to divert attentions from the city-built line to Main and Amity Streets, Flushing. He knew that it would hurt his business and he tried procrastination of the fateful day.

Before long we will probably have to drop all of these plans now under way and go back to where we were two years ago. And in the meanwhile, the money that seemed available then for the building of a city-built line will have slipped out of our hands.[99]

Several hundred Third Ward area residents attended a PSC hearing on August 9, at which Roe presented a petition signed by seven thousand people. However, nothing was being done to lease the LIRR's tracks or to extend the subway. Representatives of the Queens Borough Chamber of Commerce met with PSC Commissioners Travis H. Whitney and Henry W. Hodge in December, urging them to act. Whitney and Hodge promised to work for the lease agreement and stated that the PSC would try to get it approved.

Subway service to northern Queens began on February 1, 1917, when the Astoria line opened. Built in conjunction with the Flushing line,[100] it reminded people east of Corona that nothing had been done to extend that line past Alburtis Avenue. PSC Secretary James Blaine Walker[101] said they should ask the LIRR why not much had happened. "The last thing I heard about that matter we were waiting to hear from Mr. Peters, President of the Long Island Railroad, we made him good offers, and he said that he was willing to meet us halfway in the proposition. That was some time ago, and as far as I know, there has been nothing done in the matter since."[102] President Peters met with Commissioners Hodge and Whitney on February 27. There was no report of progress, but discussions continued.

There was news of an agreement in March. Commissioners Hodge and Whitney, PSC Chief of Rapid Transit LeRoy T. Harkness, and Daniel L. Turner came to terms with the LIRR on March 15 and submitted the lease to the full Commission. Rental would be $125,000 for the first year with rent increasing by 6 percent each year. The Commission would consider a second fare to be charged east and north of Flushing until the line was profitable. The *Flushing Evening Journal* published the full text of the lease.

Clinton T. Roe, speaking for the North Shore Transit League, had another reason for the extra fare: "These terms have been agreed upon and I see nothing in the way now to prevent our section from receiving rapid transit which we have been entitled to for a long time. I don't believe there will be any objection to the 10-cent fare east of Flushing, because with a 10-cent fare to sections like Whitestone, Upper Flushing, Bayside and Douglaston, the taxpayers there will be able to maintain the high class residential character which these communities have had for so many years."[103]

Flushing line service to Corona began on April 21. Full service through Queensboro Plaza started on July 23 when trains began to run over the upper level of the Queensboro Bridge, connecting the 2nd Avenue El with the Queens lines. For the next quarter century, riders on both lines had the option of riding trains that provided direct service over three routes between Queens and Manhattan.

Significant issues needed to be resolved. The most serious required a major capital investment. Large sections of the Port Washington and Whitestone lines operated at grade level, with few trestles or tunnels. Before subway service could begin, grade crossings would have to be eliminated. It would be another two years before that could happen.

The opening of the Flushing line and the possibility of the lease agreement moving ahead affected the entire north shore of Queens. Land in communities from Long Island City to Little Neck and into Nassau County was subdivided, sold, and developed.

Contract negotiations were continuing and a public hearing was held on the grade crossing eliminations. Roe criticized the plan to eliminate all crossings, saying this was immediately required at a few key streets. Commissioner Whitney said more grade crossings needed to be eliminated to ensure public safety. PSC engineers identified fourteen locations and requested more time to complete their plans. Whitney then adjourned the hearing until a later date.

There was little progress though the summer of 1917. By fall, it almost appeared as if matters were going in the opposite direction. The city lacked the funding to extend the subway through Flushing, and the LIRR continued to make demands for additional payments that were disincentives for proceeding with the lease.[104]

A lease agreement finally was announced on October 16. The IRT would operate the trains that would use the LIRR's tracks; the BRT would eventually do so as well. A second fare would be charged east of Broadway on the Port Washington line, and east of College Point on the Whitestone line. The PSC would hold a public hearing on the lease agreement on October 31.[105]

The lease agreement was well received at the hearing. Borough President Connolly sought immediate action: "I wish this matter could be settled here today and that it could be before the Board of Estimate on Friday."[106]

But that's where everything stopped. On November 14, the IRT notified the PSC they wouldn't use the LIRR's tracks. "I have submitted the matter to the officers of this

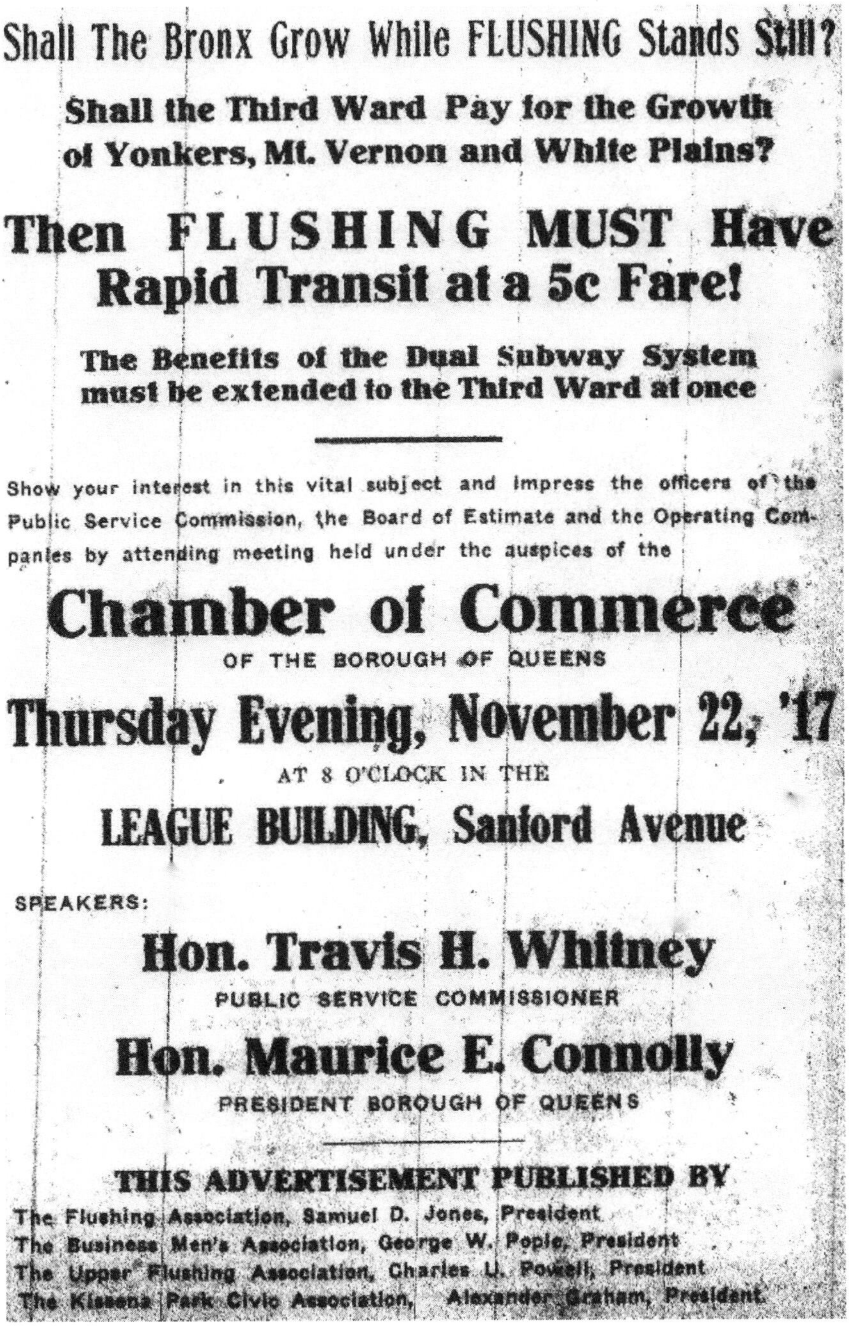

Figure 3-10. A front-page ad from the *Flushing Daily Times*.

company and am instructed to tell you that at this time we cannot undertake the proposed agreement and operation in coordination with the rapid transit line," IRT Counsel James L. Quackenbush told the PSC. "Conditions, as everybody knows, have changed greatly since this matter was discussed some months ago. It appears to our officers that it would be extremely inadequate to add operating lines to Contract No. 3 [the Dual Systems Contract] under prevailing conditions and therefore we suggest that all negotiations with that end of view be suspended at least for the present."[107]

Commissioner Whitney noted the years that had been expended in working on the lease and the support the elected officials and community groups had expressed. He moved that the PSC engineering staff return to planning for the extension of the subway into Flushing.[108] The PSC and the Third Ward were back to where they were in 1913.

The Third Ward was enraged. "It is what I suspected and I felt that they had something up their sleeves the whole time," Charles W. Posthauer stormed. "There was never any sincerity of purpose in the proposition, anyhow, and the people fell for it."[109] "I am not surprised," commented Rodman Richardson of the Third Ward Transit League. "In fact, I have known for a while that the Interborough and the BRT had refused to come in on the plan, notwithstanding statements to the contrary."[110] Ira Terry of the Third Ward Transit League indicated that his area would look to John F. Hylan, who had defeated Mitchel in the mayoral elections the previous week,[111] to provide the help needed to bring subway service to the Third Ward.[112]

About five hundred people attended a meeting at the League Building at Sanford Avenue and Union Street on November 22 to demand subway service. Whitney assured them of PSC support:

> The Commission thoroughly believes in an extension into and through Flushing as far as money will allow. If we can build the first section, we will be nearer to the construction of the second structure. The Interborough can refuse to operate an extension leased by the city, but it cannot refuse to operate an extension built by the city.
>
> When the plans are completed and bids secured the contract will be submitted to the Board of Estimate for approval. The Borough President of Queens may be depended on to be vigilant for the necessary money.
>
> Such an extension to Main Street will bring the Corona line from the further side of a swamp to a community of 30,000 to 40,000 people of great development possibility.[113]

Connolly thought consideration of the lease agreement was only suspended: "We should all work for this proposition first, because it is the only way, for years to come, at least, whereby all the sections of the Third Ward will be benefitted. Let's go ahead with this plan until we find it is absolutely impossible to get this company to consent to operate. Then we should go ahead and work for the Main Street extension."[114]

The borough president and representatives of Third Ward groups and the Queens Borough Chamber of Commerce met with IRT President Theodore Shonts in December about reviving the lease plan. Shonts said the IRT would meet with the PSC and the LIRR to see if this was possible. According to Shonts, the IRT had disagreements only with some of the agreement's terms, rather than with the plan itself.[115]

Any optimism concerning the lease was misplaced; any hope for action was mistaken. The IRT's decision on November 14 not to operate trains on the Port Washington and Whitestone lines marked the end of that plan. The focus fully and permanently returned to extending the subway to Main Street.

It wasn't until 1920 that there was any progress. As discussion of the Corona Subway Yard in the Flushing Meadows was underway at the Board of Estimate's Finance and Budget Committee meeting on June 3, Connolly called for the extension to proceed. Mayor Hylan and the other committee members agreed and passed the recommendations on to Transit Construction Commissioner John H. Delaney.[116]

Although they both supported extending the subway to Flushing, the contentious relationship between Hylan and the New York State Transit Commission, especially its chairman, George McAneny, slowed transit planning and construction. The mayor took a number of actions to obstruct the Transit Commission, including directing the *City Record*, which publishes official advertisements for public agencies, not to do so for Transit Commission requests for bids for construction projects, thereby interfering with its ability to award contracts. This hampered the building of the line.[117]

On May 12, the Board of Estimate met to vote on the construction plan. Aldermanic President Fiorello H. La Guardia moved that it be postponed until concerns over the Transit Commission's authority were resolved.[118] The plans weren't approved for another month.

The Transit Commission awarded a construction contract in November 1922. The Board of Estimate delayed action because no plans had been made for a vehicular bridge to be built along with the subway crossing over the Flushing River. This bridge would link Roosevelt Avenue and Amity Street, creating one street.

Construction contracts were finally awarded and work on the subway and the Roosevelt Avenue Bridge began on April 21, 1923. Mayor Hylan and Borough President Connolly led the groundbreaking ceremony.[119]

The line was also extended westward from Grand Central to Times Square, with service to Times Square beginning on February 19, 1927. A short stub of a tunnel was built beyond Times Square in hopes of connecting the Flushing line with the line the Board of Transportation would build along 8th Avenue. That connection was never built; the tunnel stub sat unused for eight decades.

Flushing line service to the Willets Point Boulevard station began on May 7, 1927.[120] The Roosevelt Avenue Bridge opened one week later, but the subways' extension to Flushing was again delayed. The support columns for the elevated structure were sinking into the soft land of the Flushing Meadows. A sinkhole developed. Construction stopped and about 250 feet of the elevated structure had to be demolished and rebuilt.

Piles for the new structure were driven seventy feet into the ground. More piles were driven at least ten feet deeper into the ground to provide extra support.[121] At a meeting with Flushing-area representatives, Delaney attributed this problem to the demands of the people of the Third Ward for transit relief: "It probably would have been prudent to have waited a year or so to observe how the soil would react, but speed was urged and we tried to comply with the result that we now have."[122]

George U. Harvey, the Republican candidate for Aldermanic president in 1925 (who became borough president in 1929), protested in a letter to Mayor James J. Walker: "It had taken only four years to build the first subway, twenty-five miles long; four years to fight the Civil War and four years to fight the [First] World War. After four and a half years your engineers are alleged to have discovered that there is mud in the Flushing Meadows and this is given as an excuse for further indefinite postponement of completion."[123]

The first subway train ran to Main Street on January 21, 1928. The event was marked with three days of celebrations in Flushing. Mayor Walker was supposed to assist in the operation of that first trip but was a no-show. IRT President Frank Hedley ordered Train Operator Herbert L. Parsons (who operated the first train through the Steinway Tunnels with Mayor Mitchel in 1917) to proceed. The official explanation for Walker's absence was a "previous and unexpected engagement."[124] When Walker spoke at the closing celebration at the Sanford Hotel in Flushing on January 23, he explained his absence by saying that he never expected a train operated by the IRT or BMT to be on time.[125]

Flushing had its subway, but planning to extend the line continued. The BOT devised a plan for service to Whitestone that didn't use the LIRR's tracks. Instead, they proposed a line that came off the Flushing line east of Main Street and then looped back to College Point via 149th Street and 11th Avenue.

The LIRR offered the Whitestone line to the BOT in 1928, but they declined, citing the costs involved with eliminating grade crossings, widening the line's right-of-way (it was mostly a single-track route), and the need for more stations along the line.[126] The LIRR ended the Whitestone line on February 16, 1932.

The BOT continued to include Flushing line extensions in its capital priority lists through 1945. Postwar budgets and other priorities affected the planning process and ended any further efforts to take the line beyond Flushing. Several proposals by the New York City Transit Authority would include the takeover of the Port Washington line but never made it through the discussion process.

By that time, Flushing line service had been cut back, not expanded. Service over the Queensboro Bridge on the 2nd Avenue Elevated ended on June 14, 1942. Borough President James A. Burke and other borough representatives fought this, but the city and the

BOT proceeded anyway.[127] The links between the Flushing and Astoria lines at Queensboro Plaza were taken out of service in 1949 and the other platforms and track structures were demolished; parts of the structures still stand to the east and west of the station. Flushing line riders had the ability to take one train all of the way to Lower Manhattan; since 1949, they have had to make transfers in Queens or Manhattan that added significant time and effort to their trips.

The eleven-year delay in extending the Flushing line from Corona, and the failure to widen Amity Street, still has effects. Before work on the extension had begun, its effect was felt on Flushing's real estate. Many of the buildings that are still standing in the area were either built or planned within the building lines established in Flushing's village days. Amity Street wasn't widened; the Main Street station was built within a confined area with narrow platforms and stairways. Few in the 1920s imagined how many people and vehicles would enter the area to reach the subway. Few anticipated that the Third Ward area or the rest of northern Queens would grow as it did following the opening of the Flushing line and in anticipation of the system expansion that never came.

The station entrances at Main Street and Roosevelt Avenue couldn't handle the crowds of riders who wanted to ride the No. 7 line. A new entrance was built toward the east end of the station after World War II. This entrance was also overwhelmed and was replaced by a larger entrance area in 1999.

The intersection of Roosevelt Avenue and Main Street is heavily congested due to narrow roadways and sidewalks. Many of the bus lines that enter downtown Flushing come from communities across northern, central, eastern, and southwest Queens, Nassau County, and the Bronx to link with the subway. Add to it the cars and other vehicles that enter this area and the quiet, unclogged streets of the early part of the twentieth

Figure 3-11. Looking north on Main Street toward Amity Street (Roosevelt Avenue) in 1923. (Photo courtesy of the New York Transit Museum Archives)

Figure 3-12. The same view in 2011. (Photo by the author)

century are choked with traffic and pedestrians. The New York City Department of Transportation and MTA New York City Transit are still working toward a solution.

All talk of extending the Flushing line is in a westward direction these days. After eight decades, work on an extension to 11th Avenue and West 34th Street in Manhattan is underway. Mayor Michael R. Bloomberg and others have discussed a further extension under the Hudson River to New Jersey to connect with commuter rail lines there. This is nothing new—in 1926, Daniel L. Turner proposed such an extension while serving as consulting engineer to the North Jersey Transit Commission. It just continues to show the Flushing line's ongoing and growing value to transit riders in the New York metropolitan area.

4

The expansion of the subway system helped to bring social and economic change to the Bronx. As IRT lines extended to the northern reaches of the borough and the New York, Westchester, and Boston Railway (W&B) from Hunts Point to past the city line, developers of large properties recognized the land's potential. "The faster the Interborough puts through service in operation on the White Plains [Road] line the quicker the communities adjacent thereto will develop and become thickly populated," the *Bronx Home News* noted in 1917.[1]

"These estate holdings show the high opinion with which the purchasers and their heirs regard Bronx real estate. It is only natural that the investing public, when it knows that so many business men and financiers invest their money in the Bronx, should follow their judgement and do likewise," Elmer Dean Coulter, representing the Astor Estate, wrote in 1912. "That this judgement is good is shown by the profits the original owners obtain when they sell their properties. . . . The New York, Westchester and Boston Railway, running through what is known as the 'Annexed District' . . . with branches to New Rochelle and White Plains, extends through beautiful property, ideal for home sites. With this [rail] road and the additional means of rapid transit, the Bronx should beat its past record of more than doubling its population in ten years."[2]

John Masterson Burke owned land bordered by Gun Hill Road and Bronxwood, Throop, and Burke Avenues. He established the Burke Rehabilitation Hospital in White Plains and the Winifred Masterson Burke Relief Foundation, and donated land the city needed to open parts of Throop and Burke Avenues in 1913.[3] Joseph P. Day and J. Clarence Davies auctioned off Burke's Bronx property, 1,386 undeveloped parcels of land, on June 24, 1920; the proceeds benefited both charities.

Day auctioned off other Bronx properties as well. He claimed to have sold "at least a third of the Bronx."[4] Even if viewed as hyperbole, he did sell huge amounts of land. Day advocated for expanding the Bronx's rapid transit system, seeing a connection between the transit system and increased property values. He stressed the proximity between the properties and existing and planned rail lines.

The New York State Transit Commission's 1922 plan led the Bronx Board of Trade to issue proposals. The Transit Commission proposed extending the BRT's Broadway line from 57th Street to 8th Avenue and 155th Street; the Board proposed extending it to the Bronx and running the Transit Commission's 8th Avenue–Amsterdam Avenue line along Tremont Avenue to Fort Schuyler. They proposed a line along 2nd Avenue in Manhattan to connect with the Pelham line.[5]

On November 24, 1924, Alexander Haring, Olin J. Stephens, Maurice Westergren, and Charles E. Reid of the Board of Trade met with Chairman John H. Delaney and the members of the newly formed Board of Transportation. They discussed their proposals and suggested more routes, including extending the Lenox Avenue line to the city line via the Grand Concourse, Jerome Avenue, and Katonah Avenue; connecting the 2nd and 3rd Avenue Els with the Pelham line; extending a proposed 1st Avenue line[6] to Fordham Road via 3rd Avenue, Boston Road, and Southern Boulevard, extending the IRT Broadway line to the city line and building a spur from the White Plains Road line to the city line via Boston Road.[7]

"The Bronx has before it a magnificent future, made more magnificent by the fact that from now on its growth will be largely from within and most healthy, because it shall be a natural growth," Day said at the Bronx Industrial Exposition in February 1925. "The Grand Boulevard and Concourse has been splendidly developed with a fine type of modern apartment house. Sooner or later the great building movement that has made the Grand Boulevard and Concourse the foremost residential centre of the Bronx must swing to the east into the Bronx and Pelham Parkway, which is the finest in the world. This building movement has begun already with the erection of small homes, but it is only a question of time before this movement will be succeeded by the building of apartment houses."[8]

The Grand Boulevard and Concourse was the vision of Louis A. Risse, a French immigrant. He came to the United States in 1871, becoming a civil engineer for the New York Central Railroad. Risse mapped the Bronx's Kingsbridge, West Farms, and Morrisania sections. After working in the private sector, he became New York City's chief topographical engineer, developing the Grand Concourse and playing a major role in the mapping of other parts of the city.

The BOT approved the Concourse line on March 10, 1925, running from the 8th Avenue line to Bedford Park Boulevard. The original plans called for a four-track line; one was later eliminated, a point of contention for Bronx groups. There were plans to extend the Concourse line to the Northeast Bronx, an area not served by rapid transit. The W&B served the area but didn't enter Manhattan. Customers wishing to go to Manhattan had to transfer to the IRT at East 180th Street or in Hunts Point.

A growing population required more transit service. In 1926 the Amalgamated Clothing Workers Union announced the purchase of land near Van Cortlandt Park to build apartment houses. Tenants moved into the Amalgamated Houses' first 303 apartments in 1927, starting the co-op movement in the Bronx. Amalgamated was designed by the architectural firm of Springsteen and Goldhammer, which also designed the first phase of the Workers Cooperative Colony on Bronx Park East and the Shalom Aleichem houses by the Jerome Park Reservoir with the Yiddish cooperative Heim Gesellschaft.

The Jewish National Workers Alliance sponsored the Farband Houses on Williamsbridge Road. The Typographical Workers Union sponsored buildings by East 180th Street. Four unions, including the International Ladies Garment Workers Union, sponsored the Thomas Garden Apartments on Mott Avenue (later the Grand Concourse's southern extension).[9] New apartment buildings went up along the Concourse, leading to a major increase in population and the growth of a new form of architecture, Art Deco.

The Board of Estimate approved the 8th Avenue–Concourse line connection on March 24, 1927. Despite dissatisfaction over the missing fourth track and a direct downtown routing, no one opposed the plan, but Bronx transit advocates wanted more. Highbridge and University Heights residents formed the West Bronx Taxpayers Alliance, calling for service to their communities.[10] The East Bronx Transit Committee supported a W&B extension to Manhattan's West Side via 125th Street. "This plan, if successfully carried out, would revolutionize conditions in the section. It would make possible the development of large tracts that now lie idle and would advance business possibilities in this part of the city," said Committee Chairman Alfred G. Illich.[11]

Charles P. Giraud and James M. Welsch, working with the Park Avenue Improvement Association, had another idea. *Home News* editorials advanced their concept: continue the Concourse line along 5th Avenue and Central Park South to 6th Avenue, connecting with the IND there. The *Home News* made it a recurring theme. New York Board of Aldermen President Joseph V. McKee, the Bronx Board of Trade, and the Bronx Chamber of Commerce endorsed the plan.

The BOT disagreed with Giraud and Welsch, believing that its Concourse line plan would resolve the problem of Bronx subway congestion. BOT Commissioner Daniel L. Ryan asked, "What revenue would the city derive from a line in the district running from 59th to 110th Sts. along Fifth Avenue? . . . In the main, this is a highly residential section and the present Lexington Avenue line serves it adequately. To build a subway under Fifth Avenue from 59th and 110th Streets would cost at least $40,000,000 [$1.01 billion in 2011 dollars, according to MeasuringWorth.com], with little prospect of an adequate return on the investment."[12]

Plans for other Bronx projects were examined in 1927. U.S. Secretary of Commerce Herbert Hoover appointed a group to find locations for regional airports in 1927. The Chamber of Commerce's Airport Committee chairman, Major William F. Deegan,[13] proposed a site between the tracks of the W&B and the New York, New Haven, and Hartford Railroad by the Hutchinson River. The site ranked third out of a possible seventy-two locations.[14]

Alderman Alford J. Williams and the Taxpayers Alliance of the Bronx met with Borough President Henry Bruckner[15] on December 31 to plan a meeting with the BOT on January 10, 1928, that all Bronx Aldermen would attend. They proposed a line on 1st Avenue connecting the Pelham line with a branch along Lafayette Avenue; another line along Madison Avenue, connecting with the Concourse line at 161st Street; a Concourse line extension, running north to Gun Hill Road via Mosholu Parkway and Van Cortlandt and Bainbridge Avenues; and an extension to the 8th Avenue line to the city border via Riverdale Avenue.[16]

Thomas McDonald suggested extending the 3rd Avenue El to the city line via Gun Hill Road and Laconia Avenue and a Boston Road line.[17] Edward J. Walsh, William P. Sullivan, and Max Gross discussed the Giraud/Welsch plan. Ryan promised that the proposals would be studied.

Bruckner asked whether the BOT considered new subways for the Bronx. Ryan said studies had been conducted though a decision had not yet been reached. "Can we hope for any increased rapid transit lines in the near future?" Bruckner asked. "There is nothing definite yet," said Ryan. "As it is at present the Bronx is getting $60,000,000 of the

Figure 4-1. Borough President Henry Bruckner in 1918. (*New York Sun*)

$600,000,000 [$600 million in 1928 is $14.9 billion in 2011 according to MeasuringWorth .com] to be spent upon the subways now under consideration."[18]

The *Home News* editorial board was aghast at Ryan for saying that only 10 percent of subway construction money would go to the Bronx, and unhappy that no one protested:

> The interests of the Bronx would assuredly be served best if all Bronx officials and all Bronx organizations would concentrate on a single route—the one that would do most to cut down transit congestion here—and if all these forces would then present a unified front in demanding that the route determined upon be gotten under way.
>
> We are already sure of a subway along the Concourse. Why should not every local effort towards transit betterment be combined in one huge drive for the inclusion of that subway as part of a through trunk line under Fifth Avenue, Madison Avenue or whatever downtown thoroughfare may be found most desirable?
>
> The Bronx certainly got no fair share in the $600,000,000 program.[19]

Ryan answered a letter from Albert D. Phelps, a real estate broker, protesting the borough's share of capital funding. He said the Board was considering a spur from the

Figure 4-2. Major William F. Deegan in 1921. (*New York Tribune*)

Concourse line at 192nd Street that would go east to Webster Avenue, connect with the 3rd Avenue Elevated, and continues to the 241st Street station on the White Plains Road line.[20]

The Chamber of Commerce, the Bronx Real Estate Board, and the 170th Street Merchants Association campaigned for the Giraud/Welsch plan. At the Chamber's January 26 meeting at the Concourse Plaza Hotel, Deegan, now Chamber president, appointed William A. Cokeley to chair their Public Utilities Committee.

Bruckner wanted a low-key approach. Cokeley disagreed: "We're going through with this protest in spite of the Mayor, the Borough President, the Board of Transportation and all others who object. . . . We may not do good, but we'll at least be heard sufficiently to keep them from spending $10,000,000 in this fashion again. Our idea is to see that the Bronx is not discriminated against."[21]

The BOT, unaffected by calls for the Giraud/Welsch plan, awarded contracts for the Concourse line's first section, from Manhattan to 161st Street and Ruppert Place, on January 27. Deegan and Fred Wurzbach, Board of Trade president, organized the Bronx Combined Civic Organization on January 31 at the Concourse Plaza. Cokeley would be the chairman and Wurzbach would be vice chairman. Their goal was building the Concourse line in accordance with the Giraud/Welsch plan.

Henry F. A. Wolf of the Bronx Taxpayers Association was worried: "If we take the attitude that we want the four-track line or none we may get none."[22] "We want nothing but what we are entitled to, and that we should accept nothing but that," Wurzbach responded. "We are entitled to a direct line to lower Manhattan, and we should get it. If necessary, we should organize a delegation of 2,500 to go down to City Hall and make our demands known. We don't want relief. We want a cure."[23]

More civic groups and businesspeople joined the Bronx Combined Civic Organization, but the Board of Trade withdrew on February 1. Wurzbach told Deegan that a strong Board of Trade, working separately, but with the same purpose, would strengthen efforts for the Giraud/Welsch plan. He set up a meeting with the BOT.[24]

Wurzbach assembled his committee. Leo Ehrhart,[25] an engineer who worked with Joseph P. Day to develop parts of City Island and Hunts Point, chaired. Time was short. "We must induce the Board of Transportation to change its plans before they start removing dirt for the Concourse subway," said Ehrhart. "Once that three-track subway is laid it will remain a three-track line until the end of time. Everyone knows that the third track will never have any use except as a storage yard for empty cars."[26]

The meeting was held on February 21 at the BOT's Manhattan offices. Wurzbach and Ehrhart tried to discuss the Giraud/Welsch plan but spent more time on the defensive from Delaney's comments: "This is part of the main line. If you have two tracks running all the way from 200th Street down to Fulton Street, without any change whatever[,] why is it a branch? There are only two tracks running to Washington Heights."[27]

Ehrhart responded: "We absolutely admit that we are getting a certain relief by this line, a great relief, but we feel, or know from an engineering viewpoint . . ."[28] Delaney interrupted: "Mr. Ehrhart, if you persist in that attitude, I don't want to give a certain relief to the Bronx. The Bronx is entitled to relief. The Bronx is entitled to a full line. In my judgment it is getting it. If the Bronx doesn't want it, we will take the four tracks to Washington Heights."[29]

"We don't want to lose what we have already accomplished," Ehrhart said. "We don't want to lose anything that has been accomplished."[30] All the Board of Trade members could talk about was reverse commutation, providing access to facilities like Hunter College (then in the Bronx).

Ryan discussed service expansion: "I am not violating any confidence when I say that the members of the Board have given very serious consideration to the building of another rapid transit line with express service in the Bronx, but not in the westerly end—in the central and easterly end."[31] He later said nothing was imminent, but admitted there was room for a subway line between the White Plains Road and Pelham lines to Manhattan. The Board of Trade members promised to support the BOT, largely ending talk of the Giraud/Welsch plan. Wurzbach later said that while the Board of Trade supported its concept, it was more committed to the planned line Ryan discussed.

Northeast Bronx residents and businesspeople focused on transit issues. McDonald discussed his proposed "Belt Plan" at a March 3 meeting. A meeting was scheduled for March 27 with McDonald, the Northeast Bronx Civic League, and the BOT concerning Northeast Bronx service. James Holler, the Civic League's president, knew what his area needed:

We have suffered from lack of transportation facilities for many years. It is time that we should receive recognition from the Board of Transportation and the city. Adequate facilities for our section will do what milk will do for a child. . . . We need a subway in our neighborhood. No one questions that statement. Commissioner Ryan said at a previous meeting that the section is undeveloped and cannot support a subway. . . . In answer to that statement we can point out that the Westchester Avenue east of the Bronx River was undeveloped before the subway was built on that avenue. Now that section is growing so rapidly it is difficult to keep pace with it.[32]

Altermen Thomas McDonald and Peter Donovan presented the case for the Boston Road line. McDonald said the area was growing, with plans to widen the roadway underway and ground broken for new housing: "Unless the City authorities act quickly in this matter, these thousands of people will be without the proper transit facilities and the growth of the entire section would be stifled."[33]

Clarence Beach, a Throggs Neck real estate agent, criticized the Concourse line, and asked why the Fulton Street subway was being built in Brooklyn and why it couldn't be postponed.[34] Delaney was contentious: "This Board will not change any of the plans for the subway now under construction. It intends to build all of the routes that have been authorized."[35] They argued until Delaney said, "I'll have to ask you to dismiss this gentleman. He's wasting our time and the time of those people here to be heard on the Bronx subway needs."[36]

Mary Helmbuch of the Throggs Neck Property Owners Association asked when help would come. "Back in 1924, apparently unified, the Bronx associations came before the Board of Transportation and recommended the Concourse subway, which we are about to build," Delaney said. "I want you to know that we have in mind the needs of the East Bronx, and will take cognizance of them in considering the second part of the [IND] subway plan."[37]

Work on the Concourse line's first section began in July 1928, and bids were received for its second section from Ruppert Place and 161st Street to 167th Street and the Concourse. The bids for the third section, to 175th Street, were due in September, and those for the fourth, to 183rd Street, were due in October. The bids for the rest of the line's *first* phase would be in by the end of 1928. There would be a *second* one.

On August 30, BOT Secretary William Jerome Daly told Wurzbach that Concourse line work had progressed to allow for planning an extension:

> The designing engineers have been instructed to design the northerly end of the Concourse construction at about 206th Street in such manner as to allow further extension easterly from the Concourse. Surveys and test borings have been authorized and are under way to locate a feasible route for the proposed easterly extension, so that the construction plan of the most northerly Concourse section may be designed for such a connection. Burke Avenue would be an appropriate on the easterly side of Bronx Park, if a practicable route between the Concourse and Bronx Park can be located, but no definite plan can be adopted until the information to be obtained by the surveys and borings is available.[38]

On September 1, the BOT informed Bruckner of a plan to build the line to Bedford Park Boulevard with three tracks, swing eastward as a two-track line on an unspecified route, cross Bronx Park, and run to Dyre Avenue via Burke Avenue and Boston Road.

There wasn't much reaction. McDonald said little until December. At a meeting of the Joint Committee on Public Improvements in the North Bronx, he vowed to fight for a subway on Boston Road to link with the Concourse line extension on Burke Avenue and sought another meeting with the BOT. The Board of Trade said nothing until January 1929.

The Bronx Chamber of Commerce opposed the line, according to a September 2 account, astonished that it would be built along Burke Avenue, a street they called "sparsely-populated," instead of Fordham Road.[39] Charles Goldblatt claimed that people with inside information bought property along Burke Avenue in anticipation of a subway being built.[40]

Goldblatt may have been right. Early in 1928, before the BOT's intentions were known, many parcels of land changed hands near Burke Avenue. Huge estates weren't sold, but rather many smaller properties. Apartment buildings, row houses, and commercial properties sprung up in the White Plains Road line's service area throughout the middle and late 1920s after the estates were sold.

A second wave of housing was built between 1929 and 1935, probably in anticipation of the Burke Avenue line. People saw what happened on the Grand Concourse and wanted to take advantage of the same opportunity in the Northeast Bronx. Based on reports in the *New York Times* real estate section, we know that real estate companies made numerous land purchases in the Burke Avenue / Boston Road corridor.

The Chamber of Commerce reiterated their position in early 1929. Logan Billingsley,[41] a realtor who succeeded Deegan as Chamber president,[42] said on March 28 that the plan was "rushed through official bodies in a quiet manner [because of] the friendship that exists between a certain City official and a well-known Bronxite, who has large real estate holdings on Burke Avenue."[43] He didn't name names; neither did Cokeley, still nursing a grudge. "I want to know, first, what right have they to take away the four-track subway?" asked Cokeley. "I want to know how if there is not enough money, a long spur can be spread over the most sparsely-populated portion of the East Bronx? . . . Who is behind the Burke–Dyre proposal? Who is dictating this plan? Who is the unknown and unseen power that wants such an extension?"[44]

Illich, the Chamber's vice president, sold 12,500 square feet of property on Burke Avenue early in 1928,[45] possibly before the BOT's plans were known. He criticized the line: "The very people in the East Bronx who now want the extension spur will kick about it if it is carried through. They will find that it will take them far too long to get downtown. Any layman at all could lay out a better subway route than the proposed plan. . . . It is plain that there is something behind this proposal."[46]

On April 4 the BOT approved the extension to Webster Avenue and 205th Street. McDonald led a delegation to the meeting to speak for the plan: "We are here in favor of extending the Concourse subway to Webster Avenue, but we want to particularly impress you with the urgent need of a new subway line on Boston Road. Extending the Concourse line to Webster and Burke Avenues is a necessary preliminary to further extension of the line on Boston Road to a point near Dyre Avenue. . . . The community that such a subway would serve has a population of about 100,000 people and apartment houses, now in progress will accommodate 60,000 more."[47]

Delaney responded:

When the present subway system, now under construction, was laid out, it provided for only half of the subway needs of the city. At that time this was all that we had money for. However, let me emphasize that no one realizes the need for an East Bronx subway more than the officials of the Board of Transportation. . . . With our

1925 subway construction program well under way, engineers of the Board of Transportation have constructed research work on the needs for new subway lines in the past year. They are now plotting to see what can be done in the way of constructing an East Side subway up either Second or Third Avenues, or along a private right-of-way, into the East Bronx section.[48]

This was news. The *Home News* called the statement "as gratifying as it is unexpected."[49] Wurzbach termed it "one of the greatest projects in years for encouraging the growth of the Bronx, and one in line with proposals for transit relief which we made fifteen years or so ago in advocating a subway under either First, Second, or Third Avenue."[50]

The BOT approved the specifications for the Concourse line's first phase on May 3. Anna Mahler, president of the Bronx Division of the League of Women Voters—claiming to represent the Bronx Ridge Civic Association, the Chester Improvement Association, the Northeast Bronx Civic League, the Central Chester Taxpayers Association, the Wakefield Taxpayers Association, and the Bronx Chamber of Commerce—spoke against the second-phase plan. "You do not represent the Northeast Bronx Civic League. Members of that organization are in favor of this improvement for their section," McDonald said. "The extension will be a means of providing a subway for Boston Road, and that is what the people of the Northeast Bronx want." "I spoke to James W. Holler, the President of that organization," Mahler replied, "and he told me that he was opposed to the construction of the extension of the Concourse subway to Burke and Webster Avenues."[51] Frederick S. Loewenthal objected. *He* represented the Northeast Bronx Civic League, disavowing Mahler's statement. Holler, P. B. Willis of the Central Chester Taxpayers Association, and Emil J. Cavanaugh of the Chester Improvement later denied that Mahler represented them, and spoke in support of Burke Avenue.[52]

On May 6, Bruckner brought University Heights residents to a BOT meeting, seeking a Concourse line branch in that area. Hunts Point, Clason Point, Union Point, and Throggs Neck groups formed the East Bronx Allied Association on May 20. John Moroney of the Throggs Neck Property Owners and Taxpayers Association outlined their goal of a subway line serving their communities, a campaign he led for the next two decades.

The Curtiss–Wright Corporation announced the purchase of 250 acres of land across the Hutchinson River from Pelham Bay Park on June 4. They were buying land for airports across the nation. Charles W. Cuthell, Curtiss's general counsel, stated that the airport would be "entirely for the people of the Bronx and Westchester County. . . . The airport will be a local improvement of the finest sort. It will be one of the few airports that can be built within the corporate limits of the City of New York." ". . . The site is well located," he continued, "and in selecting this land, the necessity of tearing down structures on the ground was avoided. It is in a highly strategic position for transit purposes, and the new Hutchinson River Parkway will make it easily accessible to all parts of Westchester County. . . . The field will be laid out so that it may easily be regarded as an adjunct to Pelham Bay Park."[53]

The W&B's Baychester Avenue station adjoined the site; the New Haven Railroad ran east of it. The Boston Road line would be built nearby. Bruckner compared its potential impact to an earlier Bronx project: "Airport development will undoubtedly bring other activities to the section involved. . . . When the Yankee Stadium was proposed there was some opposition to the closing of the streets, but I think that having the Stadium in the Bronx has been a great advantage to the borough. I think the Curtiss airport development will be of even more benefit to the Bronx than the Yankee Stadium has been."[54]

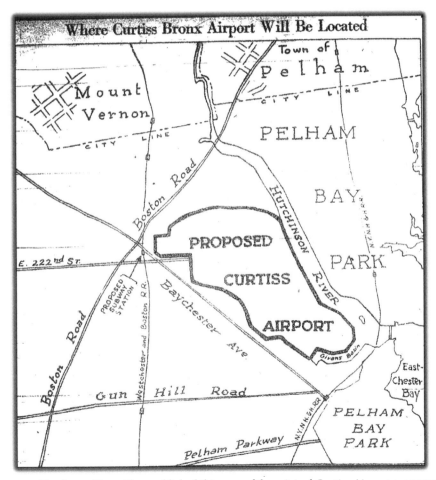

Figure 4-3. The *Bronx Home News* published this map of the original Curtiss Airport property on June 2, 1929.

News of the 2nd Avenue subway came out in August. It would run on Lincoln and Brook Avenues and Boston Road in the Bronx, linking with the Concourse line at Burke Avenue. The BOT would "recapture" the White Plains Road line at 177th Street from the IRT. The trunk line would link with it and a branch would run along White Plains Road to 241st Street. The IRT line would terminate at the Bronx Park station.[55]

The *Home News* editorial on September 3 found benefit in the Burke Avenue line, but suggested that a better route would be for it to go via Fordham Road and Pelham Parkway to Boston Road. The paper hinted that the beneficiaries were "certain real estate investors who have bought wisely and well, and with truly remarkable foresight."[56]

The areas around Fordham Road and Pelham Parkway were being developed and served by existing lines. Building a subway line through less-developed areas would have a greater impact on their development. The potential for growth and increased tax revenues along Burke Avenue and Boston Road must have influenced the BOT's thinking.

The BOT released the plan for the IND's second phase on September 15, calling for one hundred miles of new lines to be built at a cost of $938 million ($12.3 billion in 2011 dollars, according to MeasuringWorth.com), of which 38.12 miles would be in the Bronx, built at a cost of $75.9 million ($1.84 billion in 2011), with an additional $2.1 million ($27.6 million in 2011) being spent to "recapture" the northern part of the White Plains Road line.

The branches of the 2nd Avenue line planned for the North and Northeast Bronx were expected. A third wasn't, leaving the trunk line at 3rd Avenue and 163rd Street, running to East Tremont Avenue via 163rd Street, Hunts Point, Seneca, and Lafayette Avenues.

A significant portion of the Bronx routes would be elevated. The 2nd Avenue Trunk Line would be elevated from Vyse Avenue and 177th Street to its connection with the White Plains Road line. After 180th Street, the Boston Road line would go underground at Garfield Street, become elevated again at Mace Avenue, and remain elevated to the Baychester Avenue Terminal. The Lafayette Avenue branch would be a subway through Edgewater Road and Seneca Avenue; from there it was elevated. The Burke Avenue line would cross Bronx Park as part of a viaduct including a vehicular roadway, becoming elevated to link with the Boston Road line.

The new els drew the most attention. The *Home News* assailed the idea:

The elevated railway has long been regarded as obsolete. It is a killer of property values, an eyesore and a general neighborhood nuisance. It obstructs the vehicular roadways of a city that has no roadway space to spare. . . . Let them look at the horrible example of Jerome Avenue. Had the rapid transit line there been underground (as is the Manhattan section of the route) Jerome Avenue, a through north and south artery running into Westchester County, might have been a fine residential avenue, or a productive high-class business street. It has every advantage of location. It might have been pouring a maximum value of tax money into the city treasury.[57]

"How much greater would the folly of starting on new elevated lines at this late date, when the arresting and dismaying example of Jerome Avenue has been before us all these years," Billingsley fumed. ". . . It will be said that the elevated structures are cheaper than underground routes. That is true. But it is high time that all of our officials realized that cheapness and economy are not synonymous."[58] Wurzbach asked, "Why put up such antiquated structures in the Bronx? . . . Look at Jerome Avenue, especially just north and south of Fordham Road. What kind of stores do you have there today?"[59]

Aldermanic President McKee praised the overall plan in a letter to Delaney, but condemned new els:

My conviction is based on the sad experience the Bronx has suffered in this respect. Jerome Avenue was one of the great arterial highways in our borough. It might have developed into a high-class thoroughfare with valuable frontage for business of the best type. The return in taxes to the City would have been incalculable. . . . But what has happened? A short-sighted policy during a former administration dictated the building of an elevated structure and today, instead of a high-type avenue, the street for the entire length has been ruined, and is now fit only for garages and other unrestricted activities.[60]

Joseph P. Day supported els: "It should have a stimulating effect on real estate in general, and particularly on vacant and improved properties in the territories which the new lines are routed. . . . In the Bronx, the territory to receive the greatest benefit from the proposed subway along Boston Road is that section north of the Pelham Parkway and east of Boston Road. While it is served by the New York, Westchester and Boston Railway and bus lines, it should obtain added favor by reason of the Grand Concourse subway now under construction."[61] The BOT didn't seem to expect this opposition. Ryan was the only Board member to speak. He said he had nothing else to say.[62]

The BOT approved the final section of the Concourse line's first phase on September 26 and anticipated that work would soon be underway. The 205th Street Station would be the Concourse line's terminus until the Burke Avenue line was built. A tunnel was built to 205th Street and Webster Avenue, where it would run across Bronx Park on a viaduct.

The year 1929 featured a mayoral election. Mayor Walker ran for reelection against Congressman Fiorello H. La Guardia. Transit was a major topic of discussion. Walker's campaign committee issued *New York: The Wonder City*, a publication hailing the accomplishments of his administration's first four years, giving major play to the plan.

Figure 4-4. Mayor James J. Walker in 1929. (Queens Planning Commission)

The Chamber of Commerce sent questionnaires to the candidates asking their opinion of the BOT's plan. James W. Welsch, the Republican–Fusion candidate for borough president, replied:

> With all due respect to Chairman Delaney and members of the Board of Transportation and their knowledge in problems of rapid transit, I must say that they certainly did apply the fundamental principles of psychology and subterfuge to cause Bronx officials and city official[s] to focus their attention on only one phase of this very important phase of this very important engineering problem.
>
> . . . The Board of Transportation should be required to give the people of the Bronx a complete and comprehensive plan for transit lines needed in this borough.[63]

Walker was in a bind. La Guardia was no proponent of els. Opposition to them was growing. This could affect the election. He had to speak out, and speak out he did at Jamaica High School on October 2:

> Not one foot of elevated structure will be constructed unless with the unanimous approval of the citizens. . . . Since the announcement of the new plan by the Board of Transportation there has been some discussion about elevated railroads. The major part of that new program is composed of subways, but there are some elevated extensions in the outlying parts of the city. . . . I agree with the critics of elevated structures. I do not like to see them in the streets. The engineers tell me that there are parts of the city where the surface of the ground is so near the level of the sea that subway construction is impractical. . . . All new subway routes must come before the Mayor for his separate approval and therefore the Mayor will consider another provision in

the constitution which requires that the consent of the owners of the property must be obtained on every street in which a railroad is built, and the owners of the property, in the last analysis, are those who are the most directly concerned.[64]

Bronx civic and business leaders discussed the plan on October 3 at a meeting of the New York State Society of Professional Engineers and Land Surveyors at the Concourse Plaza Hotel. Arthur V. Sheridan,[65] their president, said els were "obsolete, unsightly, noisy, dangerous to traffic and a source of depreciation of real estate values far in excess of the initial saving effected in construction cost."[66]

Walker spoke again on October 19 at Evander Childs High School: "There are some who are annoyed about certain elevated structures for new elevated lines, but let me bring you the assurance tonight, if you please, speaking for myself as a member of the Board of Estimate—no little reason to assume that my mind runs along the same mind as the other members of the board—there is no necessity for running a high temperature about the proposed elevated routes. . . . There will be no elevated routes of the rapid transit line in the City, unless the people of the City want them."[67] New subways became a moot point shortly afterward, when the stock market crashed on October 26. The main effort would be completing the first phase of the IND, rather than beginning the second.

Day auctioned the Hammersley and Crawford estates in the Northeast Bronx on Election Day. He emphasized the proximity of the land to the proposed subways and Curtiss Airport. He pointed to the increased value of the Claflin estate, by the Jerome Avenue line, in a decade, and how the value of the Gleason estate, by the Pelham line, had increased by almost seven times in about two decades, seemingly answering critics of elevated lines.[68]

Walker defeated La Guardia on Election Day; Bruckner won a fourth term. In the Bronx, the Curtiss Airport Corporation bid $5,000[69] for five of the lots Day put up for auction along the western boundary of the airport. Day was also successful in selling other properties in the area. Despite the Stock Market crash, people still had big plans for the Northeast Bronx.

The BOT's second-stage construction program was poorly received, but it planned to award contracts totaling $25 million[70] in the fall of 1930 and to hold sixteen public hearings on the plan. Three hearings affected the Bronx. The first, on February 10, dealt with the 2nd Avenue Trunk Line; the Burke Avenue and Boston Road lines would be discussed on February 19; and the Lafayette Avenue line hearing would take place on February 28.

The els had some supporters. August F. Schwarzler of the Bronx Real Estate Board said that his group and the Board of Trade supported them, particularly in the East Bronx. Wurzbach disagreed. The Board was "absolutely opposed to the construction of any elevated lines in the Bronx and has not changed its opinion."[71] Many realtors attacked Schwarzler, although Real Estate Board President Samuel E. McRickard gave mild support:

> There is no question that elevated lines bring about depreciation of realty values on the streets on which they are constructed. But the transportation facilities thus provided benefit all the surrounding streets that lead to the development of hitherto dormant sections. . . . Back in 1904, I was emphatically opposed to the construction of the then-proposed Jerome Avenue "L." The difference in cost between a subway line and an "L" was so great that the problem was reduced to the question "will the West Bronx take an elevated line or will it go without rapid transit?" . . . Under these circumstances, I finally gave my approval to the Jerome Avenue "L." I realize now that the unsightly elevated structure has destroyed Jerome Avenue. But it had benefited and led to the development of the surrounding streets, such as the Concourse, Fordham Road and University Avenue.[72]

Schwarzler's justification for els was the problems with building subways in swampy areas. Wurzbach called Schwarzler's argument "a very weak excuse. If engineers can build tunnels under rivers, certainly subways can be built under marshy lands."[73]

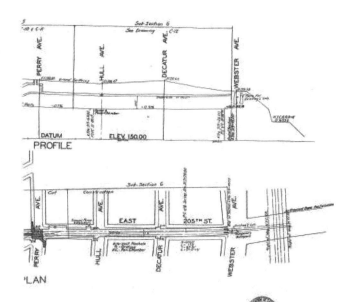

Figure 4-5. A contract drawing for the Concourse line, showing the future plans for the extension to Burke Avenue. (Courtesy of the New York Transit Museum Archives)

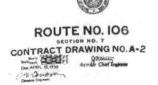

ROUTE NO. 106
SECTION NO. 7
CONTRACT DRAWING NO. A-2

Wurzbach led the delegation to the February 10 hearing, saying, "Don't scrap the elevated lines in Manhattan to bring them to the Bronx. They are a detriment to property values. You took them down on Sixth Avenue between 53rd Street and 59th Street and as a result property values increased threefold. Although the Bronx is extremely anxious for transit relief, let me assure you that we would sooner wait ten years more than to have a 50-year heritage in the form of an unsightly 'L' structure."[74]

Hundreds attended the February 19 hearing. Future BOT Commissioner Charles V. Halley, Jr., proposed something different:

Buildings along the proposed transit route in the North Bronx would not have to be shored up as in the lower Bronx and Manhattan. . . . The builders could also work in an open "cut," which would not have to be covered over as the Concourse subway tunnel was. The traffic congestion in the north Bronx is not so great at present that it could not be diverted to other streets to cut down the expense of subway construction. . . . The money saved in this manner would greatly cut down the difference between the cost of the elevated line that the Board of Transportation proposes, and the subway that the Bronx civic organizations hold to be an absolute necessity.[75]

"We are unalterably opposed to overhead structures. They may have been useful at one time, just as the horsecar was at one time, but that time is past," McDonald said. ". . . This board knows that the people of my district advocated the construction of a subway up Boston Road. We are grateful to the board for giving it to us, but instead of having it terminate at Baychester Avenue as now proposed, we are here to demand that it be extended to Dyre Avenue and 233rd Street. . . . I know a number of builders who are desirous of starting a huge apartment house development in Edenwald and are merely waiting for some assurance from this Board that transit will be provided."[76] Delaney said nothing; Ryan thanked everyone for attending, promising that their views would be taken into consideration.

Day now criticized els:

Improved transit facilities go hand in hand with population growth. The Grand Concourse subway now building is a big step forward in Bronx history. In its broad aspects and without reference to details the proposed subway plan announced last fall by the Board of Transportation is a thoughtful and intelligent one. It is not enough to say that these proposed new subways in the eastern section of the Bronx would be a good thing. They are an absolute necessity. . . . And when I use the word "subway" I mean subway and I do not mean elevated railroads! The time is coming soon when elevated railroads will be as obsolete as overhead telephone and trolley wires. I have never known a case where an elevated structure did not injure the value of abutting property, and I have never known a case where a subway did not improve real estate value along its route.[77]

More testimony against els was heard at the third hearing. Bronx Public Works Commissioner William J. Flynn wrote to the BOT for Bruckner, who had said little: "We have learned our lesson, and should not, under any circumstances, sanction a further extension of the elevated lines."[78] Ryan stated that no decision would be made until the hearing process ended in late March. A citywide policy would be developed.[79]

Bruckner himself refrained from making any public comment until September: "It is difficult to believe that the engineers who planned the new East Bronx subway suggested that elevated structures should be made part of the new system. It is the more inconceivable since a movement had been on foot both in the Bronx and in Manhattan to get rid of the subway and elevated train supporting contraptions for the past several years."[80] The BOT and its engineers had much to evaluate, a process that continued through February 1932.

The Board of Estimate approved a street-closing plan for the airport in 1929; the Curtiss Airport Corporation announced that work would start in March 1930. Little was done; people asked what was happening. Curtiss was waiting for the federal government to dredge the Hutchinson River, thereby allowing for construction of a seaplane base and providing landfill to even out the land.[81]

The Taxpayers Alliance of the Bronx protested. At a meeting on June 11, James F. Donnelly called it a "subterfuge" and sought an investigation.[82] Max Just, another Board member, said Curtiss placed the airport land for sale and had no plan to build.[83] Alex B. Mayer, the Airport Committee chairman, defended Curtiss, saying the stock market crash affected its plans. Schwarzler justified waiting for Hutchinson River landfill due to the landfill costs.

"The report that we have offered our Bronx property for sale is without the slightest foundation in fact," said William F. Carey, Curtiss president. "It has never been so offered since we acquired it; it is not now on the market, and we have no present intention of offering it for sale."[84] The federal government said dredging would take place, but Charles Loos, the project manager, wouldn't set a start date. "Despite rumors that the property is up for sale, the Curtiss–Wright Airports Corporation has at no time offered it for sale. The airport's exact boundary had to be determined, due to the swampy nature of the land. Dredging would solve that matter.[85]

Sites Curtiss had purchased in the North Beach and Idlewild sections of Queens turned out to be more preferable for airports. The city acquired them despite strenuous protests from the Bronx. North Beach Airport was dedicated on January 5, 1935; it was renamed for Mayor Fiorello H. La Guardia in 1939. The first commercial flight left New York International Airport on July 1, 1948; it was renamed for President John F. Kennedy in 1963. The Bronx property was mostly undeveloped until the 1950s. Most people are unaware of its history, only remembering a place young people visited for adventure. As strange as it may seem today to some people that an airport was planned for the site, it probably would have been as strange for people in 1930 to think a housing development the size of Co-op City's size would be built there.

The BOT's revised plans were made public on February 28, 1932.[86] The Burke Avenue line was intact; the Boston Road line was changed. The Board would connect it with the White Plains Road line by West Farms, but how it would run into the Northeast Bronx was different. It proposed using the W&B's local tracks above 180th Street. This would reduce construction costs, but also later play a major role in the discussion of transit issues in the Bronx.

There was little discussion of the new plans. There was no coverage in some newspapers and no public reaction reported; the IND's first phase was endangered, possibly because the city was in such financial distress. Walker and Delaney were looking for new sources of funding but wouldn't raise the fare, which remained at five cents until 1948.

City Comptroller Charles Berry met the representatives of the major area banks to sell bonds on January 8, 1932, without success. Economic conditions worsened and Walker was enmeshed in the scandals that would drive him from office later that year. The IND's first phase had to be completed. It was hoped the Concourse line's first part would be operating at the start of 1933, but in fact it would take much longer.

A major step was taken to develop the Northeast Bronx on September 21. The New York State Board of Housing announced plans for five housing developments for working-class families around the city. One of them was the Hillside Houses, to be built along the Burke and 2nd Avenue lines on land along Boston Road in Eastchester.

Hillside was sponsored by Nathan Straus, Jr., a former state senator and a member of a family prominent in business, political, and philanthropic circles. His uncle, Oscar, was the chairman of the New York State Public Service Commission when it was the agency planning the subway system.[87] Straus served in the State Senate from 1922 to 1928, the presidential administration of Franklin Delano Roosevelt, and the mayoral administration of Fiorello H. La Guardia. After he died in 1961, the *New York Times* eulogized him as follows: "All forms of pomposity were poison to Nathan Straus. Born to wealth and social prestige, he spent his life crusading for slum clearance, civil rights and the amelioration of urgent community problems."[88]

Nathan, Jr.'s grandfather purchased the Hillside Houses land in 1887.[89] His father bequeathed it to him. It was unused, and he wondered what to do with it. One night in Boston, he read a newspaper article by Andrew J. Eken of the Starrett Brothers and Eken construction firm. According to Straus:

[Eken] thought that the real future of the building business was not in the construction of more hotels and apartment houses, but in the construction of housing.

Figure 4-6. Nathan Straus, Jr. (Straus Historical Society Inc.)

He went on to say that he had studied the subject both here and abroad, and that he was confident that large project would rise, offering better living conditions at lower rents than had been available in the past.

His investigation had convinced him that such projects should not be located on expensive land in the slums of our cities, but should, instead, be built on sites of vacant land, available in large tracts at relatively low cost, at the outskirts of the cities.[90]

Straus contacted Eken and they began their work.

The visionary Clarence S. Stein was Hillside's architect. Along with Henry Wright, he designed the landmark Sunnyside Gardens and Phipps Gardens houses in Queens and similar developments elsewhere. Stein wanted to develop modern layouts, believing in communities with open spaces, as opposed to using standard street grids.[91]

The new mayor opposed Hillside Houses. James J. Walker had resigned due to the scandals sweeping the New York City government. Aldermanic President McKee replaced him until a new election was held in November. When the Reconstruction Finance Corporation (RFC) provided a loan to Hillside covering two-thirds of the project's cost, McKee protested: "There is no reason for the Bronx housing scheme. We have no shortage of housing in that borough. Actually, we find that nearly every house has at least one vacancy. We have no slum conditions in the Bronx either."[92]

The groups Straus termed "most of the real estate interests and practically all of the small speculative builders in the Bronx"[93] supported McKee. The New York Times editorial board and groups like the City Club supported Hillside.[94] McKee blocked the

Figure 4-7. Acting Mayor Joseph V. McKee with his press secretary, Charles E. Keegan, in 1932. Keegan served as an alderman and City Council member from 1935 to 1953. He was one of the Burke Avenue line's primary advocates. (*New York Evening Post*)

RFC loan, but support for Hillside grew after he left office. The Public Works Administration granted $5 million in January 1934; construction began that April.

Things weren't going well for the IND. The 8th Avenue line's first segment opened on September 10, 1932, but the Concourse line had no opening date. Aside from *Home News* editorials, there was little discussion of Burke Avenue. It was speculated that a minimal amount of funding could put the Concourse line and parts of the Queens Boulevard line into service,[95] but work didn't continue until Comptroller Berry sold $10 million ($165 million in 2011 dollars, according to MeasuringWorth.com) in corporate tax notes in December 1932.

New Year's Day in 1933 brought change to City Hall. Surrogate John P. O'Brien defeated McKee to complete Walker's term. On January 19 the Board of Estimate appropriated $1.46 million ($25.5 million in 2011 dollars, according to MeasuringWorth.com) to operate twenty-two new route miles on the IND, including the Concourse line. Delaney had lobbied for funding, arguing that it cost more *not* to operate these lines or maintain the tunnels than to begin service.

Concourse line service began on July 1 with little fanfare. Mrs. Edward Molloy of 3199 Bainbridge Avenue, the first rider at 205th Street, said, "I am a property owner and a resident of Bedford Park, and I am interested in the Concourse subway line from the standpoint of the good it will do for my community."[96] What celebration there was took place at a luncheon held at the Concourse Plaza two days earlier, followed by a tour of the line led by Delaney and Ryan, accompanied by Mayor O'Brien.

The scandal that drove Mayor Walker from office affected the whole city government. There was major turnover on the Board of Estimate. Judge Samuel Seabury's Moreland Act Commission investigated other city officials, including Borough President Bruckner and his chief aide, Public Works Commissioner Flynn. Newspaper articles implied that Flynn was the real power in the borough president's office.

Seabury wanted Bruckner and Flynn to resign or be removed from office. The Bronx County Democratic Party leadership nominated James J. Lyons as its candidate for borough president; he was elected in November.

Lyons was a successful leather salesman from University Heights. Though he was involved in civic affairs, this was his first public office. It was the only office to which Lyons would be elected. He served as borough president until 1962. When he took office, Franklin Delano Roosevelt hadn't yet completed his first year in the White House; he left at the end of the second year of the Kennedy administration. No other borough president has ever served as long.

Lyons brought his salesman's training with him. A 1940 *New York Times Magazine* profile said he "is using the same kind of sales tactics to 'sell' the Bronx as a combination of Byzantium, Biarritz and the Swiss Alps. As he views his situation, there is no basic difference between the Bronx and shoe leather. Now, as in the old days, his method is to

Figure 4-8. James J. Lyons in the 1930s. (Photo courtesy of the Bronx County Historical Society)

break down sales resistance by repeatedly hammering home the fine points of his product and keeping it constantly before the public."[97]

The city had a new mayor. With Seabury's support, Fiorello H. La Guardia ran against former Mayors McKee and O'Brien and won, starting a tide of change. Lyons was the one Democrat on the Board of Estimate at that time. Despite his occasionally professed admiration for La Guardia, Lyons was a frequent thorn in the mayor's side. One issue on which he was particularly nettlesome was Burke Avenue.

Bronx transit advocates revived in 1934; Hillside provided further argument for extending the Concourse line. The *Home News* noted this: "[Burke Avenue] furnish[es] convenient and direct rapid transit service for the great number of families who will tenant the Hillside Homes now under construction on upper Boston Road." The Chamber of Commerce now urged the BOT to proceed with the line.

Lyons asked the BOT to start work on Burke Avenue on May 19. Writing to George F. Mand, president of the Chamber of Commerce from 1931 to 1953,[98] he said that he thought the Board of Estimate approved the plan, but "to make certain, I am again taking the matter up with the Board of Estimate . . . so that if prior action taken does not carry with it adoption, we may get the necessary action from the Board."[99]

He also wrote to his colleagues the following:

The only facility now provided is a bus line operating in Boston Road from Dyre Avenue to Allerton Avenue and then westerly of White Plains Road. The nearest

Figure 4-9. Mayor Fiorello H. La Guardia. (Queens Planning Commission)

rapid transit being the New York, Westchester and Boston Railway located from 1,000 to 3,000 feet to the east, with stations too far apart to be of use to the properties in the vicinity of Boston Road and the elevated portion of the Lexington Avenue subway running in White Plains Road which is over 1,000 feet to about a mile and one-half to the west of this portion of Boston Road.

At the present time a large housing development is under construction to the westerly side of Boston Road, between Wilson Avenue and Eastchester Road [Hillside], and this housing project when completed will provide accommodations for about 1,600 families.

The private properties adjacent to each side of Boston Road and Baychester Avenue have not been developed to any great extent, due to the lack of proper transit facilities, and it is very doubtful that they will ever be developed unless rapid transit lines are constructed. These properties for the most part lend themselves to high class development and such development will enhance taxable values to a marked degree and be of great benefit to the city at large.[100]

Lyons proposed a resolution asking the BOT to proceed. La Guardia said he wanted to study the line further; there was no vote. Lyons tried a second resolution on September 29 but met the same fate.[101] La Guardia wanted more time. This continued into early 1935. Noting Hillside's upcoming opening, the potential for additional growth in the area, and the need for transit service to the Northeast Bronx, Lyons again asked for action.

La Guardia wanted the motion postponed at the Board of Estimate's January 18 meeting. Lyons protested: "This resolution merely indicates our approval of the extension. It doesn't involve money." "Well, you know this Board isn't going to authorize this without approval of the Board of Transportation," said La Guardia. "But there is nothing accomplished by sending it back to the Board of Transportation," Lyons replied.[102]

Delaney said no action would be taken on any line before the 6th Avenue subway. Lyons wanted Burke Avenue to be a priority, but the BOT prioritized the 6th Avenue line ahead of it and the Board of Estimate approved that a week later. Lyons abstained.

Commissioner Halley scheduled a conference on Burke Avenue on February 13. Lyons would lead a group from the Bronx Civic Congress to meet with Delaney at the conference. He met with representatives of the civic and business groups in the borough a week earlier to organize for the event.

Delaney wasn't happy. Responding to the Board of Estimate resolution, he said, "While I am here, I will exercise my own judgment concerning transit routes," noting that the Board of Estimate had no legal authority to adopt or construct subway lines or order the Board of Transportation to do anything. They could act only on BOT recommendations.[103]

"I feel certain that the governing body of the City should not be subservient to Commissioners who are appointed by the Mayor," Lyons answered. "If the law reads that way, it should be amended. The language of this resolution is definite and if the Board will not adopt a route, legislation should be invoked to correct the situation."[104]

Delaney promised to discuss the resolution with the BOT, but noted problems with local elected officials controlling the transit system: "I would have no objection if the elected officials would take over all responsibilities for laying out transit routes, but while I am here I want to exercise my own judgment. I don't think you will ever get any transit at all if you leave it to elected officials."[105]

Lyons, Delaney, Commissioners Halley and Frank X. Sullivan, Bronx Consulting Engineer Leo Ehrhart, and Bronx Public Works Commissioner Robert L. Moran toured the area on May 21. They looked at the planned route and one Ehrhart suggested— continuing on Burke Avenue and connecting with the W&B's local tracks, near the Baychester Avenue station, and running to the Dyre Avenue station, south of the city line. The Board members liked Ehrhart's plan.[106] It looked like a victory for the Northeast Bronx.

The impending opening of the Hillside Houses and plans for Curtiss Airport affected Delaney's thinking. He could justify the construction of two unidentified stations along Burke Avenue, but "until the Hillside Homes development came along, there wasn't enough business here to develop a good bus line" along Boston Road.[107] Ehrhart made the airport a selling point, noting that proximity to the W&B's Baychester Avenue station made it accessible to Midtown Manhattan.

Lyons and Arthur V. Sheridan reported on this at the May 27 meeting of the Bronx Civic Congress. Lyons felt he had won Delaney over, but despite what Delaney said about Hillside's impact on the BOT, the Board was considering a plan taking the subway further from Hillside. The Board members thought Hillside residents wouldn't mind the additional walk—they would. Ehrhart's plan created a wedge issue.

Hillside's opening ceremonies were held on June 29. Governor Herbert H. Lehman, Senator Robert F. Wagner, Aldermanic President Bernard S. Deutsch, Borough President Lyons, Nathan Straus, Jr., and Joseph P. Day spoke. Mayor La Guardia was attending the Police Department–Fire Department baseball game at the Polo Grounds and didn't arrive until later.[108] Lyons spoke for extending subways to the area, hoping that adequate transportation would be provided to the Hillside Houses.[109]

The New York, Westchester, and Boston Railway faced severe financial problems. It lost money throughout the 1930s, defaulting on its bonds on January 1, 1936. A W&B bond-holders committee, led by stockbroker Irving A. Sartorius, issued a reorganization plan in December. They believed a W&B takeover wasn't possible until the city's transit system was unified. They wanted to keep it going by issuing new bonds to finance operations while cutting costs and stopping all capital projects except for two bridges in the Northeast Bronx.

The W&B tried to reduce costs by reducing service, but Bronx community groups led by Harry Lesser, both counsel to a number of associations and president of DeWitt

Clinton High School's PTA, complained; the Transit Commission blocked the plan. The W&B was allowed to raise fares in July 1936, but that didn't solve their problems.

When the proposed city capital budget was released on December 16, it included a number of Bronx projects. Lyons obtained funds for projects that included constructing a viaduct crossing Bronx Park linking East 205th Street and Burke Avenue, but the Concourse line extension wasn't part of La Guardia's capital budget. Lyons wrote to La Guardia about the omission on March 6.

Delaney replied to Lyons. The route would cost $9.5 million[110] and take forty-eight months to complete. It followed Ehrhart's plan, running from Webster Avenue and 205th Street to Burke Avenue and Eastchester Road to the W&B. There was no explanation as to why this budget item was hard to find. Seemingly, all was going well.

Or maybe not. Halley invited a group of Bronx civic and business leaders to his office and told them that a decision on Burke Avenue would be made at that week's Board of Estimate meeting: "It is up to the Bronx civic groups to urge the Board of Estimate to appropriate the $5,700,000[111] which will be needed at this time for the construction of the new subway up Boston Road."[112]

Having taken Halley's advice, a parade of elected officials and community group leaders attended and spoke about the potential for growth in the communities to be served by Burke Avenue. The Board approved the funding a week later, reverting to the 1928 plan, running via Burke Avenue and Boston Road to Baychester Avenue.

Halley met the Northeast Bronx representatives again on April 6; $300,000 was available for planning and legal work. Plans for at least one line segment would be ready for Board of Estimate action by the end of the year. This included property appraisal along Burke Avenue in order to obtain consent or easements from landowners. Halley said the BOT thought Ehrhart's plan was the best for the line. If an agreement with the W&B wasn't possible, the Board would consider a parallel route.[113]

The BOT sent a new plan to the Board of Estimate on May 25. A model of the viaduct across Bronx Park was prepared. It would go underground by Bronx Boulevard, run under Burke Avenue to Eastchester Road, where it would turn northeast and go to Kingsland Avenue.[114]

Things should have come together. The subway line many people had worked on for years was going to the Board of Estimate. There were few objections to the viaduct connecting 205th Street and Burke Avenue, mostly coming from area baseball players, who would lose the one diamond in the area at the time, which was in the path of the viaduct.

Ehrhart's plan had consequences, though. When Delaney presented it to the Board of Estimate on June 18, Lyons asked why Ehrhart's route was proposed. Delaney said that the original line was abandoned due to "natural difficulties" and increased costs.[115] The Unity Taxpayers Protective Association and the Boston Road Subway Committee opposed the plan. They thought it would take the line through a

Figures 4-10 and 4-11. Two views of the Board of Transportation's model of the planned viaduct that would have been built for the Concourse Extension and vehicular traffic across Bronx Park. (Courtesy of the New York Transit Museum Archives)

less-populated area, away from the Hillside Houses, which would make it more useful to Westchester residents than Bronx residents. Louis Elkins, the Boston Road Subway Committee's chairperson, said the new routing would bypass areas along Boston Road where property valuations rose in anticipation of the new subway.[116] Petitions circulated by the Boston Road Subway Committee opposing Ehrhart's plan were sent to the other Board of Estimate members and the BOT.

Figure 4-12. The *Bronx Home News* ran this map on May 22, 1935, showing the two options under discussion for the route of the Concourse Extension. The dotted line on Boston Road represents the original plan. The dashed line east of Boston Road is the routing suggested by Leo Ehrhart.

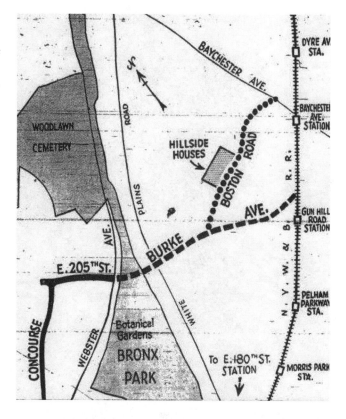

Figure 4-13. Supporters of the original plan for the Burke Avenue line at City Hall on June 18, 1937. (*Bronx Home News*)

The Board of Estimate hearing lasted three hours. Elkins and his committee presented petitions with 3,500 signatures. Their signs read, "We want a subway on Boston Road," "Why rescue a bankrupt railroad at the expense of taxpayers?" and "Why build a five-cent fare subway for Westchester residents?"[117] Lesser spoke for opponents of Ehrhart's plan, criticizing Delaney's belief that the original plan was more expensive than purchasing the W&B's local tracks would be. "I must interrupt," Delaney responded. "The statements that are being made are totally erroneous. The Board of Transportation has no thought of connecting, leasing, buying, or using the tracks of the New York,

Westchester and Boston. The terminus of the subway extension will, however, be within 25 feet of the railroad."[118]

Straus suggested approving the line as far as Burke Avenue and Boston Road, leaving the rest for future study. Lyons agreed, but that met a storm of opposition. No vote was taken. Lesser was a lone voice of support: "This could be laid over for two months as the controversial part of the route is concerned, and everybody could go out of here smiling."[119]

La Guardia tried bringing the meeting to order: "This mob scene does not do anybody any good. This is the only country in which people like you are given a hearing at all. Please don't spoil it with a mob scene."[120] Lyons said this behavior didn't reflect the feelings of the people of the Bronx: "Some may have overstepped in the heat of the controversy. We don't want Chairman Delaney to think that we're opposed to transportation."[121]

Loewenthal, representing the Edenwald Taxpayers Association, supported Ehrhart's plan: "We have been fighting for transportation in Edenwald for 20 years. This opposition comes from those who have lived along an existing subway line. We have nothing in Edenwald. It costs us 15 cents to get Downtown. This is what I would call an eleventh hour monkey wrench."[122]

Hillside's representatives contended that Ehrhart's plan required a longer walk to the subway. Delaney was unsympathetic. He thought it would do more to develop the area: "I don't think that it is good policy to put a subway along Boston Road. Even those people [Hillside residents] would have only three blocks to walk to new route. There is no reason to go any other way than we are going, and you might just as well abandon the rest of the route if you do."[123] A vote would be taken a week later.

The Boston Road Subway Committee held a rally on June 20. About one thousand people from eleven civic groups attended. Many would attend the next morning's hearing. Straus asked why taxpayers were asked to save "a decrepit and bankrupt line. . . . Get up on your hind legs and demand your rights!"[124] "Unfortunately at this time the [W&B] stands in the background as the proposed beneficiary to offer us, out of its wreck, insolvency, and bankruptcy, its two tracks, either for sale or lease, in conjunction with the City-owned subway," Lesser said. ". . . We are told that it is more economical to lease the right of way to build an independent line. Simply to be told so blindly is not legal and does not appeal to good logic."[125]

Divisions widened; more groups spoke up. The Allied Civic Associations of Old Eastchester, a coalition of Northeast Bronx civic groups, became the lead group supporting Ehrhart's plan. "We have conducted a comprehensive and thoroughly accurate house to house survey of the entire area between the zone of adequate service of the White Plains subway and Pelham Park," their statement read. "The results of that survey give conclusive evidence that the route sponsored by the Board of Transportation will give service to the greatest number of people, now wholly without adequate rapid transit service." ". . . We further contend that the opposition to this route has a selfish motive," it continued. "The list of associations mentioned by the opposition, with the exception of Hillside [Houses], is all grouped within, or very close to, the zone of adequate transportation of the White Plains subway, and wouldn't be benefited at all by the extension of the Concourse line up Boston Road to Baychester Avenue."[126]

Louis Elkins wrote to La Guardia. "We are delighted with Mr. Delaney's statements and feel that so far as the use of the railroad tracks is concerned, the matter is closed, but there are certain inconsistencies to this statement that we feel it is our duty to call to your attention."[127] He claimed that the BOT wanted the right-of-way and had surveyed the W&B's property.

It was difficult to vote in that highly charged atmosphere; the Board of Estimate deferred to July 9 to allow La Guardia and Lyons to tour the area. Comptroller Frank J. Taylor asked Delaney what the Board of Estimate's role was in establishing new routes. Delaney response was succinct: "Nothing." "We can reject it or approve it, that is all?" Taylor asked. "Yes," Delaney responded.[128] ". . . I appointed Chairman Delaney and I take the responsibility for anything he does," said Mayor La Guardia.[129]

La Guardia and Lyons visited the area on July 8, joined by Ehrhart, Straus, and Sullivan, walking Ehrhart's route and the 1,500 feet from the Baychester Avenue station to Hillside. La Guardia gave wouldn't discuss his view: "It's the same argument that may

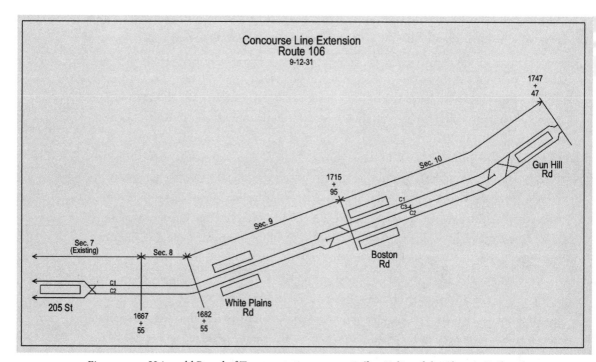

Figure 4-14. Using old Board of Transportation papers, Jeffrey Erlitz of the Electric Railroaders Association prepared a track diagram showing the alignment and stations for the section of the Concourse Extension from 205th Street to Gun Hill Road.

be advanced wherever a subway route is proposed. You always find opponents to a route if it does not go past their front doors. Subways, as you know, cost many millions of dollars, and you can't have one running under every street."[130] The Allied Civic Associations met that evening at Breinlinger's Hall on Boston Road.[131] A crowd of one thousand people supported Ehrhart's plan.

A large crowd attended the July 9 Board of Estimate meeting. When Loewenthal tried to speak, La Guardia stopped him, saying he wasn't helping his cause.[132] Lyons raised Straus's compromise, but Manhattan Borough President Samuel Levy and Queens Borough President George U. Harvey said they wanted new subways in their boroughs if there was no agreement. His colleagues wanted Lyons's decision. "I want subways in the Bronx," he said. "Due to this unfortunate difference of opinion existing, the entire subway route is threatened with delay. Perhaps it would be better if a compromise could not be reached so that the route could only be constructed up to Boston Road, leaving the controversial part to be settled at a later date. However, in view of the fact that we may lose the subway entirely if we do not adopt the route as recommended by Chairman Delaney, I vote yes."[133] The resolution passed unanimously.

The Allied Civic Associations celebrated. Louis Elkins was happy a subway would be built, but he claimed that "a serious mistake has been made in not including Boston Road in the route for the Concourse extension." ". . . It is my honest opinion that the first train will not have left the Eastchester Road station of the new subway before the people will realize this mistake," he continued. "I venture to say that when the Westchester and Boston Railroad unloads its thousands of Westchester County residents at the new terminal of the Concourse subway at Kingsland Avenue, there will be no seats left for Bronx residents. . . . Today's vote is a great victory for Westchester County residents who will receive a five-cent fare at the expense of New York City taxpayers."[134]

Lyons was satisfied that *any* subway would be built, but "it was through my efforts that the provision for the construction of the Bronx subway extension was included in the Capital Outlay Budget. I was disappointed at the difference of opinion existing among the people of the Northeast Bronx, although I could understand both sides of the question. However, I was much concerned that the controversy would result in a stalemate and that the Bronx would lose the subway extension entirely, inasmuch as other Borough Presidents were anxious for subway routes to be constructed in their boroughs."[135]

Delaney reported that groundbreaking for the Concourse line extension would take place, but there were problems. According to Comptroller Taylor the city's financial status affected the capital budget; the W&B's financial problems worsened. Federal Judge John C. Knox, overseeing the line's bankruptcy proceedings, ordered Judge Edwin L. Garvin and James L. Dohr, its receivers, to close its New Rochelle–Port Chester Division. The last trip ran on October 31; service on the rest of the line was assured only through December.

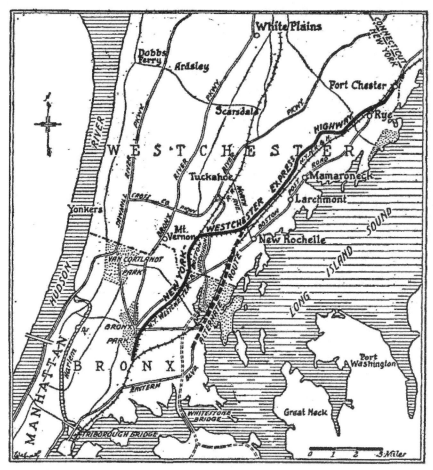

Figure 4-15. The *New York Times* published this map of Robert Moses's plan for the Express Truck Highway on December 1, 1938. The route that the New England Thruway would eventually follow is shown as a dashed line.

This was particularly felt in the Northeast Bronx. Westchester had transit alternatives; there was none in the Bronx until Burke Avenue service began. It was hoped the BOT would take over, but Delaney, for unclear reasons, insisted he had no interest in doing so.

New York City Parks Commissioner Robert Moses advanced another plan. He wanted to build new parkways and highways and wanted the W&B for one connecting the Bronx and Westchester, using use land set aside for a highway between Pelham and Port Chester that had been halted due to funding issues.

Moses's plan is largely forgotten. However, it inadvertently provided the impetus to extend the subway system into the Northeast Bronx.

Moses wrote to Garvin, who wanted to sell the W&B for use as a parkway, on November 5. "The answer to the parkway is definitely no. The right-of-way has no value whatsoever for this purpose," Moses answered. "My own offhand opinion is that the right-of-way might be useful as a through truck route because more and more attention must be given to express truck roads."[136] He discussed the "Express Truck Highway," suggesting that Garvin approach La Guardia with it. A few days later, Delaney advised La Guardia of the BOT's lack of interest. He didn't think revenue from use of the W&B's tracks would fund a rail line's operating costs, so he endorsed Moses's concept.[137]

The impending end of W&B service, along with Moses's plan, spurred Bronx groups to action. The Allied Civic Associations of Old Eastchester met on December 2 to discuss plans, including working with the towns in Westchester to keep the W&B operating and encouraging the city to acquire it for use as a rail line. They supported a plan drawn up by William E. Schramek, the leader of Westchester groups wanting to save the W&B, calling for the creation of an authority to operate the railroad.[138]

The Regional Plan Association issued proposals for steps to link railways with other transit services in 1927. Their *Plan for New York and Its Environs* called for a larger commuter network. The RPA wanted to extend the W&B into Manhattan, running across 125th Street to the West Side with connections to other lines. Harold M. Lewis of the RPA prepared a report on the W&B for the Harlem Board of Commerce in 1929 proposing an extension along 125th Street, linking with existing and proposed north–south lines.[139]

The RPA wanted the W&B to keep operating:

Nothing could be more short-sighted and better calculated to add to the present confusion of the commuting service than to take the easy way of the proposed sabotage of existing rights-of-way.

. . . By means of an extension, however, in New York City these lines would become primary instead of secondary commuting facilities and eventually serve as an integral part of a united system of transit for Long Island, Westchester County and Metropolitan New Jersey. . . . It is obvious that the continued use of [the W&B] for suburban rapid transit will serve the best interests of the region.[140]

The RPA made proposals that affected discussion of Northeast Bronx transit service, calling for the 2nd Avenue El trains to run "over the Bronx section of the [W&B] by constructing a short cross-over from the Interborough track in Bronx Park [the White Plains Road line] to the 180th Street station; direct platform changes between trains could be made at one or more stations."[141]

The W&B's bondholders demanded tax relief; only New Rochelle seemed willing to help. Nothing came from a meeting of Westchester town mayors and corporation counsels on December 16.[142] Saying he had no choice, Judge Knox ordered the W&B to cease service on December 31: "I have no more right to extend the service than I have the right to give part of the road's cash to a mendicant in the street."[143]

Bronx and Westchester officials and groups fought to keep the W&B running while searching for a long-term solution. Following the RPA's suggestion, the Allied Civic Associations asked the city to study incorporating the Bronx section of the railway into the subway system. However, there was a real danger that its right-of-way wouldn't be available for the BOT to connect it with the Concourse line extension or any other subway line.

5

Buy Land Now, Ride the Subway Later

In the early decades of the twentieth century, real estate developers saw the benefits of buying land along the route of subway lines that were proposed, planned, or built. One company with that foresight was Wood, Harmon, and Company.

William E. Harmon, his brother, Clifford B. Harmon, and their uncle, Charles E. Wood, founded Wood, Harmon in Cincinnati in the 1880s. They each invested a thousand dollars in land in the Cincinnati area. William had a plan for marketing the land: "It wasn't easy to buy land in those days. The first payments were always so high that a man with little money could not meet them. So most folks went on wanting land, but they didn't buy any. I worked out a plan by which even the smallest wage-earner could buy a building lot. All the purchaser needed was one dollar to pay in cash and a few cents to pay each week. It was simply the installment plan applied to real estate and I was sure it would work."[1]

The plan worked; Wood, Harmon bought more land in the Midwest and along the East Coast, moving to New York City in 1898. The Brooklyn Development Corporation, with William serving as president, bought sixteen large properties in Brooklyn and elsewhere in the region to be developed. Wood, Harmon marketed the subdivided lots.

Wood, Harmon promoted what were suburban areas of New York City ahead of subway construction. There areas are now neighborhoods like Flatbush, Midwood, Bensonhurst, and Harlem. It invested approximately $4 million in Brooklyn by 1909, accumulating what they termed 20 percent of the borough's available land. Some of Brooklyn's last farms in a huge belt of land from Bensonhurst to Canarsie were purchased. William E. Harmon saw that the best way to market property was to take advantage of the area's rapid transit and rail system.[2]

Harmon saw what would happen in the rest of the city as the subway system grew: "Since the present plans of the transportation companies began to mature values have materially increased, and it is certain that they will continue to improve with great rapidity as the people come to a full realization of what the combination of all the surface and elevated railways, with consequent quick transit and cheap fares to all of the suburbs, means to this borough as a whole."[3]

These properties were marketed with an emphasis on access to transit. In the case of their largest piece of property, five hundred acres in Rugby (east of Flatbush), Wood,

Figure 5-1. William E. Harmon in 1909. (*Brooklyn Daily Eagle*)

Harmon committed to building homes near Utica Avenue, the north–south street that bisects it, as a means of persuading the BRT to extend a trolley line to the area and to provide a free transfer to the Fulton Street Elevated.[4] William E. Harmon became one of the main advocates for building a rapid transit line along Utica Avenue.

Wood, Harmon succeeded elsewhere in Brooklyn. Land bought near the nascent Brighton Beach and Culver lines and the Long Island Rail Road's Manhattan Beach line was developing. Other properties were near where the BRT's West End and Sea Beach lines and the IRT's Nostrand Avenue line would be built in the next decade.

Harmon emphasized the rapid transit system in press releases to real estate sections of newspapers, stating that vacant lands along subway lines were more dependable assets than were improved properties in other sections of the city.[5] He campaigned to extend rapid transit to areas his company developed and marketed.

With the first subway line under construction and plans being made to extend it to Brooklyn, Harmon wanted to ensure that areas his company had a stake in benefited. When the planning process that led to the awarding of the Dual Systems Contracts was underway, he was in the forefront of the campaign in Rugby and East Flatbush to have a line built along Utica Avenue.

Utica Avenue runs from Fulton Street in Bedford–Stuyvesant to its juncture with Flatbush Avenue in Flatlands, intersecting many of Brooklyn's primary east–west streets. There have been many proposals to build subway lines along Utica Avenue, though the type of construction and routing has changed. It could have been part of all three

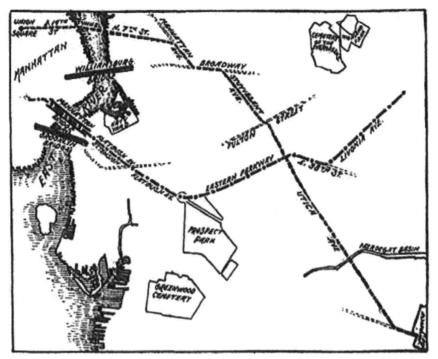

Figure 5-2. The *Brooklyn Daily Eagle* published this map on February 13, 1910, showing the Utica Avenue line as an extension of the 14th Street–Eastern District line.

subway systems. Early proposals called for the line to be connected with IRT or BMT lines. It was part of the Board of Transportation's plans for the second phase of the IND. At times, it was proposed to link with the IRT's Eastern Parkway line, which was built to allow for a spur tunnel to be built along Utica Avenue, similar to how the Nostrand Avenue line was built, a mile to the west.

Planning work done in 1910 for Utica Avenue coincided with work on the Eastern Parkway line. The two lines would have crossed; the mezzanine of the Eastern Parkway line's station appears to be built to allow for a north–south line to cross over its platform levels.

The 1910 plan called for an elevated line to be built south of Eastern Parkway, as did most subsequent plans. Unlike those in other areas of the city, East Flatbush and Rugby residents at the time embraced building an el through their neighborhoods. The East Flatbush Taxpayers Association agreed to get the consent of property owners required to allow for construction, and hired engineers to work on a plan for the line.

George J. Luhn, the chairman of the Railroads and Transportation Committee of that association, presented a petition in favor of the line to the Public Service Commission, stating, "We are not asking too much to be given what other sections already have. We are not only willing to have this proposed line built at our expense, as a gift to the

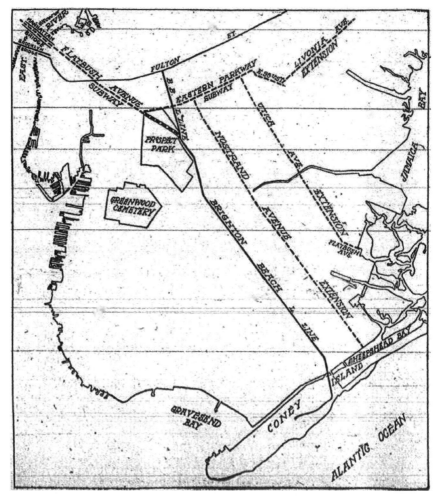

Figure 5-3. On April 3, 1910, the *Eagle* ran this map showing the Utica Avenue line as a branch of the Eastern Parkway line.

City of New York, but are anxious for it and wish to urge you to give it most favorable consideration as speedily as possible."[6]

Harmon and three other realtors, Frederick W. Rowe, William C. Demarest, and Henry Roth, wrote to the PSC: "We hereby agree that we will take a lease to operate [the Utica Avenue line], paying interest and a sinking fund of 1 percent on the cost of the Flatbush Avenue portion and a nominal rental on the balance. Should our proposition be considered favorably by you we will organize a company in such form that will be satisfactory to your commission and the Board of Estimate and make the necessary formal application for the obtaining of this lease."[7]

Utica Avenue property owners wanted to be assessed to pay for constructing an elevated line. Wood, Harmon was among them. "It seems to me the Public Service Commission should take immediate action concerning the building of the subway on

Figure 5-4. George J. Luhn in 1909. (*Brooklyn Daily Eagle*)

Eastern parkway and Utica avenue," William H. Milnor of Wood, Harmon told the *Brooklyn Daily Standard Union.* "It is not dependent upon the City's credit in any credit in any sense. Moreover, any delay in authorizing the work is a serious menace to the proper development of Brooklyn."[8]

East Flatbush and Rugby groups attended the PSC meeting on June 16 to present the plans for the el. William T. Donnelly, the architect who prepared them, was inspired by German railroad structures. They included his concept for the Church Avenue station and a solid elevator structure limiting the noise that would emanate to the surrounding community.[9] Donnelly said he prepared his plans at "the request of a well-known real estate company, which is one of the petitioners for this hearing."[10]

Allied Subway Association President Gilbert Elliot discussed the benefits the line could bring to Brooklyn, suggesting that it could be further extended to the Rockaway Peninsula. Flatbush Taxpayers Association President John J. Snyder talked about how construction of the line could contribute to the development of Jamaica Bay, then under consideration.[11]

Wood, Harmon marketed their land in Rugby on the basis that the subway was coming before the PSC had acted, taking out full-page ads in the *Eagle* and the *Brooklyn Daily Times* on June 24. Readers were told the subway was coming and that they should buy land right away at reduced costs. The ads took a very hard-sell approach ("Oh, you stupid New Yorkers"), showing how the value of other properties they sold in advance of other subway lines had increased.[12]

The PSC approved the assessment plan on July 14. Commissioner Edward M. Bassett's report stated that the line would "extend from the Hudson River to Jamaica Bay and yet

Figure 5-5. William T. Donnelly's plan for the Church Avenue station on the Utica Avenue line, as published in the *Brooklyn Daily Eagle* on June 17, 1910.

its length would only be 11.32 miles. It would directly connect the Fourteenth Street district of Manhattan with Williamsburg, upper Brooklyn, and an immense area of inexpensive land lying south of Eastern Parkway." He continued: "At regular express subway speed of twenty-six miles per hour trains could run from the corner of Broadway and Fourteenth Street, Manhattan to Eastern Parkway, the beginning of the unbuilt section, in 14.5 minutes. The route would not only open a new field to population, but would also take people who work in the Fourteenth Street district directly to inexpensive homes without carrying them through downtown Manhattan and Brooklyn."[13]

Capacity was further incentive for building a route directly to Manhattan, instead of connecting the route with the Eastern Parkway line. Even in 1910, there was concern that Eastern Parkway, with one branch operating to East New York and the other along Nostrand Avenue to at least Flatbush Avenue,[14] could be overcrowded. A direct route along Utica and Stuyvesant Avenues was more practical for the PSC.

The Board of Estimate approved the line on September 30, 1910. One person opposed it; Jacob Suydam, a Utica Avenue property owner, felt landowners had too great a cost to bear in financing construction. Aldermanic President John Purroy Mitchel, serving as acting mayor in William Jay Gaynor's absence, stated, "We are only approving the route. The assessment of the property holders may come up in the future. Then you can make your complaint."[15]

The PSC went to work. A photograph in the *Brooklyn Daily Times* of December 2, 1911, shows its engineers conducting surveys at an unspecified intersection along the route. People bought land in Rugby and East Flatbush near the proposed line. Throughout 1910, 1911, and 1912, real estate sections in the Brooklyn and citywide newspapers ran accounts of land purchases in the area.

While property owners and civic and business groups along Utica Avenue welcomed the building of an elevated line, those along Stuyvesant Avenue had the opposite reaction to building a subway. They spoke out during the spring of 1913.

Henry Weismann, the Stuyvesant Avenue Property Owners Association's counsel, spoke in opposition to the route at a State Appellate Court hearing on May 13. He claimed subway construction and subsequent operation would create vibrations that would be a nuisance to residents and reduce property values. His group suggested building the line a block to the east on Reid Avenue. Former PSC Commissioner Bassett, representing the Utica Avenue property owners, said the vast majority of property owners along the entire route supported its construction.

"Just think what the building of this line means to people in Brooklyn and other parts of this city as well," Bassett, appalled at the opposition, later said. "Why, it will bring one of the most sparsely settled territories in the city within sixteen minutes' ride of Broadway and Fourteenth Street, Manhattan. A similar radius would come somewhere south of the Harlem River in Manhattan. Look at the development there and think of what this means to Brooklyn."[16]

The Stuyvesant Avenue Property Owners prepared a response at a meeting on May 15: "It involves tearing up of our street for years, the building of a four-track line, practically up to our cellars and foundations, the destruction of our beautiful trees, the immense inconvenience and damage to all of us and the noises and vibration incidental to the operation of fast express trains underground, not to speak of the unsightly stations with their outpouring of passengers during evening hours. Reid Avenue is only too willing to have the subway and there it belongs."[17]

William Barclay Parsons testified for the Stuyvesant Avenue routing, saying that Reid Avenue would add additional turning movements, slowing the trip and increasing costs. Some Reid Avenue property owners testified, saying that they didn't want the subway either.[18] That prompted Stuyvesant Avenue representatives to try locating Reid Avenue landowners who would support them. They found sixty property owners.[19]

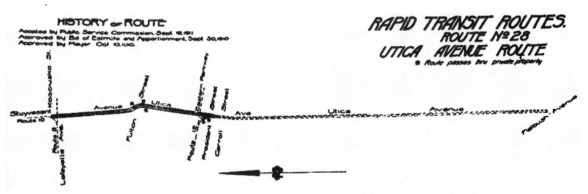

Figure 5-6. The New York State Public Service Commission's map of the Utica Avenue line from its *Annual Report* for 1912.

The Stuyvesant Avenue issue stopped the process cold, to the annoyance of Utica Avenue line supporters. "Just selfish," said Clarence B. Smith, a Fulton Street realtor. "The only protest is from the abutting owners on Stuyvesant Avenue. Everyone else in this section is in favor of the subway and particularly those owners on the streets that cross Stuyvesant Avenue. The Stuyvesant Avenue people all want a subway, but not on their street."[20]

The Stuyvesant Avenue property owners prevailed. The Appellate Division sent the matter back to the PSC, saying, "We think that the facts shown fall short of proof that the public need which could warrant the invasion of a residential street with jeopardy to private property rights. We are therefore constrained to deny the motion."[21]

Plans for the line were withdrawn and a connection with the Eastern Parkway line was again considered, despite concerns about overcapacity. Even then, the line wasn't an immediate possibility; it wouldn't be taken up until the Dual Systems Contracts lines were completed and the city could afford the costs of construction and operation.

The assessment plan's supporters continued their efforts. With PSC support, Assembly Member Almeth W. Hoff filed a bill in March 1915 enacting the assessment process. Alvah W. Burlingame, Jr., filed similar legislation in the State Senate. The Assembly passed the bill on March 23; the State Senate did the same on April 24. The PSC authorized planning work.

In the summer of 1915, PSC engineers were developing a plan for the line,[22] but complications arose. The Stuyvesant Board of Trade, representing the area of Utica Avenue north of Eastern Parkway, met on October 26 to protest the assessment plan. They felt the line should be incorporated into the Dual Systems Contracts and the city should pay construction costs. Magistrate John F. Hylan, in his role as president of the Allied Taxpayers Association, spoke and encouraged the group in their efforts.[23]

Despite the enabling legislation and the PSC's support, work leading to the construction of the line went too slow for its supporters. To encourage a faster process, the Utica Avenue Subway Extension League was formed at a meeting in Rugby on January 13, 1916. William E. Harmon was the keynote speaker. He expressed his frustration about the seeming lack of progress and the gossip that must have been going on at the time:

> We have struggled for three years to put through a rapid transit plan that once demonstrated, would forever free New York City from the cost of future transit extensions into the suburbs. We have made some progress. We have been promised co-operation time and again. The net result, however, has been distressingly insignificant. The Public Service Commission, or its employees, are continually setting forth the insinuation that this is a Wood, Harmon movement. The insolence of those subordinates would lose them their positions were they with ordinary business corporations.

We have finally decided to lay the whole situation before the taxpayers and ask for their cooperation.[24]

The PSC had reason to go slowly. A precedent was being set and it wanted to have a full plan in place before going to the Board of Estimate for authorization. Smaller-scale private investment had already taken place. The Henry Morgenthau Company led a group of investors, including Colonel Jacob Ruppert (future owner of the New York Yankees), in funding construction of the Intervale Avenue–163rd Street station on the IRT's new Bronx line in 1910.[25] Developers today receive zoning variances for building subway station improvements,[26] but building a whole line segment was an entirely new issue.

An assessment plan was no sure thing. Bronx Borough President Cyrus Miller opposed a major assessment plan in his borough in 1910: "It seems to me that in many cases the rapid transit system is like a bridge between two thriving communities. It is a thing which touches immediately the land of only a few persons in each community, but its ulterior benefits are felt by the entire community. For that reason, it has been found just to have the cost paid by the whole community and not by the few persons whose property is affected immediately. It seems unfair, at any rate, to charge the whole cost on the community through which the road runs."[27]

This may have affected the Board of Estimate's thinking. As PSC Chief Engineer Nelson F. Lewis and Deputy Chief Arthur S. Tuttle were preparing the assessment plan

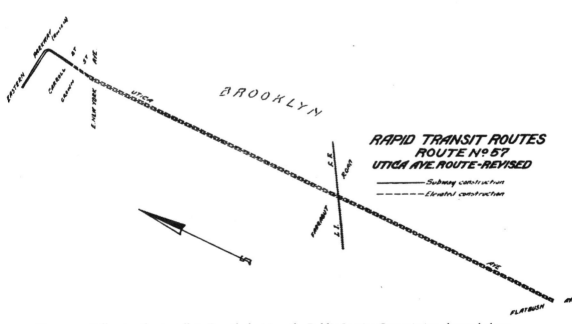

Figure 5-7. Following the Appellate Court's decision, the Public Service Commission changed plans for the Utica Avenue line. This is a map from its *Annual Report* for 1914.

for Utica Avenue, the Board asked Lewis and Tuttle to "lay out an area of benefit for the construction of a rapid transit line in Utica Avenue, between Eastern Parkway and Flatbush Avenue in Brooklyn."[28]

Tuttle proposed six assessment zones in expanding radii from each potential station. Owners of the 46,111 properties in the area would pay based on how near the zone was to a station. The PSC was considering doing the same for the Brooklyn–Queens Crosstown line and a subway line serving central Brooklyn. This was seen as a test case for the concept of assessment plans. Mayor Mitchel and the Board of Estimate had qualms, possibly harking back to Borough President Miller's earlier concerns. Work on the plan slowed.

The concept of assessments experienced additional problems in 1918. A July 25 hearing on a plan for the extension of the 7th Avenue line through Lower Manhattan financed by assessments brought out a crowd in protest. The Board of Estimate laid over the proposal, and after that there was little action on similar plans.[29] When the New York State Transit Commission was created, ostensibly becoming the lead agency on transit planning, momentum slowed even further. Although George McAneny, the chairman, supported assessments, there was opposition on the Commission, most notably from LeRoy T. Harkness. City Comptroller Charles L. Craig also opposed assessments.[30]

William E. Harmon had largely retired from his real estate company, now called the Harmon National Real Estate Company, in 1924. Without his voice, the assessment plan was less of a priority in Rugby and East Flatbush, although interest in building the Utica Avenue line remained strong.

There was little progress in building the line during John F. Hylan's administration, despite Alderman John J. Campbell's statement that the mayor regarded it as his "pet," which must have surprised Hylan's neighbors in Bushwick, who were frustrated by the lack of identifiable results in building the 14th Street–Canarsie and Brooklyn–Queens Crosstown lines. On June 18, 1924, Campbell told the Rugby Civic Association that work would proceed once the mayor effectively gained control over subway planning and construction with the formation of the New York City Board of Transportation.[31]

That didn't happen. The closest Utica Avenue came to being part of the first phase of the IND was a station on the Fulton Street subway line. Community and business groups and elected officials in Rugby, East Flatbush, and Crown Heights met at P.S. 135 on February 17, 1926.[32] Groups in bordering areas sought an extension of the Nostrand Avenue line to Sheepshead Bay. Over the next few months, competition developed as the supporters of one line saw the other as being an impediment toward achieving their goal.

In July 1927, Brooklyn Borough President James J. Byrne sent a telegram to the Rugby Chamber of Commerce to tell them that a line on Utica Avenue would be included in a new subway program,[33] an early sign of planning for the IND's second phase. The BOT and the Utica Avenue groups had the same idea: a revival of the Utica / Stuyvesant line, with the northern leg connecting with an extension of the yet-unbuilt 6th Avenue subway in Williamsburg.

BOT Chairman John H. Delaney discussed this concept at a meeting with Flatbush groups on January 13, 1928. The Flatbush Chamber of Commerce suggested building a line to Sheepshead Bay via Stuyvesant, Utica, and Flatbush Avenues, Avenue U, and Bedford Avenue. Nostrand Avenue line advocates objected, thinking that it would prevent an extension of their line. Delaney suggested a compromise plan, swinging the Utica line toward Nostrand Avenue farther to the north and then turning south toward Sheepshead Bay.[34]

News came out about the IND's second-phase lines in the spring of 1929. Initial reports had the Utica line, referred to as the Utica Avenue–Crosstown line, heading east into Brooklyn from the 6th Avenue line and south via Union and Stuyvesant Avenues to Utica Avenue. It would then run south to Fillmore Avenue, turn west, connect with the Nostrand line and go to Sheepshead Bay, turn west again and run as far as Sea Gate, the gated community at the tip of Coney Island, via Emmons, Neptune, and Surf Avenues.[35]

When the full second-phase plan was officially unveiled in September, the Coney Island leg wasn't included; the rest of the line was amended. It would run to Avenue S, turn west, go to Nostrand Avenue, turn south, and run to Voorhies Avenue. It was a branch of the trunk line planned to cross Brooklyn and Queens, connecting with the 6th Avenue–Houston Street and 8th Avenue lines in Manhattan.[36]

While the response to the route was generally positive, one component ran into a brick wall of opposition, as it did elsewhere in the city. There were no objections to the construction of an elevated line two decades earlier, but there were objections now. Representatives of twenty-three Flatbush civic and business groups met at Oetjen's Restaurant on Church Avenue on October 21 to map plans to oppose els. "We must fight unalterably for subways. Let it be subways or nothing," said the Flatbush Gardens Civic Association's Frederick Boyd Stevenson. "Brooklyn has been at the tail end of every kind of improvement, and it is time that the two and a half million people in our borough demanded what was coming to them. If the City can afford to give Manhattan subways it can afford to do the same for Brooklyn."[37]

Aside from the reduced costs of building an el, the BOT believed there was a problem with building a subway south of Eastern Parkway due to groundwater levels. Allyn S. Crumm of the Flatlands Civic Association didn't agree:

If they can build subways under the river it ought to be very easy out here.

Elevated structures certainly would kill the valuation of property. We do not want the subway if we have to have the "L."[38]

The BOT hearing was held on February 14, 1930, at its Manhattan office. Former Flatbush Chamber of Commerce President John J. Snyder stated that decreased property tax revenues would offset any savings achieved in building an el.[39] Hugo Sesselberg of the Flatlands Civic Association cited Aldermanic President Joseph V. McKee's pledge that no other elevated lines would be built in the Bronx due to protests, and asked why that wasn't the case in Brooklyn.[40] A BOT hearing on the Nostrand Avenue line's extension and the Avenue S leg of the Utica line on March 3 attracted many of the same groups, all of whom had the same message.

The funding issues that nearly crippled the IND's first phase stopped the second; opposition to elevated lines didn't help. The only work on the second phase that took place came when the Fulton Street subway was built. The Utica Avenue station was built to allow for a transfer with what would have been the Utica line's Fulton Street station. Parts of two platforms, four roadbeds, and passageways connecting the two stations were built that would have allowed for work on the Utica line to go on without disrupting Fulton line service. Transfer stairways were built at the Fulton line station, but were removed when the station was rehabilitated in the 1990s.

The advocates for the Utica line continued their work and the BOT continued to plan for it. The Board's priority lists from the 1930s through the 1950s included different iterations. The proposal for the connection to Nostrand Avenue disappeared after 1929. All subsequent plans had it operating along Utica and Flatbush Avenues to Avenue U, and for the Nostrand Avenue line to be extended to Sheepshead Bay. All proposals until 1951 kept it as an IND line. The BOT then revived the concept of connecting it with the Eastern Parkway line, despite earlier concerns about whether it had the capacity to handle Utica Avenue line trains.[41]

The proposals for the Utica Avenue line survived the BOT. Capital plans issued by the New York City Transit Authority in the 1950s and the Metropolitan Transportation Authority in 1968 included it as an Eastern Parkway line branch. The will was there, but the money wasn't. The people who purchased the land that Wood, Harmon and other realtors sold likely did well with their investments, but it wasn't the subway that allowed them to profit.

The service area for the Utica Avenue line was one part of New York City that Wood, Harmon invested in that didn't get a subway built through it. Staten Island was another.

Staten Island's one physical connection with the rest of the city is the Verrazano-Narrows Bridge, which connects it with Brooklyn. It was one of Robert Moses's last projects, with its upper deck opening on November 21, 1964, and the lower deck on June 28, 1969. Staten Island has one rail line, the Staten Island Rapid Transit (SIRT), now the Staten Island Railway, part of the MTA New York City Transit system, running from the St. George Ferry Terminal to Tottenville at the island's southern tip. Two lines for-

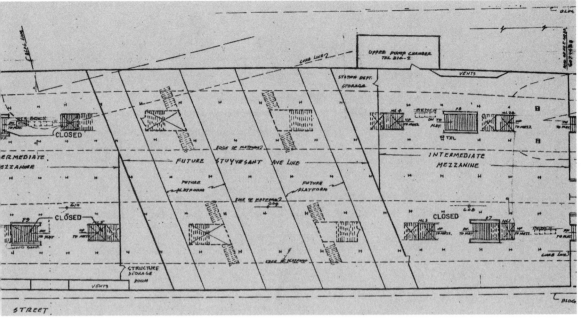

Figure 5-8. A diagram of the Utica Avenue station on the Fulton Street line showing the space left for the Utica Avenue Crosstown line. (Courtesy of the New York Transit Museum Archive)

merly branched off, running along the borough's northern and southern shores; passenger service on those lines ended on March 31, 1953.[42]

It was not for a lack of desire that those lines weren't connected with the subway system. A number of proposals were made over the last century to do so. Work began on a rail line in the 1920s but was halted, triggering a series of events that contributed to the downfall of John F. Hylan's mayoral administration.

Unlike in Rugby, where Harmon campaigned for the Utica Avenue line, his company focused on selling land, using plans for subway service as a selling point. Wood, Harmon marketed much of the land it owned on Staten Island as "Little Farms." Properties were laid out larger than what would be found in Rugby or other locations in Brooklyn—two lots deep and two lots wide, enabling a property owner to build a house and use the rest of the land for cultivation. Fruit trees were planted.[43]

This land was developed near the SIRT's Annadale, Prince's Bay, and New Dorp stations. Advertisements noted their accessibility to the SIRT and the ferry to Manhattan, and referred to a tunnel that would be built from Staten Island to Brooklyn, connecting the SIRT and the BRT's 4th Avenue line. Wood, Harmon wanted people to believe the subway was coming. Other property was advertised as "South New York," noting possible subway connections. There were many who thought that would happen, as Staten Island's elected officials and civic and business groups had been seeking subway service.

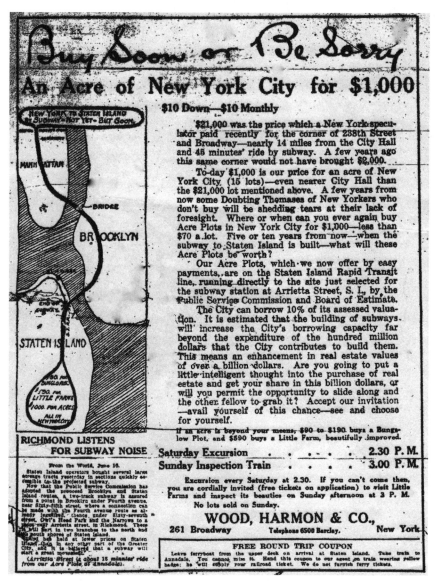

Figure 5-9. This Wood, Harmon advertisement for "Little Farms" appeared in the June 28, 1912, edition of the *Brooklyn Daily Eagle*.

The completion of the Arthur Kill Bridge between Staten Island and New Jersey in 1888 brought the Baltimore and Ohio (B&O) Railroad to the island and an expansion of its commercial facilities. Erastus Wiman, a Canadian businessman and land developer who led the Arthur Kill project, sought a tunnel between Staten Island and Brooklyn, expanding the rail system through Long Island and into New England.

Wiman didn't get far, but interest in rail service from Staten Island grew. As work for the first subway line in Manhattan went on, planning began for the next phase of subway construction. City Comptroller Bird S. Coler[44] called for a line to be built to southern Brooklyn that would eventually be extended to Staten Island, which Coler believed would become a highly urbanized community.[45]

Coler discussed this with the Staten Island Chamber of Commerce, inspiring them and others to participate in the Board of Rapid Transit Commissioners hearing on May 10, 1900. David J. Tysen, president of the Citizens Association of Richmond Borough,[46] spoke, claiming that transit from the island hadn't improved in half a century. W. Allaire Short called for an overall plan to relieve the congested parts of the city by making sparsely settled areas more accessible. Erastus Wiman called for the development of freight lines between Brooklyn and Staten Island.[47]

Most proposals for the southern Brooklyn line, which evolved into the 4th Avenue line, called for a Staten Island extension. One of its strongest advocates was Brooklyn Borough President J. Edward Swanstrom. He believed that a southern Brooklyn line would open up more of Brooklyn to expansion than would any other line, and that expansion to Staten Island was a logical step. In a letter to the RTC Board, Swanstrom wrote:

> The selection of this route is demanded by the needs of both Brooklyn and Staten Island and is recommended by its adaptability to the purposes I have mentioned. In the first phase, the construction of a tunnel under Fourth Avenue is practically free from engineering difficulties, because the roadway is unusually wide and in addition is without railroad tracks. Furthermore, it terminates at the narrowest part of the Narrows, so that a subway connecting the Boroughs of Brooklyn and Richmond and thus uniting the five boroughs with lines of steel, could be constructed with a minimum of expense. Such a tunnel would be of incalculable value to this borough.[48]

The 4th Avenue line had significant support in Brooklyn, and the BRT wanted to build it. It would serve as the trunk route for the West End, Sea Beach, and Culver lines and eventually replace the el on 3rd and 5th Avenues. Wood, Harmon used those lines to market their properties in Marlboro and South Marlboro.

The 4th Avenue line proposal gave momentum to groups seeking subway service to Staten Island, as evidenced by Staten Island Borough President George Cromwell's statement in 1908:

> We think we feel that aside from the benefit the pushing of the Fourth Avenue tunnel across to Staten Island gives to ourselves, that it is a very great thing for the welfare and advance of the interests of the City of New York as a whole. We think what confronts us, one of the great troubles the confronts the City of New York at the present time is the very serious issue of congestion in its business centers downtown, and we think that Staten Island has to offer thousands and thousands that toil downtown to make this city great, the best outlet of any that can be found in a radius

from City Hall. We have an area of 60 square miles, large portions of which are still treated as farm lands whereas, in other directions, I believe are easily three times what they are with us. It therefore would be to the advantage of those who are looking for homes to turn their steps in the direction of Staten Island.[49]

Staten Island's representatives saw the 4th Avenue line as an important step toward getting subway service. Like Swanstrom did, civic groups in Brooklyn saw the extension as a means of garnering more support for their line, and reached out to their counterparts on Staten Island for their ongoing support.[50]

Cromwell led three hundred people at a Public Service Commission hearing on January 11, 1911, to support building the line. Henry P. Morrison of the Richmond Chamber of Commerce spoke in support of building the line: "Hasten our Richmond tunnel and you will have regulated congestion with a baseball bat. Every dollar of subway money heretofore expended has been to increase rents in localities where rents are already high. Hasten the building of this subway and you will introduce the poor man to cheap land."[51]

Manhattan Borough President George McAneny proposed an extension from Brooklyn to Staten Island that day. The line, designated as Route No. 51, would run as a spur from the 4th Avenue line in the area of 66th Street and run under 67th Street to the Narrows, cross to Staten Island, and break into two branches. One would turn

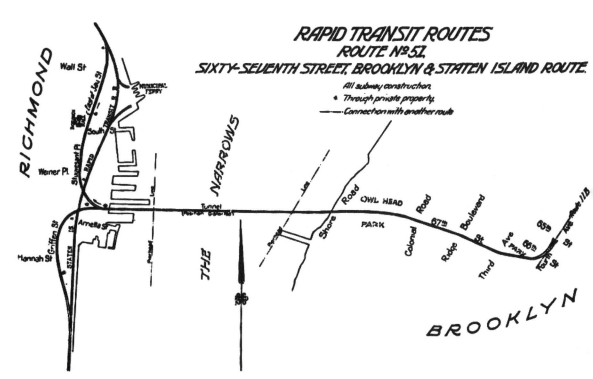

Figure 5-10. The PSC's 1912 diagram for Route No. 51.

north and run under Stuyvesant Place, linking with the SIRT's North Shore line at the intersection of Jay Street (now Richmond Terrace) and DeKalb Street (now Schuyler Street). The other branch would turn south and link with the SIRT's Main and South Beach lines at the intersection of Bay and Minthorne Streets.

McAneny's plan was approved by the PSC on June 14, 1912, the Board of Estimate on July 11, and Mayor William Jay Gaynor on July 16. It was on Dual Systems Contracts and PSC maps, but not in the construction contracts for the BRT. The consent from property owners that was needed to carry out construction work was never sought; nothing happened beyond the planning stage. Like the Utica Avenue line, this plan was held for future construction.

As the 4th Avenue line was built south toward Bay Ridge, tunnel portals were built between the 59th Street and Bay Ridge Avenue stations. This would allow work on the Staten Island branch to take place later, minimizing service disruption. The portals open to the railroad tracks running under the 4th Avenue line, giving riders their only glimpse of daylight along that line.

In February 1916 the Staten Island Chamber of Commerce revived Wiman's plan to build a freight line to Brooklyn. They called for a tunnel that would be used by both subway and freight lines.

When the contract for the construction of the BRT's Brighton Beach line from Grand Army Plaza to Malbone Street (now Empire Boulevard) went before the Board of Estimate on March 17, 1916, Calvin D. Van Name, who had succeeded Cromwell as borough president, objected: "I must refuse to vote in favor of any appropriation of $1,300,000 for transit purposes in any other borough, while Richmond has to bear its share of paying $1,000,000 [$21.1 million in 2011 dollars, according to MeasuringWorth.com] of interest and amortization charges without getting any benefit from them. I am doing this on the unanimous request of the 100,000 residents of Staten Island."[52]

Mayor John Purroy Mitchel responded by saying that it wasn't good policy for a Board of Estimate member to "jimmy" improvements for his borough by attempting to stop improvements elsewhere.[53] The funding was approved, but Van Name's statement was evidence of growing impatience on Staten Island.

Efforts on behalf of that borough continued into the mayoralty of John F. Hylan. At a meeting at Staten Island Borough Hall on January 24, 1919, Van Name cited Hylan's support for additional transit service and held weekly meetings as part of an ongoing campaign. PSC Chief Engineer Robert Ridgway promised to take action on the plan for Route No. 51 by the end of the year.

Frustration grew with the process of building a subway between Staten Island and Brooklyn; a movement developed to build a line directly to Manhattan. At a February 18 meeting at Borough Hall, Louis L. Tribus, president of the Chamber of Commerce and Chairman of the Staten Island Subway Committee, outlined a proposal for two routes. The first was an all-tunnel route, traveling under Ellis Island on its way to

St. George. The second would run to New Jersey, operating as an elevated line along that state's shoreline before crossing the Kill Van Kull in a tunnel to Staten Island.

"In making this application, the Staten Island Subway Committee expresses the unanimous wish and the undivided judgment of the people of Staten Island that such a subway would be to the greatest advantage of the City at large and of the Boroughs of Manhattan and Richmond in particular,"[54] the Committee said in a statement.

The plan lacked support from City Hall. "There are certain people in Staten Island who want to appropriate $30,000,000 for a subway system in that borough. Those who are conducting this agitation know full well that they will never be able to get this sum—at least not at that time or in my mind," Mayor Hylan said.[55]

When Van Name's resolution calling on the PSC to study a tunnel from Manhattan came before the Board of Estimate, Comptroller Charles D. Craig wasn't encouraging: "This city can't do it for at least five years and we ought to be perfectly frank with the people of Richmond and tell them so. When the present contracts are completed, there won't be one penny for other subway work. Why not tell the people of Staten Island so?"[56] The Board of Estimate's Transit Committee supported Route No. 51, and wouldn't support the resolution because that line was already established.

The Board of Estimate voted on October 3 to ask the newly established Transit Construction Commission to study their report, conduct studies, and plan for a subway route. Assembly Member Frank Curley and John Sherlock Davis of the Brooklyn Chamber of Commerce led representatives of Staten Island, Brooklyn, and Queens business groups to call for the construction of a freight tunnel connecting Staten Island and Brooklyn. Van Name protested this request.

"You needn't worry about that. We're all against a freight tunnel. I am sure that everyone on the board will be against such a proposition," Hylan said. Queens Borough President Maurice Connolly agreed: "Let's settle this question right now. I move [for] the adoption of a resolution that it is not the sense of this board that a freight tunnel be combined with the proposed passenger tunnel."[57]

This would turn out to be totally contrary to the actions that Hylan and the Board of Estimate would take for most of the next six years. Nonetheless, the Transit Construction Commission undertook the study and reported to the Board on May 11, 1920.

The report submitted by John H. Delaney and Daniel L. Turner looked at seven options. There were plans for three tunnels between Manhattan and Staten Island (two of which were submitted by the Staten Island Subway Committee). Two were for tunnels connecting Brooklyn and Staten Island (one which was Route No. 51). A sixth option called for extending the 4th Avenue line from its terminal to a temporary ferry terminal at the foot of 95th Street with a tunnel to Staten Island being built later.

Delaney and Turner ruled out the New Jersey shoreline plans on the grounds that an interstate project was fraught with legal and financial issues. The third Staten Island–Manhattan tunnel, which would have swung more toward Brooklyn and Governors

Island, was also ruled out due to financial, construction, and operational issues. They thought there would be problems with providing ventilation and emergency access in a tunnel of such length.

The options for the extension of the 4th Avenue line were viewed as most practical because they would be built from the closest point between the two boroughs. Delaney and Turner shied away from them because no preliminary engineering work had been done there, as opposed to plans for Route No. 51, which took advantage of work that had been done for a tunnel in that area that had been built by the Board of Water Supply.[58] Turner thought that a bridge would be the most practical for developing freight and passenger connections between the two boroughs, but would require more money and time to build.

Delaney stayed with Route No. 51: "It is my judgment that the most practical, as well as the least costly plan of connecting the Borough of Richmond with the rapid transit facilities of the Greater City is by means of a tunnel under the narrow waters separating Staten Island from Brooklyn, carrying the line to a connection with the Fourth Avenue Subway and operating the trains via that route until such time as a separate or additional route may be required by increase in population in Richmond and South Brooklyn."[59]

Delaney and Turner found any consideration of a combination freight and passenger line to be impractical "except with the clear understanding that the freight service would be extremely limited and controlled entirely by passenger service requirements. It would be impractical to attempt to route any through freight trains over such a route, even though connections with trunk line railroads were provided."[60] They noted that a separate freight tunnel would add to the project's cost, but still was more practical.

Support for a freight tunnel soon materialized. Just a week after Hylan told Borough President Van Name of his opposition to it, he expressed support for it. The reason was Jamaica Bay. Despite New York City's fame for having one of world's greatest natural harbors, for many years plans were circulated to turn Jamaica Bay into a separate seaport. A further incentive of the Utica Avenue line was that it could be extended there.

The plan for a freight tunnel under the Narrows took life as part of the Jamaica Bay plan. After a series of meetings with Hylan, Delaney sought and received permission from the U.S. Department of War and the Army Corps of Engineers in January 1921 to build the tunnel.[61] Hylan and the Board of Estimate changed their original policy, seeking clearance from the state legislature for both passenger and freight tunnels, with the freight lines connecting to the B&O system in New Jersey. Legislation was approved on April 13, 1921.

More priority was given to building connections with the rail networks serving the rest of the region and to providing commercial access to the Jamaica Bay seaport. It

NEW YORK CITY, SUNDAY, APRIL 4, 1910.　　THREE CENTS

HOW JAMAICA BAY IS TO BE MADE INTO A GREAT INNER HARBOR

The Story of a Wonderful Project That Will Revolutionize Shipping, Industrial and Real Estate Interests

Figure 5-11. This rendering of a plan for Jamaica Bay appeared in the *Brooklyn Daily Eagle* on April 20, 1910, with the headline "How Jamaica Bay Is to Be Made into a Great Inner Harbor."

didn't appear as if much thought was given to passenger convenience. Arthur S. Tuttle, now the Board of Estimate's chief engineer, discussed routes for the tunnel, downplaying Delaney and Turner's report: "In the selection of a route for the tunnel under the Narrows, the fact that heavy freight must be carried through it must be given first consideration. We shall have to choose a route offering the easiest possible grade."[62]

This resulted in more discord between the Board of Estimate and the Transit Commission. At a meeting on December 21, McAneny said they would cooperate with

Mayor Hylan in building separate passenger and freight tunnels, but wouldn't support a mixed-use tunnel, fearing this would delay the subway being built.[63]

"You may be assured that we will proceed with our plans for the building of a passenger tunnel, either to be independent of or linked up with some enterprise of that character, without any delay," McAneny said. "Our ability to carry out that plan will, of course, depend on the co-operation of the Board of Estimate and Apportionment. I do not think that there can be any reasonable doubt that the development of Richmond ought to be put away to the front of the plan for the future development of the city."[64]

The Board of Estimate put its plan into direct conflict with that of the Transit Commission by voting for a mixed-use tunnel a week later. This situation was made more complicated by the plans of the Port of New York Authority (later the Port Authority of New York and New Jersey), bypassing Staten Island. On December 31, they issued a plan for a tunnel running between Greenville, New Jersey, and Bay Ridge, Brooklyn.[65]

As with the Transit Commission, Hylan viewed the Port Authority as a challenge to his authority; further, he had another reason to support the city's plan for the Narrows Tunnel, making other enemies in the process. "In his speeches and in public hearings, he managed to convey a sense that his efforts were motivated less by the benefits of the project than by a passionate desire to block the activities of the Port Authority (whose creation he had opposed), and by antagonism to the 'foreigners' of New Jersey (as he called them)," Jameson W. Doig wrote in *Empire on the Hudson*, a history of the Port Authority. Since the Narrows project could not be linked to the nation's railroads without cooperation from New Jersey, Hylan's rhetoric undermined prospects for its success. Moreover, the railroads said that they would not be willing to use the tunnel—at least not at the level of charges needed to amortize very large capital costs."[66]

Undeterred, Tuttle defended the city's plan: "In dealing with [the city's plan], the press has apparently taken the Narrows Tunnel as one fostered by the Board of Estimate and Apportionment on a political basis aimed in part to circumvent the Port Authority effort to secure recognition and in part to secure an unfair advantage over New Jersey, and were it not for the fact that a strong protest has gone up from Staten Island against the Port Authority project it is perhaps questionable whether or not the proposed Narrows Tunnel would have come into the limelight as strongly as it has."[67]

The Citizens Union filed suit to stop the mixed-use tunnel, contending that a huge amount of money would be wasted on an impractical scheme.[68] The Transit Commission viewed the plan as infringing on its legislatively mandated authority and voted for its own route. They called for the extension of the 4th Avenue line from its Fort Hamilton terminal to Staten Island, connecting with the SIRT in Rosebank, and branching off to the north and south.

Mayor Hylan and the Board of Estimate ignored that proposal, viewing the Transit Commission as infringing on *their* authority. Hylan broke ground at the foot of Bay Ridge Avenue for the Brooklyn shaft of the Narrows Tunnel on April 14, 1923. He called the tunnel "the great key to the greater development of Jamaica Bay, which in time will make New York the greatest port in the world. We have some opposition by the newspapers against this great connecting link, but that criticism has not been constructive."[69]

Hylan led a similar groundbreaking for the Staten Island shaft of the tunnel on July 19. LeRoy T. Harkness, a member of the Transit Commission, criticized the mayor and the Board of Estimate for proceeding without resolving who would use the tunnel: "No contracts have been let out for its operation and so far as freight is concerned, if and when the tunnel is completed, the City will be at the mercy of railroad companies in fixing the terms of the lease. So far as transit is concerned, this tunnel is a complete misfit."[70]

Controversy continued as the two shafts approached completion, with construction of the main section of the tunnel to follow. In the seventh year of the Hylan administration, this was the only transit construction project not associated with the Dual Systems Contracts. Groundbreaking for the first IND line was still months away.

A *New York Evening Post* editorial criticized the Narrows Tunnel: "Thus the city is confronted squarely with a crucial question. It's as if a fairy held a gift in each hand and said 'which will you have—a tunnel you don't need or a couple of subways you do need?' Incredibly as it may seem, New York is about to reject the subways and take the tunnel."[71]

The remaining Dual Systems Contracts were delayed while work on the Narrows Tunnel went on and Hylan and the Transit Commission fought for control. After the mayor made accusations of wrongdoing on the Commission's part and demanded its removal, Governor Alfred E. Smith authorized a Moreland Act Commission to investigate and determine what actions were needed. Justice John McAvoy was appointed to head the probe.

When Hylan learned that McAvoy would be investigating both his and the Transit Commission's accusations, he originally refused to participate. Governor Smith said Hylan had no choice:

> The subject matter of the charges of the Board of Estimate and Apportionment is within the scope of the wider inquiry I have directed. I trust you will lay before Judge McAvoy, when he requests it, the proof of the charges you say you are prepared to proceed with. When he clears this matter up, we will have taken a long step to remedy the intolerable conditions of which you so bitterly complain.
>
> The ability, integrity and standing of Justice McAvoy gives full assurance that the investigation will be conducted in a thorough, fair and dignified manner. No procedure under him will play into any hands. I am clear that the welfare of the people requires complete investigation only to the extent required by law and conclude to cooperate with Justice McAvoy fully in the public interest.[72]

McAvoy's Commission worked through the beginning of 1925, including Hylan's testimony on Christmas Eve. He put full blame on the ongoing problems on the Transit Commission, McAneny in particular, and the IRT and BMT. McAneny replied with equally strong testimony against Hylan.

McAvoy reported to Governor Smith on February 6, 1925. Whom he found to be culpable for the delays in transit construction was obvious: "The Transit Commissioners are not chargeable with the failure to build the much needed new subway lines or extend the existing subways. The repeated and persistent refusals of the Mayor and other members of the Board of Estimate and Apportionment to adopt proposals for the validation of new routes and to approve construction of routes already validated or provided for in the dual contracts of 1913, completely frustrated provision for increased transit facilities."[73]

The report was specific about the Narrows Tunnel: "The plans for the Staten Island tunnel now being built for both freight and rapid transit service at a great cost to the City of New York should be changed to provide for a proper rapid transit tunnel which may be more speedily and economically constructed. Such amendment to present legislation as it is appropriate on this subject should be enacted to accomplish this result."[74]

Mayor Hylan was vacationing in Florida when the report was issued. Upon hearing the news, he attacked McAvoy: "In whose interest was Commissioner McAvoy working?"[75] Aside from William Randolph Hearst's newspapers, he had little support. Most other papers blasted him on their editorial pages. He was politically vulnerable. Tammany Hall polled voters on his run for a third term.[76]

State Senator Courtland Nicoll and Assembly Member Samuel H. Hofstadter took McAvoy up on his call for legislation. They filed bills limiting the tunnel to passenger service. The Assembly approved the legislation on March 24; the State Senate followed the next day. It went to Governor Smith for his signature and he scheduled an April 20 hearing to obtain input on what to do.

In the weeks before the hearing, Hylan and the Board of Estimate implored Smith to veto the legislation. Ignoring the need for subway service to Staten Island, the mayor threatened to abandon the project: "I don't see how the city could afford to build a tunnel from Staten Island to Brooklyn exclusively for rapid transit. It would cost $38,000,000 [$983 million in 2011 dollars, according to MeasuringWorth.com] and there are only about 133,000 people on Staten Island who could use the tunnel—hardly enough to warrant the cost of its construction."[77] Hylan led a contingent up to the Albany hearing and spoke, calling for a veto. Port Authority Chairman Julian A. Gregory and Consulting Engineer George W. Goethals[78] were among the speakers supporting the veto. Hylan's efforts were to no avail: Smith signed the bill.

Work on the tunnel stopped. Within days, much of the engineering staff was laid off; those who remained were there to maintain records through the end of the year.[79] An office was maintained at Shore Road and Bay Ridge Avenue in Brooklyn until 1931.[80]

Questioning the constitutionality of the Nicoll–Hofstadter bill, Hylan still wanted to proceed. However, support for his plan was deteriorating, even in the part of the city that would most benefit by construction of the tunnel. The Staten Island Chamber of Commerce passed a resolution on April 25 stating that they wouldn't support a court case against the bill. "The Chamber does not see where anything would be gained by lengthy law suits brought for the purpose of having the Nicoll–Hofstadter bill declared unconstitutional," said Chamber President Anton L. Schwab. "Such litigation would be nothing more than expense to taxpayers, loss of time and no tunnel for Staten Island. Therefore, the Executive Committee passed a resolution urging cooperation by officials by putting through the passenger tunnel."[81]

Governor Smith stood by his veto and McAvoy's report. Hylan continued his attacks. He used the occasion of the groundbreaking for the first section of the 8th Avenue–Washington Heights line on March 14—the first major subway project that was not part of the Dual Systems Contracts—to launch an attack on Commissioner Harkness.

Hylan announced his candidacy for a third term on May 5, running regardless of whether the Democratic Party's leadership supported him. A resolution seeking Board of Estimate control of the Narrows Tunnel project was passed. They would build it wide enough for freight traffic were the Nicoll–Hofstadter bill overturned.[82]

The five Democratic county leaders met at the New York Athletic Club on July 25. Queens Borough President Connolly, David S. Rendt of Staten Island, and John H. McGooey of Brooklyn supported Hylan. Tammany Hall's George W. Olvany, the Manhattan leader, and Edward J. Flynn of the Bronx opposed him, although no formal vote was taken.

Olvany and Flynn subsequently announced their support for Manhattan State Senator James J. Walker in early August. A split developed on Staten Island, where a group aligned with Tammany Hall supported Walker. Governor Smith announced his support for the challenger on August 13.

The split between Smith and Hylan had been developing for some time. Smith had aspired for the mayor's office in 1917, but was pushed aside for Hylan, and ran for Aldermanic president instead. While he admired how Hylan had worked to achieve his law degree and subsequent accomplishments, Smith had little respect for the mayor otherwise. Smith's biographers, Norman Hapgood and Henry Moskowitz, quoted him as saying, "I do not think it is fair to the people of New York that a man with so little intelligence should again be their mayor, and I am personally ashamed to have the city represented by him."[83]

The month leading up to the Democratic primary on September 15, 1925, was filled with strong language. Hylan positioned himself as a political outsider, attacking Walker, Smith, Tammany Hall, and the Transit Commission. Walker and his allies responded by saying that Hylan had accomplished nothing since taking office. Walker won easily, carrying Manhattan and the Bronx by huge margins and narrowly winning Brooklyn. Hylan barely carried Queens and Staten Island.

Walker won the general election with a promise to build more rapid transit, but how this would be accomplished on Staten Island was unclear. The price tag for restarting the Narrows Tunnel was daunting and talk turned toward building a bridge. Board of Transportation Chairman John Delaney harked back to the report he and Daniel L. Turner had issued with the Transit Construction Commission in 1920. Fearing Department of War disapproval of a bridge, he wanted to resume work on a tunnel.[84]

The bridge plan gained support on Staten Island and throughout the city as a whole, though. It was given a name, the Liberty Bridge, memorializing the military personnel who had died during World War I. The engineering firm of Robinson and Steinman prepared plans for the bridge at the urging of Staten Island and Brooklyn civic groups, calling for a structure strictly for vehicles. They took Delaney's word that the BOT wanted to build a subway tunnel and so didn't include tracks in the plans.[85]

There was considerable discussion over which direction to go, so much so that the Flatbush Chamber of Commerce scheduled a debate on the issue for October 20, 1926. Hylan spoke for the tunnel plan, attacking Governor Smith for playing into the hands of a "special group of financiers who are interested in the development of the New Jersey Meadows" by signing the Nicoll–Hofstadter bill, "the most dastardly action that had been perpetrated against Brooklyn and Queens."[86]

Many people expressed an opinion on building a crossing to Staten Island, though not Mayor Walker. All he promised Staten Islanders was that their borough would be provided with greatly improved transit facilities "before the end of the current city administration."[87] Responding to a question about whether he supported the Narrows Tunnel or the Liberty Bridge, he said, "That is purely an engineering question. I shall advocate whatever our engineers advise."[88] He would make no commitment as to what would be built or how it would be paid for.[89] When the BOT released the plan for the IND's second phase in September 1929 there was just a reference to a "proposed vehicular tunnel." There was no plan for a rail link between Staten Island and the other boroughs.

A new plan to extend rapid transit to Staten Island did come a few months later, but not from a New York City agency or its government. Frank Hague, the mayor of Jersey City, New Jersey, met with Charles F. Kerrigan, Mayor Walker's assistant; John Sullivan, Walker's engineering adviser; and Dock Commission Clerk John McKenzie. Hague proposed building a line that would run from St. George to the Bergen County–Hudson County line. It would run along the SIRT's North Shore branch and Hudson County Boulevard (now John F. Kennedy Boulevard). The line would connect with the Hudson

Figure 5-12. The Boulevard Subway
Plan. (*Jersey Journal*)

and Manhattan Railroad at the Exchange Place station; a subsequent extension would run to Fort Lee, New Jersey, connecting with the George Washington Bridge.[90]

Walker and Hague met the next day to discuss the Boulevard Subway Plan (as it was known). No commitment was made; New York City's elected officials seemed to shy away from the plan.[91] Hague's plan faded away after a few days of coverage. There was no further advancement of a plan to extend subway service to Staten Island during the remainder of the Walker administration.

The lack of an official plan was not due to a lack of effort by the groups representing Staten Island or their elected officials. The Staten Island Chamber of Commerce, the Staten Island Taxpayers Association, and other groups supported a new plan put forth by the Richmond Chapter of Professional Engineers in April 1931. The engineers proposed building a two-track tunnel from Staten Island to Brooklyn. Rather than connecting it with the 4th Avenue line, they called for it to run north through Brooklyn to connect with the IND in the area of the Smith–9th Street station, then under construction.

W. Burke Harmon, William E. Harmon's son, the Harmon National Real Estate Corporation's president, spoke for the need to build the line and improve connections with New Jersey: "For more than a generation, the problem of Staten Island's growth has been this: How can the island gain a real increase in population without subway connection with New York proper, and how can such a costly improvement become a reality until Richmond has a population large enough to justify it?"[92]

Borough President John A. Lynch forwarded the plan to Mayor Walker and the BOT for consideration. No action was taken. When the BOT finally proposed a new plan, Interim Mayor John P. O'Brien was awaiting the beginning of Fiorello H. La Guardia's administration. The BOT submitted four separate route proposals to the Board of Estimate on November 28, 1933. Route Nos. 120, 121, 122, and 123 were variations of what had been proposed twenty years earlier for traveling between Staten Island and Brooklyn. What happened when they reached Brooklyn was different.

Each route would terminate at a station in the area of the 4th Avenue line without a direct connection to it. Passengers would need to transfer to that line to go farther. Route No. 120 would terminate at the Bay Ridge Avenue station. Route No. 121 would be built with a future eastern extension in mind, terminating at 5th Avenue and 61st Street, allowing for a transfer to the 59th Street station. Under the plan for these two routes, an adjoining freight tunnel would be built, reviving that aspect of John Hylan's Narrows Tunnel plan. Route No. 122 was similar to Route No. 120, and Route No. 123 was similar to Route No. 121, but neither included a freight tunnel.

It did appear as if Route No. 123 was the preference of the Board of Estimate. They advanced this proposal by approving on July 15, 1936, an application to the federal government for a loan of $47 million to finance extending the IND's Smith Street line from an unidentified location between 4th Avenue and 9th Avenue (Prospect Park West) to Staten Island. The BOT filed the application covering the application. There is no report of anything further being done, possibly because the BOT had other ideas for an IND connection.

The BOT's 1937 capital plan included funding for the maintenance of the Narrows Tunnel's shafts. Its plans from 1938 through 1943 included a line to Staten Island that wasn't a branch of the 4th Avenue line, but rather an extension of the IND's Smith Street line, running along Fort Hamilton Parkway and 10th Avenue. At 10th Avenue, this line would have split into two branches, with one continuing on 10th Avenue in Bay Ridge and the other running along 65th Street to the Narrows and onto Staten Island, linking with the SIRT.

From 1943 to 1945, the BOT revived Route No. 51, calling for a branch from the 4th Avenue line. From that point on in the BOT's existence, there were no further proposals for a Staten Island line, nor would the New York City Transit Authority issue any. The furthest the Metropolitan Transportation Authority went was a vague promise in 1968 that didn't come to pass: "In the immediate years ahead, population increases and densities are not expected to require major new construction; however, planning will be undertaken looking to the future when a high-speed, direct rail tunnel link will provide for the needs of this Corridor to the to the year 2000."[93] Studies to revive transit service along the route of the old North Shore line have been carried out, but still nothing has come of them.

The Staten Island and Brooklyn shafts for the Narrows Tunnel still lie under the shorelines of both boroughs. John F. Hylan, who led the groundbreaking for both, made unsuccessful attempt to revive his political career during the 1929 mayoral and the 1934 gubernatorial campaigns. He was appointed to serve on the Children's Court in 1930 and served there until his death on January 12, 1936. He passed away from an attack of angina pectoris at his home in Forest Hills after becoming ill on a Long Island Rail Road train. Plans for a freight tunnel connecting Brooklyn and New Jersey are still under discussion.

William E. Harmon died on July 15, 1928. He had retired from his real estate business in 1924 and focused on charitable activities. The Harmon Foundation, which he founded, was renowned for its support of the artists of the Harlem Renaissance. After his death, it became known that Harmon had made numerous gifts to "great writers, obscure poets, unsung heroes and good children" under the pseudonym of "Jeremiah Tingle."[94]

One of the last major tracts of land Wood, Harmon had purchased that hadn't been fully developed was in the Midwood section of Brooklyn. Originally owned by the Ditmas family, it was purchased by the city for use by the Board of Higher Education, becoming the site of Brooklyn College. According to Mrs. William Good, the primary advocate on the board for this purchase, what made this site so attractive was its accessibility to public transit.[95]

6

Ashland Place and the Mysteries of 76th Street

When talking about the New York City subway system's unbuilt lines, someone will inevitably bring up the existence of the 76th Street station on what would have been the IND Fulton Street line's extension into eastern Queens. Supposedly located in Ozone Park, the station and line segment are alleged to have been built during the 1940s.

The plan to extend the Fulton Street line into Queens as a subway was approved by the Board of Transportation and the Board of Estimate along with the Burke Avenue line in 1937. When these plans were dropped in favor of connecting it with the Fulton Street Elevated in Ozone Park in 1949 there were no protests. What controversy there would be arose years later for much different reasons.

The BOT proposed the Fulton Street subway as the replacement for the elevated line the BMT and its predecessors operated since the late 1880s, first to the Brooklyn/Queens line and then to Lefferts Avenue (later Lefferts Boulevard) and Liberty Avenue in Ozone Park in 1915. The plan for the Fulton Street subway was also a step beyond what was advocated by groups in Brooklyn, to connect it with the BMT's subway lines south of the DeKalb Avenue station at that time.

The Fulton Street Elevated began service in 1888. It would turn downtown Brooklyn into a major commercial district serving the whole city, and promoted the growth of the adjoining residential communities. Trains ran over the Brooklyn Bridge to a terminal across Park Row from City Hall from the time that service began.

But that's as far as it went, despite some work that actually took place to connect it with the BRT's Nassau Street line south of the Chambers Street station. Anyone wanting to travel farther needed to transfer to a branch of the 2nd and 3rd Avenue Els at an adjacent terminal, or to trolley lines in the area. After 1904, riders could transfer to the IRT at its Brooklyn Bridge or City Hall stations or to the other subway lines as they were built through the area. These were not direct transfers, nor were they free.

After the Dual Systems Contracts were approved and construction began, attention turned to next steps. One was the Ashland Place connection, linking the Fulton Street El with the Brighton Beach line south of the DeKalb Avenue station. Plans initially called for a ramp to be built off the el between St. Felix and Cumberland Streets in Fort

Greene into a tunnel leading to the connection, allowing trains to run farther into Manhattan, along either the Broadway or Nassau Street lines. A short connecting tunnel can be seen from Manhattan-bound trains on the Brighton line between the Atlantic Avenue and DeKalb Avenue stations.

The BRT wanted the connection built as part of a series of capital improvements in downtown Brooklyn.[1] It had significant support in Brooklyn and Queens. The Broadway Association, a Manhattan business group, wanted the mezzanines of the BRT's 34th Street station expanded, anticipating the ridership that would come to Midtown because of the connection.

Several issues led to the connection not being built and the IND's Fulton Street subway being built. The Public Service Commission and the BRT saw it as a short-term solution. As the Dual Systems Contract lines were built, there were concerns about congestion at the DeKalb Avenue interchange slowing train movement between downtown Brooklyn and Manhattan. It was feared that routing Fulton Street trains through that interchange would add to congestion, limiting the track capacity through DeKalb Avenue. These fears were borne out and several major capital projects were needed to rebuild the interchange and connect the BMT's Culver line with the IND's Smith Street line.

The PSC sent plans for the Ashland Place connection to the Board of Estimate on January 27, 1917. The Board's Transit Committee held a hearing on April 13. Preliminary approval was given that spring, but work stalled. Bronx Borough President Douglas Mathewson, chairing the Committee, and the other members had concerns about whether there was enough funding to proceed.[2]

The full Board voted to allow preliminary engineering work to commence on the Ashland Place plan on June 15; Mayor John Purroy Mitchel approved it on June 27. By the time these approvals were given, though, the United States had entered World War I. Fighting the war took priority over all capital projects. Before the year was over, John F. Hylan was elected mayor.

After a long delay, the Transit Committee passed a resolution approving the Ashland Place plan on February 25, 1919, but that's as close as it got to implementation. The resolution went before the full Board on March 14; Hylan had it tabled for further study and summed up his attitude toward transit projects in doing so. "You know that I have been away on a little vacation and have not had time to familiarize myself with this proposition," he told the Board. ". . . An improvement may be ever so necessary, but the first thing to be considered is how we are going to get the money to pay for it. There are some bills in Albany that will cost the city $21,000,000 [$273 million in 2011, according to MeasuringWorth.com] if they go through. We must take these things up carefully and proceed slowly, even though the Ashland Place connection may be one of the most important."[3] Consideration of the connection went so carefully and slowly that it was never built.

Over Brooklyn Borough President Edward J. Riegelmann's objections, the Board of Estimate deferred action on April 4. John H. Delaney, in his role as transit construction

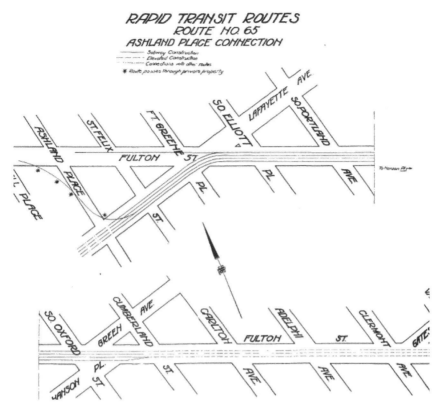

Figure 6-1. The New York State Public Service Commission's 1917 plan for the Ashland Place connection.

commissioner, announced that the plan was being withdrawn on May 29. While he favored connecting the Fulton Street El with the subway, he wanted a different plan.[4] Delaney thought the contract with the BRT provided too great a benefit to the company to provide a service that it should operate strictly on its own merit.[5]

The BRT was tiring of waiting for the connection to be approved. The longer the wait, the less reason there was to go ahead. With the connection of the Brighton and 4th Avenue lines at DeKalb Avenue approaching completion, causing congestion through that junction, there was less benefit in building it: Fulton Street trains would only add to the congestion.

There were several proposals to extend the Fulton Street Elevated, once below street level, past Ashland Place and toward Manhattan. The PSC wanted to extend the line along Lafayette Avenue, past Flatbush Avenue, and onto Livingston Street, connecting with the BRT's Broadway line south of the Whitehall Street station. Short tunnels were built south of that station in anticipation of a future extension.

Delaney announced the Transit Construction Commission's plan on December 7, 1919. It would have the el enter a tunnel near the intersection of Fulton Street and

Vanderbilt Avenue, running under Fulton, Livingston, Court, and Washington Streets to the East River. In Manhattan, it would run under Ann Street and Park Row to a connection with the Broadway line at its City Hall station, which was being built with lower-level platforms to allow for future connections.

With these plans under discussion, the BRT had more reason to delay work. It needed to purchase up to three hundred steel subway cars to operate on Fulton Street to replace the wooden cars in use. These cars were viewed as unsafe to operate in tunnels after similar ones were destroyed in the Malbone Street crash in November 1918.[6] With the BRT facing the financial difficulties that would force it into receivership, reorganizing as the Brooklyn–Manhattan Transit Corporation in 1923, the purchase of subway cars was impossible, even when the Board of Estimate approved the Ashland Place connection on October 1, 1920.

There the plan sat. Mayor Hylan and the state's Transit Commission had conflicting proposals for a connection between the Fulton Street El and the subways. The BRT had concerns about the decreasing benefits of the Ashland Place connection and didn't have the resources to do anything. There was no real progress until the creation of the Board of Transportation in 1924 and the release of the plan for the first phase of the IND in March 1925. The IND's 8th Avenue line was planned to run into Brooklyn onto Fulton Street and connect with the Brooklyn–Queens Crosstown line. No connection with the Fulton Street El was announced.

The direct connection with the Crosstown line didn't survive the summer[7] and the BOT didn't formally announce a plan to build a Fulton Street subway line as part of the IND until March 31, 1927. There was no connection planned with the el in downtown or central Brooklyn. It would continue as a subway to Alabama Avenue in East New York. BOT Chief Engineer Robert Ridgway would investigate the routing of the subway east of that point. To the delight of many groups in Brooklyn, the only thing planned for the el was its demolition.

The question left open was what to do with the eastern extension of the line. Decades passed before it was answered. After considering ideas for building a subway along streets that included Atlantic and Liberty Avenues,[8] Ridgway proposed that the subway line be connected with the el on Liberty Avenue in Ozone Park as part of the IND's second phase plan in 1929. The major difference with what would later be built was that it would extend from Lefferts Boulevard, continuing eastward along Liberty Avenue through Richmond Hill South, Jamaica, and Hollis, connecting with an extended Jamaica Avenue elevated line and continuing to Springfield Boulevard in Queens Village. In May 1930, the plan for the route of the subway through East New York was set, running under Liberty Avenue, not making the connection with the el until reaching 80th Street.

That plan didn't last long. Beginning with the BOT's 1932 capital plan, the Fulton Street line was pointed toward southern Queens, with an extension to Rockaway Bou-

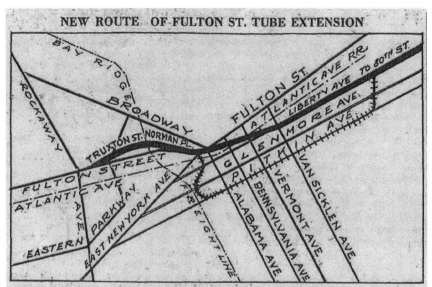

NEW ROUTE OF FULTON ST. TUBE EXTENSION

The heavy black line shows new route of Fulton St. subway link connecting with Liberty Ave. "L." The line veers off Fulton St. at Truxton St., passes over the Bay Ridge Freight Railroad, and then takes a diagonal course through private property to the intersection of Vermont and Atlantic Aves., where it passes under the L. I. R. R. at a depth sufficient to permit the railroad to be subwayed above it and continues to Liberty Ave. at Van Sicklen. From that point it will continue as a subway to 80th St., Woodhaven, where it is to connect by ramp with the "L" structure. From Euclid Ave., eastward, it is laid out as a subway under the existing "L."

Figure 6-2. The *Brooklyn Daily Eagle* ran this map diagramming a new plan for the Fulton Street subway on May 18, 1930.

levard near the Brooklyn / Queens line. There would be a further extension, although it was not identified at the time.

IND service to Brooklyn began on February 1, 1933, with trains running along the Smith Street line to Bergen Street and then to Church Avenue in October.[9] Construction work on the Fulton Street subway began. Financial considerations affected what the BOT could do to expand service. In a letter to Mayor La Guardia shortly after he took office in 1934, Chairman Delaney explained how funding problems affected the BOT's ability to carry out capital work:

> The work of construction and equipment of the new subway system is almost totally suspended because of the lack of money.
>
> More than two thousand engineers, draftsmen and less skilled employees have been discharged during the last two years, and hundreds more must go.[10]

Delaney explained why city funding could be used for the capital projects that the BOT wanted to proceed with (extending the Fulton Street line to the Rockaway Avenue station in Brooklyn, and completing the Houston–Essex Street, Brooklyn–Queens Crosstown, and Queens Boulevard lines) and discussed where funding existed: "The only recourse apparent to me is a loan from the Federal Government. Application for such a loan amounting to about $23,000,000 [$386 million in 2011, according to MeasuringWorth.com] has been made and all the engineering preliminaries have been completed. This sum would enable the board to complete the structure and line equipment of unfinished portions of the new subway."[11]

Speaking to the Brooklyn Civic Council on May 13, 1935, Delaney promised that the Fulton Street line would "eventually" be built into Queens, but again said the city had insufficient funds to do much. This condition was further exacerbated by the cost of merging the three subway systems.[12] Negotiations had begun, but an agreement was still more than five years away.

The beginning of Fulton Street subway service on April 8, 1936, was marked by ceremonies at the Kismet Temple in Bedford–Stuyvesant and its terminal for the next twelve years, the Rockaway Avenue station. Mayor La Guardia was at the controls of the first train for a moment and then stood and rode on the trip to and from Rockaway Avenue from the Hoyt–Schermerhorn station. Once there, he promised to extend service to Queens without specifics: "We'll extend this line to Queens and then tear down the Fulton Street Elevated as soon as we cut down red tape and eliminate bureaucracy and stubborn politics."[13]

Demolishing an elevated line was a priority for area community groups, elected officials, and the *Brooklyn Eagle*. Herbert L. Carpenter, who chaired the Kismet Temple event, was one of the primary advocates for demolition, chairing a citywide committee for elevated-line demolition, seemingly regardless of whether these lines were still needed.

On July 15, 1937, the BOT submitted a plan to the Board of Estimate that included Route 110-B, an extension of the Fulton Street line from the yet-to-open Broadway–East New York station (opened in 1946) to Linden Boulevard at 101st Street in the Ozone Park section of Queens, via Pennsylvania Avenue and Linden Boulevard.[14]

A contract was signed in 1937 to conduct surveys along Fulton Street and Pennsylvania and Pitkin Avenues with the Meserole City Surveying Company. Although Route 110-B was the authorized plan, a second surveying contract was signed with Walter I. Browne Inc. to survey the area that would be needed to connect the Fulton Street subway and elevated line to the subway yard that would be built in the area. The BOT made contingency plans based on city finances.

The BOT's capital construction plans for 1938 called for the Fulton Street line to be extended in two phases. It would initially be extended to Linden Boulevard and 106th Street, with a connection to the Long Island Rail Road's Rockaway Beach line, which would be purchased from the LIRR. In the second phase, it would further extend along Linden Boulevard to 229th Street in Cambria Heights, close to the city line.

Fulton Street El service ended between Manhattan and Rockaway Avenue on May 31, 1940. A party led by Borough President John J. Cashmore boarded the last Manhattan-

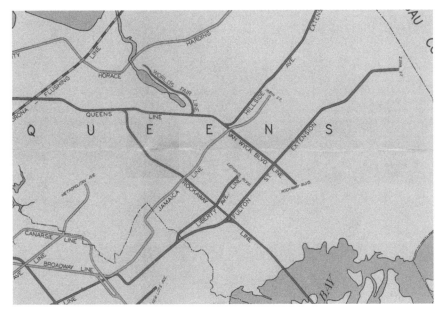
Figure 6-3. The Fulton Street Extension as planned in 1938.

bound train at the Court Street station, rode to the Park Row Terminal, and then, joined by La Guardia, Delaney, and members of the City Council and the BOT, rode back to Rockaway Avenue.

At Rockaway Avenue, about two thousand people heard the mayor tell them that demolition of the el would turn Fulton Street into "a splendid boulevard."[15] Earlier in the day, Herbert L. Carpenter led what was described as a "funeral procession" along the length of the route.[16] A mock funeral was held at 5th Avenue and 25th Street in Sunset Park, in front of the entrance to Green-Wood Cemetery, to celebrate the end of the Fulton Street and 5th Avenue Els and the Broadway Ferry branch of the Broadway–Brooklyn line, which also ended service that day.[17] Lost in the celebration was recognition of both the impact that the el had in developing the city and the services those lines provided.

The Fulton Street line's extension was included in all BOT capital plans through 1945. Little construction work was done, though. The line wouldn't be extended to the next station, Broadway–East New York, until December 30, 1946. The only short-range extension planned was to the Grant Avenue station, the last stop in Brooklyn. In its coverage of the opening, the *Brooklyn Eagle* noted that the extension to 229th Street was still in the BOT's long-range plans, but it depended on resolving the city's financial condition.

There was no further discussion of extensions to eastern Queens. When the next segment of the Fulton Street line opened on November 29, 1948, it was to the Euclid Avenue station. No mention was made of any extensions. When the BOT voted to extend

1888 Fulton St. Progress 1940

BROOKLYN EAGLE

BROOKLYN, N. Y., FRIDAY, MAY 31, 1940

Sketched by Lawrence Lustig, Pratt Institute '40

DREAM REALIZED—Artist's conception of how Fulton St. will appear, looking west toward Borough Hall, with the elevated structure removed. Ornamental poles and modern trolley tracks and cars, suggested by the Downtown Brooklyn Association, will preserve for shoppers, with the subway, all present transit facilities. With this broad thoroughfare, Downtown and Central Brooklyn are expected to undergo a rejuvenation.

BROOKLYN TAKES ANOTHER GREAT STEP FORWARD

Tonight, at long last, exactly 52 years, one month and six days after the first chugging, screeching steam locomotive pulled its string of bright yellow cars along the new Fulton St. Elevated Line, another epic event in the creation of the Brooklyn of Tomorrow will take place. On the stroke of midnight, the final, dingy green electric train will grind its way into the Rockaway Ave. station.

Immediately, it will be possible to start work on demolition of six miles of the structure, the ugly Black Spider which for half a century has cast its shadow over the heart of Brooklyn and its evil spell over the slums it helped create.

As part of the unification of the Brooklyn-Manhattan Transit system with the city lines and at an estimated cost of $2,000,000, the facades of Fulton St. stores and office buildings, hidden for years in gloom, will be revealed in the light of day and a broad, unobstructed main thoroughfare opened to traffic.

Culminating a civic campaign of many years, in which the Brooklyn Eagle was the crystallizing force, removal of this blight on the borough is, without doubt, one of the greatest single forward steps taken here since the opening of the Brooklyn Bridge on May 24, 1883.

Authorized by the Board of Estimate, with Mayor LaGuardia firmly behind it, demolition of the ancient elevated structure will be no simple task. Borough President John Cashmore's engineering staff, under Consulting Engineer Philip P. Farley, has drafted maps and specifications for the complicated razing and the condemnation order has been signed by Supreme Court Justice Charles C. Lockwood.

But in the years this monster on stilts has held nine miles of Brooklyn's principal business street in its tentacles, trolley, light, telephone, power and fire alarm system wires have been strung on it. Now they must be relocated. Poles must be erected to hold the trolley wires; most of the others will be buried, a complex task because of telephone wires already underground and the subway.

There will be a transition period, it is true, in which patience will be necessary. But after this metamorphosis, Fulton St. will emerge from its aged chrysalis a newer, brighter and better thoroughfare.

Figure 6-4. A page from the *Brooklyn Eagle*'s special section celebrating the end of service on the Fulton Street El in downtown Brooklyn on May 31, 1940.

the line on July 6, 1949, they had gone back to the plan to build the route proposed in 1929, a connection to the Fulton Street El line at the 80th Street–Hudson Street Station and running to the Lefferts Boulevard Terminal stop. The el segment west of the subway link would be demolished.

The Board of Estimate approved this proposal on November 17. The only person to speak against it was Milton Jarrett of the City Line Civic Association (City Line was the name of the community on the Brooklyn/Queens border). Reading a letter written by Frank Lissner, the group's president, to Mayor William O'Dwyer, Jarrett focused on the houses in his community near Liberty Avenue that would be demolished to build the tunnel portal and the structure linking the subway and elevated lines. His alternative was to extend the subway under Pitkin Avenue to connect with the Rockaway Beach line, still being run by the LIRR, just to the west of Aqueduct Racetrack, part of the BOT's plans from the 1930s and 1940s. This argument had no impact on the Board. Work on the connection proceeded and it opened for service on April 29, 1956. Four weeks later, the connection to the Rockaway Beach line opened, which was built from the el on Liberty Avenue.

The possibility of extending Fulton Street line service was raised again in 1963. The New York City Transit Authority proposed using a spur tunnel that runs off the Fulton Street line east of the Euclid Avenue station—where Route 110-B would have run, and where some think a longer tunnel exists—along Pitkin Avenue and Linden and Merrick Boulevards to Springfield Boulevard in southeastern Queens.[18] Connections with the Rockaway line would be maintained by building a new transfer station where the new line and the Rockaway line met near Aqueduct Racetrack. As an alternative, the TA proposed extending the elevated line on Liberty Avenue to follow the route to Springfield Boulevard.[19] The proposals received little comment and quickly faded away.

Construction of the Fulton Street subway in Brooklyn and the plans to extend it across Queens didn't inspire the passion that other lines did. The main interest it stirred in Brooklyn was as a replacement for an elevated line that some viewed as being antiquated. The program for the opening ceremony at the Kismet Temple made as much note of the need for efforts to demolish the elevated structure as that for the new subway line itself. There wasn't much interest in Queens because the area it would have served hadn't yet been developed to the degree Brooklyn was. Extending the Queens Boulevard line and connecting the subway with the Long Island Rail Road's Rockaway Beach line were much greater priorities in that borough.

The most interest in the proposals to extend the line came after the last proposal was issued in 1963. The interest was not on the part of civic and business groups or elected officials seeking to get a new subway line built; instead, it's on the part of people who believe that something *was* built.

There is a school of thought among students of subway history and railfans that a tunnel was built eastward along Pitkin Avenue as far as 76th Street in Ozone Park, where a station was supposed to have been built.[20] There are little clues that encourage this thinking. For instance, there is a board in the signal tower at the Euclid Avenue station showing part of this extension, including the 76th Street station. The spur tunnel

Figure 6-5. Looking west on Pitkin Avenue from 76th Street. (Photo by the author)

that the TA proposed to use in 1963 is visible from the Fulton Street subway as it turns toward the Liberty Avenue connection.

There is absolutely no question that the BOT wanted to build the extension of the Fulton Street line to 229th Street, and would have if they had the financial resources to do so. There's no doubt that preliminary engineering work took place. But that's as far as things went.

The proposals to build the Burke Avenue and 10th Avenue lines provide testament. Elected officials like James J. Lyons or Edward Vogel objected to projects proceeding while work on their favored line didn't. In 1938 Lyons tried to stop funding of the conversion of the Elks Club building at 110 Livingston Street in Brooklyn into the New York City Board of Education's headquarters. While Lyons didn't succeed, there is no doubt that he or the *Bronx Home News* would have protested had work on the Fulton Street extension gone on while work on Burke Avenue hadn't. Vogel or the *Brooklyn Eagle* would have complained about this work starting and stopping while the Culver–Smith Street connection or the 10th Avenue line went unbuilt. Others would have protested on behalf of their communities. There are no reports of any protests having taken place.

Second, there was no coverage in any newspaper about work on a tunnel running from just east of Euclid Avenue to 76th Street having started, taking place, or stopping without completion. The subway system is filled with tunnel segments built to ensure that work would continue on a new line without disrupting existing service. This enabled the Archer Avenue line to be built in Queens decades later. It used track ramps from the Queens Boulevard line in the 1930s to facilitate later construction of a line to be built along Van Wyck Boulevard.

Tunnel segments for unbuilt second phase IND lines went only so far as to avoid interfering with the operation of the line in service while the new line was being built. They weren't built to run from the Fulton Street line to Pitkin Avenue and 76th Street. Building a line between Euclid Avenue and 76th Street would have meant building a tunnel a little more than half a mile long.

If work started and stopped without comment by the city government or the BOT, without any promise that work would resume, there would have been an immense uproar from the elected officials and community and business groups representing the area where work had taken place. In the case of the Fulton Street line, there would have been significant coverage in the area newspapers, particularly the *Brooklyn Eagle*, the *Long Island Star-Journal*, and the *Long Island Press*. The *Bronx Home News* or *New York Post* would have complained about the money being wasted without the Burke Avenue or Tremont Avenue Crosstown lines being built. All of them advocated for expanding the subway system throughout their existence[21] and condemned what they saw as wasteful spending. There were no articles or editorials of any kind about the

Figure 6-6. This *Brooklyn Eagle* photograph from January 20, 1916, showed the Brooklyn Bridge ramp going toward the Chambers Street station.

Fulton Street line. If work took place, it would have happened in complete secrecy, which would have been impossible at any time on a project of this magnitude. There were no articles published about ground being broken for an extension.

More than three decades earlier, the *Eagle* protested a project's abandonment. Work had started on a project connecting the BRT's elevated lines running over the Brooklyn Bridge (including the Fulton Street El) with its lines on Nassau Street at the Chambers Street station. Work stopped and never resumed.[22] The *Eagle* covered this in 1916. It's hard to imagine the *Eagle*, the *Press*, or the *Star-Journal* not reporting the abandonment of a half-mile subway tunnel built out to 76th Street in the 1940s.

Another indication that nothing was built comes from a lack of subway infrastructure in the area of Pitkin Avenue and 76th Street. There are no pump rooms or anything else proving that subway construction had taken place. Southern Queens has a very high water table, a constant problem throughout that area. Without pumping facilities, it's likely any tunnel under Pitkin Avenue would have long since caved in.

The final indication that no major work ever took place comes from the fact that no final authorization came from the BOT and the Board of Estimate. Communications from the BOT and the New York City Planning Commission in 1944 and 1945 indicated that the extension hadn't been formally authorized under the terms of the New York State Rapid Transit Law up to that time. There is no record of this authorization ever having been given to do any work.

The public hearing for the project completing work at Euclid Avenue didn't take place until September 21, 1945.[23] The BOT was struggling to find funds to extend the Queens Boulevard line by one stop. They wanted to build the connection between that line and the 60th Street Tunnel, the Culver and Smith Street lines in Brooklyn, and the White Plains Road and Dyre Avenue lines in the Bronx. They still wanted to construct the 2nd Avenue line. These projects all had higher priority than extending the Fulton Street line to 76th Street and points east between the completion of work on Euclid Avenue and the Board of Estimate's approval of the connection with the Fulton Street Elevated in 1949. It is difficult to imagine any other work on Fulton Street taking place, given the city's financial concerns and the interest that existed in building these other lines in different parts of New York City.

Prior to the eastward extension of the Flushing line's Main Street station in the 1990s, there was similar talk of a tunnel running beyond that station. When construction work began, all that was found was a lot of dirt and water, sewer, and utility lines that were missing from city maps. Having said all of this, it's also obvious that the mystery of the tunnel to 76th Street won't clear up until a major construction project requires extensive excavation along Pitkin Avenue. But that's not likely to happen any time in the near future.

7

To the City Limits and Beyond

The Metropolitan Transportation Authority's East Side Access (ESA) program is the most substantial expansion of New York's commuter rail system since the Long Island Rail Road extended into Pennsylvania Station a century ago. Using the 63rd Street Tunnel's lower level, trains will run from the Sunnyside Yards in Queens to a new station built at Grand Central Terminal. This is a new version of a route proposed in the MTA's 1968 "New Routes" program, planned to run from 63rd Street to a terminal at 3rd Avenue and East 48th Street. The revised line will allow riders to transfer between the LIRR, subway, and Metro-North Commuter Railroad trains.[1]

The idea for ESA dates back generations. A number of proposals for commuter rail networks dwarfing it were made early in the twentieth century, creating systems connecting the routes serving New York, New Jersey, and the subway system.

William Gibbs McAdoo, president of the Hudson and Manhattan Railroad Company (H&M), was a major advocate for creating an interstate network. Born in Cobb County, Georgia, McAdoo attended the University of Tennessee. Admitted to the bar in 1885, he set up a law practice in Chattanooga and became counsel to several railroad lines.

McAdoo's work with the railroads piqued his interest. He bought a controlling interest in the Knoxville Street Railway Company, upgrading it and changing it from mule-driven to electric operation, a rare occurrence at the time.[2]

McAdoo moved to New York in 1902, forming a partnership with another William McAdoo, a former congressman from New Jersey, assistant secretary of the navy, and New York City police commissioner. He hadn't lost interest in transportation, becoming involved with a dormant project to build a commuter rail line between New York and New Jersey.

McAdoo made numerous trips by ferry between the two states and thought about building a rail tunnel connecting them. In his autobiography, *Crowded Years*, he wrote about telling an associate, John Randolph Dos Passos,[3] about this and being told about earlier attempts to connect the two states.

DeWitt C. Haskins began work on the original project in the 1870s. He ran out of funds and encountered legal problems. A tunneling accident claimed twenty lives, and work ceased in 1882. Other attempts to restart the project were made without success.

Figure 7-1. William Gibbs McAdoo. (*Wikimedia Commons*)

Dos Passos served as a director of the Hudson Terminal Railroad Company, another group trying to build the tunnel. Three thousand feet of one tunnel running toward Christopher Street in Greenwich Village had been built. When McAdoo told Dos Passos about his interest, Dos Passos responded, "Why not take hold of ours and build it?"[4]

Financing was found, and McAdoo began the work of completing a rapid transit line. The tunnels to Christopher Street opened on February 25, 1908; service to the Hudson Terminal in Lower Manhattan began on July 19, 1909. The line connecting the H&M's lines in New Jersey opened on August 2, and the junction connecting the uptown and downtown tunnels opened on September 20. The H&M's uptown line was extended to its terminal at 6th Avenue and East 33rd Street on March 10, 1910.[5]

McAdoo wanted to do more. The uptown tunnel allowed for a branch line to be built to the East Side from the 9th Street station. He wanted to extend the H&M to the new Grand Central station. Even before H&M service to Lower Manhattan began in 1909, McAdoo considered the potential for connecting his line with the subway system at the Hudson Terminal.[6] He saw other opportunities.

The Interborough Rapid Transit Company, the Brooklyn Rapid Transit Corporation, and the New York State Public Service Commission were in a slow dance to expand the subway system. The PSC wanted to build. The IRT and BRT didn't seem to be in a hurry, since they didn't have competitors who would push them to move ahead.

Now they did. As the H&M's work in Manhattan approached completion in early 1910, McAdoo proposed expanding it. The PSC's Tri-Borough Plan routes would be connected with the H&M's lines. The uptown branch of the H&M would continue to

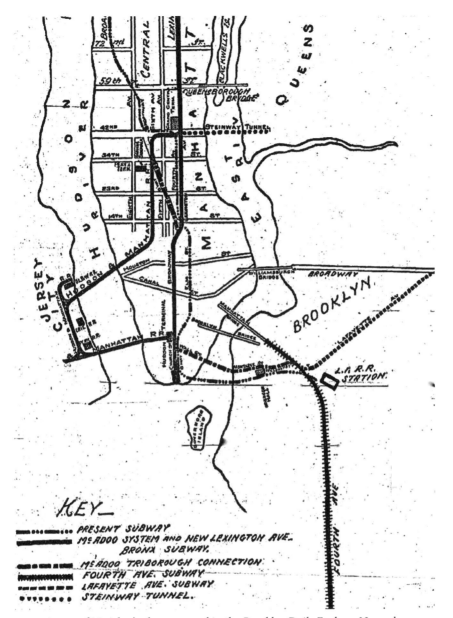

Figure 7-2. A map of McAdoo's plan appeared in the *Brooklyn Daily Eagle* on November 19, 1910.

Grand Central Terminal, connecting with the Tri-Borough Plan's Broadway–Lexington Avenue line. A downtown connection would be developed at the Hudson Terminal.

PSC Chairman William R. Willcox saw potential in McAdoo's proposal: "I have not had time to make a study of the proposition presented by Mr. McAdoo, but one thing is apparent and that is that a responsible company is ready to undertake the operation of the tri-borough system with certain minor modifications."[7] Mayor William Jay Gaynor didn't comment on McAdoo's proposal, but Aldermanic President John Purroy Mitchel and Comptroller William R. Prendergast saw it as a step forward.[8] Brooklyn Borough President Alfred E. Steers had reservations; he wanted more details on the Broadway–Lafayette Avenue loop line.[9]

McAdoo campaigned for the franchises, touring 4th Avenue in Brooklyn on November 23 to develop a plan for that line. In response to Borough President Steers's concerns, he promised to return to study the Broadway–Lafayette Avenue line and other parts of Brooklyn.[10]

McAdoo planned a second phase for what he called the "Independent Subway." He wanted to extend the 4th Avenue line to Staten Island, continue the Broadway–Lafayette Avenue loop line to Queens via Lafayette, Bushwick, and Jamaica Avenues, and construct branch lines from the Eastern Parkway line to Jamaica Bay via Utica Avenue, to Sheepshead Bay via Nostrand Avenue, and to East New York via Livonia Avenue.[11]

There was little response. McAdoo and Willcox met on December 13. Willcox stepped back from his praise of McAdoo's plan, speaking of the benefits of a "regulated monopoly."[12] He was now leaning more toward new proposals that the IRT and BRT made in the wake of McAdoo's plans.

A frustrated McAdoo spoke at a City Club luncheon on December 3:

> The Public Service Commission of this district has developed some years to preparing a plan which would solve the subway problem in New York, not only for the present, but for a reasonable length of time in the future. I think the plan can be

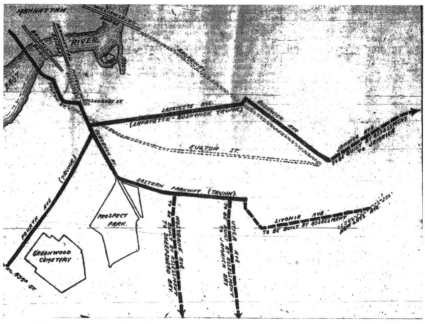

Figure 7-3. This map showing McAdoo's proposals for routes to be built as part of the IND appeared in the *Brooklyn Daily Eagle* on November 26, 1910.

bettered in some respects, but I am frank to say also that you can appoint a hundred bodies of committees of engineers or of citizens and ask them to study the subway problem, and submit a plan, submit suggestions, and submit specifications and I will guarantee you that no two of them will be in accord as to the route or as to the specifications, or as to anything, but I think that the duly constituted authorities under the law are the people to make that plan and that plan is here, and you are at a point where you can do something with it unless you allow yourselves to be talked out of it, or allow the plan itself to be talked to death.[13]

The H&M then withdrew its bid. "We have become convinced that it is futile for us to unite with the city authorities to provide an independent system unless the city authorities are fully determined that an independent system is wanted for the city," McAdoo wrote to Willcox. "In short, there can be no competitive bids between this company and the Interborough on independence or monopoly. It seems to us essential that one policy or the other shall be decided upon before further progress can be made."[14]

McAdoo spoke at the annual dinner of the trustees of Brooklyn Heights' Plymouth Church on January 11, 1911: "The welfare of the people as a whole must, as it should, be the determining influence. The time has come when the *real* people must be considered. The views of civic bodies and interested persons must not be taken too seriously. The real people are the masses, who use the subways most, and it is their interest, because they are the most affected, which should have the most claim. . . . Once the City begins to construct the Independent System progress in every direction will be easier and it will be easy to secure better terms that the City ought to have."[15]

McAdoo then left the country for "health reasons." He wouldn't discuss anything after his return. The H&M didn't withdraw its plans to extend to Grand Central until 1920, after seventeen separate proposals. The Board of Estimate, the PSC, and the Transit Construction Commission declined to grant permission, fearing the H&M would interfere with the extension of the Flushing line from Grand Central to Times Square.[16] By then, McAdoo had left the H&M to become secretary of the treasury during Woodrow Wilson's administration.[17] After seeking the Democratic nomination for president in 1920 and 1924, he moved to California and was elected to the U.S. Senate in 1932.[18]

McAdoo's efforts to operate subways did not succeed, but they probably did produce the results the PSC wanted. The IRT and BRT made offers to expand their systems. They were beginning to take the steps toward what would become the Dual Systems Contracts.

Daniel Lawrence Turner's concept of building subways ahead of population growth was most clearly seen in the proposals he drew up in the 1920s and 1930s; his influence, as exemplified by the ESA, is still felt. The plan he prepared for the Transit Construction Commission in 1920 proposed extending subway lines to the city line in Queens and the Bronx and to Staten Island's western shore. Once Turner became the consulting engineer for the New York State Transit Commission (NYSTC), he tried to reach the suburbs.

The NYSTC released Turner's Queens Parkway plan, a proposal for a line into eastern Queens, in 1923. It was an east–west line running from 9th Avenue and West 23rd Street in Manhattan into Brooklyn, mostly operating along Greenpoint and Metropolitan Avenues, and into Queens along Penelope and Jewel Avenues and Black Stump Road (now 73rd Avenue) to near the city line. A further extension to the suburbs is easy to envision. Most of the line in Queens would be built in "open cut" style—below street level, but not in a tunnel. The line would be built with an adjoining parkway and parkland. What Turner had in mind would look like Mosholu or Pelham Parkways in the Bronx with a subway between the main roadways.

BRT lines in Brooklyn—parts of the Brighton Beach line and most of the Sea Beach line—were built this way, as were parts of the New York, Westchester, and Boston Railway. It reduced construction costs and was a reasonable alternative in constructing new lines. "Subways are prohibitive in cost, and elevated subways, while they develop a district eventually, are a blight," Transit Commissioner LeRoy T. Harkness wrote. "The ideal method has seemed to be the depressed open cut such as the Brighton Beach line in Brooklyn. That line gives splendid service and normal building development continues on both sides right up to the banks of the open cut."[19]

Turner wanted to build the line in an open area, with residential and recreational areas developing around it. His view was not different from that of Nathan Straus, Jr., Clarence Stein, and Andrew J. Eken with the Bronx's Hillside Houses:[20] "In addition to providing the population with rapid transit, a parkway line also provides the same population with a park, just as conveniently accessible to them as the rapid transit line itself is accessible. In other words, a playground and breathing space for the children is provided at the front door of the homes. This great advantage can be obtained for the people, as will subsequently appear, at a very little cost over an elevated line, and at a very much less cost than a subway line through the same territory."[21]

Turner discussed the growth the Queens Parkway line would generate:

Given rapid transit, the area east of Queens Boulevard alone, even if restricted to an average population of about 60 per acre gross, which would mean a suburban type of development, with for the most part one or two family dwellings, could house 300,000 people. . . . The area made accessible by these 12 miles of rapid transit in Queens, would therefore, under housing conditions are superior to those of people living the present rapid transit areas of the Bronx or Brooklyn, giving homes to half a million people.

Even if a more intensive apartment house development were to result along practically the entire parkway line, the objections to such a type of development would

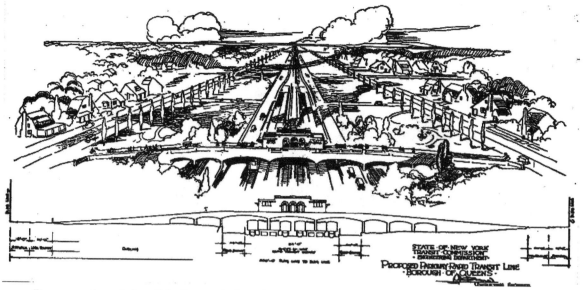

Figure 7-4. A rendering of the Queens Parkway line.

be greatly minimized by reason of the fact that these apartments would have in front of their doors a parkway following the rapid transit line. In other words, simply by crossing the street, there would be ample playground and breathing space for the children.[22]

The Queens Parkway line didn't go beyond the proposal stage. Not long after, the Board of Transportation proposed its own east–west route, the IND's Queens Boulevard line. However, other proposals creating new subway systems within Manhattan, radiating out through the other four boroughs and into New York City's northern and eastern suburbs and New Jersey, followed.

Henry M. Brinckerhoff proposed a system serving the city and the suburbs. He was a partner with William Barclay Parsons in the company then known as Parsons, Klapp, Brinckerhoff, and Douglas. "Let us first free our minds of our habitual ideas of New York as Manhattan Island and think rather of the great surrounding district extending even outside of the five boroughs of Greater New York," Brinckerhoff said in a paper presented at a meeting of the New York Section of the American Society of Civil Engineers on November 17, 1920.[23] He called for east–west lines running from New Jersey through to Long Island, as well as lines running into the northern suburbs and a north–south line running from Staten Island to New Jersey's northern counties.

Daniel L. Turner spoke about his concept of having rapid transit precede population growth, which was not inconsistent with Brinckerhoff's plan. George McAneny, who would become NYSTC chairperson, agreed with Brinckerhoff.[24] At a Transit

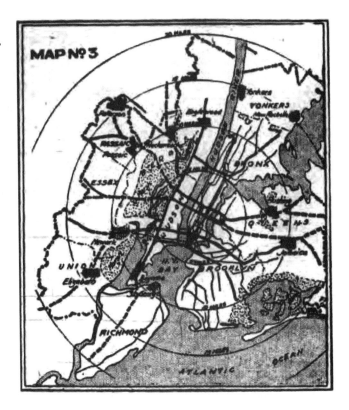

Figure 7-5. This map of Brinckerhoff's plan appeared in the December 11, 1920, edition of the *New York Evening Post*.

Commission hearing on May 24, 1922, McAneny and Turner discussed building a new suburban rail terminal at 4th Avenue (now Park Avenue South) between East 32nd and East 33rd Streets.[25] He wanted to relieve overcrowding at Pennsylvania Station and Grand Central Terminal.

In June 1922 Turner was appointed as the chairperson of a NYSTC staff committee tasked with planning for a system serving suburban riders and relieving overcrowding of the subway lines. Rather than developing one central terminal, the committee expanded on Brinckerhoff's proposal. The Metropolitan Transit System (MTS) plan was released in April 1924.

Two loop lines in Lower and Midtown Manhattan were the center of this system. One went under 57th Street on the north and Battery Park on the south. Along the West Side, it would go along Washington Street, West Broadway, Hudson Street, and a "super street" to be built between 9th and 10th Avenues. The East Side route would run along Front Street, the Bowery, and a "super street" to be built between 2nd and 3rd Avenues.

Connections with the LIRR would be developed in Lower and Midtown Manhattan. A second, larger loop would establish connections to the New Jersey commuter lines. The East Side line would be extended to the Bronx, linking with the northern commuter lines at a station at 149th Street. Stations in the city would create additional rapid transit service for local riders.

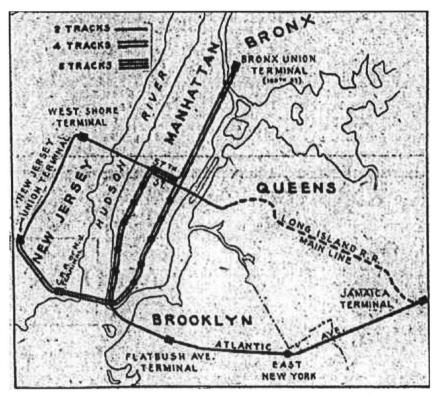

Figure 7-6. A map of the Metropolitan Transit System plan. (*Brooklyn Daily Eagle*)

Turner estimated that the MTS would cost approximately $687 million to build ($18.9 billion in 2011 dollars, according to MeasuringWorth.com), with costs divided between the localities and railroads.[26] No schedule was set for construction; Turner thought the project's benefits were short-term and, accordingly, should be funded on a pay-as-you-go basis: "There will be many direct beneficiaries of the System, apart from the passengers who use it daily to and from work. All of these beneficiaries should share in the cost as well as the riders. Furthermore, the System will not serve more than the present generation. Later generations will have their own facilities to provide. Therefore, the System should be paid for now to the greatest extent possible, not passed on for those in the future to pay for."[27] Turner foresaw suburban sprawl in the New York metropolitan area well before anyone thought of the phenomenon or the expression describing it.

Two other Transit Commissions drew up plans building on what Turner and his committee proposed. Henry M. Brinckerhoff, serving as consulting engineer for the Westchester County Transit Commission (WCTC), and John F. Agar, its chairperson, thought Westchester lines should not terminate at 149th Street. Brinckerhoff believed it was impractical due to the required transfers.[28] He proposed continuing trains along Madison Avenue to Murray Hill as a "deep tunnel" line (similar to what the MTA is

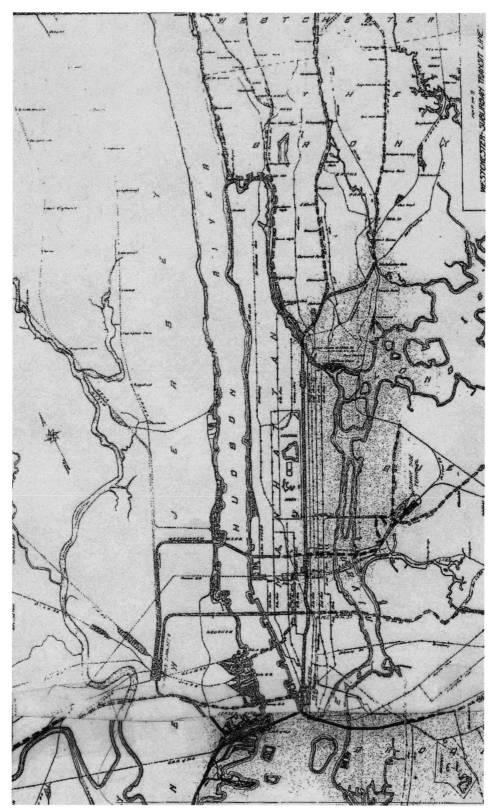

Figure 7-7. The WCTC plan.

doing with the ESA). Some trains would terminate there; others would go on to a terminal at City Hall. Further extensions would connect with the LIRR in Brooklyn, the Central Railroad of New Jersey in Jersey City, and the SIRT in St. George via the New Jersey connection.

Turner also went beyond the MTS. Serving as consulting engineer for the North Jersey Transit Commission (NJTC), along with having similar positions with the NYSTC and the BOT,[29] he helped to develop an NJTC plan for a commuter subway system establishing direct links with the existing New York City subway system.

The core of the NJTC plan was the Interstate Loop line, running north to south from Weehawken to Jersey City in New Jersey and Park Row, Mulberry Street, Lafayette Street, Irving Place, and Lexington Avenue in Manhattan. The northern leg would run along 57th Street; the southern leg would run along Washington and Barclay Streets. The Interstate Loop would be built as a "deep tunnel" line on the East Side. Fourteen stations would have been built in New Jersey, and nine would have been built in Manhattan. Turner estimated it would cost $185 million to build ($2.26 billion in 2009 dollars).[30]

The NJTC also proposed extending New York City subway lines to New Jersey. Three routes were extensions of IRT lines and the fourth was from the BMT. Two of the IRT connections were links to the Lexington Avenue and Broadway–7th Avenue lines in the area of the Battery. The third was an extension of the Flushing line from its yet-to-open Times Square terminal to Bergenline Avenue in New Durham. The report called for extending the BMT's 14th Street–Canarsie line, yet to be built to its terminal at 8th Avenue, to Hoboken.[31] A full rapid transit line was planned for northern New Jersey, taking advantage of the new river crossings expected to be built across the Hudson River.

The NYSTC had started to examine extending the IRT to New Jersey when the NJTC report was released.[32] Initially, focus was given to the connections at the Battery, but it would eventually be given to extending the Flushing line to New Durham. Laws authorizing that extension were discussed in the legislatures of both New York and New Jersey[33] and had support from Midtown Manhattan business groups.[34] The NJTC released a report on the feasibility of this route on June 1, 1927.

The New Jersey Legislature passed the legislation, but the plan went no further. The $33 million cost ($837 million in 2011 dollars, according to MeasuringWorth.com) of building the extension may have been too much of a burden for both states, which first needed to respond to local priorities.

The BMT opposed extending the 14th Street–Canarsie line to Hoboken. "If you would consider the merits of the proposed extensions, there is at present no need for an added feeder from the B.M.T. into New Jersey," said BMT Vice President Travis H. Whitney. "But when we consider the rapid growth of Brooklyn and the almost stagnated expansion of the transportation facilities to match the increase in population,

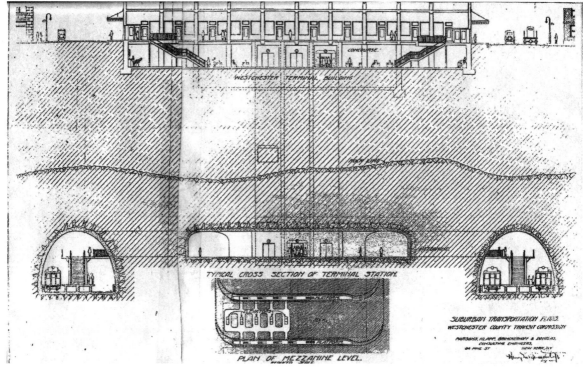

Figure 7-8. A cross-section of the WCTC "deep tunnel."

there is no doubt that B.M.T. extensions are better concentrated in this borough for the present."[35]

The New York State Suburban Transit Commission, a legislative group evaluating all the plans, held a hearing at City Hall on July 16, 1925, seeking additional input. LIRR Vice President George LeBoutillier opposed the MTS, believing it was redundant to the operation of the LIRR. He thought more could be accomplished by providing additional subway service to Queens. James A. McCarthy of the Fifth Avenue Association called for the line to be built from Westchester to connect with the LIRR's tracks and run into New Jersey. James W. Dansky of the Eighth Avenue Business Men's Association thought there wasn't enough subway service on the West Side (the start of service on the IND's 8th Avenue–Washington Heights line was seven years away). He proposed building the Westchester line down the West Side. Lawson H. Brown of the Brooklyn Chamber of Commerce wanted the Westchester route extended to connect with the LIRR in Brooklyn.[36]

W&B President Leverett S. Miller expressed reservations with the WCTC plan in December 1925. Brinckerhoff and Agar had envisioned the line running into Lower Manhattan. Miller's thinking was more in line with the MTS concept of having the line terminate at a station in the Bronx. He thought this would reduce transportation costs and actually make the trip easier for his riders.[37]

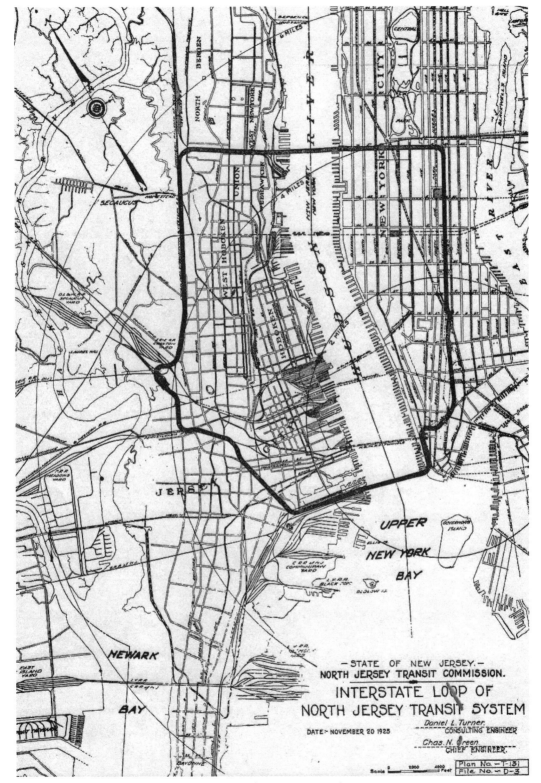

Figure 7-9. The North Jersey Transit Commission's Interstate Loop line.

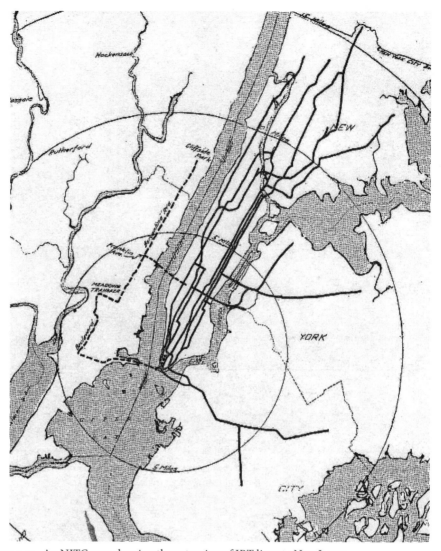

Figure 7-10. An NJTC map showing the extension of IRT lines to New Jersey.

Miller thought he had had a better idea. On February 4, 1926, he proposed a W&B extension from its terminal at 133rd Street and Willis Avenue in the Bronx to St. Nicholas Avenue and West 125th Street in Harlem, connecting with the subway and elevated lines intersecting 125th Street. Miller thought this would decentralize and better distribute suburban riders in Manhattan. He believed most W&B riders were already traveling to points north and west of Grand Central Terminal, and that this would make travel easier for them. No consideration was given to cost or financial arrangements.[38]

The final WCTC report was released on April 26, 1926, following up on earlier proposals. It called for trains from the New York Central Railroad, the New Haven Railroad, and the W&B to run into a tunnel from a station at 149th Street, allowing for a transfer to the IRT and then continuing downtown as a "deep tunnel" line under

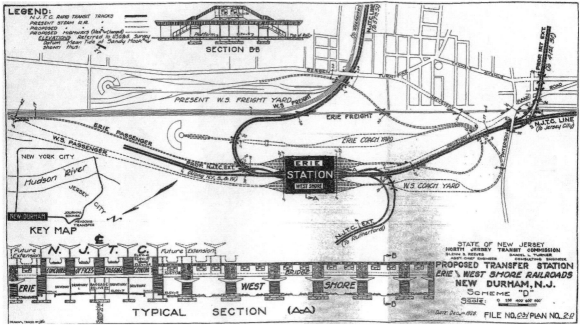

Figure 7-11. This North Jersey Transit diagram for an unbuilt railroad terminal from 1926 includes an extension of the Flushing line from Manhattan (*upper right*).

Madison Avenue. A branch line would serve Grand Central Terminal, allowing for transfers with the subway lines there. Other trains would run to the City Hall area via Madison Avenue, Broadway, University Place, and West Broadway.

Brinckerhoff estimated the project's cost at $150 million ($1.82 billion in 2009 dollars) for a four-track line, and $95 million ($1.15 billion in 2009 dollars) for two. He stressed the connectivity this line could have with intersecting transit lines on the way to City Hall, and pointed out possible connections with the development of further extensions connecting with the LIRR in Brooklyn, the Jersey Central Railroad, the H&M in Jersey City, and the SIRT in Port Richmond and St. George.[39]

Cost was again the daunting factor. There was little chance the Westchester County Board of Supervisors would take action, given the investments they were making in other public works projects, including their county's highway system.[40] The WCTC plan was tabled[41] and not considered again until 1928, without any change in its fate.[42]

Interest in developing a suburban transit system went on. On June 9, 1927, Agar led a delegation of Westchester representatives to meet with George S. Silzer, the chairperson of the Port of New York Authority, to discuss commuter rail concerns. After trying to get Brinckerhoff's plan funded within their county, Agar and his group knew that a more regional approach was needed and turned to the Port Authority for help.

The Port Authority had received a request from the New Jersey Legislature to play a role in the development of a suburban system. Out of this came the Suburban Transit

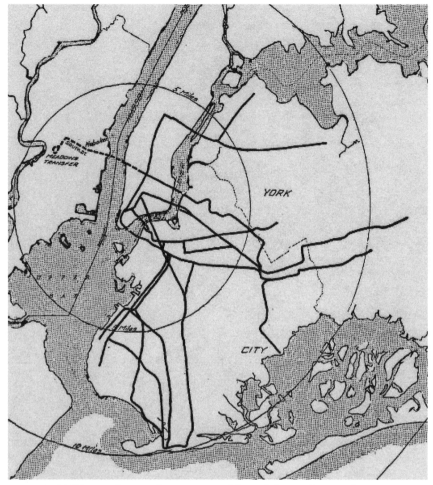

Figure 7-12. An NJTC map showing the extension of the 14th Street–Canarsie line to New Jersey.

Engineering Board (STEB), which would examine the proposals and develop a master plan. The engineers from the local Transit Commissions, the BOT, and the Nassau County government participated; Turner was its chairperson. The STEB carried out an origin/destination survey of Westchester County commuters and evaluated a survey done in New Jersey by the NJTC.

One of its findings was that north–south New Jersey service was as desirable as service to New York City.[43] This was reflected in a NJTC plan that harked back to Jersey City Mayor Frank Hague's Boulevard subway line.[44] A route was proposed that would run from Port Richmond on Staten Island and then connect with the SIRT's North Shore line, via the then-proposed Bayonne Bridge, and with Manhattan via the then-unbuilt George Washington Bridge. The Palisades route would connect with cities along the Hudson River, the H&M, and lines proposed by the NJTC.[45] The NJTC later called for two other New Jersey rapid transit lines, one connecting Paterson, Passaic, and Newark and the other running from Hackensack to Newark via Rutherford.[46]

The proposal for rapid transit tracks on the George Washington Bridge was part of the plans of both the STEB and the Port Authority. A 1926 Port Authority report stated:

> As a result of our studies it now appears quite feasible . . . to build the bridge initially for highway traffic only, but with the provision, at a small extra expenditure, for the future accommodation of rail transportation or additional bus passenger traffic. . . . If and when accommodation for rail passenger traffic or for bus passenger traffic, across the bridge becomes necessary, two or four lanes, or tracks, or either form of such traffic can be added on a lower deck. . . . The question as to whether, and to what extent, rail passenger traffic should be provided for on the bridge is still under consideration, and the cooperation and advice of the transit authorities in the two States has been sought in order to arrive at a satisfactory solution.[47]

Drawings accompanying the report showed two or four tracks built as part of a lower deck. As we've seen, that solution has not yet been achieved.

That was not the only Hudson River crossing considered. Along with the Interstate Loop plans was a proposal to build a bridge crossing the river to enter Manhattan at West 57th Street, but it ran afoul of the federal government. The Department of War wanted to have a vertical clearance of 200 feet above the river at its center and 185 feet at its pierhead lines. The plans for the 57th Street Bridge called for a 175-foot clearance at its center. The additional price of increasing the bridge's height made it less feasible, and

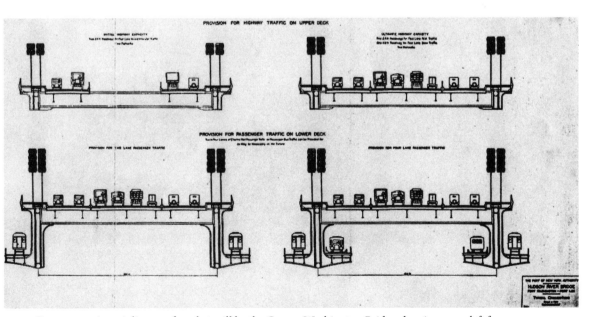

Figure 7-13. A 1926 diagram for what will be the George Washington Bridge showing room left for rail traffic.

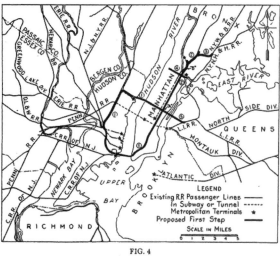

FIG. 4

PROPOSED FIRST STEP OF SUBURBAN RAPID TRANSIT SYSTEM

Figure 7-14. The first step of the Regional Plan.

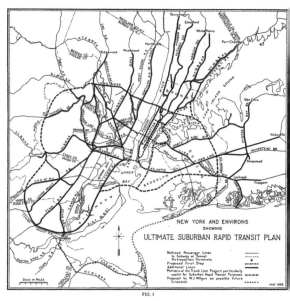

Figure 7-15. The second step.

ultimately made a bridge 121 blocks to the north in Manhattan more viable.[48] While the idea was considered, no proposal for tracks on the George Washington Bridge ever advanced beyond the planning stage.

The Regional Plan of New York looked at developing an overall transit network. Harold M. Lewis, their executive engineer, working with Daniel L. Turner, developed a report, *Transit and Transportation*, incorporated some aspects of the earlier plans, brought back some of Turner's proposals for the subway system, and set the framework for the proposals to expand the subway system that the BOT would issue over the next decade.

New versions of the Queens Parkway line were considered. One connected it to the Queens Boulevard line in Elmhurst, near the Woodhaven Boulevard–Slattery Plaza station. Another went into eastern Queens via Union Turnpike, rather than Black Stump Road. The Interstate Loop and other NJTC lines were discussed with a Midtown extension to the LIRR and a northern extension under 3rd Avenue, linking with the three commuter rail lines serving Westchester in the Bronx at the 149th Street Union Station first called for in the MTS Plan.

As a second step, the Regional Plan proposed rapid transit links crossing the George Washington Bridge, to Brooklyn to link up with the LIRR, and from Staten Island using the Narrows Tunnel. The plans for the Staten Island line also called for new western connections to New Jersey and an eastern extension to link with the LIRR in southeastern Queens.

"All means of transportation should be planned to furnish direct routes not only to the older business centres but to the new ones which are arising or may be expected to develop," Lewis wrote. "Short hauls between residences and places of work will do much to relieve congestion."[49]

The STEB proposed variations of the Interstate Loop with connections to the LIRR in Brooklyn and Queens. They made no proposals for Westchester connections, feeling that schedule and operational adjustments at Grand Central Terminal were what was needed to relieve congestion on the northern routes.[50]

The Committee on the Regional Plan for New York and Its Environs followed both its plan and the STEB's with a proposal a month later to build a terminal in the Long Island City section of Queens, over the Sunnyside Yards. This would enable connections between the STEB's line, the LIRR, the subways at Queensboro Plaza, and the northern commuter lines, which would use the Hell Gate Bridge to reach Queens and the Sunnyside Yards.[51]

The STEB released additional reports on ridership counts. No action was taken, due to the Depression's effects on commuter traffic and transit funding.[52] The NJTC issued a report in 1931 reiterating the routes proposed in its earlier plans and discussing further extensions into the northern, western, and southern reaches of its service area.[53] The STEB analyzed ridership trends, but ceased planning activities until ridership levels justified resumption of that work.[54]

The shortage of funding didn't stop people from proposing commuter rapid transit systems. In 1936, New Jersey's legislature passed a resolution asking the Port of New York Authority to report on ways to connect the counties adjoining the Hudson River with New York City via rapid transit. The Port Authority responded with a revised version of the STEB plan.

The PA's Interstate Loop would run to 6th Avenue and West 51st Street and then westward to New Durham, where it would meet the Erie Railroad, which would be electrified to serve Manhattan. A spur in New Jersey would run to Staten Island, linking with the SIRT in Port Richmond. Connections with the LIRR and the northern commuter lines, and a north–south line in Staten Island connecting the SIRT's Tottenville line with the line coming from New Jersey were proposed as a second phase.

The Port Authority estimated the cost of the plan's first phase at $187 million ($92.6 billion in 2011 dollars, according to MeasuringWorth.com), which wasn't there to be spent.[55] It would be more than two decades before the Port Authority would operate rapid transit service.

The Regional Plan Association built on the Port Authority's plan with one of its own a year later, calling for a northern extension of the Interstate Loop, under 2nd Avenue to 149th Street and linking with the New York Central Railroad. They revived the plan for a terminal in Queens, running a spur into that borough, where it would link with the LIRR, the subways and extensions of the New Haven Railroad, and the W&B running from the Hell Gate Bridge. This was seen as a way to revive the W&B, which had ceased operations at the start of the year.[56]

The Interstate Loop was again proposed in 1957. The Metropolitan Rapid Transit Commission, created by the state legislatures of New York and New Jersey, proposed a new version connecting with the BMT's Broadway line by the Battery and north of the 57th Street Station. The line would make transfers with the H&M and the commuter rail lines in New Jersey. It was estimated that the line would cost $400 million to build ($3.05 billion in 2009 dollars).[57]

The Port of New York Authority played a primary role in the organization of the Suburban Transit Engineering Board and issued a suburban rapid transit plan in 1937, but did no more until the 1960s. The H&M was in bankruptcy in 1961; the system McAdoo and Dos Passos succeeded in building was in decline.

The Port Authority bid $20 million ($150 million in 2011 dollars according to MeasuringWorth.com) for the H&M and budgeted to spend more. The plan also involved improving linkage with the commuter rail lines in New Jersey and discontinuing the ferry lines that the railroads still operated across the Hudson River.[58] This led to a significant change in Lower Manhattan.

Plans for the World Trade Center then called for it to be built along the East River, in an area bordered by Fulton Street, South Street, Old Slip, and Pearl Street. As part of the Port Authority's plan, it would be built along the Hudson River, with the Hudson Terminal and other buildings in the area demolished to make room for it.

Despite protests by area property owners and businesspeople who would be displaced by the World Trade Center's construction, the plan proceeded. New York Governor Nelson A. Rockefeller and New Jersey Governor Richard J. Hughes reached an agreement on January 22, 1962, for legislation to enable the purchase of the H&M by the Port Authority. The Port Authority took over operation of the H&M on July 26, 1962, with that line becoming known as the Port Authority Trans-Hudson Corporation (PATH).

Daniel L. Turner retired in 1933, following the end of the Suburban Transit Engineering Board's planning work. He died on March 12, 1942, leaving a huge legacy in the development of the transit system in the New York metropolitan area. With the construction of the East Side Access program and the 2nd Avenue subway now in progress, springing from plans he helped to develop eight decades ago, that legacy continues to grow.

8

The Battle of the Northeast Bronx, Part 2

The New York, Westchester, and Boston Railway's last trip arrived in White Plains at 12:40 A.M. on January 1, 1938. One hundred fifty members of the Allied Civic Associations and other community groups met with John H. Delaney and Charles V. Halley, Jr., on January 12. They wanted the Board of Transportation to obtain the W&B's Bronx tracks and resume operations. Delaney said he didn't think it would be profitable.

Preliminary engineering work for Burke Avenue was underway. A field office opened at 3238 White Plains Road; the BOT awarded a contract to John S. Fitz Associates in 1937 to locate building lines along the route. Surveys were done along the New York Central's right-of-way in Bronx Park for the viaduct crossing the park. It would consider obtaining the W&B's tracks after that, if they were still available.[1]

But would they be available? Robert Moses's plan had gained momentum. At his urging, James J. Lyons, Arthur V. Sheridan, and other officials inspected the right-of-way on February 5 to consider its use as an express truck highway with a bus line stopping by old W&B stations. Moses stated that "pleasure cars" could also use it.[2] The Board of Estimate allocated $5 million for Burke Avenue on February 17, but Bronx and Westchester groups still sought the W&B's revival.

Mayors Dominic Amato of North Pelham and Harry Scott of New Rochelle stated that all options for the W&B should be explored before Moses's plan. Frederick G. Schmidt, majority leader of the Westchester County Board of Supervisors, equivocated: "Of course, what we need most is the railway, but if it is impossible the establishment of express highways on the railroad bed might be the solution."[3] Supervisor Harold W. Davis thought a "fast trolley system" was feasible.[4] The United Civic Association of the Bronx supported Moses's plan.[5]

The *Bronx Home News* supported a "rapid transit bus line" connecting with the Burke Avenue line: "The express bus service is an especially important feature of the project, for the N.Y., W, and B. (and its right-of-way) by all means should be retained for transit purposes.... Rapid transit, by all means, should come first, but the truck highway plan, as such, has considerable merit."[6]

Some Westchester real estate brokers opposed Moses's plan. Leo O. Rostenberg of White Plains said, "The communities along the railroad are essentially residential, and represent investments of many millions of dollars. Trucking would certainly hurt these fine communities just as it ruined the fine residential character of the Boston Post Road."[7]

Westchester State Senator Pliny W. Williamson sought the W&B's reactivation:

> If the villages and cities affected by the railroad desire to form some kind of an inter-community authority to take possession of the railroad, I am willing to assist by presenting the necessary legislation in Albany . . .
>
> . . . Everything within reason should be done to revive the railroad. It should be done for humanitarian reasons and to save the homes and assessed valuations along the line.[8]

Assembly Member Peter Quinn sponsored a resolution calling for a legislative committee to study resuming W&B service. He didn't believe that a state authority was useful. The economy would make difficult the sale of bonds to operate the revived rail line:

> Our only hope is in evolving a plan whereby the receiver appointed by the Federal Court and the bondholders can be persuaded to surrender their interests in return for the bonds of a State Authority at a considerable discount on the face amount of their present outstanding obligations.
>
> This plan would obviate the need of selling any bonds and would remove all problems of financing from the already involved situation.
>
> The only and best way to work out such a plan and reduce it to the form of a legislative measure is through the agency of a committee of the Legislature with authority to confer with all the interested parties and receive from them official offers for the surrender of their holdings in return for the bonds of a state authority.[9]

Bennett E. Siegelstein spoke as a representative for a Westchester homeowners group who claimed they had the financing to keep the line in operation.[10] The New York, Westchester, and Boston Company's Employees Protective Association, representing former employees, wrote to Senator Wagner, seeking help.

The Allied Civic Associations of Old Eastchester met at Breinlinger's Hall on March 10. William E. Schramek reported that state legislators would file bills calling for an authority to operate the W&B if the Westchester Board of Supervisors wanted it. They did; despite his earlier opposition, Quinn filed matching legislation creating the Westchester and Bronx Railroad Authority. The legislation passed and went to Governor Lehman for his signature.

Mayor La Guardia opposed the bill, feeling it shifted funding responsibility to the City Council and Bronx borough president.[11] Lehman vetoed it, saying, "It is unwise to have government create a public benefit corporation with the color of governmental authority and sanction for the purpose of acquiring and operating a private railroad through several communities which has since been forced to discontinue its services."[12]

Figure 8-1. The *Bronx Home News* ran this 1938 photograph of preliminary engineering work on Burke Avenue on March 19, 1946.

Williamson wrote to Lehman in July:

The closing of the railroad December 31, 1937, has caused serious inconvenience to those who founded their homes and established their businesses along its line. If its operation be not renewed, that inconvenience will result in actual reduction in value of the real estate in the zone of the service of the road. Such value falls not alone on the owner of an affected plot, serious though that be; as loss of taxable valuation, it spreads across each of the tax districts involved and so lays a charge across an entire community. . . . I respectfully suggest to you appoint a committee from all of these municipalities suffering from the discontinuance of the railroad.[13]

Lehman agreed: "I see no objection . . . to the appointment by me of an unofficial committee, provided that the Mayors or governing bodies of the municipalities desire it. As you point out, the committee would understand that no funds [were] available for their work from the state, from the county of Westchester or from the city of New York."[14]

Moses criticized the Committee in a letter to Garvin:

With the assistance of various City and State executives with whom I have been working on such matters, I offered a reasonable solution of the problem. This was opposed by various people including some cheap political fellows in Westchester and smart aleck lawyers who told the former commuters on this road that they had some magic way of reviving it. The Commission appointed by the Governor on the nomination of various municipalities, was the most ridiculous I have seen in a long time....

... So far as I am concerned, and speaking for the competent and intelligent engineers of the City and State who worked on this plan, I am getting sick of being the voice crying in the wilderness. I see no other future for your right of way excepting as a toll truck highway.[15]

Moses had stronger words in a letter to George Mand:

The fact of the matter is that they do not know what they are talking about, and there is no talent on the Regional Plan at the moment worth listening to or bothering about.

If they had any really first-rate men these men would have been absorbed into our big public construction program long ago, and would be earning a living instead of sitting up in an ivory tower drawing pretty pictures and telling busy officials how to do their work.[16]

Figure 8-2. William E. Schramek and Pliny W. Williamson. (*Yonkers Herald Statesman*)

Herman W. Johnston wrote to La Guardia for the Allied Civic Associations:

As the representative of the taxpayers along the route of the Westchester and Boston in the Northeast Bronx, the Allied Civic Associations of Old Eastchester protest and stand ready to fight the adoption of any such plan that Commissioner Moses proposes to convert the right-of-way into a toll truck highway.

. . . The right-of-way of the Westchester and Boston is a natural rapid transit route and its 25 years' use has developed the northeast Bronx to an extent that obligates the City of New York to furnish transportation to its citizens. The City now has the opportunity to preserve this route for future transit use that will save millions of dollars in a few years.[17]

Moses learned that Lehman asked La Guardia for nominees, and so contacted the mayor on July 22. He suggested that La Guardia nominate him and other highway advocates (including Delaney, "because he can explain the uselessness of this road for rapid transit purposes"):[18] "Obviously, recent attempts of Westchester politicians led by Senator Williamson and others to rehabilitate the old railroad and make the New York–New Haven people and the Receivers think they can still get a lot of money for their broken down road. It is quite obvious that Governor Lehman is simply playing politics with this issue and joining Williamson. . . . This railroad will never run again and it is simply spoofing the old commuters to tell them that it will."[19] Lehman appointed Moses and City Planning Commissioner Rexford Guy Tugwell; Albert Ritchie, a New Rochelle lawyer, was elected chairman. Herman W. Johnston and George Mand were also appointed. They toured the W&B right-of-way in December to have Moses's plan explained to them.[20]

Preliminary work on Burke Avenue continued, but Manhattan Borough President Stanley M. Isaacs proposed its removal at the Board of Estimate:

I am moving for the elimination of this item because I think it is unnecessary. I think it is unsound policy on the part of the City to extend subways to the outlying regions and thus to drain populations from the center of the city—or in this case from the South Bronx.

I believe the transportation question could be better handled by a proper system of bus line feeders to our main subways, with interchangeable feeders. By going in for the construction of unnecessary feeders, the City merely increases the deficit for subway building. One of the reasons advanced in favor of this situation is the fact that the Hillside development is built there. It could be served by buses.[21]

Lyons protested; Isaacs's resolution failed. Deputy Mayor Henry Curran voted for La Guardia, and Comptroller Joseph McGoldrick supported Lyons; City Council President A. Newbold Morris supported Isaacs.

Figure 8-3. City Council President A. Newbold Morris in 1940. (*Long Island Star Journal*)

The W&B's infrastructure was disappearing. After a hurricane devastated New York and New England on September 21, New Haven Railroad crews removed rails, ties, and ballast from the W&B's New Rochelle–Port Chester branch to repair their lines. Ritchie protested, but he couldn't stop this from happening.

The City Planning Commission deleted all but $185,000 ($2.95 million in 2011 dollars, according to MeasuringWorth.com) of Burke Avenue's funding from the 1939 capital budget in November, while funding another Moses project, the Circumferential Parkway, connecting Brooklyn and Queens (an unwieldy name later changed to the Belt Parkway). Outraged, Lyons blamed Council President A. Newbold Morris: "[The funding cut] will deprive the North Bronx of transit facilities. . . . It is another of Newbold Morris' brainstorms based on a lack of information and knowledge of the situation. . . . It was used simply as a method to reduce the budget to provide for a circumferential parkway in Brooklyn."[22]

Johnston, speaking for Allied Civic Associations, protested:

When [Burke Avenue] reached the stage where we were assured that the contracts were to be let before the first of the year, along came a persuasive Commissioner of Parks with a scheme to "doll up" Brooklyn with a circumferential parkway and a complacent Board of Estimate very graciously handed over to him the money that had been set aside in this year's capital outlay budget. . . . Our organization is determined to fix the responsibility for this treatment at City Hall. The Northeast Bronx is not just another community waiting for [a] rapid transit facility.

It has within a year lost a first class railway service, the New York, Westchester and Boston Railroad, upon whose service the entire community was built up. To a large area affected by the closing of the W&B the promise of speedy construction of the Burke Avenue subway was the only factor to counteract the depressed values in the properties when the railroad abandoned its tracks.[23]

The Allied Civic Associations met on November 15 at Evander Childs High School. They advertised the meeting with a leaflet with the headline "STOLEN. Your help is needed in restoring the Burke Ave. SUBWAY to the Capital Outlay Budget."[24]

"The Board of Estimate cannot find $5,000,000 [$65.3 million in 2011 dollars] to cover necessary expenditures for the next year for [the] Burke Avenue subway, yet it did find nearly 30 millions for a parkway [$1.03 billion in 2011 dollars], which will never benefit the thousands of residents of the Northeast Bronx who must have transit facilities," Herman W. Johnston wrote to the Northeast Bronx civic groups. "Much as these North Bronx people appreciate Commissioner Moses' efforts to build parks and highways, they realize that work on them must be deferred until certain necessary transit facilities are provided for the Northeast Bronx."[25]

Approximately nine hundred people attended. Lyons, Mand, Loewenthal, and Council Member James A. Deering encouraged them to attend the Board of Estimate hearing the next day; many went.

With Morris chairing, Lyons made a motion to restore funding. "My motion is not for approval of [the $5 million]—it merely states that it is the sense of this board that the Burke Avenue extension be restored to the budget. By adopting my motion, you will let these people know that you are in favor of it," Lyons said.[26] Morris said the Board of Estimate couldn't vote on an individual item.

Lyons wouldn't accept this: "We are here demanding from the Board that you will again take this matter up and put it back in the budget. Every other borough has benefited, but here are thousands crying for transportation. The Westchester and Boston Railroad has been abandoned, leaving them without means of travel and they are pleading for consideration and hoping you will return this item to the budget so that construction may be started."[27]

Brooklyn Borough President Raymond V. Ingersoll noted that Burke Avenue was only deferred. "We had that $5,000,000 in the 1937 budget and in the 1938 budget, and now it is in the distant future, although Brooklyn has about $20,000,000 for subways for 1939," Lyons responded.

"At various public meetings the Borough President of the Bronx has been reported as saying that the President of the City Council moved to strike out that $5,000,000," Morris said. "That is a direct misstatement and also a violation of one of the first principles of orderly procedure of this board. What transpires in executive session is supposed to be confidential. That is supposed to be a violation of what I consider ethics.

However, I don't hold the Borough President of the Bronx to the same rules of conduct as I do the other members of the Board."[28]

Members of the audience hissed. Morris continued: "We were discussing the circumferential highway and I asked Mr. Lyons to telephone the Board of Transportation to see if $5,000,000 could be cut out of subway construction funds. He did so, and there was no suggestion that any specific item be eliminated."[29]

"We expected that $5,000,000 would be eliminated from the general transportation program, but it came to us in a different form," Morris went on to say. "We never contemplated this. All boroughs should have the same treatment. I consider that it would be unfair not to do it that way."[30] He characterized Lyons's accusation as "very unfair,"[31] and called him a "pie-eyed piper of Hamelin."[32]

"The statements I made were based on facts and I don't withdraw one iota of them," Lyons responded. "You withdrew $3,000,000 for the new Appellate Division courthouse and you withdrew $5,000,000 for the Bronx Extension and then you told me to telephone John H. Delaney and he said he would prefer to take it out of the lump allocation. I then returned and asked you to rescind the action that had been taken."[33] He made a motion to restore Burke Avenue's funding but was ruled out of order.[34]

Deputy Mayor Curran said money was in the budget for Burke Avenue: "The Planning Commission has put up $185,000 for the next year. The balance $10,000,000 is listed under Table 1 as expenditures after 1939, as I read it. . . . If the Burke Avenue line were to be abandoned, it would be silly to put in even one penny. The City Planning Commission has put in the amounts possible to spend next year."[35] "The people of the Bronx do not want $185,000 in the budget this year," Lyons protested. "They want a subway. That's not progress."[36]

Other projects took priority—constructing a new Queens Borough Hall, erecting a hangar for La Guardia Airport, purchasing the Elks Building in Downtown Brooklyn for use by the Board of Education, and planning the Circumferential Parkway. "Homes that cost $10,000 are worth only $2,000 now because it is impossible to travel since suspension of the Westchester, Boston railroad service. The city will lose much more. We have expected this subway for 20 years and we should have it before someone else is given a fancy highway around Brooklyn," said Lillian Britton of the Burke Avenue–Eastchester Road Association.[37]

Ingersoll defended the Circumferential Parkway by pointing out that the Bronx received $12 million in state funding for parkways. The Bronx residents chanted, "We don't want parkways! Give us a subway!"[38] "There are no transit facilities in the Northeast Bronx. This subway is an investment," said the Board of Trade's Thomas V. Tozzi. "It will be comparable to what happened on the Concourse. Help these people."[39]

Before his election to the Board of Aldermen,[40] Charles E. Keegan was Mayor McKee's press secretary as well as vice president and general manager of Hillside Houses. Joseph

E. Kinsley was a World War I veteran and Fordham graduate who was elected to the State Assembly when he was twenty-five years old in 1923, and the Board of Aldermen in 1929. They became the Council's most tenacious advocates for Northeast Bronx subway service.

Keegan and Kinsley, along with their Bronx colleagues, Salvatore Ninfo, James A. Deering, and Michael J. Quill (also Transport Workers Union chairman), brought the fight to the Council. Keegan and Ninfo filed legislation on November 22 restoring the Concourse line extension to the capital budget.

"Thousands of residents in the northeast area of the Bronx are now being deprived of adequate transportation facilities," said Ninfo. "There is no reason why people who bear their share of the burden of taxes and assessments equally with the other residents of the city, should not share equally in the benefits of suitable transportation."[41]

The Bronx Council Members sought the resolution's immediate adoption, which required their colleagues' unanimous consent. Joseph Clark Baldwin of Manhattan objected, because Burke Avenue would serve the Hillside Houses. He opposed building tax-exempt housing at taxpayer expense, followed by subways serving them; instead, he wanted subways built in congested parts of the city.

The Bronx Council Members met with Baldwin, seeking his support. He wouldn't budge. He understood the need for the line, but wanted more discussion,[42] asking if Hillside would benefit from Burke Avenue's opening. "Twenty years before Hillside Homes was ever thought of, the people up there asked for a subway and the BOT was even then in favor of it," Keegan said.[43]

The City Council debated the resolution on November 29. Baldwin's opposition continued:

Important principles are involved. We all realize the necessity for adequate transportation, but you can't take these isolated spots and build subways to them. I know that this is a long-standing question, but you can't spend $5 million now—you haven't got it.

We have to study the placement of housing developments. To spend the money that has been put into Hillside Homes and then to have to build transportation to it is expensive. We know this $5,000,000 is not available, and to adopt this resolution is an empty gesture. I am not opposed to transportation for the Bronx at the proper time, but the time to take this up is when there is a general plan. Trying to force the hand of the Board of Estimate now is a mistake.[44]

Ninfo, Keegan, and Kinsley objected. "This matter has been up for twenty years. There are nearly 50,000 families in the Northeast Bronx and most of them live in small homes. This is not a question of Hillside Homes," Ninfo stated.

"This subway extension is not just for Hillside Homes as Baldwin insists. . . . There are only 1,400 families there and as a former officer of that corporation I know the

$5,000,000 was not thought of for that project," said Keegan. "But there are 50,000 other families up there, as has been pointed out. They have paid their share for the transportation for other parts of the city. They were doing that twenty years before Hillside Homes were designed. This promised subway has been in the budget twice and was taken out as a convenience to the Mayor and to save embarrassment to the Mayor in his plan for a pretty parkway in Brooklyn and Queens."

"The only time you get to the Northeast Bronx is when you are on your way to the Yale Bowl to see the Yale and Harvard game," Kinsley said. "It is all right to say that we haven't got the money, but the Bronx has taken a kicking around not only on this but on other things, particularly by the City Planning Commission, even in such matters as the zoning at the old Protectory site [the location of the Parkchester development]. Why don't you come down to the common people? If we don't get this subway now, it will not be built for five years."[45]

The bill was approved by a vote of twenty-one to three vote, but Burke Avenue was now included in a group of subway improvements. Lyons blamed it on La Guardia: "The people of the Bronx are getting the foot with a fine Italian hand on the Burke Avenue extension."[46]

Lyons claimed that the Bronx was fooled into believing Burke Avenue had been funded, as there was no specific budget line, a decision made in a secret Board of Estimate session excluding him and Queens Borough President Harvey. La Guardia replied:

Hm! Well this is a most silly statement. There was no action taken by the Board of Estimate on Monday, because there was no meeting of the board. Naturally the Mayor has to confer with the Comptroller and the President of the Council about items in the budget, and any action that must be taken by the board.

As to the Bronx extension of the Independent Subway, there is only one man in the city responsible for its elimination and that is Mr. Lyons. He traded it in for the circumferential parkway in Brooklyn and Queens, and I can show you his vote on this.

There isn't any Italian hand this time—it was instead sort of a dumb-skull.[47]

"The Mayor is more unfair than he usually is in saying that I traded the Burke Avenue extension for the circumferential highway," Lyons retorted. "The action on this controversial project was determined at one of the private conferences of the Board of Estimate, and the Mayor was unable to hold these members who usually follow his bidding like Charley McCarthy against the persuasive Commissioner Moses. . . . I do not think that I am the only man interested in the Burke Avenue extension, as I know more than 50,000 families are clamoring for transportation up there."[48]

"The money was taken from us to give another borough a highway that starts nowhere and leads nowhere," Keegan said on December 1. "The action of the Board of Estimate yesterday is a further indictment of promising politicians and their practise of promising anything during a campaign and then running out on their promises when performance is due."[49]

Fearing that there wasn't enough subway construction money for Burke Avenue, Northeast Bronx civic groups attended the Board of Estimate's December 2 meeting. The budget now allocated $3,754,980 for the Burke Avenue line ($49.1 million in 2011 dollars, according to MeasuringWorth.com). Lyons supported the budget, stating that it provided a "good start."[50]

Robert Moses was proceeding with planning for the express truck highway. On November 25, he sent his proposal to Ritchie. The highway would cost $32 million to build ($1.1 billion in 2011 dollars); subsequent funds would come from tolls. Ritchie had established a subcommittee to evaluate proposals in September. Schramek and George Mowbray represented Westchester; Mand and Johnston represented the Bronx. Schramek was chairman, and he was blunt about the priorities: they wanted "trains, not trucks."[51]

Moses was unhappy that the subcommittee's response to him was publicized:

This was a confidential memorandum, but Ritchie without talking to me gave it to the press, and the result was a howl from certain groups in Westchester who said that the old commuters were being betrayed by wicked slickers from the city . . .

. . . The committee, headed by Albert Ritchie[,] does not seem to be a particularly effective one and it has a decidedly political background. The trouble is that certain people in Westchester have promised former New York, Westchester and Boston commuters that they will revive this defunct railroad and somehow make it run again. . . . My opinion is that the only thing to do with this committee is let them stew around for a few months while they completely exhaust the notion of reviving the railroad.[52]

A few months went by, but without the results Moses expected. Northeast Bronx and Westchester groups continued to work for Burke Avenue and for the W&B's acquisition. The Allied Civic Associations started 1939 with a petition drive calling on the city to purchase two of the line's tracks.

Loretta M. Pierce discussed the petition drive's aims:

The Westchester and Boston Committee of the Allied Civic Associations has studied the transit needs of the Bronx and the civic groups are determined that not only must this section of the Northeast Bronx have rapid transit, but that the most economical and practical way to accomplish it is by the acquisition of two tracks of the Westchester and Boston from East 180th Street to Dyre Avenue.

With 55,000 isolated people of the northeast Bronx clamoring for relief from rapid transit worries, the committee feels that rapid transit, rather than commuter service is the sole solution.[53]

Connecting the W&B with the White Plains Road line was a matter of urgent discussion. The Allied Civic Associations submitted the Regional Plan Association's plan to Schramek, believing this would accomplish their goals. They scheduled a meeting for January 13 at Breinlinger's Hall. There was worry that the New Haven Railroad would remove more tracks from the right-of-way, making the chance of restoring rail service more remote.

"Commissioner Moses, working under the assumption the Westchester and Boston couldn't possibly be made to run profitably, visualized the part the right-of-way could play in handling long distance truck traffic, and proposed his toll truck highway to be built under a state authority," said an Allied Civic Associations official. "It is essential that every effort should be made to determine if there is any possibility of using the railroad that cost $1,000,000 a mile [$32.6 million in 2011 dollars], is admittedly one of the finest roadways in the country, and was instrumental in building the property values by many millions of dollars, before that involvement is junked to allow the expenditure of $18,000,000 for the construction of a truck highway [$586 million in 2011 dollars]."[54]

It snowed on January 13, but over three hundred people attended the meeting. J. J. Mulholland, secretary of the Holy Name Society of the Church of the Nativity, read a letter to Mayor La Guardia favoring the Allied Civic Associations plan. He read the response Moses wrote in reply:

The Mayor has given me your letter of December 22 with reference to the New York, Westchester and Boston Railway. I am frank to say that I can see no possible way of reestablishing service on this road. There are, however, other members of the Committee appointed by Governor Lehman, who have a contrary view and they are going to exhaust every effort in the next two or three months to establish the soundness of their position.

If at the end of that time they have failed, I shall move that the committee consider the conversion of part of the railroad into a toll bus and truck route.[55]

The audience booed, and Mulholland responded:

This is not what the people of the Northeast Bronx want. We are seeking to correct an intolerable transit situation. Many thousands of names have been affixed to petitions and briefs submitted, which tell better than mere words the need of this facility to bear them to and from their work.

The ardor of those who invested their savings in small homes and business enterprises along this route is being sorely tried, and we hope that you will find us a way out.[56]

Professor Harold M. Holton, the Allied Civic Associations president, discussed their proposal: "The City of New York can give us a five-cent fare downtown and will give it to us if we demand it strongly enough. It is a natural for in these days of depleted debt margin, it saves millions of dollars. . . . It is a plan that can be put into operation practically immediately."[57]

Holton compared their plan to the one for Burke Avenue: "Present traffic figures also indicate that the Independent lines may shortly carry their capacity without any track extension, and it is a fact that the Second Avenue El does not carry its capacity. It has been pointed out that this route substantially dividing the area east of the White Plains [Road] line, is the natural path of transit service to this section."[58]

Working with the Allied Civic Associations, former BOT Commissioner Halley represented property holders claiming that their land's value diminished after the W&B closed. "The residents of the Northeast Bronx are not tax dodgers. . . . When the Westchester and Boston closed, Chairman Delaney refused to run a shuttle line from Dyre Avenue to 180th Street because of an estimated loss of $25,000 a year [$405,000 in 2011 dollars]," William E. Johnston said. "A loss to the City of many times that sum in depreciated tax values was disregarded. Apparently the City expected to be at a loss in taxes because of the closing of the Westchester. They will learn better. Now is the time to pound home to the City officials that we must have transportation to replace the Westchester and Boston or else we must be granted a heavy reduction in assessed valuation."[59]

Holton detailed his group's plan on February 15. He called for connecting the White Plains Road line and the W&B at 174th Street and keeping the Burke Avenue option open:

> By the inclusion of more than $3,000,000 in the 1939–1940 Capital Outlay Budget, the City of New York has signified its intention of furnishing a West Side rapid transit connection. This is by the Burke Avenue extension of the Independent Subway. Construction of this extension should be started shortly and this spur can be in operation in less than two years.
>
> This subway spur can and should be extended to the tracks of the Westchester and Boston at the Gun Hill Road station [of the W&B], where it can be tied in, and subway cars of the Independent system operated on and over the tracks of the Westchester and Boston to Dyre Avenue.[60]

Lyons wrote to Delaney, asking when work would begin. When he didn't receive an answer, Lyons again wrote and got an unwanted answer. Pre-engineering work had been done for about a year, but hearings on the construction work weren't held. Bids had to be advertised and construction contracts awarded. The $3,754,980 allocated for the Concourse Extension was one-third of its possible cost. The Board of Estimate had to allocate more money. How things proceeded depended on the BOT, which had little inclination for action. Completion was projected for 1944 at the earliest.[61]

The W&B owed $313,150 in back taxes to the city ($5.07 million in 2011 dollars). The Allied Civic Associations asked the mayor to take it over, with Johnston stating:

Parks Commissioner Moses has proposed a plan to utilize the Westchester and Boston right-of-way from New Rochelle to East 174th Street to be financed by a State Authority empowered to borrow money for the acquisition of the right-of-way and construction costs. The total estimated cost of the Moses toll truck highway is approximately $18 million of which $1.5 million is allocated for the purchase of the right-of-way from New Rochelle to East 174th Street.

If Moses, through a State Authority, acquires title to the Westchester and Boston for use as a toll highway, there will be further decline in real estate values on property adjacent to the highway, necessitating a still further cut in assessed valuation.

The City, faced with a tax loss of $200,000 a year [$3.24 million in 2011 dollars] because of the lack of transportation, can only retrieve that annual loss by furnishing rapid transit on the right-of-way of the Westchester and Boston.[62]

Ritchie's Committee met with Westchester officials in White Plains on February 27. New Rochelle Mayor Scott suggested that the Port of New York Authority be asked to consider operating a rail service. Johnston supported the idea, but was unhappy it had been made public, fearing Moses's response: "In view of Commissioner Moses' plan for a toll truck highway along the right-of-way of the railroad, it is to be expected that he will do everything he can to block any such arrangement at the White Plains meeting."[63]

The subcommittee examined the RPA's plan, the Williamson / Quinn plan Governor Lehman vetoed, and the Sartorius Committee plan.[64] The subcommittee thought Sartorius's plan was the most feasible, as it had a financial plan they felt would provide funding for a new railroad. They urged the start of negotiations with the city government, the Westchester towns, and the New Haven Railroad on implementing the Sartorius Committee and Allied Civic Association proposals.

Ritchie's report, made public on March 25, called for legislation authorizing a Port Authority study on reopening the W&B. The Port Authority told the Committee they lacked funding to carry out a survey, but that "if they were requested by the legislature to make the survey and study, they would be glad to do so and submit their recommendation."[65] Moses dissented; Schramek was one of five committee members who didn't sign the report.

The report noted that attempts to have a private company reopen the W&B failed because the New Haven Railroad wouldn't sell power at a reduced rate to a new operator, and wanted to be paid $110,000 annually for use of the tracks between Hunts Point and 174th Street ($1.78 million in 2011 dollars). This was a significant increase over the $40,000 paid by the W&B ($648,000 in 2011 dollars).[66]

The Committee wanted Mayor La Guardia to act: "The City has not yet agreed to the proposal as to that portion of the tracks lying within the City, nor can it be said that there is a prospect that it will do so in a reasonable time, if at all. On its face, this plan would seem to have the virtue of reason as it would serve a portion of the Bronx which is not now adequately served with rapid transit facilities."[67]

Moses protested to Governor Lehman:

The Committee was appointed to investigate all possible uses of the abandoned New York, Westchester and Boston Railroad Company. If it had been stated, when the appointment of this Committee was under consideration, that the only purpose was to attempt to revive the railroad, I am quite sure that several members of the Committee wouldn't have accepted appointment, and this applies particularly to the members appointed by the Mayor of New York City. There could be no better evidence of the fact that other plans for the abandoned railroad were contemplated than that the Chairman of the Committee and the Sub-Committee Chairman asked me to prepare a report on the use of the abandoned railroad as a toll truck and bus route connection with the so-called Pelham–Port Chester right of way in Westchester County, that such a report was prepared, that it was issued to the public by Mr. Ritchie in spite if the fact that it was meant only for committee consideration, and that it was agreed that this plan would be taken up seriously by the Committee after it had exhausted all efforts to revive the railroad as such.

In the course of a number of a number of years of public work, I have never been connected with such a fact-finding committee which functioned so badly. The entire approach to the subject was tricky and demagogic. No effort was made to get at the actual facts. On the contrary, it was indicated to groups of commuters and others interested in the revival of the railroad that the Committee had some magic plan to make the railroad run again in the face of the palpable and obvious figures that this could not be done without imposing a heavy burden of public expense in both Westchester and New York City.[68]

The Westchester towns supported the Committee's recommendations. Time was short. Garvin wouldn't wait much longer to either sell the W&B to another operator or dispose of it for other purposes. Bennett E. Siegelstein contacted Westchester's representatives, expressing interest in taking over the line. He didn't think Lehman would allocate $25,000 for a Port Authority study ($405,000 in 2011 dollars). Schramek didn't sign Ritchie's report for just that reason, thinking that a plan for a private takeover was better than a Port Authority takeover.

There was doubt about Siegelstein's group. The Allied Civic Associations still saw Moses as a roadblock to them and the Port Authority survey with his plans. Loretta M. Pierce said:

There is no reason to doubt Siegelstein's prediction of the bill to finance the study of reopening the W and B by the Port Authority.

The ability of [Siegelstein's group] to obtain the co-operation of the City of New York is of paramount importance. To date, all attempts to reopen the road as a Westchester commuter railroad have been met with the statement of Commissioner Moses, as spokesman for the Mayor, that he is in favor of a toll truck highway on the right-of-way.

The Allied Associations do not believe that Commissioner Moses would inject his toll truck highway into the picture if he personally believed that the railroad would be successfully operated. . . . If and when the railroad is sold at foreclosure, the City of New York should be the highest bidder, for as an integral part of the City transit system, the W and B has its greatest value.[69]

The New Haven Railroad announced a major increase in service to Grand Central Terminal to start on May 1. It was meant to provide access to the World's Fair, but the addition of twenty-eight new trains was permanent. Ritchie stated that he would continue the fight to reopen the W&B, but the New Haven's action reduced the need for it.[70]

His committee knew about the vandalism and theft that had taken place and how the W&B's equipment was removed to repair the New Haven after the 1938 hurricane, and was concerned about what would happen if no action was taken.[71] The *Home News* reported that the Allied Civic Associations wrote to the BOT asking for a start date for Burke Avenue. The BOT responded that while planning work would be completed by the end of the year, "it is not possible to state at this time when bids for the construction of the Burke Avenue extension will be advertised."[72]

The Allied Civic Associations discussed the issue at Breinlinger's Hall on June 27. Council Members Kinsley, Deering, and Ninfo and Mount Vernon Alderman John K. Miller addressed the 650 attendees. Kinsley endorsed the purchase in his remarks:

The New York, Westchester and Boston at this moment is a darned good bargain for the City of New York. The entire road can be bought literally for a song.

If Bob Moses' proposed toll truck highway could be a self-sustaining project, then the same structure as part of the City transit system would be much more so.

You taxpayers up here must not lose sight of the fact that upon your success in this fight depends the success of the Bronx. Success for a section like this means success for the whole Bronx. Your Councilmen are with you in this fight. We pledge our support for you now as well as before election.

As the *Bronx Home News* said in a wonderful editorial today: "Build the Burke Avenue Subway—Now," and while it is being built, tie it up with the Westchester and Boston to furnish the transportation you are fighting for. Build it now.

. . . Not only has the City done nothing to remedy that situation, but on top of that has added to your taxes. While your taxes were going up, the value of the homes and stores you have built have gone down.[73]

The Northeast Bronx would "use every means, including a march to City Hall and another to the polls,"[74] to save the W&B "in the face of the announced intention of eventually spending millions. . . . It is a criminal waste to destroy one of the best railroads in the country,"[75] Johnston said.

Mand wrote to La Guardia on June 28:

We have long sincerely recommended that the City of New York acquire rights to at least two of the tracks of the New York, Westchester and Boston within the City limits for ultimate use as an extension to the Burke Avenue route of the Independent Subway. At the time that we first made this recommendation, or at least extended our support to the idea, there was still a possibility of this railroad being rehabilitated and placed under private operation. Subsequently as you know, all efforts to bring about a reopening have failed, and at this date there is every indication that it will be totally dismantled and the right-of-way devoted to some other uses.

In our opinion the possibilities of using this road not only for extending the Burke Avenue Line if and when that improvement is completed, but in addition for the purpose of giving immediate relief to the people of North East Bronx who have been deprived of transportation, should be revived immediately. It would seem that the property can be obtained without any considerable outlay, and its devotion to the immediate transit needs could very readily be worked out with one of the existing operating systems, and which are part of the unification program.

There is an aroused public opinion in our community, because [thus] far there has not been any indication on the part of the City that these serious recommendations have been accorded any critical consideration, and there is an earnest demand for action before it is too late.[76]

The summer of 1939 was a confusing time for the Northeast Bronx. Money was allocated for Burke Avenue, but no one knew whether work would begin. Ritchie's Committee recommended a Port Authority takeover of the W&B's tracks, but they had no money to act. The easiest and cheapest way to provide subway service—incorporating the W&B into the subway system—was discussed, but La Guardia and Delaney seemed to have no interest in acting, despite previous intentions of doing so. The right-of-way could be turned into a highway, with no prospect of action on the Burke Avenue line being taken for years.

The Transit Commission discussed the subway system's unification on August 22. Loewenthal, speaking for the Burke Avenue Subway Extension Committee, told the Commission, "We of Eastchester protest loudly at the extension of the W and B lines from the transit unification plans."[77] Transit Commission Chairman Robert Fullen ruled him out of order, but William J. Mulligan, the BOT's associate counsel, said, "It is not about the Board of Transportation's neglecting the Westchester and Boston. Negotiations are in progress for the acquisition of the roadbed of the railroad."[78]

This raised eyebrows at Parks Department headquarters. Moses wrote to Delaney asking if the BOT was considering using the W&B's right-of way.[79] The BOT acquired at least some of the W&B's tracks in 1932 as an alternative to building the 2nd Avenue line's Boston Road branch; since W&B service ended, the BOT denied any desire to use it. Delaney told Moses what their interests were:

> I had several interviews with Judge Garvin and Mr. Dohr, Receivers, the last one being several months ago, when they said they had a favorable offer to purchase the catenary system and other copper wire, and proposed to ask the Court for permission and sell the equipment, if the City were still of the same mind that the property would not be purchased for railroad operations. I told them there was no change in the attitude of the Board of Transportation, or as far as I knew in the attitude of any other public official regarding the purchase of the railroad and equipment, and I would have no objection to removal of the catenary system. They inquired about the right-of-way, roadbed, rails, bridges and stations north of Allerton or Burke Avenues, and suggested that they should negotiate with the Comptroller. I reminded them that the unpaid taxes amount to $330,000, and that those taxes might be settled by conveying the right-of-way to the City.[80]

Delaney told City Comptroller Joseph McGoldrick about his conversation with Garvin and Dohr. McGoldrick began talks while Judge Knox postponed action.

Delaney wanted things done as quickly and quietly as possible to obtain the W&B for the least cost. Publicity would bring about a reaction in the Bronx, forcing the BOT's hand. He was also likely concerned that Moses would accelerate his efforts to acquire the W&B for the highway if he knew of the BOT's intentions.

"We have not reconsidered the Burke Avenue route, our intention always being to acquire the New York, Westchester and Boston right-of-way if it could be obtained without undue cost," Delaney told Moses. "To cover our intention, we tentatively projected extension of the route from Burke Avenue northerly alongside of the railroad right-of-way, but we stopped all plans at the point where our railroad would enter the right-of-way. Delaney said McGoldrick would acquire the entire right-of-way."[81] He advised McGoldrick to proceed slowly, fearing that "agitators in the neighboring district"[82] would demand the reactivation of the W&B.

That's what happened. Council President Morris, and Borough President Lyons and his Queens and Staten Island colleagues, George U. Harvey and Joseph A. Palma, supported the purchase. Roderick Stephens of the Board of Trade also expressed support.

The Burke Avenue Property Owners and Businessmen's Association and the American Society of Italian Descendants rallied at the old Burke Mansion on Cruger Avenue on September 12. Five hundred people attended. Council Member Ninfo urged the crowd to work with the proponents of the W&B's purchase to achieve a common goal; Council Member Deering questioned the city's sincerity about building the line.[83]

Budgetary concerns clouded all planning. War was raging in Europe and Asia. Mayor La Guardia, fearing its impact, capped capital budget items: "In renewing the previous authorization for the extension of rapid transit in the Northeast Bronx, may I suggest that the item be so worded so as to afford the greatest latitude to cover the method ultimately decided upon."[84]

The W&B's receivers asked Knox for permission to dismantle it on June 30. Kinsley, the Chamber of Commerce, the Allied Civic Associations, and the Board of Trade received a stay until October. Kinsley wrote to La Guardia:

That date is rapidly approaching, but as yet the residents of the Bronx have received no definite word from any person in authority in the Executive branch of the City Government as to the City's attitude in the matter, except for the statement made by Chairman Delaney of the BOT in a letter to the Bronx Board of Trade. In that letter he said that he was in favor of the acquisition of the New York, Westchester and Boston Railroad above Burke Avenue, to tie in with the proposed Burke Avenue extension of the Concourse subway, if and when completed.

The Burke Avenue subway is now almost one year behind [the] schedule anticipated when appropriation was made for it. From present indications it is doubtful when construction thereof will begin, let alone be completed. In the meantime, the northeast Bronx is without proper, direct transit connections. A community which was as established and developed because of the then existing Westchester and Boston Railway now finds itself practically isolated. Realty values have depreciated. Business has suffered heavy losses. The natural development of the area has stopped. Immediate attention to the transit needs is necessary to prevent even greater injury to that district. The Burke Avenue extension is a vital improvement, but at best its completion is three years away. Even then, it will not serve the City north of its now proposed terminus. On the other hand, the Westchester and Boston property is idle, but can be easily, quickly, and cheaply rehabilitated. It can be obtained, in my opinion, for a very low price. It can only be sold as vacant real estate, most of which is composed of interior lots, many of them far below. Against its cost, taxes of $400,000 can be charged. Pending unification, the city can operate it as an independent line terminating at 180th Street on one end and at [Dyre] Avenue on the other. After unification, it can be connected with the Lexington Avenue line by a short trestle. A short extension of the proposed Burke Avenue line would connect the Westchester and Boston roadbed with the Concourse subway.

As I believe you are familiar with this part of the transit needs of our Borough, and as time is of the essence, may I ask that you personally investigate the merits of the proposed solution?[85]

The City Planning Commission held a hearing on the capital budget on October 2 at City Hall. Over one hundred Bronx organization representatives attended, along with Keegan, Kinsley, and Ninfo. While Burke Avenue's funding remained in the budget, there was something new: the $3,754,000 could pay for it *"or other suitable facilities."*

Keegan and Kinsley strongly criticized this new wording at a CPC hearing on October 10. "We request that you strike out the phrase 'or other suitable facilities' so that the appropriation will be set up without ambiguity and there will be a definite mandate to the Board of Transportation to go ahead with this work," said Keegan. "People in the Bronx are tired of paying extra fares to get to their work, only to find the Board of Transportation going ahead with construction in other boroughs where they have so much transit that the streets threaten to collapse because of the tunnels and subways being bored through."[86] "Frankly I do not know what they mean and I must say that it appears to be a most unorthodox method of budget making," Kinsley said. "If they include buses or trolleys, or an overhead El structure, then they should be eliminated, but if they hold out the possibility that the City [would] acquire part of the New York, Westchester and Boston . . . then I say that clear indication that intention be given and the door not [be] closed without hearing at length from all concerned."[87]

No decision was reached at the October 6 hearing. Judge Knox adjourned it until November 10 to allow negotiations to continue. The city planned to demolish major parts of the 2nd and 9th Avenue Els, angering Bronx transit advocates, who wanted more service, not less. Burke Avenue line advocates met on October 25 at Evander Childs High School. Council President Morris and Council Members Keegan, Deering, and Ninfo attended.

When Morris was invited, no one apparently remembered that he supported eliminating Burke Avenue from the capital budget in 1938. Morris inflamed the seven hundred people in attendance by saying it would cost more and take longer to build than they thought—$16 million and five years. The city didn't have the borrowing capacity. He supported connecting the W&B with the subway system. Morris was showered with catcalls, but spoke for over an hour. Many people walked out; those who remained passed a resolution urging an immediate start to work on Burke Avenue.[88]

Reaction to Morris's speech dramatized divisions. Chester Civic Association President Emile J. Cavanaugh telegrammed him the following: "Thank you for your courageous stand last night at Evander Childs High School in defense of the plan to purchase the New York, Westchester and Boston Railroad for immediate transportation to the long suffering people of the Northeast Bronx."[89] Johnston wrote for the Allied Civic Associations: ". . . The North East Bronx salutes a man with courage to state the facts about the Burke Avenue subway situation to a public that had been led stray."[90]

Paul Trapani, the Burke Avenue Property Owners and Businessmen's Association's secretary, wrote to Council President Morris:

This organization regrets the fact that the meeting sponsored by it on Wednesday, October 25, 1939, ended so abruptly and uproariously.

Of course, you and we can understand the great shock and disappointment that most of the audience must have experienced as a result of this city would again have to further delay the construction of the Burke Avenue subway extension of the 8th Avenue Concourse line.

We all feel that what you said was contrary to our expectations and we wish to state further that the City of New York could safely appropriate 3 million dollars per year for a total of 15 million for the estimated cost of starting construction of the Burke Avenue Subway Extension immediately. . . . We are more resolved than ever to continue and encourage our efforts and pressure to see that we do get what we have so long been promised.[91]

Morris answered Trapani: "I wish that I could have come up to your meeting with a brighter message but I don't believe in trying to fool people by political speeches. As I said at the time, it would have been easier for me to promote the project for that section of the Bronx than discourage it."[92]

Cavanaugh criticized Ninfo and Keegan for attacking the insertion of "or other suitable facility" in the budget line: "This association condemns your action relating to your attack on the phrase 'or other suitable facility' attached to Project T-12 relative to the Concourse line extension. You are hereby looked upon as an enemy of immediate transportation for the people of the Northeast Bronx and we in meeting feel that you are not worthy of support for re-election."[93]

The Allied Civic Associations met at Breinlinger's Hall on November 1. According to Holton:

The Northeast Bronx is fighting mad. More than 50,000 people in that area have been without transportation of any kind except poor bus service for more than 22 months. . . . Now that they have been practically assured that the City is ready to buy the Westchester and Boston, and institute rapid transit to the City Line, they do not propose to take any chances on having the program upset at this time.

They know perfectly well that every possible move is being made to prevent the City acting on the Westchester and Boston until after the Burke Avenue line is built.

They know that the Burke Avenue Subway extension is at least five years away and when it is built it will only serve a small part of their area unless it is extended to the City Line, which is not now planned. . . . Rapid transit can be installed almost immediately on the Westchester and Boston under unification and that they can have downtown service before the Burke Avenue line is built, if the City is permitted to act.[94]

Johnston requested police protection before the Allied Civic Association's meeting (noting the reaction to Morris's speech),[95] called Keegan's accusations "malicious and slanderous,"[96] and tore up a check from W&B bondholders he said was for the Association's newsletter, the *North Bronx Civic Voice*.[97] He later claimed that all four tires on his car were deflated while he was speaking at the meeting, and theorized that he was the victim of political reprisals for advocating for the W&B purchase.[98]

A. J. Woodworth, the Allied Civic Associations' vice president, spoke about the Burke Avenue line:

> The Allied Civic Associations have always led the fight for the Burke Avenue Subway, are now and always will be in favor of that extension.
>
> We have never been in favor of holding up the Burke Avenue Subway, which will serve the Hillside development, of which Charles E. Keegan was manager, but have favored the extension via the tracks of the Westchester and Boston to Dyre Avenue.
>
> Now that the Westchester and Boston is closed, about to be dismantled and can be bought for a fraction of its cost, the Allied Civic Associations are backing the administration in its efforts to make possible the financing of the purchase of the railroad.
>
> This step is essential if the Northeast Bronx is to have immediate transit relief, as it is perfectly plain to anyone who cares to investigate that there is no change in the margin under the debt limit for the start of construction of the expensive Burke Avenue Subway for a number of years.[99]

Keegan and Ninfo were invited; both stayed away. Keegan responded to the charges. He supported the W&B's purchase, but had other priorities: "I am for the immediate construction of the Burke Avenue extension and if funds are available for the acquisition of that portion of the Boston and Westchester that can be used to serve our transit needs."[100]

Judge Knox held the next hearing on the plan to dismantle the W&B on November 10. He would give the order to go ahead on January 5, 1940, if a plan wasn't settled.

The Burke Avenue Property Owners and Businessmen's Association continued their fight. Paul Trapani wrote to La Guardia and Morris:

> The plans for the construction of the City Independent Subway System for the Bronx included an extension along Burke Avenue to Kingsland Avenue. The Board of Transportation has already completed work plans and is ready to start work to-morrow.
>
> As you know, the Burke Avenue Subway Extension is now in the capital outlay budget for 1940, but, following the sum allotted for this subway is a clause reading "or other suitable facilities." This clause has been inserted through the efforts of a small group of paid publicity agents and Bond Holders of the N.Y. Boston and Westchester Line as an attempt to get the City to buy this railroad and discourage the

people of the Northeast Bronx in their fight for the subway extension. . . . The people of the North East Bronx have been promised this subway for the past 12 years, but all the promises so far have been mere promises. We insist that the City keep its pledge.[101]

A preliminary agreement was reached on November 17. The city would pay up to $2.5 million for the line, absorbing $1.3 million in claims. John Delaney admitted that pressure was felt: "This is not a business deal. The City is being forced into it by public pressure."[102]

Response to the deal varied. The Allied Civic Associations and the Eastchester Civic and Taxpayers Association were happy; Trapani telegrammed Council President Morris:

We of the Burke Avenue Property Owners and Business Men's Association request an immediate hearing before Hon. Fiorello H. La Guardia, the Mayor of the City of N.Y. so that we can prevent conclusive proof before him that the advocates of the New York, Westchester and Boston Railroad have misrepresented certain pertinent facts and further to offer him facts and evidence that the immediate construction of the Burke Avenue subway extension will benefit of at least 80% of the residents of the Northeast Bronx and further to explain the sinister motives behind those civic workers who in the past have striven to obtain the immediate construction of the subway along Burke Avenue, but are working for the diversion of funds who should rightfully be used for the immediate construction of the Burke Avenue subway extension.[103]

La Guardia told Kinsley in November that while he thought the price the city was paying for the right-of-way was "a little high," the purchase would take place and there was little chance Burke Avenue would be built as a result.[104]

The Board of Estimate held a budget hearing on November 23. Kinsley spoke for the purchase; Keegan and P. A. Maele of the Burke Avenue Property Owners and Business Men's Association spoke for the Concourse Extension.

"Or other suitable facilities" remained in Burke Avenue's budget line. Lyons was determined to get it deleted and the line built. He reminded his colleagues of Delaney's previous statement that the BOT had no intention of using the right-of-way, feeling that it "indicates plainly that the Board of Transportation and the Board of Estimate were fully cognizant of the possible use of the New York, Westchester and Boston Railroad at the time that the Burke Avenue route was adopted but that the taxpayers at that time were definitely assured that it would have no bearing on the Burke Avenue extension. Therefore, it is my firm belief that any change from the assurances given the taxpayers at the public hearing would be a breach of faith by the Board of Estimate." He continued, ". . . I, therefore, move to strike out from the Capital Budget the phrase 'or other suitable facility' and to add the line: '. . . for the acquisition of the New York, Westchester and Boston Railroad with an allocation of $2,500,000.'"

Lyons feared that "or other suitable facilities" would divert funds for Burke Avenue to projects outside the Bronx: "I do not think that the people of the Northeast Bronx should be deluded by the inclusion of any indefinite and ambiguous clause as 'or any suitable facility' with the possibility of jeopardizing all transit facilities for the Northeast Bronx."[105]

The Board of Estimate approved the budget on November 30 without amendment. Lyons voted against it, criticizing "people who were vociferous on behalf of the Burke Avenue subway extension until recently, when they became strongly vociferous in switching to the Westchester and Boston."[106] He made a motion to change "or other suitable facility" to an item funding the W&B's purchase. Only Queens Borough President Harvey supported him.

The debate carried over to the City Council's December 11 capital budget hearing. Keegan wanted the phrase deleted from Burke Avenue's budget item. He didn't want the money used for the W&B:

> Along the Burke Avenue route, assessed values have been raised in the expectation of an extension being built from the Concourse subway. Property owners up there have been paying these increased assessments for almost 16 years. A condition has now arisen in which a certain group of people desire that the City acquire the W and B, a defunct railroad.
>
> While the people I represent do not wish to deprive their neighbors of transit, they insist that this railroad not be acquired at the expense of the Burke Avenue subway, and even if the City plans to do it by this means, it cannot legally do so.[107]

Kinsley reiterated La Guardia's comments. There was little possibility of the Burke Avenue line being built; converting the W&B for rapid transit could be easily accomplished. Johnston stated that using the W&B would benefit more people than would the Burke Avenue plan. Representatives of the Westchester towns served by the W&B wanted their part of the line reactivated with a rail service linking with the subway at Dyre Avenue. McGoldrick and Delaney met with the town officials on December 20, promising cooperation.

January 1, 1940, was the second anniversary of the end of W&B service. Knox wanted resolution and Moses wanted to build the highway. Time was running out. Knox extended the deadline for one week on January 5, providing the impetus to make a deal. At a conference of the Board of Trade attended by Kinsley, Mand, Stephens, Holton, and Maskell E. Fox, La Guardia announced an agreement for the area between 174th

Street and Dyre Avenue. If the city wanted the tracks to Hunts Point to connect with other lines, a separate deal needed to be reached with the New Haven Railroad, which never happened.

The money came from Burke Avenue's funds. La Guardia said that the city wanted to build the line, but the cost, which he put at $16 million ($489 million in 2011 dollars, according to MeasuringWorth.com), and time needed to complete it, made the purchase more viable. The contract restoring rail service to the Northeast Bronx was signed on January 9. There was no direct connection to another subway line (and wouldn't be for seventeen years), requiring riders to transfer to the White Plains Road line at East 180th Street. A separate fare would be charged to transfer between lines.

Keegan objected to the extra fare; he felt it whittled away at the five-cent fare.[108] Johnston wrote to Morris on January 17:

> It is needless to say that the great number of people living along the line of the railroad are elated at the prospect of rapid transit being restored to the Northeast Bronx. . . . It may be enlightening to you that I have yet to talk to a person in our neighborhood that has expressed the slightest objection to paying an extra five cent fare for a limited period of time to facilitate rapid transit service. We are entirely antagonistic to Mr. Keegan's recently published threat against a ten cent fare. We understand Mr. Keegan's motives fairly well.[109]

The W&B purchase went to the Board of Estimate on February 6 without specifying a connection: "The operation will be by means of a shuttle service between the Dyre Avenue station at the northern end of the route, and the 180th Street station, at the southern end of the route, for some period of time, until it is deemed to authorize and construct another route southerly to a physical connection with an existing or new rapid transit line."[110] As the subway system hadn't yet been unified, the line would be part of the IND.

Halley warned about budget priorities: "Millions of dollars of Federal funds are spent on airports and highways, but not one cent for rapid transit facilities."[111] The *Home News*, concerned about White Plains Road line congestion after Dyre Avenue service started, asked the city to acquire the rest of the W&B's Bronx tracks to connect with the Pelham or other lines.[112] Paul Trapani wrote to the mayor on March 4 for the Burke Avenue Property Owners and Businessmen's Association:

> As we stated to you before, we do not object to the purchase of the Westchester and Boston railroad by the City, but, not at the expense of another delay on the start of construction of the Burke Avenue subway. This is the third time that this subway extension has been included in the capital outlay budget and the third time that much needed transportation project has been postponed and funds diverted.

We still feel that the only solution for the transit problem for the Northeast Bronx is the Burke Avenue Subway Extension, more so now, with the demolition of the 2nd Avenue Elevated a reality and with the operation of the Westchester and Boston Railroad. Both will add considerably to the congested Lexington Avenue Line.

We ask you to reconsider before it is too late. We ask you to investigate the present overcrowding and slowing up of I.R.T. trains during rush hours, because of the inability of those lines to absorb additional trains.[113]

The Board of Estimate approved the purchase on March 7. Lyons abstained, citing the additional fare. Michael Moses spoke for the Burke Avenue Property Owners and Businessmen's Association: "[The Board of Estimate] voted to extend the Concourse Subway along Burke Avenue. We celebrated that fact and even had a victory dinner, thinking that a 25-year campaign had at last been accomplished. Now we are offered a broken-down, abandoned railroad which few of us can use and we are expected to be content. I tell you, gentlemen, that we want subways and we will fight this matter to the finish."[114]

"Like many others in the Bronx, I would like to see a subway built but the fact remains that the money for this line is not available an even if it were, it would take at least six years to build," Kinsley said. "With the transit situation in the Bronx in the deplorable state that it is, the valid question, it would seem to me is how soon transit service can be installed."[115]

Johnston said the extra fare was less than what W&B riders had paid; he hoped a connection could be built in five years. Lyons vowed to continue to advocate for the Burke Avenue line, believing that both it and Dyre Avenue were needed. No one knew it would take another seventeen years to connect the Dyre Avenue to with another subway line. With the town and city governments in Westchester still fighting for W&B service, Judge Knox granted another extension.[116]

Delaney and Dohr signed the agreement to purchase the line for $1,785,000 ($28.6 million in 2011 dollars) in McGoldrick's office on April 17. Equipment and trains from the 9th Avenue El would be used. Efforts continued for Burke Avenue. On June 22 the

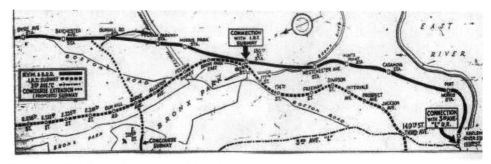

Figure 8-4. The *Bronx Home News* published this map on January 7, 1940, to explain the possible connections that could be made with the New York, Westchester, and Boston Railway's right-of-way.

City Council passed Keegan's resolution asking the BOT and the Board of Estimate to include funding for Burke Avenue in the 1941 capital outlay budget.

The CPC sent the 1941 capital budget to the Board of Estimate and the City Council in November without mentioning the Concourse Extension. Sheridan was the lone voice against it. Protests came from along Burke Avenue and the area's elected officials. Another meeting was held on November 14 at Evander Childs High School, sponsored by the Bronx Division of the Community Council of New York. The Civic Council members organized the meeting to ensure the largest possible turnout when the capital outlay budget went before the Board of Estimate.

Hyman Bravin, an attorney from the Hillside Houses, chaired the meeting, stating that the W&B's purchase and the opening of the Dyre Avenue line did nothing for their area. Lillian Britton of the Allied Civic Associations pledged her group's support. A resolution was passed calling for work to continue on Burke Avenue: "The City Administration's present position that the re-opening of the New York, Westchester and Boston right-of-way will provide ample transit facilities for our section of the Bronx is untenable and indicative of bad faith."[117]

The City Council passed the capital budget on December 28 without funding Burke Avenue. Mayor La Guardia gave his report on the city's budget to the City Council on January 8, 1941, without mentioning the line.

The Burke Avenue Property Owners and Businessmen's Association met in February at the old Burke Mansion. Bravin announced plans to send representatives to all civic association meetings in the North Bronx to solicit their support and read a letter to his group from Newbold Morris, who had encouraging words this time: "It is hoped that under municipal operation [of the transit system] sufficient savings can be made so that more tax revenues can be used for the financing of such important projects as the Burke Avenue extension."[118]

There are no reports of Robert Moses's reaction to not being able to use the W&B's right-of-way to build a highway. Did he lose interest once John Delaney said the BOT wanted it, moving on to his next option, what became the New England Thruway? A 1940 report issued by Moses's Triborough Bridge Authority, *Vital Gaps in New York Metropolitan Arteries*, didn't mention the highway.

But there are hints that he remembered. Lyons experienced significant problems in getting public housing built in the Bronx after the end of World War II. He had to fight Moses, also the city construction coordinator, to get anything built. Could Moses's methods in building the Cross Bronx Expressway, his unwillingness to change its route and its subsequent impact on the Bronx, be traced to his reaction to his losing the W&B's right-of-way?

The New England Thruway opened in 1958 on a different route, years after it might have had the original highway been built. Possibly coincidentally, but definitely symbolically, the last exit before leaving the Bronx points toward the intersection of Boston Road and Connor Street, where Herman W. Johnston—one of the leaders of the Allied Civic Associations of Old Eastchester, the main proponents of the conversion of the W&B's right-of-way into a subway line and among the main opponents of the Express Truck Highway—once lived.[119]

The Bronx's focus shifted to the paid transfer issue. The city government and BOT wanted to charge the extra fare until a connection was built between the Dyre Avenue line and another subway line, which the BOT said would happen in another five years. It was not until May 6, nine days before Dyre Avenue service began, that La Guardia and the BOT relented; the free transfer was adopted on May 13.

The first train ran from Dyre Avenue at 11:25 A.M. on May 15. Unlike the quiet circumstances marking the start of Concourse line service, there was a ceremony at the Church of the Blessed Nativity on Secor Place, at which La Guardia, Lyons, and Delaney spoke, followed by a parade from Breinlinger's Hall to the Dyre Avenue station attended by thousands of people.[120] A block party was held that evening.

Mayor La Guardia received many expressions of gratitude for the opening of the Dyre Avenue line and the elimination of the second fare. He said that it "makes up for some of the kicking around we get at other times."[121] When New Rochelle Mayor Stanley Church sought rail service from Dyre Avenue into Westchester, La Guardia wasn't encouraging: "I have all that I can do to clean streets of New York city, and I can't run Westchester."[122] While Westchester bus service ran to the Dyre and Baychester Avenue stations and the New Haven provided more service on its routes, the W&B's service into Westchester was never replaced.

Figure 8-5. The *Mount Vernon Daily Argus* ran this picture of the Dyre Avenue line's opening ceremonies on May 16, 1941.

Halley said there was still much to do, questioning why subways were built in Queens but not along the Burke and Tremont Avenue lines. He called on Mayor La Guardia to obtain federal funding. Kinsley and a new colleague, Louis Cohen, succeeded in getting their resolution calling on the BOT to provide funding for Burke Avenue. The city had a budget surplus of $2,113,745 ($32.3 million in 2011 dollars), which the Council Members wanted to use to provide funding for the line.

The BOT ranked Burke Avenue twelfth out of twenty-seven items on their 1941 capital priority list. The Jerome Avenue–Lenox Avenue connection was second on the list. A connection between the Dyre Avenue and Pelham lines (using more of the W&B's right-of-way) ranked eleventh, one ahead of Burke Avenue. The BOT believed there was only an urgent need to build the first five lines on the list.[123]

This didn't sit well with Burke Avenue's strongest advocates. Lyons vowed to fight to get the line funded. Mand called on the various Bronx groups to unite to speak out to obtain more service for the borough. Nonetheless, it was the last time the BOT took action on Burke Avenue.

On October 22 the CPC held a hearing on the 1942 capital budget, which didn't include Burke Avenue. Lyons and other Bronx representatives spoke for the line. Kinsley talked about how Parkchester was built without thought of the area's overall needs. He discussed the Northeast and East Bronx's transit needs with Delaney, and received only a promise that the BOT would investigate. Sheridan blamed Burke Avenue's absence on the W&B purchase: "Neither the Board of Transportation nor any City agency originally favored the acquisition of the New York, Westchester and Boston subway route as a substitute for the Burke Avenue subway. However, organized pressure from the section in question forced the purchase of the defunct facility. Desirable though it may have seemed to some, it was obvious to public officials generally and to most persons that the reorganization and use of the Westchester and Boston route would indefinitely postpone, if not prevent, the construction of the Burke Avenue [line]."[124]

Despite Lyons's protest, the Board of Estimate approved the capital outlay budget on December 4. Three days later, America was at war, and action on many capital projects became less of a concern.

Final victory was years away in May 1942. Most of the battles that turned the tide hadn't been fought, but the city was already planning projects and programs to be implemented after the war's end. This resulted in the BOT's 1944–48 Postwar Plan. It was very ambitious, with a projected cost of $905 million,[125] but without mention of Burke Avenue.

Reaction was quick. The Burke Avenue Subway Extension Committee stated, "When this war is over, we of the North Bronx will remind the members of this Commission of their obligations to the people of the North Bronx."[126] Chief Engineer Thomas B. Dwyer stressed the need for the extension of the Concourse line and other Bronx lines. Lyons continued to lobby for the inclusion of Burke Avenue and other transit services for the borough in the city's plans without success.

"A sterile, complacent, non-Bronx or anti-Bronx Board of Transportation has completely failed to indicate any interest or display any vision in considering the dire need of new transit facilities for the East Bronx, the North Bronx or the West Bronx," Lyons later complained. "The present Board of Transportation seems to feel that when the Bronx obtained the makeshift Boston and Westchester they got all they were entitled to and all they are going to get."[127]

During the war there was little funding available for capital projects. Some Burke Avenue advocates, like Keegan and Bravin, were in military service. A few continued the fight for the line at home. Lyons wrote to Delaney in the summer of 1943, asking him about its status in light of its omission from the 1944–48 Postwar Plan. Delaney replied on September 3, "The Burke Avenue Extension is legally alive, but its status or condition may be reasonably diagnosed as a state of suspended animation. . . . The route and general plan of construction adopted in 1937 will continue [to be] valid indefinitely unless the Board of Estimate's resolution of approval should be repealed or modified at some future time."[128]

"Suspended animation" was usually seen in comic books. It gave the borough president another opportunity to sound off on the effect of "or other suitable facilities": "I am happy to say that I vigorously opposed this amendment and voted against it. I predicted that it meant the demise of the badly needed Burke Avenue extension of the Concourse line. . . . Subsequently the Bronx was given the makeshift Bronx and Westchester elevated service which appears to be the death knell of the Burke Avenue extension."[129]

The Bronx Joint Committee, representing thirty-eight civic associations across the borough, met at the Board of Trade's offices in November 1943. Intending to discuss the need for highway projects, they spent most of the time considering rapid transit projects. The Burke Avenue line was a priority, but other lines were discussed, including the 2nd Avenue line, the Tremont Avenue Crosstown line, and the Jerome Avenue–Lenox Avenue connection.[130]

Their plan, issued on January 12, 1944, called for Burke Avenue to be linked with the 2nd Avenue subway, extending from Manhattan via Alexander, 3rd, Melrose, Washington, and Webster Avenues, across Bronx Park, and along Burke Avenue and Gun Hill Road to Kingsland and Bartow Avenues. Burke Avenue was not the Committee's priority. Their priority was starting work on the 2nd Avenue subway,[131] which was a story in itself.

9

It's impossible not to write about New York's unbuilt subway lines without discussing the 2nd Avenue subway. The question of when it would be built has been asked for more than eighty years. It's being partially answered with the construction of a segment east and north from the Lexington Avenue station on the 63rd Street line to 96th Street and 2nd Avenue, one step in a process that has lasted the entire twentieth century and into the twentieth-first century. There have been *at least* thirty-eight separate official proposals for additional lines serving the East Side of Manhattan, issued by every agency with the responsibility for planning the expansion of the rapid transit system in the New York metropolitan area.

The Metropolitan Street Railway Company, operators of many trolley lines in Manhattan and the Bronx, proposed a subway system running from the Battery to the Bronx along the East and West Sides of Manhattan in 1904. The East Side line would be built along William Street, New Bowery,[1] and 3rd Avenue; the West Side line would be built along 7th, 8th, or 10th Avenues and Greenwich Street. The lines would operate along the New York Central Railroad's Putnam Branch to Van Cortlandt Park in the Bronx.[2]

The IRT responded to the Metropolitan's proposal as it did with other competitors: by purchasing the company, on December 22, 1905. They had leased the 2nd, 3rd, 6th, and 9th Avenue elevated lines from the Manhattan Railway Company in 1902 for a period of 999 years.[3]

The Board of Rapid Transit Commissioners (RTC) and its chief engineers, William Barclay Parsons and George S. Rice, addressed the need for trunk lines on the East Side. Parsons considered building a north–south line on the East Side, and studied the avenues east of Madison Avenue in 1903. He ruled out 2nd and 3rd Avenues because of the presence of elevated lines:

An examination of the traffic returns of the Second and Third avenue elevated railways shows that the passengers per station on the Third avenue line are more than twice as numerous as those on the Second avenue line, and that the bulk of the travel on the Third avenue line comes from points along or west of it. A line west of Third avenue, or under Lexington Avenue, for instance, would thus supply the most urgently demanded transportation facilities, and would best serve to relieve the present congestion on the most crowded elevated line on the east side.[4]

Parsons also saw an advantage to building a 1st Avenue line. More residential and business growth would be coming and this street offered the most direct route all the way downtown.[5]

Parsons and Rice both saw the role the 2nd and 3rd Avenue Els were playing in their service areas. They knew service demand would grow. The two RTC plans from 1905 called for lines on 1st, 3rd, and Lexington Avenues from Lower Manhattan to the Bronx, connecting with lines to be constructed in that borough.

Many RTC proposals were authorized for construction, easing the way for subsequent plans to become reality. When the New York State Public Service Commission began to supervise transit planning in 1907, its plans would continue to include the 1st and 3rd Avenue lines, but other streets were studied, too. The PSC and the IRT considered a line along Madison Avenue. The PSC's Tri-Borough Plan called for the construction of a line along Broadway and the length of Lexington Avenue, independent of the original IRT line to the Bronx, running the length of Lexington Avenue and splitting off to run along the Pelham and Jerome Avenue lines.

The IRT wanted to run to Brooklyn, using tracks to be built over the Manhattan Bridge and along 4th Avenue. As its existing subway line was built through downtown Brooklyn, space was left for connections with both the 4th Avenue and Manhattan Bridge lines and a line planned for Lafayette Avenue.[6] Knowing that the RTC's proposed lines were authorized for construction contributed to the IRT thinking the Lexington Avenue route was better than the one along Madison Avenue. IRT President Theodore F. Shonts outlined his reasoning to the PSC on July 14, 1910:

> Lexington Avenue can be tunneled at once, because legal consents have been obtained and all other legal conditions fulfilled, thus avoiding a delay of many months,

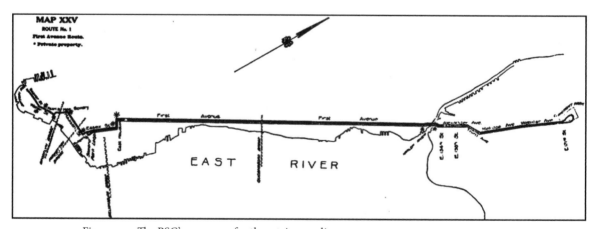

Figure 9-1. The PSC's 1909 map for the 1st Avenue line.

possibly of two years, in acquiring the right to use Madison Avenue, and, in addition, better physical connections can be made between the present subway in Park Avenue and a new subway in Lexington Avenue.

. . . Lexington Avenue better divided that portion of the City between Central Park and [the] East River than Madison Avenue, which lies only one block east of the Park, where the residents are not so much in need of subway service as are the more crowded residents nearer to Lexington Avenue, and the Lexington Avenue extension will also give better facilities for the Grand Central Depot, the Belmont Tunnel [which would be used by the Flushing line beginning in 1915],[7] and the Hudson and Manhattan tunnels, when constructed.[8]

When the Subway Committee of the Board of Estimate proposed the Dual System contracts, this line had evolved into the eastern trunk of the IRT "H," the route of the Lexington Avenue line as we know it from Lower Manhattan to the Bronx.[9]

With work on the Lexington Avenue and 7th Avenue lines underway, consideration was given to additional trunk lines. Daniel L. Turner included two Manhattan lines in the Transit Construction Commission plan of 1920. He proposed an East Side line from the Harlem River to the Battery along Madison Avenue, 5th Avenue, Greene Street, and Church Street, with connections to lines traveling to the other boroughs. Turner called for the line in his plan to be built primarily with six tracks: "The Fourth Avenue–Lexington Avenue line is now heavily overcrowded. The neighborhood around the Grand Central Terminal area is rapidly building up. Large increases in hotel facilities are being planned. Numerous extensive office building projects are taking form. In a relatively short time the existing subway will be wholly unable to meet the transit requirements of the East Side of Manhattan and in particular the Grand Central neighborhood. Consequently, to meet this pressing demand, the proposed Madison Avenue line will have to be placed under construction in the near future."[10]

Turner saw the need for a greater expansion of West Side service, though. He proposed an eight-track line along 8th and Amsterdam Avenues. The State Transit Commission's 1922 plan had two West Side routes but no East Side line. The first was the 8th and Amsterdam Avenue line to Washington Heights, intended to allow for a direct link with the Flushing line, not yet extended to Times Square. The second route would extend the BRT's Broadway line north from the 57th Street Station via Central Park South, Central Park West, Central Park North, and 7th Avenue (now Adam Clayton Powell, Jr., Boulevard). Track ramps were built as the Broadway line was constructed, anticipating an eventual northern extension.[11]

The NYS Transit Commission waited two years to propose an East Side line, but this line wouldn't be part of the existing subway system. Instead, it was part of Turner's Metropolitan Transit System plan, his concept for connecting commuter lines from

Long Island, New Jersey, and the northern suburbs. Turner called for a north–south line under a new street to be built between 2nd and 3rd Avenues.[12]

Mayor John F. Hylan issued a more ambitious plan affecting the East Side in August 1922. He called for a line from City Hall to the Bronx via 1st and Webster Avenues and Boston Road, with a southern extension to Brooklyn.

These plans were caught up in the battle for control of the subway between Hylan and the Transit Commission, which stymied efforts to expand the system. The Board of Estimate wasn't willing to proceed; to the Transit Commission's frustration, they waited until July 1, 1924, to take any action on new subways. That was when the Board of Transportation and its chairman, John H. Delaney, took the lead role in transit planning.

Hylan's plan sparked interest among the business groups who saw a 1st Avenue line as the way to promote growth. "First Avenue more than any street in Manhattan lends itself to the speedy building of a subway at this time, and if a trunk line should be built through First Avenue (it is wide and has no overhead structure above Twenty-Third Street) relief would be quicker than from [the] building of a subway in any other part of the city,"[13] Samuel J. Bloomingdale, president of the Bloomingdale Brothers department store, wrote to the Transit Commission.

With the motto "First Avenue Subway First," Bloomingdale and other property owners formed the First Avenue Subway Association on April 7, 1924, at a luncheon at his store.[14] They believed the 1st Avenue line would have more of an impact than the 6th Avenue line, which had a higher priority in the planning process.

Representatives of this group, along with business and realty groups from Manhattan and the Bronx, met with the BOT on July 25 to discuss the 1st Avenue line. They had petitions supporting the line and promised to share in construction costs. Delaney asked the representatives to meet with the property owners to determine how many of them would participate in an assessment plan. Newspaper articles over subsequent weeks ran stories on owners who were willing to join. However, the BOT's plans for the IND didn't include an East Side line.

The First Avenue Subway Association protested to Hylan and Delaney. "The east side has been entirely ignored in the plan which has been submitted," Managing Director Irwin L. House wrote. "The congestion on the east side is as great as exists on the west side and the money that it will cost to build the west side route with the Fifty-Third Street extension [the Queens Boulevard line] could be used to greater advantage if expended on the east side."[15] Charles M. Estabrook, a transit engineer hired by the Association, feared that if the East Side was neglected then, it wouldn't get an additional subway line for another twenty years.[16]

The Transit Commission got around to discussing expanded East Side subway service in June 1925. Writing in the June 12 edition of the *New York Times*, Major General John F. O'Ryan, a Commission member, discussed a plan for a subway line on 3rd

Avenue. Turner called for the demolition of the 3rd Avenue El and the widening of the street to allow for the construction of a six-track line. The line would run from the City Hall area to the Harlem River, with at least three tracks linking with the 2nd and 3rd Avenue Els. O'Ryan and Turner saw 3rd Avenue becoming a second Park Avenue.[17] The Merchants Association of New York called for the construction of a 3rd Avenue line as part of an overall position paper opposing the IND.[18] This was as far as the 3rd Avenue line proposal went, with the BOT controlling the planning process.

The lobbying efforts of the East Side groups paid off when news of the plans for the second phase of the IND appeared in April 1929. While the Utica Avenue–Crosstown line and the Nostrand Avenue line extension in Brooklyn drew the most attention, Delaney, trying to avoid making a definitive statement, did say that another route to be built was an East Side trunk line, operating along 2nd or 3rd Avenues, or a private right-of-way between those two streets. They favored 2nd Avenue but did not make a final choice.

The line would run from an unnamed downtown location to the East Bronx. Mayor James J. Walker requested the routing to allay the fears of East Bronx residents that they were neglected due to the BOT's earlier approval of the extension of the IND Concourse line via Burke Avenue and Boston Road.[19]

A route was selected after two years of planning for the East Side Trunk Line. It was originally proposed to run from Houston Street to the Bronx via 2nd Avenue, connecting with the White Plains Road line. The mid-block routing was ruled out; land acquisition costs for the line and the new street were too steep. Building it on 3rd Avenue brought it too close to Lexington Avenue; 2nd Avenue brought it closer to areas not served by rapid transit.[20] Connections to the 53rd Street and 6th Avenue–Houston Street lines were considered.

Within a few weeks, the route was extended south to Water and Wall Streets and split into three branches in the Bronx. The original connection to the White Plains Road line at 177th Street was retained. A second branch would run along Boston Road to the Northeast Bronx, linking to the Concourse line extension at Burke Avenue and the Curtiss-Wright Corporation's planned airport. Responding to Mayor Walker's concerns, a third branch would be built along Lafayette Avenue, serving the East Bronx. No track connection would be built at 53rd or Houston Streets, but there would be a spur line built along East 61st Street connecting the 2nd and 6th Avenue lines.

The response to where the routes would be built was largely positive. Samuel J. Bloomingdale spoke for the proposal and looked forward to when the elevated lines in his area would be gone:

The plans for the Second Avenue line will dramatize a development which parallels the growth of any community from frontier town to city . . .

. . . When the east side is completely equipped with subsurface transit, the day will be at hand when added light will be given to the splendid new buildings on Second and Third Avenues, and the unsightly elevated structures will be merely on of the reminisces of the oldest inhabitants.[21]

Complaints in the Bronx, Brooklyn and Queens were directed toward the BOT's plans for new elevated lines. There were concerns in Manhattan over building a route connecting the 2nd and 6th Avenue lines on East 61st Street, rather than 57th Street, a much wider thoroughfare. On the other hand, the 57th Street Committee of the Fifth Avenue Association spoke against running the branch along that street and supported using East 61st Street.[22]

The greatest desire was for work to begin. The First Avenue Association, a group of businesspeople and realtors that included Bloomingdale, organized to promote growth along the East Side, began a campaign to achieve that goal. A series of speakers supporting the proposed route attended the BOT's public hearing on the trunk line on February 10, 1930. Philip J. Healey Inc. carried out preliminary engineering on 2nd Avenue from East 30th Street to the Harlem River.[23]

Delaney wanted to begin work on that line, as well as the Utica Avenue–Crosstown and South Queens Trunk Lines. However, finances affected the BOT. They needed to finish a component of the IND's first phase, the 6th Avenue–Houston Street line, feeling

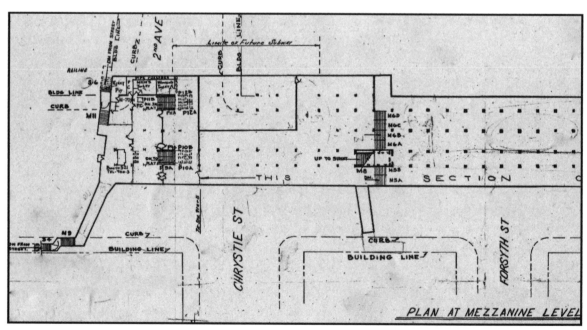

Figure 9-2. A diagram of the mezzanine of the 2nd Avenue station on the 6th Avenue–Houston Street line, showing the room left for the 2nd Avenue line to go through and a transfer station to be built. (Courtesy of the New York Transit Museum Archives)

it was necessary to relieve pressure on the 8th Avenue line.[24] The 2nd Avenue station on this line was built to allow for a transfer with the 2nd Avenue line.

The 2nd Avenue line was included in the Board's next capital plan, released in February 1932. The White Plains Road line connection was gone. A connecting line running on 34th Street between 2nd and 10th Avenues had been added, the only time the BOT proposed this. The Northeast and East Bronx lines were retained. It was still significant on paper, but that's all it was—a plan on paper. Despite the ongoing efforts of the East Side and Bronx organizations to start work, no action could be taken.

The city government didn't help. The Subway Committee of the First Avenue Association met with Acting Mayor Joseph V. McKee that fall to urge that he obtain a Reconstruction Finance Corporation loan for the line. McKee wanted to cut $50 million from the budget ($823 million in 2011 dollars, according to MeasuringWorth.com); he wouldn't do anything that would add to the city's obligations.[25] Federal funding would later help to build the first phase of the IND in Fiorello H. La Guardia's administration.

The start of work wasn't imminent, but some people supported actions that led to the contraction of East Side transit service. Not wishing to wait for construction of the trunk line, the First Avenue Association advocated for demolition of the 2nd Avenue El. Their main effort throughout the 1930s seemed to be advocating for the demolition of the elevated, rather than building the subway.

The 2nd Avenue Trunk Line took on less importance for a time in the late 1930s. It ranked fourteenth on the Board's 1938 capital priority list. The line itself shrank. While a connection from 2nd Avenue to the BMT's Broadway line was proposed for the first time, the trunk line was now only a two-track line, with one route proposed for the Bronx, along the borough's southern shore. Other lines took on greater importance in the Board's capital plans. Proposals for the extensions of subway lines in Queens ranked higher.

The BOT's capital plans from 1939 through 1941 brought on a change in the plans for 2nd Avenue. For the first time, there was a proposal to operate to Brooklyn, running under Water Street and Coenties Slip, connecting with the Fulton Street line at the Hoyt–Schermerhorn Street station.[26] Construction of the 2nd Avenue line to Brooklyn and southern Queens remained a priority for many years.

One capital budget item ranked higher by the BOT was demolishing the 6th Avenue El. The city government was listening to the groups calling for the demolition of the els. Comptroller Joseph V. McGoldrick announced that the demolition of the 2nd, 6th, and 9th Avenue and Fulton Street elevated lines would be in the 1939 capital budget.

The BOT had wanted to demolish the 6th Avenue Elevated for years to facilitate construction of the 6th Avenue subway. It would be difficult building even if the el weren't there, as it needed to be built around the Hudson Tubes below 33rd Street and above and below other tunnels and pipelines along the length of the street. The Transit Commission considered the demolition at a hearing on September 29, 1930.

The IRT and the Bronx Chamber of Commerce opposed this. McKee, then Aldermanic president, opposed building new elevated lines, but he also opposed this action: "While I believe that everything should be done to enhance the value of real estate in our city, when there is any question between real estate value and the convenience of the people, I prefer to take my stand on the side of the people."[27] McKee thought the 8th Avenue line should be completed before demolition started. The BOT would have to wait.

The Board of Estimate authorized demolition on August 3, 1938. The Transport Workers Union opposed this, fearing the loss of jobs, but had little help. The last train ran on the evening of December 4 and demolition began. Joseph P. Day auctioned off the structural steel.[28]

Attention turned to the other elevated lines. The Transit Commission held a hearing on October 26, 1939, attended by a large group of civic and business group members and elected officials from the Bronx and Queens and the Transport Workers Union. Assistant Corporation Counsel Leo H. Brown made the city's case for demolition. Council Member Joseph Kinsley criticized any effort to reduce rail transit service in the Bronx. John Gannon of the Bronx Chamber of Commerce stated that demolition "without adequate substitute transportation is contrary to the public good. There can be no justification for any procedure which will add to the already overcrowded East and West Bronx subways."[29]

The hearing continued on October 27. Brown again spoke, showing how bus service could replace elevated service. Charles V. Halley noted the lack of alternatives to elevated service: "I believe that before the Transit Commission gives the City the right to demolish these two elevated lines, which are admittedly antiquated and an eyesore, but still useful, some definite guarantee should be made as to a substitute for the people of the Bronx."[30]

Despite those objections, the Transit Commission approved demolition on February 21, 1940. George F. Mand of the Bronx Chamber of Commerce protested. "The decision of the of the Transit Commission as regards demolition of the Second and Ninth Avenue elevated structures is astounding and will meet with the general condemnation of the people of the Bronx," Mand stated in a press release. ". . . They intend to crowd people into already overtaxed lines or otherwise inconvenience them. And why?"[31]

The Board of Estimate took up the demolition plan. Despite a huge crowd of Bronx residents and businesspeople and members of the Transport Workers Union who showed up on March 14, 1940—not everyone could be admitted to City Hall—demolition was approved. Bronx Borough President James J. Lyons and Manhattan Borough President Stanley M. Isaacs cast the only dissenting votes after a public hearing that lasted more than five hours.

The Bronx Chamber of Commerce and fifty affiliated groups took the demolition plan to court, but Justice Edward S. Dore of the State Appellate Division ruled against their application for an injunction on June 9. Mayor La Guardia personally began demolition on the uptown section of the 2nd Avenue El on February 17, 1941.

The Board of Estimate voted to end service on the rest of the 2nd Avenue El on May 28, 1942. Bronx Borough President Lyons and Queens Borough President James A. Burke cast negative votes. Burke set off fireworks after Manhattan Borough President Edgar J. Nathan, Jr., said scrap metal from the elevated structure should be used as part of the national defense effort. Burke implied that scrap metal from the 6th Avenue Elevated line had been sold to Japan, which used it for military purposes.

Burke wanted to continue 2nd Avenue El service over the Queensboro Bridge, where it connected with the Flushing and Astoria lines. He knew this was an important service to his constituents that wouldn't be replaced if the el were demolished. A decade would pass before BOT proposals called for 2nd Avenue subway service into northern Queens.

Burke was also protesting the point made that opposing demolition was unpatriotic since it kept scrap metal from being used for the war effort. It didn't quite have the result he wanted. Stanley Isaacs, now a member of the City Council, protested. "I am going to inform the Borough President of Queens that at my request, when the contract for the demolition of the Sixth Avenue Elevated was considered in December, 1938, I asked the board to include in that contract a prohibition against the export of that metal," Isaacs said. "First, because of a present loss to the city, there were alternate clauses put in that contract, but later at my assistance the contract provided that not one ounce of that steel could be exported to Japan or to any one else."[32]

"To my own personal knowledge, Mr. Isaacs stated the exact facts," said Delaney. "I investigated them on behalf of the Board of Transportation, on the assertions that have been bandied about from one orator's list to another. There never has been one pound shipped to Japan, of either the Sixth Avenue or any other elevated. All of it has been sold to our own local companies."[33]

Both Isaacs and Burke were correct. The BOT and city government hadn't sold scrap metal from the 6th Avenue El to Japan or the other Axis powers—someone else had. Two years earlier, the *Brooklyn Eagle* investigated what happened to the 6th Avenue El's steel. Borough President Isaacs's resolution was in effect: the Harris Structural Steel Company, which did the demolition work, was restricted from selling the steel to a "foreign agency." Accordingly, they sold it to the Bethlehem Steel Corporation.

The *Eagle* contacted Bethlehem: "No effort had been made to keep the 6th Ave. elevated steel apart from other scrap, and that sheets, plates, bars and girders made from the combined converted metal had gone to various destinations. Japan and the European countries, which before the [British] blockade, included Germany, were among Bethlehem's best export customers at the time."[34]

Isaacs called the *Eagle*'s article "misleading and inaccurate,"[35] but said that while Harris Structural Steel lived up to the terms of the contract, once Bethlehem converted it to other forms for export, it could have gone to Japan or Germany for military purposes,[36] which was the point of the article.

When the Board of Estimate approved el demolition in Manhattan and Brooklyn on June 6, 1940, Isaacs again sought to bar export of the steel. Brooklyn Borough President John Cashmore offered a further amendment earmarking the scrap metal for sale to Great Britain and its allies. This resolution was enacted.

Lyons's and Burke's arguments in 1942 came to naught, although Delaney admitted that "there is no doubt that the people in Queens are going to be inconvenienced."[37] Demolition began on July 7, 1942, and was completed on September 30. The structural steel from the els was recycled and used to construct the Grumman Aircraft Corporation's plant in Bethpage, New York, and to build Grumman's F6F "Hellcat" fighter airplane.[38]

The fate of the scrap metal from the 6th Avenue El received further notoriety after e.e. cummings's 1944 poem "plato told" was published ("it took a nipponized bit of the old sixth avenue el: in the top of his head: to tell him"). The use of the scrap metal from the other elevated lines in Manhattan and Brooklyn demolished in 1940 and 1942 has been forgotten or lumped in with what happened to the 6th Avenue El.

Some derived huge benefits from the demolition of the elevated. Alexander Nobler Cohen wrote in *Fallen Transit*, his study of the 2nd Avenue El and subway, that "property owners prophesized that demolishing the El would lead to a surge in real estate activity and a revitalization of the neighborhood."[39]

2nd Avenue *has* changed, with high-rise office towers and apartment buildings replacing low-rise structures from Gramercy Park to East Harlem. The character of the retail properties changed as well. There was a spillover effect on adjoining streets, accelerating after the 3rd Avenue El service ended in 1955.

But the 2nd Avenue El's riders didn't benefit. They had a longer walk to crowd onto the Lexington Avenue line. Demolition affected the entire transit system. The tracks on the Queensboro Bridge providing a connection for the Flushing and Astoria lines were gone as well. Burke's and Lyons's fears were correct. Removal of the tracks from the bridge removed access to the East Side that Queens riders need. It took operational flexibility away from both lines, now necessary with the huge growth in population in northwestern and northeastern Queens. It further overloaded the Lexington Avenue, Flushing, and Astoria lines.

Cohen noted that customers of the elevated lines had little support. The First Avenue Association, professing to speak for the needs of the area, didn't want to wait for the work on the subway to begin to demolish the el. State Senator Frederic René Coutert and Assembly Members Stephen J. Jarema and MacNeil Mitchell (two decades later, Mitchell, as a state senator, investigated what happened to funding ostensibly earmarked for the 2nd Avenue subway), representing the East Side in Albany, filed legislation facilitating demolition. Elected officials and civic and business groups from Queens and the Bronx wanted to save the 2nd Avenue El, but had little support from their colleagues and risked being called unpatriotic while the Second World War was in progress.

With the nation's resources devoted to fighting the war, the BOT had fewer resources to devote to subway expansion. All they could do was plan for when victory was achieved. In a letter to Louis Cohen, chair of the City Council's Finance Committee, BOT Secretary William Jerome Daly had reported that while no funding was available for construction, they were planning for 2nd Avenue line service to the Bronx, running eastward along Lafayette and East Tremont Avenues to Throggs Neck, with connections to the Concourse line at either 161st Street or Claremont Parkway, a connection to the Dyre Avenue line via a spur at Hunts Point Avenue and 173rd Street, or a connection to the Pelham line in Hunts Point.[40]

In his annual message to the City Council on January 5, 1944, Mayor La Guardia said:

> The preparation of engineering plans for the Second Avenue Subway has not been interrupted. The work continues. The engineering plan entails an expenditure of $500,000 out of a total spent for engineering plans on the projects mentioned above [new rolling stock, platform lengthening, etc.] of $3,400,000. The plans for the first ten sections of the Second Avenue subway up to 125th Street will be ready by the end of this year. The plans will be available and ready when financial conditions permit. I do not anticipate that it will be in the immediate future. The total estimated cost of the Second Avenue line is $250,000,000 [$5.6 billion in 2011 dollars]. With extensions now under study, the total new system exceeds $360,000,000 [$8.16 billion in 2011 dollars].[41]

2nd Avenue would become the key component of all capital plans. The BOT believed the primary need was for a new trunk line accommodating additional riders from the other boroughs instead of an outward extension of the subway system.

The first postwar plan, issued in May 1942, was meant to be implemented between 1944 and 1948. The 2nd Avenue line would be built in two phases. The first, extending from Coenties Slip to the Bronx via 2nd Avenue to Water Street, received top priority. The Bronx routing wasn't specified. The Brooklyn routing, connecting with the Fulton Street line, was ranked nineteenth on the Board's list. In August 1944, BOT General Superintendent Philip E. Pheifer prepared a service plan to be implemented once 2nd Avenue and other improvements being proposed were completed. Pheifer's plan called for a realignment of many IND and BMT lines, with at least fifty-six trains per hour operating along 2nd Avenue.[42]

Figure 9-3. The 2nd Avenue line in a 1948 map. A branch route into northern Queens and a connection to the Concourse line in the Bronx would be added in subsequent years. (Courtesy of the New York Transit Museum Archives)

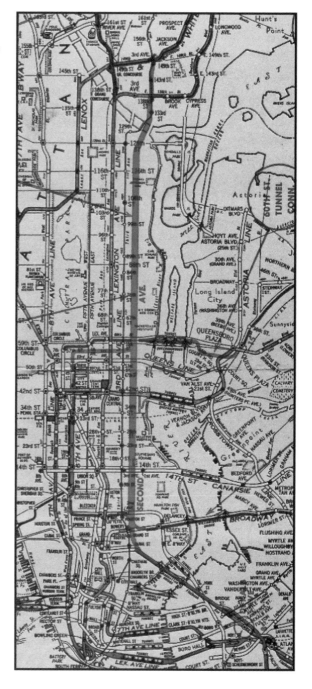

Pheifer also discussed a new connection to be built in Lower Manhattan. Links were planned between the 2nd Avenue, 6th Avenue–Houston Street, and Nassau Street lines, and the BMT trains crossing the Manhattan and Williamsburg Bridges.

A second postwar plan was released in August 1945. The Manhattan routing was unchanged. A specific Bronx route was proposed, running along the borough's southern shore to Harding Avenue in Throggs Neck. There was no Brooklyn route proposed, although the Board planned for service to that borough. Subsequent proposals built on Pheifer's 1944 plan.

Both William O'Dwyer, who succeeded Fiorello La Guardia as mayor in January 1946, and General Charles P. Gross, whom La Guardia appointed to replace John H. Delaney late in 1945, believed 2nd Avenue was the key component of any subway expansion plan, one of the few issues on which O'Dwyer and Gross agreed. Gross saw 2nd Avenue as necessary to relieve the overloading that the north–south lines were experiencing in Manhattan. He knew building the line was not possible without increasing BOT revenue, either through the farebox or tax subsidies.

Mayor O'Dwyer would take the steps toward raising the fare to provide more revenue for the operation of the system, but he first looked to the state government for financial support and an exemption from the city's debt limit to sell bonds to meet capital needs. He used a new subway expansion plan featuring 2nd Avenue as a selling point.

The plan was the brainchild of Colonel Sidney H. Bingham, a longtime BOT and IRT engineer and planner O'Dwyer appointed to the Board.[43] Released to the public on December 14, 1947, Bingham's plan was the most ambitious proposal for 2nd Avenue. He called for a six-track line to run from Lower Manhattan to the Bronx. Expanding on Pheifer's plan, he proposed the Chrystie Street connection, using three different East River crossings, the Williamsburg and Manhattan Bridges and the Montague Street Tunnel. It would establish connections with eight separate BMT branches serving Brooklyn and Queens, the 6th and 8th Avenue lines in Manhattan, and the Pelham line in the Bronx, which would be converted to an IND / BMT line, enabling more Lexington Avenue line trains to serve the White Plains Road, Jerome Avenue, and Dyre Avenue lines.[44] Like Pheifer did, Bingham prepared a service plan identifying the existing routes that would run along 2nd Avenue.[45]

Bingham's concept for 2nd Avenue had more connections with other lines than it had in previous plans. BOT Chairman William Reid[46] discussed why so much emphasis was placed on that line. "The need for a new Second Avenue Subway has not been sufficiently emphasized," Reid told the *New York Times* in 1948. "That line is not needed primarily to handle Manhattan traffic but to relieve the congestion caused by numerous feeder lines going into the older Manhattan lines."

". . . What we really need is not more subway lines to serve the city's outlying areas, but a new Manhattan line to absorb the feeders that pack into the existing Manhattan lines," he continued. "The present situation is like taking four pipes ten inches in diameter and jamming them into one pipe ten inches in diameter. A new Second Avenue line is the answer to that."[47]

Emphasis in transit planning had been consistent with Daniel L. Turner's belief in extending the system ahead of population growth. The way Queens, Brooklyn, and the

Figure 9-4. Colonel Sidney H. Bingham. (*Yonkers Herald Statesman*)

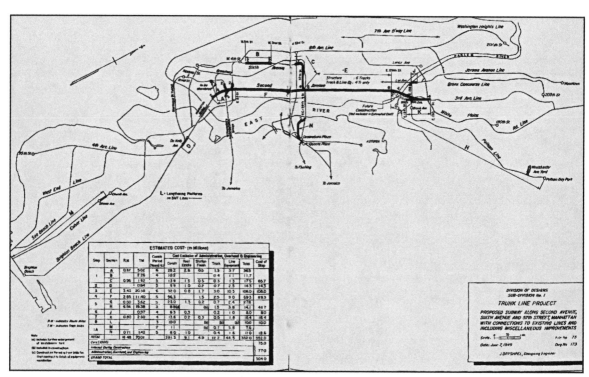

Figure 9-5. A Board of Transportation diagram from 1949 showing the 2nd Avenue line plan. In subsequent years a branch line to Queens would be added.

Bronx were growing justified that. But great strain had been placed on the system's interior, the Manhattan trunk lines.

Financial constraints restricted the BOT. The city could borrow up to 10 percent of the average total assessed real estate value over the previous four years for capital projects. Mayor O'Dwyer sought an exemption from the state legislature to finance capital work. An amendment to the state constitution was needed, which required authorization by state voters in a referendum after being approved twice by the legislature. An initial vote failed in 1948, but it was approved in 1949 and 1950. It would go to the voters in 1951.

On August 29, 1950, a hearing was held in the office of Manhattan Borough President Robert F. Wagner, Jr., concerning a BOT proposal to demolish the section of the 3rd Avenue El between Chatham Square and the Battery. Bingham, who became BOT chairman in January after Reid became deputy mayor, said the structure was outdated and cost too much to upgrade. The BOT used their own inaction to maintain the infrastructure as an excuse for demolition. Staten Island Borough President Cornelius A. Hall and Council Member Isaacs opposed the proposal, citing its impact on their constituents due to the overcrowding of other subway lines. Another council member, Robert Weisberger, and Rev. Arthur G. Keane of the Roman Catholic Church of St. James spoke for demolition. Rev. Keane attacked demolition opponents, calling them people with "very beautiful sunburns and $100 suits." He asked if they wanted "private cabs to their doors" for their ten-cent fare.[48] The BOT and Board of Estimate agreed; 3rd Avenue El service to South Ferry ended on December 22.

Two days after the hearing, Mayor O'Dwyer resigned to become ambassador to Mexico, and City Council President Vincent H. Impellitteri would be elected to serve the rest of his term. Impellitteri campaigned for the bond issue and the 2nd Avenue line. The next BOT capital plan was released on June 22, 1950, to be financed by the 1951 bond issue. The 2nd Avenue line was the lead item, with a branch to Queens from East 76th Street planned to use the Long Island Rail Road's right-of-way to link up with either their Rockaway Beach or Port Washington lines.

The city's financial status continued to raise concerns for the BOT's plans. Comptroller Lazarus Joseph warned against adding new debt, including the bonds authorized by the 1951 constitutional amendment. City Budget Director (and future comptroller and mayor) Abraham D. Beame stated that the city could allow for $235 million ($2.86 billion in 2011 dollars) to pay for all permanent capital improvements, but he thought financial issues needed to be dealt with first.[49] This allowed for work on smaller projects, but it affected projects like 2nd Avenue. Bingham said he would push for the allocation of funding above what Joseph and Beame said was available. It was questionable whether the Board of Estimate would authorize such expenditures, given the city's financial concerns and the short-term needs of the system.

The BOT final capital priority list in July 1952 called for eight routes and was approved by the Board of Estimate that fall. The main feature of these proposals was the latest iteration of the 2nd Avenue subway with the Chrystie Street connection. It also allowed for connections to the Concourse and Pelham lines in the Bronx and an option for further connections into Queens from Woodside.

The expansion of the BMT's DeKalb Avenue station and the rebuilding of the track and switches systems north and south of the station took priority over the rest of the line. This was crucial for the operation of BMT trains through downtown Brooklyn, as it resulted in easier movement of trains in and out of Brooklyn. Over the long term, it would facilitate movement through the Chrystie Street connection to 2nd Avenue, but it required the closing of the Myrtle Avenue station, the next stop north of DeKalb Avenue, one of several stations closures that took place in that era.[50]

The ambitions of the summer of 1952 didn't survive the fall. The BOT expressed concern over their ability to move ahead. There was, a Board spokesman told the *Times*, a shortage of engineers necessary to carry out design work: "Scores of these professional men have left [the BOT] for better paying posts in the outside business world. There may be some delays in our construction program if this outside competition continues."[51] The New York City Transit Authority became the agency operating the subway system after 1952 and continued to issue plans for the expansion of the subway system.

The TA established its own capital priorities in July 1953, which didn't include steps to maintain or upgrade the structure of the 3rd Avenue El. Instead, they were planning to end el service in Manhattan. It would cost $1.5 million a year to operate ($12.6 million in 2011 dollars),[52] and this didn't include what was needed to upgrade the seventy-five-year-old structure. Since the spring of 1952, there had been no service on the el on weekends, holidays, or at night. TA engineers and executives believed that the structure had a useful life of only another five years. Service on the branch of the el running from Chatham Square to City Hall ended with one last trip at 6:49 P.M. on December 31, 1953. The end of the rest of the line in Manhattan was coming.

When the TA issued its capital plan, its president, Hugh J. Casey, told the Board of Estimate that much of the money provided by the 1951 bond issue had gone to other projects. Additional funding would be needed for 2nd Avenue. The TA wanted to build that line but had no idea as to when work would actually begin, despite hopes for a 1957 start.

The 3rd Avenue Elevated ran between Manhattan and the Bronx until 1955. Following on the TA's plan, Robert Moses, as city construction coordinator, advised Robert F. Wagner, the new mayor, that the el should be demolished below 149th Street. Bronx groups protested to Wagner, but he wouldn't take a position: "The [TA] is given sole purpose to determine whether any transit facilities shall or shall not continue to operate."[53]

Sentiment against demolition in the Bronx wasn't unanimous. The Bronx Board of Trade, for one, supported it: "Faced with dwindling patronage, diminishing revenues, mounting deficits and the prospects of extending more than $80,000,000 [$905 million in 2011 dollars] to rehabilitate the railroad structure, the TA has no alternative . . . if it is to avoid an increase in fare."[54]

The TA held hearings at their headquarters in Brooklyn on June 4 and 5. Twelve speakers from the Bronx opposed demolition; the Board of Trade spoke for it, with Joseph F. Addonizio, its executive director, expressing the opinion that demolition might accelerate work on the 2nd Avenue line. The majority of demolition proponents came from Manhattan.

On July 15 the TA Board voted four to one in favor of demolition. Rehabilitation of the el's structure would cost approximately $80 million; the TA would achieve an annual savings of $2.4 million ($27.1 million in 2011 dollars) by demolishing it.[55] The end of service was scheduled for December 31; legal and legislative efforts delayed the last day of operation until May 12, 1955. After service ended, the elevated structure was dismantled. As with the earlier elevated lines, the structural steel was recycled, in this case for the third tube of the Lincoln Tunnel.[56]

One part of the 2nd Avenue line the TA wanted to start work on was the Chrystie Street connection. This would be the link between the 6th Avenue–Houston Street line and the BMT lines crossing the Manhattan and Williamsburg Bridges. Grand Street would be the one station in that segment. The TA asked the city to fund this project on July 9, but the start of work on the main part of the line was no longer on the horizon.

Charles L. Patterson, who replaced Casey as TA chairman in July 1955, issued a report at a Board of Estimate hearing on September 22. Patterson told the Board members that the start of construction of the 2nd Avenue line was "about ten years off"[57]—working on the existing system and dealing with the TA's financial issues would come first.

The report, which responded to Board inquiries concerning the extension of the IRT's Nostrand Avenue line in Brooklyn, made it clear: "No new lines or extensions should be undertaken until the major portion of the modernization program has been completed, and such construction should only be undertaken if it can shown to be self-sustaining."[58]

This was frustrating to the representatives of the 2nd Avenue line's service area. Council Member Isaacs and a Queens colleague, Robert E. Barnes, criticized the use of the funding ostensibly earmarked for 2nd Avenue to maintain the existing system. Barnes called it a "disgraceful double cross"; he wrote to State Senate Majority Leader Walter J. Mahoney and Assembly Speaker Oswald D. Heck, asking for a legislative investigation into how the bond issue money had been spent.[59] State Senator MacNeil Mitchell[60] sought authorization for a hearing on what had happened to the $500 million from the 1951 bond issue ($4.33 billion in 2011 dollars).

Twenty years earlier as an Assembly member, Mitchell supported demolishing the 2nd Avenue El. As a state senator, he was interested in what happened to the money meant to pay for the subway that would replace it. Mitchell soon found that people knew bond issue funds were never specifically earmarked for one subway line. "Where the $500,000,000 or most of it went—nearly $400,000,000 has already been spent or committed—is one of the worst-kept 'secrets' in city affairs," the *New York Times* editorialized. There had been "no breach of faith with the people."[61]

Mitchell's hearing was held on March 8, 1957. Patterson made it clear that the 2nd Avenue line wouldn't be built with funds from the 1951 bond issue. Other system needs—the purchase of the Rockaway Beach line and its integration into the subway system, the completion of the Fulton Street subway, the DeKalb Avenue project, the connection of the Dyre Avenue and White Plains Road and the Culver and Smith Street lines, platform lengthening, subway car purchases, and other work needed to rehabilitate an aging system—took precedence. "It would have been a tragic mistake for the city to have embarked on the trunk line program [the 2nd Avenue line] as planned at the expense of denying capital funds for the improvement and modernization of the existing rapid transit systems," Patterson testified.[62]

With that, aside from the Chrystie Street / DeKalb Avenue section, most of the 2nd Avenue line went into the "state of suspended animation" John H. Delaney told James J. Lyons the Burke Avenue line was in during the 1940s. The Board of Estimate allocated $10,227,400 ($100 million in 2011 dollars) on October 25, 1957, to begin work on Chrystie Street; ground was broken on November 25. Mayor Wagner announced that the Grand Street station would be built using ramps and a minimum amount of stairs to provide access for the senior citizens who lived in the area.[63]

The construction of the Chrystie Street connection required a northern subway extension. The TA announced plans to extend the 6th Avenue line north to 57th Street on January 30, 1962. Although this extension would be used for a future system extension, its purpose then was to handle the additional number of trains coming up 6th Avenue from Chrystie Street without running to Upper Manhattan or Queens.

Chrystie Street line service began on November 26, 1967, completing the work started in the 1950s with the reconstruction of the track system at DeKalb Avenue. It completed the IND / BMT merger that began with the Queens Boulevard / 60th Street connection in Long Island City and the Culver / Smith Street connection in Brooklyn in the 1950s. Two 6th Avenue line routes used Chrystie Street to reach the Manhattan Bridge and run along the Brighton Beach and West End lines in Brooklyn; a new 6th Avenue route, the KK line, used Chrystie Street and the Williamsburg Bridge to connect with the Broadway–Brooklyn line. This was the most significant change in subway service in decades. The opening of the Chrystie Street line led to other changes in the system. Four new routes began service, and five others experienced significant revisions.

In a span of about five weeks in 1968, two plans were released that harked back to the BOT's old plans for 2nd Avenue. The first was a report for the TA by the engineering firm of Coverdale and Colpitts. They revived the plan to use all of the New York, Westchester, and Boston Railway's right-of-way, connecting it with the Dyre Avenue line at East 180th Street. It would branch off on Burke Avenue to the Co-op City housing development, being built on land meant for Curtiss Airport. Another branch would connect with the Pelham line, bringing back part of the BOT's plans from the 1940s and 1950s.

A third branch would use part of what remained of the 3rd Avenue El, running along Washington Avenue to 198th Street, where it would connect with the el and run to Gun Hill Road. The el segment south of 198th Street would be demolished. In Manhattan, Coverdale and Colpitts proposed connecting the 63rd Street line with the 2nd Avenue, 6th Avenue, and Broadway lines.

On February 28, 1968, the newly formed Metropolitan Transportation Authority (MTA), which included the TA, the suburban railroads, and the Triborough Bridge and Tunnel Authority, issued its "New Routes" plan, succeeding Coverdale and Colpitts's proposals.[64] "New Routes" brought back components of past BOT and TA plans, and incorporated some of the Coverdale and Colpitts schemes. The 2nd Avenue line was included, starting in Lower Manhattan, linking with the Chrystie Street line at Grand Street, which would be rebuilt as a four-track station, and running into the Bronx. In the Bronx, it would run on the unused part of the New York, Westchester, and Boston Railway's right-of-way to link with the Dyre Avenue line. A branch from the south would connect with the 63rd Street line going toward Queens; one from the north would connect with 63rd Street, going to the 6th Avenue and Broadway lines.

The MTA wanted to avoid the problems of the BOT and the TA. Dr. William J. Ronan, the first MTA chairman, stressed the need to move ahead. "We must act decisively and with courage, recognizing that years of study and review have already helped forge and temper this program," Ronan told the Board of Estimate on August 12. "The plan before you is practical and 'doable' and meets present and future needs. . . . We are little interested in stocking libraries with more studies. We want to bring people the transportation they deserve."[65]

That didn't happen. City Council Member Robert A. Low wanted the line built on 1st Avenue. Robert W. Haack, the New York Stock Exchange's president, and Edmund F. Wagner, the president of the Downtown–Lower Manhattan Association, wanted it extended to the Battery.[66] The Downtown–Lower Manhattan Association proposed an extension around the tip of Manhattan to serve the Battery Park City development, then in the planning stage.[67]

Figure 9-6. The Grand Street station on the Chrystie Street line, a two-track station, would be rebuilt to handle four tracks, allowing for transfers to the 2nd Avenue line. (Courtesy of the New York Transit Museum Archives)

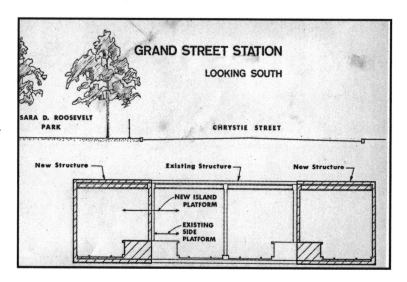

Shortly after Ronan's speech, three city agencies asked for changes in the plan for 2nd Avenue. The City Planning Commission, the Transportation Administration, and the Bureau of the Budget issued a joint report to the Board of Estimate on August 14 calling on the MTA to build it with two tracks and to construct it using the "deep tunnel" method.[68] On September 18 Mayor John V. Lindsay and the five borough presidents called for this to be done with limited stops.

The Board of Estimate approved the overall plan on September 20, but 2nd Avenue had a long way to go. Funding issues weren't resolved and there were more objections to its routing. Manhattan Community Board No. 4, acting on a request by Borough President Percy E. Sutton, held a public hearing at City Hall on March 4, 1969. Council Member Low and U.S. Representative James H. Scheuer led the speakers.

Scheuer opposed the construction of a "two-track high-speed line" and called for inclusion of local tracks.[69] Low felt that the BOT's original plans didn't anticipate the growth that 1st Avenue and the area to the east experienced.[70] Jack Sissman of the New York State Liberal Party called the 2nd Avenue line "a rich man's express, circumventing the Lower East Side with its complexes of high-rise low- and middle-income housing and slums in favor of a silk stocking route."[71]

The issue of Lower East Side service took on a life of its own. Borough President Sutton and Representative Edward I. Koch (eight years before becoming mayor) called on the MTA to reroute the line or run a spur line to serve that area. Ronan questioned the cost and benefits of the plan.[72] The calls for an eastward routing had Mayor Lindsay's support. His transportation administrator, Constantine Sidamon-Eristoff,[73] called on the MTA to reconsider its plan for the 2nd Avenue line's downtown routing: "If this route is reasonable and financially feasible, it should be done.... Our preliminary work shows that shifting the route to Avenue A or B would add only a minute to travel time, serve additional population and be fairly close in cost to [the] direct line recommended by the Metropolitan Transportation Authority."[74]

The Board of Estimate scheduled a hearing for July 24 to review the MTA's plans. Sutton was pessimistic about his plan being adopted: "It would seem that the Wall Street boys with their paid ads have done an effective job of routing and have defeated the little people of the Lower East Side."[75] That feeling was groundless. After a seven-hour hearing, the Board rejected the MTA's plan. Only Queens Borough President Sidney Leviss and Brooklyn Borough President Abe Stark[76] voted for it.

The MTA reconsidered its plans for 2nd Avenue, a process lasting through the end of 1969. Comptroller Abraham Beame grew frustrated with the time it was taking to come up with a new plan and issued a statement on January 21, 1970, criticizing the MTA for the delay. Lindsay's office also pressed for action. The MTA issued a plan for a spur route a week later. Nicknamed the "Cuphandle," it would run east from the 2nd Avenue line at Houston Street to Avenue C and then turn north and run to meet the 14th Street–Canarsie line.

That may have ended that issue, but another issue was festering. Ever since Lindsay and the borough presidents called for what Representative Scheuer later disparaged as a "two-track, high-speed line," there were concerns in Manhattan over the number of Midtown and Upper East Side stops. It became a full-fledged controversy in September 1970. Ronan stated that no station locations had been set and hearings on the locations

Figure 9-7. Senator Jacob K. Javits, Governor Nelson A. Rockefeller, U.S. Secretary of Transportation John Volpe, Mayor John V. Lindsay, Congressman Edward I. Koch, and MTA Chairman William J. Ronan break ground for the 2nd Avenue subway on October 27, 1972. (Photo courtesy of the New York Transit Museum Archives)

Figure 9-8. A view of the 2nd Avenue line segment built between East 99th and East 105th Streets. (Photo by the author)

would be held, but John T. O'Neill, the TA's chief engineer, stated there would be six stations, located at 34th, 48th, 57th, 86th, 106th, and 125th Streets.

The absence of stations at 72nd and 96th Streets drew protests. Sutton held a hearing on the issue on October 6. Ronan declined to attend, although Justin Feldman, an MTA representative, stated that no decision had been made concerning the number or location of stations. Assembly Member Stephen C. Hansen expressed the belief the station locations were being kept secret until it would be too late to alter the plans.

This controversy went on for close to a year. A station was added at 72nd Street, which failed to satisfy many East Side residents. "While we are gratified that the MTA now accepts our previous request for a station at 72nd Street, which will serve the important New York Hospital Medical Center, we cannot understand why the MTA fails to provide such an equal facility for the Metropolitan Hospital Center at 96th Street," William J. Diamond, the chairman of Manhattan Community Board No. 8, said at an MTA hearing at Hunter College on September 15, 1971.

"... It is important to remember that in the early 1940s before most of the large high rise apartment houses were built on Second and Third Avenues, that the area between 34th Street and 126th Street had been served by the Second Avenue elevated line and the Third Avenue elevated line in addition to the Lexington Avenue IRT and trolley car service," he continued. ". . . With the removal of these two lines the east side lost a total of 28 mass transit stations. . . . Even with the addition of a 96th Street station, the east side will still have only one-third the number of subway stations that it had thirty years ago when its population was much less than it is today."[77]

Ronan announced on October 3 that a station would be built at 96th Street. The question of how the construction of 2nd Avenue and the other "New Routes" routes would be paid for remained to be answered.

Governor Nelson A. Rockefeller thought he had the answer. In March 1971, he announced he would seek approval for a $2.5 billion sale of bonds on the ballot in November ($13.9 billion in 2011 dollars). The money derived from the bond sale would help to finance the "New Routes" projects as well as other transit and highway projects across the state.

Despite a heavy advertising campaign for the bond issue, it failed at the ballot box by nine hundred thousand votes, attracting little support in New York City. Even though the bond issue would finance expansion of the transit system and maintain fares, many remembered the promises made in 1951 and forgot the work that was done.

The 2nd Avenue project continued while other projects withered away and the fare went from thirty to thirty-five cents. Money remained from a 1967 bond issue, and federal funding was available. On June 21, 1972, President Richard M. Nixon announced that a $25 million[78] Urban Mass Transportation Administration (UMTA) grant would be provided to the MTA for 2nd Avenue.

Governor Rockefeller, Mayor Lindsay, Senator Jacob K. Javits, Borough President Sutton, and U.S. Secretary of Transportation John Volpe broke ground for one of the two uptown segments of the line at a ceremony at 2nd Avenue and East 103rd Street on October 27.[79] The MTA celebrated the groundbreaking at East 103rd Street by issuing a brochure, titled *The Second Avenue Subway Line . . . The Line That Almost Never Was*, tracing the history of the line back to Daniel L. Turner's Transit Construction Commission plan of 1920. The uptown segments would run between East 99th and East 105th Streets and East 110th and East 120th Streets.

More changes were sought. Bronx Borough President Robert Abrams proposed a new routing that would have the line run eastward along Whitlock Avenue to serve the Parkchester housing development and then north to Co-op City.[80]

Work on 2nd Avenue proceeded slowly. Leftover parts of the 2nd Avenue El's structure along with unmapped water and sewer lines and utility ducts were discovered. They weren't on any street diagrams or blueprints, and these elements needed to be removed or relocated before heavy construction started.[81]

Another ceremony began work on a different 2nd Avenue segment that fall. Lindsay and Ronan broke ground at Chrystie Street and Canal Street for a segment that would run south under the Manhattan Bridge and adjacent to the new Confucius Plaza housing development to Chatham Square in Chinatown.

The question of funding for the 2nd Avenue line and the other "New Routes" lines remained unanswered. Governor Rockefeller proposed another bond issue. Authorization for the sale of $3.4 billion in bonds ($18.3 billion in 2011 dollars) would be sought in November; $1.35 billion ($7.26 billion in 2011 dollars) would go toward the new subway lines and maintain the thirty-five-cent fare. New York City voters supported the bond issue this time, but it wasn't enough to overcome opposition in the suburbs and upstate. Ronan still expected transit system expansion to proceed.

With construction of the three segments of the 2nd Avenue line underway with a 1981 expected completion date, the Department of City Planning and the Municipal Arts Society studied how to integrate development along 2nd Avenue and build stations on the subway line. Its view was that "the logic for locating new subway entrances in buildings and plazas is simple, straightforward, and clearly in the public interest. . . . The opportunity to carry such logic into effect came with the construction of the Second Avenue Subway. A new subway does not merely move masses of people from point to point but new pedestrian traffic and 'opens up' new territory as surely as the westward push of the railroad once did."[82] In their report, *Humanizing Subway Entrances*, the Second Avenue Study Group proposed zoning changes in the areas near stations, which would facilitate the construction of plazas and arcades where station entrances would be located.

Figure 9-9. The City Planning Commission wanted station entrances on the 2nd Avenue line built into plazas and arcades. Areas along 2nd Avenue were zoned for that; buildings were erected to allow for the construction of entrances. An example is this plaza at East 33rd Street and 2nd Avenue. (Photo by the author)

In the last week of 1973, as the Lindsay administration was winding down, the Board of Estimate enacted zoning regulations establishing "Transit Land Use Districts," formalizing the study. Comptroller Abraham D. Beame, the incoming mayor, embraced this concept. With the new zoning regulations in effect, new buildings were erected in the Transit Land Use Districts with off-street areas for station entrances within property lines. These are still visible at many points along 2nd Avenue, and the zoning regulations remain in effect.

Mayor Beame, Governor Malcolm Wilson (who replaced Rockefeller after he resigned (he would later become vice president to Gerald Ford), and the MTA's new chairman, David L. Yunich (who replaced Ronan in May 1974), officiated at a ceremony marking the start of work on a fourth segment in the East Village on July 25, 1974. This segment would be built between East 2nd and East 9th Streets. Bids would be opened for work on a fifth segment between East 50th Street and East 54th Street. "Planners have been beating around the mulberry bush with this line since 1920," Yunich said. "It's fundamental to the future development of New York if we want to entice business and manufacturers to come in. . . . It's a gross injustice to refer to this as simply a Second Avenue line when in fact it is a new interborough system with connections to Queens, the Bronx and Brooklyn."[83]

Funding remained an issue. In October 1974, UMTA Administrator Frank C. Herringer warned against using federal funding to offset operating deficits: "I don't think that we should structure a national transit program to save the 35-cent fare or any fare. I'd hate to see the capital program grind to a halt in order to maintain the 35-cent fare."[84]

Budgetary concerns were wearing "New Routes" down. Yunich, Beame, and the Board of Estimate met on October 31 and announced that the 2nd Avenue line would be delayed until at least 1986.[85]

A week later, Yunich announced further delays. The completion dates for the "Cuphandle" line and routes in other boroughs were extended to the 1990s. Work on 2nd Avenue continued, but the line would not be completed until 1988. When asked if the new delays canceled some lines, Yunich said, "I think that when a project is put off that far, it's a polite way of saying 'not in our lifetime.'"[86]

Mayor Beame announced further delays to 2nd Avenue in 1974 and revealed that only part of the line would be built. Completion was now scheduled for 1992. Despite the work on the two line segments in East Harlem, the only part of the route to be into service would be the segment from Lower Manhattan to 63rd Street, connecting with the tunnel to Queens. Work continued on the 63rd Street line, which would eventually lead to the construction of the first 2nd Avenue segment.

Even that cutback might not be enough. On January 4, 1975, CPC Chairman John E. Zuccotti stated the city was $700 million short of the $2.5 billion ($10.5 billion in 2011 dollars) needed for capital work and fare stability. Then came the financial crisis that beset the city and state in the mid-1970s. On September 25, 1975, citing the lack of state

Figure 9-10. Mayor Abraham D. Beame, Governor Malcolm Wilson, and MTA Chairman David L. Yunich breaking ground for the East Village segment of the 2nd Avenue subway on July 25, 1974. (Photo courtesy of the New York Transit Museum Archives)

funding, Beame directed the MTA to cease work on the East 2nd Street–East 9th Street segment. The city financed this work anticipating reimbursement from the state, but none came. The East Harlem and Chinatown segments were completed, but the East Village segment was filled in and paved over.

A new effort was made for a transit line on the East Side of Manhattan in the late 1980s. Using a federal grant, the MTA undertook the Manhattan East Side Alternatives Study (MESA) in 1995. MESA looked at options including reviving 2nd Avenue, restoring trolley service (now called Light Rail Transit) to the East Side, creating a busway along 1st or 2nd Avenues, or improving the signal system of the Lexington Avenue line so that it could handle more trains.[87]

By 1999, MESA leaned toward a scaled-down version of 2nd Avenue, connecting with the 63rd Street line and running to 125th Street. Mayor Rudolph W. Giuliani supported it, although he wanted higher priority given to extending the Flushing line to the west to serve the Jacob K. Javits Convention Center on West 34th Street and a proposed sports complex.[88]

The shortened 2nd Avenue line was opposed on the East Side and in the Bronx. A group of elected officials, led by Representatives Eliot L. Engel and Carolyn B. Maloney, Public Advocate Mark Green,[89] and Manhattan Borough President C. Virginia Fields wrote to MTA Chairman E. Virgil Conway, calling for a full-length line to be built. Sheldon Silver, the speaker of the New York State Assembly, also supported the full-length line.

Figure 9-11. The Lexington Avenue Station on the 63rd Street line was built to be a four track station with temporary tiled walls. Wooden walls have been installed while the platform is rebuilt to create a transfer with the 2nd Avenue line. (Photo by the author)

Forty of the forty-five speakers at the MESA public hearing on September of 1999 called for the full-length line. The MTA issued a statement in the *Federal Register* on March 22, 2001, stating that they would focus on the full-length line. After public hearings on May 12 and 13, 2003, that option was selected. Representative Anthony D. Weiner summed up the feelings of the public hearings' participants when he said, "This is going to be noisy, this is going to be dusty, and there are going to be people who have their dishes shaking off of their cabinets during part of this work, but at the end of the day, I think that we can't live without the 2nd Avenue subway."[90]

A new groundbreaking took place for the 2nd Avenue line in the lower East Harlem tunnel segment on April 12, 2007, the same segment Governor Rockefeller and Mayor Lindsay broke ground for three decades earlier. Governor Eliot Spitzer and MTA Chairman Peter Kalikow led the ceremony.

The 2nd Avenue line will be built in four segments. The first, now under way, runs south from 96th Street to connect with the 63rd Street and the Broadway lines. The Lexington Avenue station on the 63rd Street line was built as a four-track station, with the side of the platform used by 2nd Avenue trains walled off from the side used by Queens Boulevard line trains. The walls are being removed and the station rebuilt to allow for transfers between the two lines. Completion is scheduled for 2016.

The 2nd Avenue line's next phase will utilize the two East Harlem segments and run to Park Avenue and East 125th Street, meeting the Metro-North Railroad and the Lexington Avenue line. Subsequent segments will be built to 2nd Avenue and Houston Street and then to Hanover Square in Lower Manhattan. The fate of those segments, as with every other plan in the past, rests on what funding is available in the future.

But that's a story for another time.

10

Other Plans, Other Lines, Other Issues in the Postwar Years

General Charles P. Gross began his tenure as Board of Transportation chairman on January 7, 1946, by announcing his plans to modernize the system. Lengthening platforms, buying new trains, installing escalators, improving lighting, and paying down debt took priority. Without financial resources, greater emphasis was being placed on upgrading the existing system. No commitment was given to raising the fare.

Gross knew the system needed to expand. It couldn't be done without increased funding, through the farebox, increased borrowing powers, or city and state financing. He wasn't even sure an increase of five cents was enough. At a meeting of the Queens County Transit Alliance on April 25, Gross said a five-cent increase could not provide for a system expansion sufficient to meet the city's growth potential. A lack of funding had prevented the expansion of the Fulton Street subway to Ozone Park and the completion of the first phase of the Queens Boulevard line, its extension to 179th Street.

Speaking at a conference sponsored by the Commerce and Industry Association of New York on November 12, Gross said, "Unless something is done to provide for necessary extensions to the system, the whole subway problem itself, most notably in Manhattan itself, the whole problem will blow up in the city's face."[1] He thought "the present two to two and one half-hour rush hours could be stretched to three and one-half to four hours"[2] if this didn't happen.

O'Dwyer, Gross, and Queens Borough President James A. Burke finally broke ground for the extension of the Queens Boulevard line to Hillside Avenue and 179th Street on May 5. Financing future work was on everyone's mind. "Digging here, we might hit gold and solve all the city's financial problems," O'Dwyer said.[3]

No gold was found, and the Queens Boulevard line never extended eastward from Jamaica. The Flushing line didn't extend beyond Main Street and no subway tunnel was built to Staten Island. It would be almost a half century before there was official discussion of building a subway line to La Guardia Airport, and thirty years until a rail link to Idlewild Airport was considered. When it was finally built to John F. Kennedy International Airport, it was the AirTrain, built and operated by the Port Authority, charging a separate fare. From 1929 to 1945, any proposal for the Utica Avenue line had been as an IND line. From then on, it would only be considered as a branch of the IRT's Eastern Parkway line.

The BOT notified the Board of Estimate that a fare increase was needed on October 20. The system's operating costs were increasing and the capital needs were still there. They were also facing demands for salary increases from the Transport Workers Union.

The Board of Estimate held a hearing on the fare increase at City Hall that began on the morning of February 11, 1947, adjourned at 11:20 P.M., and resumed the next morning. The City Council's chambers were used to handle the overflow crowd. The Board rejected the proposal, with only Staten Island Borough President Cornelius Hall voting in favor. O'Dwyer recognized the BOT's need for more funding and said he would ask the state legislature to authorize a referendum authorizing the city to sell $400 million in bonds that would be exempt from the city's debt limit to provide the necessary financial support.

Advocacy for the Burke Avenue line took on new life when O'Dwyer assumed office. The *Bronx Home News* ran a full-page article on March 19, 1946, reminding readers of what happened before the war. It included a 1938 photograph of the preconstruction work on Burke Avenue, possibly the only photograph published of this, and reminded people about the sale of the New York, Westchester, and Boston Railway's right-of-way sale. (In an interesting juxtaposition, one advertisement on that page was for a rally at James Monroe High School against the proposed Cross Bronx Expressway.)[4]

George Mand of the Bronx Chamber of Commerce wrote to Gross asking what his intentions were for Burke Avenue. Gross wasn't encouraging, saying it was too close to the White Plains Road and Dyre Avenue lines to justify building. Mand appreciated his honesty, but questioned Gross's reasoning: "It is a fact . . . that the Board of Transportation as such laid out this line while the White Plains Road line was available and the Dyre Avenue line in operation as the New York, Westchester and Boston Railway—both common, especially with the latter affording better service than today—so that it will be only natural to find public opinion hard to convince that the existence of these facilities justifies the abandonment of this project at this late date."[5] Gross would speak at the Bronx Board of Trade luncheon on April 18 at the Concourse Plaza Hotel. The Burke Avenue line's supporters hoped they would finally get a positive response.

Gross had good and bad news. More trains would be put into service at the 177th Street–Parkchester Station on the Pelham line, making it easier for the residents of that growing area to use the subway. Express service would come to the Pelham line, and there would be increased express service on the Lexington and 7th Avenue lines. Platforms would be lengthened at IRT local stations, enabling longer trains to run, thereby increasing capacity.

His bad news concerned Burke Avenue:

The board has received a number of inquiries as to the construction of the Burke Avenue extension of the Concourse Line of the Independent Division of the subway system. I am informed that this extension to the IND Division was planned about 1937, in order to provide some rapid transit service in the section of the East Bronx contiguous to Burke Avenue. As designed, the extension would serve the territory between the White Plains Road line of the IRT Division and the Dyre Avenue Line, operated on the route of the old New York, Westchester and Boston Railroad. . . .

. . . The acquisition of the New York, Westchester and Boston Railroad right-of-way has materially altered the situation as to transit in this section and there appears to be at this time no immediate necessity for the construction of the Burke Avenue extension. Studies by the engineering staff of the Board indicate that the maximum distance to either the White Plains Road Line or the Dyre Avenue Line along Burke Avenue is less than 3,500 feet. The construction of the Burke Avenue Line, therefore would be to some extent a duplication of existing facilities. It is estimated that it would cost approximately $16,000,000 to construct the Burke Avenue extension. It would be difficult to justify the expenditure of this sum for the Burke Avenue Line when there are more pressing problems for which the board, because of the financial limitations of the City, is unable to make any provision at this time.[6]

Gross undoubtedly wanted that to be the final word; the elected officials and community and business officials didn't. Borough President Lyons took the occasion of the Board of Estimate's August 1 vote on the extension of the Queens Boulevard line to 179th Street and Hillside Avenue to protest the fact that Burke Avenue hadn't been funded.

Hoping this was the beginning of a major effort to expand the transit system, rather than a step toward completing the IND's first phase, Lyons voted for it, but not without mentioning a sore point: "The Burke Avenue Extension plans are all ready. Formerly, it had top priority on the subway construction program, but during the La Guardia Administration, the people of the Northeast Bronx were sold down the river in the form of the Boston and Westchester Railroad. This caused the Burke Avenue Extension to be bypassed."[7] It wasn't just Burke Avenue; there was also no plan to connect the Dyre Avenue line with another subway line.

Financial pressures on the BOT grew, and there was no help on the horizon. O'Dwyer's Special Transit Committee wanted the fare increased to eight cents, and brought that measure to the Board of Estimate. The mayor had come to a realization that had apparently escaped his predecessors—the five-cent fare was draining the city's financial resources at a time when there were many needs in all five boroughs. "We cannot continue to drain our current revenues to pay increased transit wages and costs at the expense of other vital services," the committee stated to the mayor in their report. "We cannot continue to neglect our sick and unfortunate and progressively strip other essential city services from maximum potential public usefulness just to pay transit employees wages and other operating costs."[8] The Board of Estimate denied Gross's request of $5.5 million for a pay increase for transit workers; O'Dwyer would later state that a hospital improvement program would not take place without a fare increase.[9]

The relationship between O'Dwyer and Gross was different from that between Fiorello La Guardia and John Delaney. When Gross sought to appoint Edward F. Durfee as director of transit safety, O'Dwyer took steps to block the selection.[10] Gross's advocacy for raising the fare was a sore point and he accused O'Dwyer of interfering in negotiations between the Board and the Transport Workers Union. O'Dwyer responded by saying, "My paramount concern at all times, has been the improvement of service, the strengthening of safeguards for the riding public and better labor relations. My several recommendations to those ends have been rejected." He went on to say he would hold the BOT responsible for any issues that had a negative impact on the people of the city.[11]

Two other BOT members, Colonel Sidney H. Bingham and Frank X. Sullivan, supported O'Dwyer. After a meeting with the mayor on September 19, Gross resigned. O'Dwyer appointed William Reid—who had worked for the city government in financial positions since the Mitchel administration, and was O'Dwyer's fiscal adviser and chairman of the Special Transit Committee—to replace Gross.

The CPC took a similar position in releasing their capital budget for 1948: "We believe that such action has now become imperative not only to relieve the city budgets and make it possible to advance other improvements but to assure safe and proper operations of the transit system."[12]

O'Dwyer wanted to raise fares. Realizing that approval by the voting public was unlikely, he asked the state legislature to approve an amendment to the Rapid Transit Law allowing the BOT to raise fares without a referendum. He also asked for an increase in the real estate tax to provide additional funding.

In order to show what additional financial support could accomplish, O'Dwyer and the BOT released a new subway expansion plan on December 14, 1947. Developed by Bingham,[13] a long-time IRT and BOT engineer, the plan called for a six-track trunk line on 2nd Avenue, with connections to lines serving the Bronx, Queens, Brooklyn, and other parts of Manhattan, as well as bringing back extensions that were part of previous BOT plans. The one new component was a link that would connect the Jamaica Avenue and 14th Street–Canarsie lines in East New York. Bingham also prepared a service plan, showing how the system would change once all the components of the plan had been built.[14] The new capital plan coincided with the TWU's endorsement of the fare-increase proposal. With the Board of Estimate rejecting funding for a salary increase, it was the best way to provide for increased salaries.

Mayor O'Dwyer's financial package was not acted on until the end of February 1948. Governor Thomas E. Dewey and the legislative leadership indicated their support for increasing fares, but the proposal to increase real estate taxes was opposed by Republican legislators from Queens, fearing its impact on individual homeowners.[15]

Figure 10-1. (*Left to right*) Brooklyn Borough President John Cashmore, Mayor William O'Dwyer, and Board of Transportation Chairman William Reid at ceremonies marking the opening of the Euclid Avenue station on the Fulton Street line on November 28, 1948. (Brooklyn Public Library, Brooklyn Collection)

The funding package passed on March 29 reflected that. The legislature authorized a fare increase without requiring a referendum, and empowered the city to increase gross receipts taxes on businesses. O'Dwyer wanted to wait until after the 1949 mayoral elections to raise the fares, probably concerned about it being an issue in the campaign. He felt the package that was enacted "would place the sole and entire burden on the great majority of people who could least bear it alone."[16] However, the needs of the system were too great to wait any longer. In a radio speech on April 20, O'Dwyer announced the fare would increase to ten cents on July 1.

The BOT issued another plan for subway expansion in 1948. It wasn't as ambitious as those issued earlier in the decade, but it was major in scope. The Board was equally concerned about upgrading the existing system. Reid had submitted the plan to the City Planning Commission in October. The CPC didn't provide much help in obtaining funding and Reid turned to the Board of Estimate:

The Board of Transportation requests your Honorable Board to do what the City Planning Commission did not do, that is, provide the funds requested.

The Board takes this opportunity of calling your attention to the amounts not only needed to completely rehabilitate the present transit facilities during the next six years, but also to point out the urgent need of beginning immediate construction of the Second Avenue feeder line. This new line is needed to relieve the intolerable conditions existing at the present time in the other feeder lines in Manhattan and to make possible full utilization of the lines in the outlying areas of the City, which is now not possible because of the bottlenecks due to insufficient trunk lines in Manhattan.[17]

Financing remained a concern. Reid noted that O'Dwyer opposed use of the additional fare revenue to pay down the debt. He wanted to use the revenue from the increased business tax revenue for that. Reid also opposed a proposal that the city's sales tax be raised from 2 percent to 3 percent to provide additional capital funding: "If this were done, the cost would fall on the rider in large part, as it is primarily the seven million daily riders who are paying the city's sales tax. Real estate would escape the charge almost entirely although real estate, as well as the rider, benefits because of the city's rapid transit system."[18]

The BOT couldn't proceed with its capital plans. Under constitutional restrictions, the city could only borrow up to 10 percent of the average total assessed real estate value over the previous four years for capital projects. As Reid's letter pointed out, he wanted to see an increase in real estate taxes, but that wasn't happening.

The fare increase was an issue in the mayoral campaign, but not to the extent that O'Dwyer may have expected. Representative Vito Marcantonio, the American Labor Party's candidate, did attack him, fearing that an increase to fifteen cents was already being planned. He promised to roll the fare back to a nickel. Former City Council President Newbold Morris touched on it, but only to question what riders got for the additional nickel. Morris's main transit issue was in the Bronx.

Competition existed between community groups, elected officials, and newspapers in each borough over capital funding and city services. The Bronx groups fought against the city building airports in Queens, rather than on the Curtiss Airport site. Borough President James J. Lyons protested that the Queens Boulevard line was being extended while the Bronx subway projects were not going forward. The feeling was reciprocated in Queens.

As such, it was no surprise when a group from the Bronx led by Arthur V. Sheridan and George Mand toured the Queens Boulevard line project in June 1948, Sheridan said that while they were impressed, "There's only one thing the matter with that extension, and that it's in Queens instead of the Bronx."[19]

Queens was entering a period of massive postwar expansion beyond what was happening in the Bronx and beyond what anyone could imagine. The beginning of service in Queens as the result of the Dual Systems Contracts projects spurred residential and industrial development. It accelerated with the opening of the Queens Boulevard line between 1933 and 1937. While the financial issues that affected the expansion of the subway system in the Bronx also prevented the extension of service into eastern Queens, the impact it had was huge.

The Queens Boulevard line extended from Forest Hills and Kew Gardens to Hillside Avenue and 169th Street in Jamaica in 1937. This triggered the massive development in that line's service area that the Bronx's elected officials, business leaders, and civic groups anticipated had the Burke Avenue line been built. While the elected officials and civic and business groups in Queens were disappointed when the extension of the subways to near the city line didn't happen, what was built resulted in the growth of that borough that continues to this day; 179th Street became a major transit hub and remains a vital entry point to the subway system for the people who moved into eastern, northeastern, and southeastern Queens and Nassau County.

What attracted a lot of attention in 1948 was the BOT's plan to extend the 2nd Avenue line to the South Bronx, with a transfer connection to the 3rd Avenue El. This would lead to the demolition of the el below 149th Street. Indirectly referring to Burke Avenue, Reid said the 2nd Avenue/Pelham line connection, coupled with additional service along the White Plains Road and Jerome and Dyre Avenue lines, would provide the level of service the North Bronx needed.

This was a variation of the plan for the 2nd Avenue line the BOT proposed for the second phase of the IND in 1929, but using connections to existing lines to provide service to the Bronx. The Pelham line connection was the alternative to the Lafayette Avenue line; the additional Lexington Avenue line service routed to the White Plains Road and Jerome and Dyre Avenue lines would replace the two other branches.

This changed the discussion of Bronx transit service. No one liked the appearance of the elevated structure on 3rd and Webster Avenues. Many Bronx groups made their feelings about those structures clear twenty years earlier when the BOT proposed building new ones. However, they also knew the el provided service that wouldn't be easily replaced if demolished. Along with wanting new service, they needed to fight to hold on to what they had.

The Bronx's response was typified by a *Post and Home News* editorial, titled "They Give Us a Morsel, but We Want a Meal."[20] Everything the BOT proposed was viewed as positive, but the absence of the Burke Avenue and Tremont Avenue Crosstown lines seemed conspicuous to the editorial board.[21]

The Empire City Racing Association bought the Curtiss Airport site in 1949 and planned to build a racetrack seating thirty-five thousand people. One entrance would be built adjacent to the Dyre Avenue line's Baychester Avenue station. Empire City wanted a New Haven Railroad spur line built to the racetrack.

Borough President Lyons, an airport proponent since taking office, said, "Racetracks bring in tax revenue; airfields don't."[22] "During past years, the Bronx has always been Manhattan's bedroom. Now the Bronx will get back to business," Thomas Tozzi of the Bronx Board of Trade said.[23] Frank Mazzetti of the Bronx Real Estate Board noted that the property was too small for the airplanes then in use. Mand still wanted the airport to be built: "For 20 years, we have consistently fought for an airport on that site. The airport plan was in conjunction with the seaport development to make the Bronx a leading transportation center. This is regrettable."[24]

The proximity of the proposed racetrack to the Dyre Avenue line, and the plans to connect it to the White Plains Road line, was a flashpoint. "We charge that the Board of Transportation has speeded up plans to build a direct rail connection at East 180th Street from the White Plains Road line to the Dyre Avenue line to replace the present transfer so that through rapid transit service will be provided to the racehorse players visiting the Empire City track without the inconvenience of transferring from the IRT White Plains Road line to the Dyre Avenue line," Hyman Bravin wrote to O'Dwyer. ". . . The Board of Transportation proposed Bronx tinhorn special to the very entrance of the contemplated track is not needed."[25] Bravin demanded that O'Dwyer name the officials who sponsored the White Plains Road / Dyre Avenue connection and called for Burke Avenue's construction.

The racetrack issue brought renewed focus to Burke Avenue. In the week before the November 8 election, Newbold Morris made the question over the racetrack proposal and the subway service an issue in the mayoral campaign. In addition to his role on the Burke Avenue Subway Extension Committee, Bravin was the Liberal Party's manager of Morris's Bronx campaign. Bravin brought the issues he raised earlier on his own to Morris, who thought he had an issue with which he could attack O'Dwyer.

Morris charged that O'Dwyer pushed the White Plains Road / Dyre Avenue connection over the objections of Budget Director Thomas Patterson. To Morris and Bravin's view, the connection advanced only to benefit Empire City and their customers. He implied that there were improper connections between the mayor and Empire City, using Bravin's expression "Tinhorn Special"[26] to refer to Dyre Avenue, promising not to build the connection until the 2nd Avenue line was built. He would build the Burke Avenue line.

Reid said the BOT knew nothing of anything related to the racetrack. They wanted the White Plains Road / Dyre Avenue connection to serve the new Eastchester Gardens and Pelham Parkway housing developments. Patterson's objections concerned timing; he knew the connection was necessary. William Ellard, the city's director of real estate, stated that proper procedures were followed in the sale of the Curtiss Airport property.[27]

Lyons, an O'Dwyer supporter, said Morris was given a "wrong steer" on Empire City and suggested he consult with another La Guardia ally, Paul Windels, Sr., who he said was a counsel for Empire City.[28] When reporters asked for his comments, O'Dwyer smiled, said, "Silly boy," and changed the subject.[29]

Bravin viewed Morris as Burke Avenue's last hope: "The Burke Avenue extension is doomed if O'Dwyer is elected. Newbold Morris . . . has assured [the Burke Avenue Subway

Extension Committee] that if elected one of his first acts will be to assign qualified engineers to study the project. . . . If they report the need genuine, as we have long know it is, he promises he will back extension work with the full force of his administration. . . . If you want the Burke Avenue extension, vote for Newbold Morris."[30]

Morris and Marcantonio split the vote opposing O'Dwyer, who won with a plurality of the vote. An extension of the Concourse line to Burke Avenue wouldn't again be considered for two decades. The racetrack was never built; the land would sit vacant for another decade until it was later developed for the Freedomland amusement park. Freedomland would be demolished; much of that land would be used for the Co-op City housing development.

The transit system's needs increased without its financial needs being met. The infrastructure was aging; new trains and buses were needed. Diesel buses were needed to replace trolleys and trolley buses. The existing system needed work. IRT and BMT local stations had been built at a shorter length than had express stations; customer demand required their extension. The BOT hadn't connected the White Plains Road and Dyre Avenue lines and the Culver and Smith Street lines. The DeKalb Avenue interchange needed to be rebuilt in order to unclog the bottleneck impeding service on the five BMT lines then traveling through downtown Brooklyn, and to facilitate the connections that would be built with the 2nd Avenue line. And the Board now had the issue of the LIRR's Rockaway Beach line to address.

The LIRR was looking to cut costs; they wanted the BOT to take over. "The people of the Rockaways need and should have the direct benefit of the rapid transit system they have been helping to support as taxpayers of the City of New York," David E. Smucker, the LIRR's chief executive officer and trustee, wrote in the *Rockaway Review*, the publication of the Chamber of Commerce of the Rockaways, in 1949. "It is hardly necessary to point out that extension of rapid transit to the Rockaways would make this community more accessible to visitors and also would make the Rockaways a more desirable year-round residential area."[31]

The Rockaway Beach line was originally built as a grade-level line. Its tracks were elevated in the early 1940s as part of a recreational development plan developed by Robert Moses to BOT specifications in anticipation of it becoming part of the subway system.[32]

A takeover of the Rockaway Beach line was a BOT priority, but Reid wanted a change from earlier plans. The Queens Boulevard line was already experiencing the capacity problems that plague it to this day. Reid said connecting it with the Rockaway Beach lines was impossible "if we're going to provide any kind of service"[33] to Rockaway riders. Instead, it would link with the BMT's Fulton Street Elevated in Ozone Park, which would then connect with the IND's Fulton Street subway on the Brooklyn–Queens border. A $3 million savings would be achieved by connecting it to the Fulton Street line. More savings would be achieved—at least another $33 million ($417 million in 2011 dollars, according to MeasuringWorth.com)—by building the connection between the Fulton Street subway and elevated, instead of extending the subway eastward along Pitkin Avenue.[34]

As a result, the BOT wanted to connect the Utica Avenue line with the IRT. A link of that line with the Fulton Street line was no longer viable. The BOT saw that it would have the same issues with the Fulton Street line as it would have if the Rockaway and Queens Boulevard lines connected in Rego Park. There wasn't track space or passenger capacity to operate the three Queens branches and the Utica line to and from Manhattan. It was too expensive to connect to the Houston Street line. The BOT went back to the PSC's plan from the Dual Systems Contracts era, a connection with the IRT's Eastern Parkway line, despite long-standing concerns about *that* line's capacity.[35]

A new crisis then arose. A fire destroyed a trestle that Rockaway Beach line trains used to cross Jamaica Bay during the evening of May 7, 1950.[36] Twenty-nine fires had damaged the LIRR's wooden bridges since 1942.[37] The LIRR's financial state was as precarious as the BOT's. This was the last straw—it wanted to abandon the Rockaway Beach branch. Rail service would still be provided through Far Rockaway and Nassau County, a convoluted trip making rail travel impossible for many Rockaway residents.

The BOT released its next capital plan on June 22, to be paid for with the funds from the bond issue going before the public in 1951. The 2nd Avenue line was the lead item, with an extension to Queens via East 76th Street now included, using either use the LIRR's right of way to link up with the Rockaway Beach line or the LIRR's Port Washington line, reviving the old plan to link that line with the subways. Rockaway residents would have had to travel well to the north in Manhattan before heading home.

Mayor O'Dwyer resigned to become ambassador to Mexico on August 31, 1950; City Council President Vincent H. Impellitteri was elected to replace him in November. Impellitteri wanted to obtain the Rockaway Beach line and appointed a committee consisting of Robert Moses, Colonel Sidney H. Bingham, and Corporation Counsel John P. McGrath to investigate the feasibility of purchasing it. Moses was the chairman.

Much has been made over Robert Moses's impact on transit in the New York metropolitan area. There is no doubt his projects used funds that could have financed subway capital work. He wanted to obtain the New York, Westchester, and Boston Railway's right-of-way to build a highway in the Bronx. He advocated for demolishing the 3rd Avenue El in Manhattan instead of rehabilitating it, further overloading the Lexington Avenue line. He was a more effective spokesman for his agencies than was John Delaney and his successors.

Moses helped transit riders this time. He recommended the purchase of the Rockaway Beach branch to Mayor Impellitteri on May 16, 1951. The committee called for a bid of $7 million to the LIRR and the allocation of $40 million ($505 million in 2011 dollars) to convert it to a subway line. If the LIRR turned the offer down, they wanted the Interstate Commerce Commission and the New York State Public Service Commission to "compel" the railroad to put the line back into service. The last alternative was a city condemnation and takeover. The line would be linked with the Fulton Street El, and a second link to the Jamaica Avenue line, further to the north, would be considered, but was never built.

Not everyone supported this. George Wolpert of the Chamber of Commerce of the Rockaways wanted the line condemned in order to speed acquisition. A. Edward McDougall of the Queens Borough Chamber of Commerce wanted the line connected with the Queens Boulevard line despite the BOT's concerns. Brooklyn Borough President John Cashmore wanted the Nostrand Avenue line extended and the Utica Avenue line built at the same time that work was being done on the Rockaway Beach line.[38]

An unexpected protest came from TWU President Michael J. Quill. Speaking to the State Congress of Industrial Organizations convention at Lake Placid on September 8, 1951, Quill called the purchase "the greatest steal since Boss Tweed."[39] Impellitteri delayed Board of Estimate action until Quill returned to outline his charges.

Impellitteri and Moses irately demanded that Quill explain himself. Moses called the accusation "a completely irresponsible blatherskite charge. . . . I do not propose to be slandered or libeled by you." Moses went on to state, ". . . The recommendations of this committee were made solely in the public interest in order promptly to restore service in the Rockaways."[40]

Quill and his counsel, John F. O'Donnell, testified on September 13, admitting that there was no evidence of illegal action. Quill believed the responsibility for adequate service to the Rockaways rested with Governor Dewey, the LIRR, and the state government, rather than the BOT. He also thought real estate and banking interests stood to benefit the most by a BOT takeover.[41] O'Donnell repeated these charges. As an alternative, Quill and O'Donnell proposed extending the Nostrand Avenue line to the Rockaways. Bingham said this wasn't financially feasible.[42] The Board of Estimate unanimously approved the offer to the LIRR and endorsed the entire capital plan. They also approved resolutions calling for studies of extending the rapid transit system to Staten Island and the Throggs Neck and Ferry Point sections of the Bronx.

The BOT's 1951 capital priority plan was used to win support for the $500 million debt limit exemption that would be voted on as a state constitutional amendment that November. Most of the projects on this were centered on the 2nd Avenue line. The amendment easily won victory in a referendum on November 6, receiving ninety-three thousand votes more than the amendment authorizing the sale of bonds to finance the construction of the New York State Thruway.

Despite the bond issue's passage, the financial status of New York City and the BOT was tenuous. The city and state governments were considering the feasibility of an independent agency that would be responsible for its own financing to replace the Board as operator of the transit system, leading to the creation of the New York City Transit Authority.

Governor Dewey and the Republican leadership in the state legislature wanted to create the TA as part of a package to balance the city's budget that also included the establishment of a 3 percent city sales tax, an increase in real estate taxes, the deferment of the city's payment to the Teachers' Pension Fund, and the authorization of a new series of "nuisance taxes" in the city. There was discussion of a new fare increase. Mayor Impellitteri and the Board of Estimate called for the imposition of new real estate taxes, an increase of state financial aid, and a takeover of the transit system by one of the agencies Robert Moses chaired, the Triborough Bridge and Tunnel Authority.[43]

There was criticism of both plans. Assembly Minority Leader Irwin Steingut (his son, Stanley, was later Assembly speaker) said his members supported the TA's creation but opposed a fare increase. Moses said the TBTA completely opposed taking over the transit systems: "The suggested expansion of the functions of this authority is unsound and . . . other, more practical means must be found to solve the city's present financial problems."[44]

The BOT released its final capital plan in July 1952. It called for the latest iteration of the 2nd Avenue line and the Utica and Nostrand Avenue lines. The Board of Estimate voted to approve the purchase of the Rockaway Beach line on May 22, 1952. In order to help to pay the cost of the purchase and for some capital work, they voted to charge a second fare for riding the subway south of the Howard Beach station. This surcharge stayed in effect into the 1970s, to the great annoyance of Rockaway residents.

Brooklyn Borough President Cashmore questioned the Rockaway Beach line purchase, fearing that the projects benefiting his borough would get lost in the shuffle, but voted for the purchase plan after receiving assurances from Impellitteri and the BOT that this wouldn't happen. The BOT took steps to back up that assurance in the capital program. The expansion of the BMT's DeKalb Avenue station and the rebuilding of the track and switches systems to the north and south of there, meant to be a component of the 2nd Avenue line, took top priority in the plan.

The CPC's plan for the 1953 capital budget didn't include the 2nd Avenue, Nostrand Avenue, or Utica Avenue projects. Despite Impellitteri's support, the CPC didn't recommend any commitment be made until the city's financial needs had been resolved, but the city's transit needs grew. With the Baltimore and Ohio Railroad facing severe operating deficits for the Staten Island Rapid Transit, the city took the first steps to take over the SIRT's Tottenville Branch. The SIRT's North Shore and South Beach branches were eliminated and replaced by bus lines.[45] Later that month, Impellitteri formally proposed the creation of the TA, which would be financed by a new business tax and increased real estate taxes along with fare collection.[46]

The city's financial status worsened in March 1953. Governor Dewey sent his own plan to create the TA to the state legislature on March 12, noting that the TA could resolve the transit system's debts through the institution of "drastic economies" and the sale of the BOT's bus lines to private operators. The Board of Estimate called for the implementation of Mayor Impellitteri's plan, but Dewey called this action "self-defeating."[47] He would support only increased real estate taxes.

The TA Board would consist of five part-time members. The governor would name two, the mayor would name two, and the fifth would be appointed by a vote of the other four members. The Board of Estimate protested. They looked at imposing service cuts and layoffs as an alternative. Dewey responded by asking the state legislature to withhold new taxing powers from the city. Impellitteri had no alternative.[48] He and the Democratic leaders in the legislature could only protest.

Dewey signed the legislation into law on March 26, criticizing the city for not coming up with a "workable" program: "The difference between the city administration and the state government on this issue is that the city would advocate hidden taxes and living on borrowed money and I consider such a program deeply damaging to the city, both financially and morally. The people are entitled to good government, and they are entitled to know its cost right out in public."[49] Major General Hugh J. Casey, a former army engineer with a distinguished war record, would be chairman.[50] Bingham became the TA's general manager.

The Board of Estimate voted to lease the transit system to the New York City Transit Authority on June 1, 1953. Comptroller Joseph, while supporting the lease, accused the governor and the legislature of using tactics "which violate the fundamental spirit of home rule. Manhattan Borough President Wagner voted against the lease along with City Council President Rudolph Halley because he believed it would result in a fare

Figure 10-2. Major General Hugh J. Casey.

increase: "I would be against a higher fare if I were a plain businessman, employe [*sic*] or taxpayer because it is bad for the city."[51]

The TA Board allocated funding for the rebuilding of the two bridges the Rockaway Beach line used to cross Jamaica Bay. Other budget items reflected the existing system's need for upgrading. Funds were sought for new subway cars, modernized power plants, and lengthened subway platforms.

Casey announced a new capital plan. It was pretty much the same as the BOT's with one major difference: one line that had been part of the Board's plans since 1929 was missing. The Utica Avenue line, too expensive at $63 million ($730 million in 2011 dollars), especially with the emphasis on the Rockaway line, was gone,[52] not to be proposed again until 1968. Contrary to past thinking, the TA felt that the Nostrand Avenue line and its proposed extension would be close enough for many Utica Avenue line riders. Budgeted at $38 million ($441 million in 2011 dollars), it remained a priority.

The TA Board voted to increase the subway and bus fare to fifteen cents in July. Impellitteri protested, saying it was "a hasty action taken without the benefit of mature consideration." Halley, the Liberal Party's candidate for mayor, said it was the "bitter harvest resulting from eight years of incompetence in city government." Bronx Borough President Lyons thought better management and improved economic policy could save the fare. Casey replied that the fare increase was needed to operate the transit system on a self-sustaining basis and undertake deferred maintenance projects.[53] TA workers made changes in station equipment, adjusting turnstiles in the subway system to handle a new form of paying the fare—tokens. (Nickels and dimes were previously used to insert in the turnstiles; tickets were bought and deposited before that.)

The state's role in the operation of the transit system chafed at them much in the same way the Transit Commission did at the Hylan, Walker, and La Guardia administrations. Comptroller Joseph said the fare increase was "another example of state domination over city affairs."[54]

The relationship between City Hall and the TA didn't improve after Borough President Wagner defeated Mayor Impellitteri in the Democratic primary and then became mayor in November 1953. Wagner criticized the TA Board for not putting in enough time on the job, reducing service, and not cooperating with him: "The only means we have of getting information from the TA is through the newspapers."[55]

The TA's 1954 capital plan gave highest priority to completing the Rockaway line project and improving existing lines. Casey told the Board of Estimate that these projects were eating into the money provided by the 1951 bond issue. Additional funding was needed to build the 2nd Avenue line. The TA still wanted to build that line, but gave no indication as to when work would begin, despite hopes for a 1957 start.

The Northeast Bronx still waited for direct subway service to Manhattan. Bingham announced in December 1954 that the opening of the White Plains Road/Dyre Avenue connection was delayed. The new trains hadn't yet been delivered. In any event, he felt that ridership on the Dyre Avenue line "doesn't quite warrant it yet to be anything other than a shuttle."[56]

Council Member Edward Vogel got part of what he wanted on October 30, 1954, when the Smith Street–Culver line connection was put into service. The part of the Culver line that connected with the West End line would operate as a shuttle until May 11, 1975.

The relationship between City Hall and the TA Board changed with the 1954 gubernatorial elections. Governor Dewey didn't run for a fourth term, and he was succeeded by W. Averill Harriman. In his campaign, Harriman had attacked both Dewey and the TA, and his election gave Mayor Wagner the opportunity to seek change. Michael J. Quill and the Transport Workers Union sought the dissolution of the TA, with control returning to a city-appointed administrator. Neither Harriman nor Wagner wanted that, but they were unhappy with the existing system and began to discuss changes. The new TA Board would have three full-time paid members, one appointed by the mayor, one by the governor, and a chairman appointed by the two members. Charles L. Patterson,[57] a veteran railroad executive, was its first chairman.

The connection between the BMT's 60th Street Tunnel and the IND's Queens Boulevard line opened for customer service on December 1, 1955, giving the TA the ability to provide direct service between Queens and Manhattan on both the express and local tracks. The BOT hadn't seen the need for this when the first phase of the IND was built, which was a serious mistake.

The BOT's decision to connect the local tracks only with the Brooklyn–Queens Crosstown line responded to Brooklyn Borough President Guider's thinking that a huge demand for direct service between both boroughs existed.[58] It wasn't a need then; the Board realized that when the full line opened in 1937. We know that because the Board began both to plan for a new river crossing connecting with the Queens Boulevard line and to do more with the Crosstown line. A 6th Avenue line extension from West 53rd Street to Steinway Street and Broadway in Queens, connecting with the local tracks, was proposed in 1938.[59] A new Crosstown line branch was proposed, running from Long Island City to Marathon Parkway in Douglaston via 21st Street, Ditmars Boulevard, Astoria Boulevard, 104th Street, Corona Avenue, and Horace Harding Boulevard.

This was the first in a series of proposals the BOT and the TA made for new crossings between Manhattan and Queens linking with a route paralleling the Queens Boulevard line. In Manhattan, the line would connect with either the 6th Avenue or Broadway lines; the eastern terminal would range from northeastern Queens to the Rockaway Peninsula. The Queens Boulevard–60th Street tunnel connection, about 3,700 feet in length, first proposed in 1940, was a short-term action to be in service while the river tunnel and cross-borough line were built.

The BOT and TA proposed adding a branch line to their proposals for the 2nd Avenue line in the 1950s, running from East 76th Street, connecting with the Rockaway Beach line in Rego Park. Both agencies had realized Queens was developing with a population surge that the Queens Boulevard and Flushing lines couldn't accommodate. Another line was needed.

Patterson talked about what the impact of that new line would be shortly before the Queens Boulevard–60th Street tunnel connection opened: "The authority believes that the new operation can change the pattern of passenger traffic flow in midtown Manhattan and, by substantially altering travel habits by many thousands of riders, can better distribute these passengers over various lines."[60]

On July 29, 1956, Patterson discussed his view of long-range action on the *Viewpoint* program on WRCA-TV.[61] He didn't talk about the 2nd, Utica, or Nostrand Avenue lines, but rather about how the Queens Boulevard line was operating at capacity and how the borough was growing.

The plan that Patterson outlined was for a $2 billion ($20.5 billion in 2011 dollars) trunk line across Queens, possibly integrating it with the LIRR. He didn't discuss the specifics of the route, but did say it would run along the 2nd Avenue line to East 74th Street in Manhattan and under the East River to Queens. It would run north of the Queens Boulevard line to White Pot Junction in Rego Park, the point where the Rockaway

Figure 10-3. Mayor Robert F. Wagner, Jr., and Transit Authority Chairman Charles L. Patterson at a City Hall event. (Photo courtesy of the New York Transit Museum Archives)

Beach line broke away from the LIRR's main line. Patterson spoke of the subway line operating to St. Albans in southeastern Queens and Little Neck in northeastern Queens. He knew this couldn't be done right away. The plan itself would take another year to complete and it would take ten years to put the line into service.[62]

During the broadcast, Patterson was asked about what happened to the $500 million from the bonds that had been authorized for sale in 1951. "If most of that money had not been allocated for rehabilitating the existing systems and modernizing old power plants there would have been a complete breakdown of rapid transit in the city," he answered.[63] A new bond issue would be needed for the plan.

Brooklyn exploded. The Brooklyn Civic Council told the borough's legislators that it was "unthinkable" that the Queens line should be built before work began on the Utica and Nostrand Avenue lines, and called on the legislators to oppose Patterson's proposal.[64] Borough President Cashmore, saying the TA acted like "a prince in Manhattan and a pauper in Brooklyn," vowed he wouldn't support "any transit improvements that did not include Brooklyn." State Senator William Rosenblatt made the same promise on behalf of Brooklyn's state legislators.[65]

Ringing endorsements weren't coming from Queens. "The plan is fine, but it started 10 years too late. We've been fighting for a plan similar to that for 10 years and we should have had it in operation by now," said Queens Transit Committee Chairman Simeon Heller. "And now the TA wants to spend two billion dollars to complete work that should have been done years ago," said Dr. J. Simeon Smith of the Richmond Hill Taxpayers Association. "Let's get it out of 'dreamland' and get working on it now. We in East Queens need rapid transit as fast as we can get it," said Giovanni Nisita of the East Queens Civic Council.[66]

Patterson tried to walk everything back. It was a "misunderstanding"; reactions to his comments were a "tempest in a teapot." There was no specific plan for Queens—certainly nothing beyond what was planned for 2nd Avenue.[67] Patterson also pointed out that new subway lines in Brooklyn were not dead issues, but that putting the existing system into a state of good repair took precedence.[68] Nothing more was done, but the concept Patterson discussed would be brought up again. This was the first step toward lines that would be proposed throughout the 1960s.

The need for the existing system's rehabilitation increased, using up what was left of the 1951 bond issue funds. The only funding for a new line besides the Chrystie Street / DeKalb Avenue project was $500,000 ($4 million in 2011 dollars) for a new engineering study for the Nostrand Avenue line. Cashmore viewed that alone as being "a great victory for Brooklyn."[69]

The connection between the BMT's Fulton Street Elevated and the IND's Fulton Street subway began service on April 29, 1956. The connection to the Rockaway Beach line became operational on June 28, with one branch running to Beach 116th Street–Rockaway Park and the other to Beach 25th Street–Wavecrest. That line was extended to the Far Rockaway–Mott Avenue Terminal on January 16, 1958, completing the IND's first phase. The LIRR continued operating the Rockaway Beach line between Ozone Park and Rego Park until June 8, 1962. It still stands unused.[70] There have been ongoing discussions to revive it, but the residents of the adjoining communities have strongly opposed it until now; more recently, there has also been discussion of converting it to recreational purposes.

Through service finally began on the Dyre Avenue line on May 6, 1957. Unlike the pomp and circumstance of May 15, 1941, the opening event was a quiet affair, officiated by James J. Lyons, in his twenty-third year as borough president.

The TA also looked at what to do with the funding that was still available to them. Patterson said that their aims no longer involved major capital projects, but rather how "the transit system can be improved, congestion reduced at certain point and service improved,"[71] while "maintaining the 15-cent fare for as long as possible."[72]

The Transit Authority was entering the era of "deferred maintenance." Later that year, Budget Director Beame advised Mayor Wagner that the TA wouldn't be able to proceed with its more expensive capital projects even if it wanted to; there wasn't enough money left to pay for them.[73] Patterson agreed, but pointed out that "the sooner we get the things that we have asked for, the less risk of higher prices."[74]

The death knell sounded for another of the line extensions that the BOT proposed. Service ended on the last segment of the 6th and 9th Avenue Els, which ran from 155th Street and 8th Avenue in Manhattan to its connection with the Jerome Avenue line, on August 31, 1958. Extending it to link with the Lenox Avenue line wasn't feasible; as with the 3rd Avenue El, it would have cost too much to rebuild the aging structure. Patterson stated that discontinuation of the service would result in an annual savings of $230,500 ($1.79 million in 2011 dollars).[75]

By 1959, only two new projects were proposed. One was a new version of a Board of Transportation plan from the 1930s and 1940s calling for acquiring the Hudson and Manhattan Railroad's Midtown line and converting it to 6th Avenue line express tracks between the West 4th and 34th Street stations. Rather than doing that, the TA would build two new "deep tunnel" tracks for the same purpose.

The other proposal was new. The TA proposed installing a third track on the Jamaica Avenue line between the 160th Street and Eastern Parkway stations.[76] This was a cheaper way to parallel the Queens Boulevard line.[77] It would provide more service to rapidly expanding communities in southeastern, eastern, and northeastern Queens whose bus lines fed into the Jamaica Avenue and Queens Boulevard lines. No community between Jamaica and East New York may have benefitted. There was little room for new express stations along Jamaica Avenue or Fulton Street without additional construction or land acquisition. Queens Borough President John T. Clancy supported the proposal, but there was little enthusiasm or funding for it. The TA made several more proposals to build the third track before abandoning the idea.

The TA needed to find funding to support their programs while maintaining the system and purchasing new subway cars. Patterson identified three possible ways to pay for this work: raising fares, increasing taxes, or purchasing in installments.

Wagner quickly shot down a fare increase: "It is the purpose of this administration to keep subway fares down. We will fight for this in every possible way."[78] Moreover he opposed using operating funds for any capital projects.

No other sources of funding were identified and Patterson was correct about the costs of the TA getting what they were asking for. Years and decades later, it would cost much more and take more effort to upgrade a system that had been allowed to further deteriorate.

Bronx Borough President Lyons announced he wouldn't seek an eighth term in office on July 12, 1961. He had overheard President John F. Kennedy say in a phone call that he was in line for an important federal post.[79] In 1962 Lyons was appointed to serve as special assistant to the U.S. commissioner to the 1964–65 World's Fair in Queens. After suffering complications from gall bladder surgery, Lyons died on January 7, 1966.

The TA made its most ambitious proposals in a decade in 1962. On July 17 a proposal was released for a new north–south line between the 47–50th Street–Rockefeller Center station on the 6th Avenue line and 138th Street and the Grand Concourse in the Bronx. It would connect with the Pelham and Concourse lines. A new station would be built under the IRT's 138th Street–Grand Concourse station, allowing for transfers to and from the White Plains Road and Jerome Avenue lines. As with the earlier proposals to link the Pelham line with the 2nd Avenue line, the TA would rebuild the platforms and tracks on that line for the bigger IND and BMT cars.

Joseph F. Periconi, a former TA Board member and state senator, had succeeded Lyons as Bronx borough president. His response was straight out of Lyons's playbook: "Too many Bronxites who have cooled their heels at subway platforms know this improved transportation is long overdue."[80] Queens Borough President Clancy, noting his borough's population was almost half a million more than that of the Bronx, complained that the TA "should see fit to give priority to the need of the Bronx over that of Queens."[81]

The focus of the TA's overall plan was on Queens. Patterson brought back the plan that the BOT and TA discussed a decade earlier for the 2nd Avenue line, saying it would be built to allow for a route to branch off at East 76th Street and run to Queens. No terminal point was identified and Patterson said the TA would ask for funding in its 1964–65 capital plan.

That wasn't fast enough for Mayor Wagner, who up until that time had not been a strong advocate for expanding the subway system. He wrote to Patterson on August 11, asking him to speed the planning for the Queens line. Wagner supported the Bronx line, but "I certainly do subscribe without reservation to the high desirability and urgent need of expanding subway services to and within this dynamic borough which would, in my judgment, give sharp, new impetus to Queens' rate of growth and open up new vistas of development."[82]

In February 1963, the TA proposed a variation of the Queens–Manhattan plan Patterson had raised in the 1950s. The route would split from the Bronx line in Central Park and run under East 76th Street and the East River to Queens and along 34th Avenue to Steinway Street, where it would link with the Queens Boulevard line's local tracks and run to Northern Boulevard. A spur line would run along Northern Boulevard, Main Street, Kissena Boulevard, and the Long Island Expressway to Springfield Boulevard.

A second route revived the BOT's plan extending the Fulton Street line into southeastern Queens, running from the Euclid Avenue or Lefferts Boulevard stations to Springfield Boulevard via Linden and Merrick Boulevards.[83] A third component would

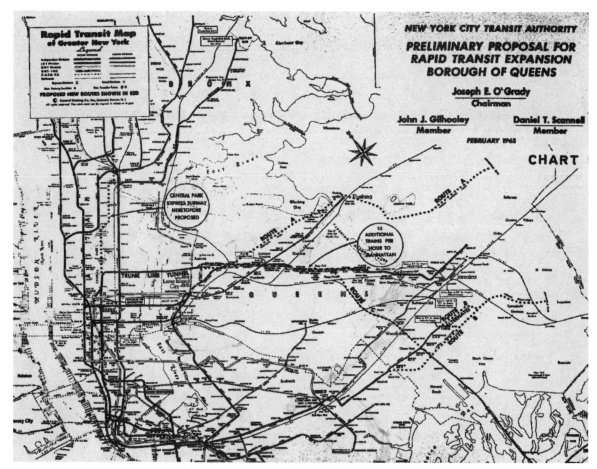

Figure 10-4. A map showing the routes proposed in the 1963 New York City Transit Authority plan.

reactivate the unused part of the Rockaway Beach line and connect the Far Rockaway and Rockaway Beach branches with the Queens Boulevard line in Rego Park.

The City Planning Commission built on the TA's plan with one of their own. Released in early May, its plan proposed a line branching from the BMT's Broadway line at 23rd Street, running up Madison Avenue to East 59th Street, where it would turn east and then split into two lines. One would go into Queens, connecting with the LIRR's Port Washington, Montauk, and Atlantic[84] lines, which would be converted for subway use. The other revived the BOT's 1940s plans extending the 2nd Avenue line into the Bronx, connecting with the Pelham and Concourse lines (this was the last time this was proposed).[85] The LIRR's station at the then-closed Belmont Racetrack would become a regional transit center.[86] It was hoped this was a new start at a regional rail system. The LIRR was also considering a new tunnel under the East River, operating to a terminal on the East Side.[87]

The TA and CPC knew there were no financing for those lines, though on October 6, 1962, the CPC released its proposal for the city's capital budget for the eighteen months

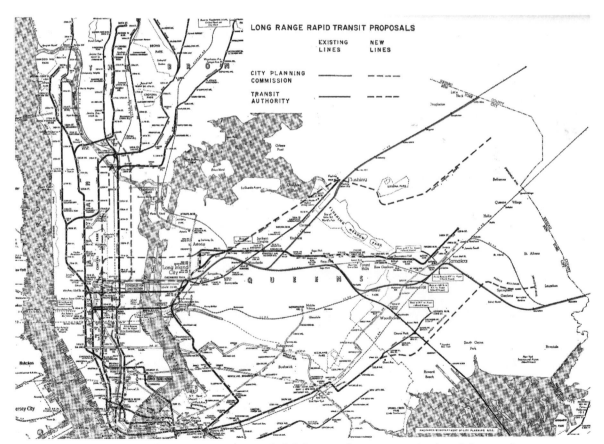

Figure 10-5. The City Planning Commission included this map showing its proposals and those made by the New York City Transit Authority in its 1963 report *Better Rapid Transit for New York City.*

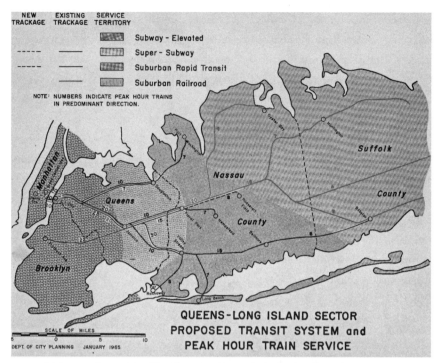

NEW TRACKAGE   EXISTING TRACKAGE   SERVICE TERRITORY

Subway - Elevated
Super - Subway
Suburban Rapid Transit
Suburban Railroad

NOTE: NUMBERS INDICATE PEAK HOUR TRAINS IN PREDOMINANT DIRECTION.

QUEENS-LONG ISLAND SECTOR
PROPOSED TRANSIT SYSTEM and
PEAK HOUR TRAIN SERVICE

SCALE OF MILES

DEPT. OF CITY PLANNING   JANUARY 1965

Figure 10-6. This map showed the City Planning Commission's plan for rail service connecting Manhattan and Brooklyn with Queens, Nassau, and Suffolk Counties.

beginning in January 1963. Although the capital budget was over a billion dollars, there were no funds for subway expansion. Funding was something the Planning Commission would try to address. Discussions with the federal government about sources of funding had begun. In the next year, the Urban Mass Transportation Act would be enacted, but nothing could be done for the time being.

The TA's plan for 76th Street was the last time building an East River tunnel that far north was proposed; its efforts thereafter turned southward. On May 24, 1963, Mayor Wagner met at City Hall with Joseph E. O'Grady (who succeeded Charles Patterson as chairman after Patterson passed away on October 13, 1962), TA Board Members Daniel J. Scannell and John J. Gilhooey, Queens Borough President Mario J. Cariello, and City Planning Commission Chairman Francis J. Bloustein to discuss the transit needs of Queens. Out of that meeting came news that a subway tunnel would be built between Manhattan and Queens, from East 61st Street in Manhattan. O'Grady hoped the CPC could identify funds allowing work to begin that summer.

O'Grady urged the City Planning Commission to provide the $850,000 ($5.05 million in 2011 dollars) necessary to begin work on the tunnel. By October, though, the route of the tunnel had changed. Citing $5 million in cost savings $42.8 million in 2011 dollars), easier grades, and smaller curves, its Board voted on October 17 to shift the tunnel north to East 64th Street. No route in Manhattan or Queens had been identified.

The Rockefeller Institute on York Avenue objected due to concerns about tunneling work and train operation creating vibrations affecting scientific work.[88] Groups including the Citizens Budget Commission, the Fifth Avenue Association, and the Queens Borough Chamber of Commerce opposed the plan, questioning the TA's claims of cost savings. They felt that transfer connections with the Lexington Avenue and 6th Avenue lines wouldn't be possible if the 64th Street line was built instead of a line along 61st Street.

The Board of Estimate and the City Council's Finance Committee held a joint hearing on the 64th Street plan at City Hall on February 23, 1964. O'Grady testified that the farther north the line was built the more the project's cost would drop. The location of the tunnel would shift if seismological tests confirmed the Rockefeller Institute's concerns. O'Grady explained the cost differential between building the tunnel at 61st Street or farther north:

> The $8.8 million [$69.2 million in 2011 dollars] additional cost of the 61st Street route over the 64th Street route is a reflection of engineering difficulties and dangers.
>
> Because of the depth of the river and the location of the underlying rock it becomes easier, less hazardous and less expensive to build the tunnel as we go north from 61st Street.[89]

The seismological tests took place over the following weeks. Led by Fordham University's seismologist, Rev. Joseph J. Lynch, test blasting took place to simulate subway construction. After receiving Rev. Lynch's report bearing out the Institute's concerns, the TA moved the location of the tunnel one block south to 63rd Street.[90]

Dr. Detlev Bronk of the Rockefeller Institute hailed the change. Others were less enthusiastic. City Council Member Robert A. Low said the tunnel was being built "at the wrong time, at the wrong place and at the wrong facilities."[91] The Citizens Budget Commission called the tunnel "leading from nowhere to nowhere,"[92] helping to give the 63rd Street line a nickname—"The Tunnel to Nowhere"—it would have for many years.

The Board of Estimate approved the 63rd Street tunnel on January 14, 1965. O'Grady said that several connecting routes in Manhattan were under consideration, including the existing 6th Avenue and Broadway lines and new routes on 2nd or Madison Avenues. The TA was also evaluating creating connections to the Queens Boulevard line or building new lines. It would take four years to build; the TA would study the possible connections that would be done in 1966. By the time work on the tunnel was complete, O'Grady expected that the connecting lines would also be ready to operate.[93] To reduce costs and save construction time, the TA planned to build the tunnel by a new method, dropping prefabricated sections into a trench dug into the riverbed.[94]

As the 63rd Street tunnel was being approved, the CPC was considering how best to use it. That January, they issued *Queens–Long Island Rail Transit*, a report incorporating elements of Daniel L. Turner's Metropolitan Transit System plan and TA proposals for expanded service to Queens. They proposed linking 63rd Street with the LIRR, creating what they called "Super Subway" service in Queens and suburban rapid transit to Nassau and Suffolk Counties.

The report proposed a new system utilizing 63rd Street, its connecting routes in Manhattan and Queens, and existing LIRR tracks and right-of-way in Brooklyn and Queens and Nassau and Suffolk Counties. New "park and ride" facilities would be built in eastern Queens and Nassau County adjacent to existing or new stations. The CPC proposed instituting zone fares, seeing the fare structure as paying for improved and faster service, in many cases a one-seat ride, as opposed to the existing bus and subway system

The CPC saw this as extending the subway system beyond the center of Queens without construction and equipment costs that stifled previous capital plans: "Extended rapid transit service in outer Queens will require a substantial subsidy from New York City due principally to the high cost of providing new facilities under the East River into Manhattan. But medium-fare super subway service, on existing railroad trackage, would result in a much lower deficit than extending new low-fare subways to the Queens–Nassau line."[95]

This tied in with work by the Special Committee on the Long Island Rail Road, set up in September 1964 by Governor Nelson A. Rockefeller to make recommendations for the LIRR's future. Chaired by the governor's secretary, Dr. William A. Ronan, the committee recommended that the state purchase the LIRR and an authority operate it. They focused on upgrading rather than expanding the existing LIRR. The one new project considered was a new East Side terminal, with Park Avenue South and East 33rd Street a possible location.[96]

This was the beginning of the Metropolitan Commuter Transportation Authority. It would become the Metropolitan Transportation Authority in 1968, with Ronan serving as its first chairperson. The CPC expanded on its plan in November, making similar recommendations for the commuter rail lines operating from Grand Central Terminal.

As his administration began, Mayor John V. Lindsay wanted to readdress the 61st Street plan. After consulting with his Transportation Council, however, Lindsay approved the 63rd Street Tunnel on March 7, 1966. The Council, chaired by Arthur E. Palmer, based its decision on the savings achieved by adopting the plan. They believed there would have been more traffic disruption along the FDR Drive had the tunnel been built under 61st Street.[97]

The TA identified a routing for the 63rd Street line in Manhattan in October 1966. It would connect with the 6th Avenue line at 57th Street, linking with the extension of that line being built north from the 47–50th Street–Rockefeller Center station. A Queens

Figure 10-7. MTA Chairman William J. Ronan and Governor Nelson A. Rockefeller at the press conference announcing the "New Routes" plan. (Photo courtesy of the New York Transit Museum Archives)

routing wasn't proposed, although plans for the tunnel now called for it to be built with two levels, the top for the subway and the second for the LIRR, providing them with the access to the East Side terminal that was discussed in 1963.

More changes were about to be proposed. In a span of about five weeks, two plans harking back to the days of the BOT's old plans were released. The first was prepared for the TA by the engineering firm of Coverdale and Colpitts, followed a few weeks later by the MTA's "New Routes" plan.

Unlike what the CPC's proposals in its report three years earlier, Coverdale and Colpitts and the MTA stayed within the framework of the existing rapid transit and commuter rail systems in their plans. Both proposed capital-intensive projects rather than trying to link the existing rail lines to expand the overall rail network at a lower cost, one of the CPC plan's aims. This may have been a crucial mistake.

Coverdale and Colpitts brought back BOT proposals from the 1940s and 1950s. They revived the 2nd Avenue line and called for connecting 63rd Street with the 2nd Avenue, 6th Avenue, and Broadway lines. Once the 63rd Street line went into Queens, a connection would be made with the Queens Boulevard line's express tracks. Branch lines would have been built from Queens Boulevard, creating a "super express" line from Long Island City to Forest Hills and a branch line along the Long Island Expressway to Bayside, running from the Woodhaven Boulevard–Slattery Plaza station. Another

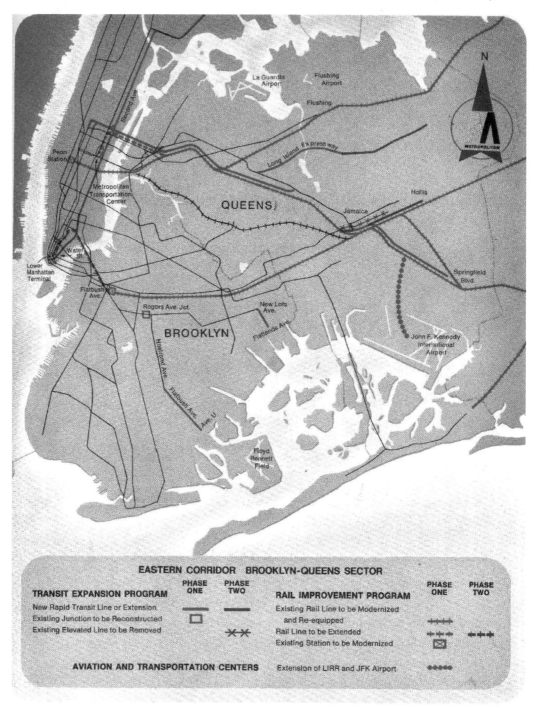

Figure 10-8. An early rendering of the "New Routes" plan as it affected Brooklyn and Queens. It was later revised to drop the extension of the New Lots Avenue line and revive the Utica Avenue line.

branch from Queens Boulevard would use the unused part of the Rockaway Beach line to connect with other LIRR lines, the Montauk and Far Rockaway branches, to reach Springfield Boulevard in Springfield Gardens.

The MTA's "New Routes" plan also revived the 2nd Avenue line and Charles L. Patterson's 1956 Queens–Manhattan Trunk Line. The need for another line across Queens was in the minds of MTA planners. The 63rd Street line's Queens route would go through Long Island City, using the right-of-way of the LIRR's main line to reach Forest Hills, connecting there with the Queens Boulevard line. Using track ramps built for the 1929 plan's Van Wyck Boulevard line, a route would be built to southeastern Queens along Archer Avenue and the right-of-way of the LIRR's Far Rockaway branch. The Archer Avenue line would also have a second level connecting with the Jamaica Avenue line, replacing the service it provided from Richmond Hill to Jamaica and running to 168th Street. Another Queens Boulevard line branch would run from Elmhurst to Bayside along the Long Island Expressway. The 1950s versions of the Nostrand and Utica Avenue lines were again proposed. The LIRR's plans for the East Side terminal were included, as well a plan for a LIRR route to John F. Kennedy International Airport.

The Concourse Extension returned in a shorter form. The MTA proposed building it across Bronx Park to meet the White Plains Road line at the Burke Avenue station and provide more service to the northeastern Bronx by extending the Pelham line to Co-op City.

Due to the 1970s financial crisis, work stopped on the 2nd Avenue, southeastern Queens, and 63rd Street lines. The other "New Routes" lines, which hadn't gone beyond the planning phase, faded away. When funding became available, the Queens lines were truncated. Service on both levels of the Archer Avenue line terminated at the Jamaica Center–Parsons/Archer Station; it began service on December 11, 1988. The 63rd Street line terminated at the 21st Street–Queensbridge Station in Long Island City, with service beginning on October 26, 1989.

The MTA examined the next steps for the 63rd Street line with the Queens Subway Option Study (QSOS). QSOS considered reviving the "super express" line to Forest Hills and two plans to use the LIRR's Montauk line to reach Jamaica. One option would turn the Montauk line into a subway line, connecting with the Jamaica Avenue line in Richmond Hill, with the existing Jamaica Avenue line terminating in Cypress Hills. The other Montauk line option kept it as a LIRR line, with subway riders transferring to the railroad at a new station in Long Island City. This was in tune with what the CPC proposed in *Queens–Long Island Rail Transit*. The Montauk and the "super express" options elicited heavy opposition from the communities the lines would run through. A fourth option, connecting the 63rd Street with the Queens Boulevard line north of the Queens Plaza station, received little opposition.

After the QSOS public hearing, the MTA Board voted for the Queens Boulevard Line Connection on December 14, 1984. Service on that connection began on January 11, 2002.

These were incremental extensions. All the maintenance programs, all the purchases of new subway cars and buses, and all the station improvements that had been postponed for years now had to be addressed. The capital improvement programs pushed during the tenures of Chairmen Richard Ravitch and Robert Kiley that the MTA implemented beginning in the 1980s started to deal with those issues; in fact, the MTA is still playing catch-up. In addition, there are new needs to address. The MTA is faced with the need to make the subway, commuter rail, and surface system accessible to disabled riders, a need no one in government or any transit agency gave any thought to until the 1980s. One hundred subway stations will be retrofit with elevators by 2020.

The concepts that planners like Daniel L. Turner and William Barclay Parsons proposed for the expansion of the transit system have remained a possibility in the minds of transit planners. On March 3, 2008, then-MTA Executive Director and Chief Executive Officer Elliot G. Sander gave the *State of the MTA* report, a series of actions expanding the regional transit system very much in keeping with Turner's Transit Construction Commission and Metropolitan Transit System plans and the CPC's *Queens–Long Island Rail Transit*.

The *State of the MTA* called for the development of a regional rail network, including the Long Island Rail Road, the Metro-North Railroad, New Jersey Transit, and Amtrak. It also discussed studying the feasibility of reviving the dormant parts of the "New Routes" plan and making use of the parts of the Rockaway Beach line that were not incorporated into the subway system in 1956, and using the old New York, New Haven, and Hartford Railroad tracks to provide passenger service to Hunts Point, Parkchester, and Co-op City.

This was before the MTA sustained major financial blows that severely affected its operations. This plan, as have earlier plans for the extension of the subway system, collided headlong with economic realities. The additional tracks across Queens are still waiting to be built, as are the Burke Avenue line, the Utica Avenue line, the Nostrand Avenue line extension, and the Narrows Tunnel. Beyond the current projects that are underway, however, little can be done beyond planning for the day when times are better.

11

One of my colleagues once pondered the question of what happened to all the ambitious plans to expand the subway system. She explained it this way: "Bad transit karma."

Terrible events always seemed to coincide with announcements of expansion plans—the Great Depression and other economic crises, both world wars, and terrorist attacks. Funds or resources that could have been used for capital programs were used to fill other needs or weren't available.

But that only starts to tell the story. The reasons why the New York City subway system hasn't grown beyond its current limits can be found in the policies and decisions of city and state administrations over the last century.

Maintaining the fare was overemphasized, and less priority was given to system maintenance and capital projects. The subway fare remained at five cents from 1904 to 1948. Opposing a fare increase played well with the electorate in campaign after campaign, but it ultimately helped to deny necessary funding to the transit system. Debts were not paid down; projects that would have maintained or expanded the system were put on hold. It had a huge impact on the Transit Authority's ability to undertake new endeavors in the 1950s and continued on from there. The Metropolitan Transportation Authority and MTA New York City Transit are still playing catch-up on capital work as a result of decisions made to defer maintenance decades ago.

After the 1970s, this was called the "Beame Shuffle," named for the budgetary maneuverings that transpired during Mayor Abraham D. Beame's administration. This might have been unfair, since there was little difference between what was being done then and in most mayoral administrations from the time the first subway line was built. More priority was always given to maintaining the fare structure than to expanding or even maintaining the system.

John F. Hylan was one such mayor. Over the years, Hylan became known as the mayor who built the IND. He certainly wanted a municipally owned transit system and advocated for the creation of the agency that supervised its construction, the Board of Transportation. Yet the six and a half years of the Hylan administration prior to the creation of the BOT were marked by a slowdown of the subway system's expansion.

Both before and during his tenure as mayor, Hylan threw up roadblocks to expansion of the system. In his history of the Dual Systems Contract, *Tunneling to the Future*, Peter Derrick pointed out that Hylan wanted to see the subway lines built in thickly populated areas, rather than in "developing farm lands."[1] Those were what William Jay Gaynor referred to as "cornfield lines" while mayor, serving what were then the outer reaches of Queens and Brooklyn, but Gaynor had the vision to understand that the city needed to expand and that the subways would facilitate that.

Mayor Hylan didn't have that foresight. While his 1922 plan to expand the subway system was more ambitious than what was issued by the Transit Commission, it was still aimed at serving the more developed parts of the city. Dr. Derrick noted that neither Hylan nor his successor, James J. Walker, had an organized city planning structure in place;[2] neither apparently wanted one. Hylan actually supported the elimination of the Standing Committee for the City Plan upon taking office. City development was carried out in a haphazard fashion. The City Planning Commission wasn't created until the administration of Fiorello H. La Guardia.

The lack of structure surely affected how planning for the subway system's expansion was conducted during the Hylan and Walker administrations. The first phase of the IND, prepared by the Board of Transportation during the Hylan administration, mostly consisted of lines built adjacent to IRT and BMT lines in areas that were already developed or developing. The one line built to serve a relatively undeveloped area, the Queens Boulevard line, triggered significant residential and commercial development in the communities that adjoined it. The areas that are least developed along Queens Boulevard are those not adjoining a subway line. Construction of what was meant to be the first phase of the Concourse line sparked significant development along the Grand Concourse, but that line closely paralleled the IRT's Jerome Avenue line. The only Concourse line station not near Jerome Avenue is 205th Street.

The IND's second phase, drawn up during the Walker administration, was reactive to political pressure. The proposal for the Lafayette Avenue branch of the 2nd Avenue Trunk Line was a response to election-year demands made of Mayor Walker. It paralleled the Pelham line to such an extent that it was later found to be easier just to consider connecting the 2nd Avenue and Pelham lines. As we saw in the land that changed hands near Burke Avenue and Boston Road in the time leading up to and following the announcement of the plans for the Concourse line extension in 1928, it's possible that insider information was being circulated about where the new subway lines would be built.

The opposition to new elevated lines led Walker to commit to building only underground lines. This promise may have helped him to defeat Fiorello La Guardia in 1929 (it may have affected La Guardia's thinking about elevated lines when he was mayor), but it would have added huge amounts of money to the cost of building subways if the city had the resources to move ahead with the BOT's plans.

It took the length of the Hylan administration and the first three years of James J. Walker's mayoralty to extend the Flushing line thirty-five blocks from 103rd Street to Main Street. Knowledge of Hylan's attitude toward rapid transit companies may have influenced the IRT and the Long Island Rail Road to back out of an agreement that would allow the connection of the subways with the LIRR's Port Washington line, thereby extending subway service into northeastern Queens, a decision that has had huge consequences. It took even longer for the Nassau Street line to be extended from the Chambers Street station to its connection with the Montague Street Tunnel and for the 14th Street–Canarsie line to be completed.

The 14th Street line was delayed because the Public Service Commission had proposed to build it through the Ridgewood and Bushwick communities as an elevated line, which was opposed by the residents of those areas. Hylan supported this view. The type of construction had to be changed. The route was adjusted, but Hylan still resisted proceeding with construction. This was due to the hostility between the mayor and the BRT / BMT (and its supporters), and between Hylan and the Transit Commission.

This wasn't a one-way grudge; the BRT / BMT and its allies gave back as good as they got. They took out advertising criticizing Hylan. BMT President Gerhard Dahl wrote a book, *Transit Truths*, that fired back at the mayor and talked about his company's desire to build more subway lines. Mayor Hylan was also continuously slammed in many of the city's newspapers. The *Brooklyn Daily Eagle* ran a series of "man on the street" interviews conducted in Bushwick, the mayor's home neighborhood, in which in which the interviewees complained about the lack of progress in subway construction.

All of this was because Mayor Hylan did not want the privately operated subway companies to control more than what they already did. When the Board of Estimate finally acted to approve the contract to complete the 14th Street–Canarsie line on October 10, 1924, Hylan commented, "It's the last thing that the B.M.T. will ever get."[3]

Hylan's goal was a single, municipally operated transit system. In his history of the subway system, *722 Miles*, Clifton Hood wrote that Hylan believed that a system operated by the city could be profitable, producing enough revenue to expand the schools, parks, hospitals, and highways. Hood noted, though, that the mayor never seemed to be able to identify the funding sources that would be needed to purchase the existing lines from the IRT and BRT or the logistics of accomplishing the purchase.[4] James J. Walker was equally steadfast in opposing a fare increase.

For Hylan, the fare was one more weapon to use against the IRT and BRT / BMT. He responded to an IRT request to raise the fare to seven cents in 1925 by saying, "They are all at the same old game of trying to increase the fare and exploit the people to the tune of sixty millions a year. If the Interborough cannot run their subways for a five-cent fare, let the Interborough turn them over to the city and we will run them for a five-cent fare. The people's money was used to build the subways and they were turned over to the Interborough and B.M.T. They take all the profit and don't even pay interest on the bonds and still they keep demanding an increased fare."[5]

One mayor who should have grasped the need to take the steps to expand the system but didn't was Fiorello H. La Guardia. His place in New York City's history is deservedly secure. But if he had an Achilles' heel, it was rapid transit. "La Guardia viewed the subways as old and thus uninteresting," Hood noted. "He did not seem to put value on the role that the Els and subways played in stimulating New York's tremendous physical expansion since the 1870s or their potential as a spearhead for further urban development."[6]

La Guardia attended groundbreaking ceremonies for subway line segments and was in the train operator's cab whenever a line opened. But he participated in the start of the demolition of an elevated line with seemingly equal, if not greater, relish. He supported the groups that wanted the immediate razing of the els rather than waiting for the construction of subway lines to replace them, without understanding the consequences of that demolition.

The service provided by the 2nd Avenue and 3rd Avenue elevated lines in Manhattan and the Bronx and the Myrtle Avenue, Lexington Avenue, and 5th Avenue elevated lines in Brooklyn, the connection of the 6th and 9th Avenue elevated lines with the Jerome Avenue line (which could have been kept in service with the construction of a ten-block connection with the Lenox Avenue line, providing service options that subway riders today don't have), and the connection of the 2nd Avenue elevated with the Flushing and Astoria lines were never replaced, at great inconvenience to their riders. If only some of the money and effort that have been put into the maintenance of the surviving elevated lines in modern times had been put into some of the lines that were demolished, some of them could have survived. Those who ride the Lexington Avenue subway can attest to the impact of the loss of the 2nd and 3rd Avenue lines.

Hood made note of Mayor La Guardia's fascination with new technology, represented by airplanes and airports. It was why the mayor was such a strong advocate for the construction of North Beach and Idlewild Airports and why North Beach Airport was renamed in his honor. By extension, it's also easy to see why Robert Moses's projects—highways, parks, swimming pools, and housing developments—fascinated him. These were new things, not extensions of old work.

No matter how closely linked John H. Delaney was to La Guardia, the Board of Transportation's capital project lists were not as attractive to the mayor. He didn't grasp the impact that new or extended subway lines would have had on parts of the city that didn't have subway service. Like Hylan, La Guardia may well have been shocked to see how the construction of the Queens Boulevard line affected the communities it served.

Subways were also old technology to Robert Moses. Many people blame him for the subway system not expanding. He certainly was no friend of public transit, except in the case of the acquisition of the Rockaway Beach line, but his impact on the subway system was more indirect.

Moses had other priorities and goals, and the ability to achieve them. He wanted something to call his own. This is not to give Moses a pass; the money spent on his projects would have been very useful in constructing new lines or better maintain existing ones. But there was never a time when he was directly responsible for taking funding away from a transit project to fund one of his own projects. Highways, parks, airports, and housing developments represented new technology to Moses. He was able to advocate for them and win support in a way that Delaney and his successors at the BOT and TA could not.

Delaney submitted ambitious capital priority lists to the City Planning Commission each year with a caveat that he was aware funding was limited. It was a self-fulfilling prophecy. In effect, the BOT submitted a wish list but did nothing to see that list become reality. Edward Vogel would complain about the ranking of the 10th Avenue line, but he was complaining about a list that was part of a letter to the CPC chairman calling for projects that would not achieve reality—in effect, a wish list. For all of Delaney's knowledge of the political system, for all of the support that he had from Mayor La Guardia, he seemed unwilling to fight to expand the system. Moses knew how to make his programs a reality and he pursued those aims.

That was the difference as the BOT planned for the postwar years. For the most part, the Board's chairmen and the early leaders of the New York City Transit Authority would not fight for their programs. William Reid was willing to speak up but he did not serve long enough to make a difference.

In writing about La Guardia's era, Charles Garrett traced the beginning of the difficulty the IRT and BRT faced with operating profitably with the five-cent fare to the World War I years, when material and labor costs rose. Costs did not decrease after the war ended. The BRT went into bankruptcy in 1918, re-forming as the BMT five years later. The IRT held on for a longer time, but was bankrupt by 1932.

Those companies were locked into the fare structure. Under the terms of the Dual Contracts, they couldn't raise fares without the city government's consent for the length of their lease with the city, which would have expired in 1966, had the system unification not taken place in 1940. But that wouldn't have happened anyway; it was too big an issue for any mayor, alderman, or City Council member.

The effect of the priority given to maintaining the transit system's fare structure cannot be minimized. Even in an era when funding sources were limited, Hylan made maintaining the five-cent fare a key talking point of his administration and campaigns.

In a series of campaign appearances shortly before the 1921 election, Hylan spoke about his views on the fare and the IRT and BRT:

The City of New York has invested a quarter of a billion dollars in creating the finest rapid transit system in the world. It was not a private enterprise in its inception, execution or development. It was an experiment in municipal ownership, conceived by the city, built by the city and paid for by the city. The city owns this rapid transit system, but has leased it to [subway] companies to operate under a guarantee that adequate service will be provided for forty-nine years at a 5-cent fare.

I have opposed an increased fare on the rapid transit lines because the contract between the private operators and the city forbids it and also because our investigation of the companies proves that there is no need or justification for such an increase of fare.

An increase in fares of three cents a passenger would amount to $180,000 daily or $60,000,000 [$754 million in 2011, according to MeasuringWorth.com] yearly. Such an increase would be a hardship to thousands of our citizens already sorely pressed to meet their daily living expenses.

The private owners of the [subway] lines want to juggle the receipts and assets of the city-owned rapid transit system so as to restore and perpetuate their enormous private profits. They never have given the people decent and adequate service as long as they have been in control; but they have squandered millions of dollars in excessive dividends, wasteful bonuses, buying useless charters and bolstering up bankrupt milked-dry transit lines.

I have no desire to dwell upon the sins of the traction rings [subway operators] of the past, but as long as I am Mayor of New York present and future fare-payers, taxpayers, and the honest investing public shall not suffer by a repetition of such misdeeds.[7]

His campaign attempted to place advertising in BRT stations that read, "You ride on this train for 5 cents because Hylan is Mayor." The BRT's advertising contractor, the Home Boroughs Car Advertising Company (whose president was none other than Joseph P. Day), refused to accept the ads, claiming that they were "offensive to good taste"; his campaign manager—John H. Delaney—took the matter to court.[8]

As the chairman of the Board of Transportation, Delaney shied away from a fare increase. Mayors Walker and La Guardia would not take that step and give the Board of Transportation cover. It was not until the administration of William O'Dwyer, who recognized the need to upgrade and expand the subway system, that there was a mayor in office who would support a fare increase and BOT chairpersons (Charles Gross and William Reid) who addressed the subject. It may have been too late by then.

The IND served the city well. Despite John Hylan's ambitions, it was never a financial success. The city needed to appropriate funding to make up the deficit. Garrett wrote that "the city, in effect, undertook to subsidize the five-cent fare; this policy, not only added to the real estate tax load, but served to limit the city's ability to borrow under its debt limit and consequently its construction of new capital projects."[9]

It was hoped that the unification of the subway system, when achieved in July 1940, would lower costs and facilitate the system's expansion. That didn't happen. The start of World War II had the same impact on costs that World War I did. "With the five-cent fare the hope of a balanced budget other than by windfalls and expedients was vain; yet the longer the fare remained fixed the more difficult it was to change it," August Heckscher and Phyllis Robinson wrote in their history of the La Guardia administration, *When La Guardia Was Mayor*. "To this dead end had come the large hopes evoked by municipal ownership of the city's public transportation system."[10]

Heckscher and Robinson noted that Mayor La Guardia was in the same position as everyone else on the matter of the fare. In his 1944 budget message, La Guardia "asserted that there was no individual in any party, and no legislative body, that would take the first step in raising the fare. He proved to be right and he seemed to feel no embarrassment in including himself."[11] La Guardia left office at the end of 1945 without doing much to increase the funding of the transit system, through either instituting fare increases or finding new sources of funding. In his time in office, William O'Dwyer seemed ready to change that mind-set, but other concerns took precedence.

The expansion projects that were "shovel ready," in modern parlance—the remainder of the IND's first phase, the Dyre Avenue line, the Culver line, and other ongoing projects—needed to be completed. The existing system's infrastructure needed upgrading. New subway cars and buses had to be purchased and the Rockaway Beach branch of the LIRR would need to be purchased and integrated into the subway system. Debt service had to be paid and labor costs rose. Instead of paying for new lines, the fare increase that O'Dwyer supported and the funds from the 1951 bond issue, out of necessity, had to address those concerns. Six years later, Charles Patterson would point out how unrealistic the plans for making use of the funds from that bond issue were.

The immediate needs of the transit system grew in the 1950s, while less concern appears to have been given to meeting them. Not until late in Robert F. Wagner's third term in office did it seem that City Hall wanted to play a role in expanding the transit system. Indeed, it appears that once Wagner regained a degree of local control of the system in 1955, he was content to let Charles L. Patterson be the only real advocate for growth. Patterson couldn't do much without substantial support from the mayor's office. The 1951 bond issue funds dwindled away without much thought as to substantial next steps.

John V. Lindsay's administration had the desire to expand the transit system, but it was at a time when control was again being returned to the New York State government with the creation of the Metropolitan Transportation Authority. The MTA's first effort to expand the rail network, the "New Routes" plan, collided with the fiscal realities of the 1970s and the need to repair an existing system that had been starved by years of deferred maintenance. Subsequent mayors and governors were shackled by those realities.

Much of the capital funding expended in the years following the Archer Avenue and 63rd Street lines and a one-stop extension of the Lenox Avenue line have gone to catching up. The existing system needed to be upgraded and modernized. It took almost eight decades for city officials to realize that people with disabilities needed access to subways and buses.

New routes had to sit and wait for a time when the leadership of the New York City and New York State governments and the governing transit agencies had the vision and incentive to move ahead and build. As with the 2nd Avenue subway, it has happened, but only in increments.

Even in a time of lowered economic expectations, what happens to the subway system now that the completion of the 2nd Avenue line's first phase and the No. 7 line's westward extension are within sight?

Three more sections of the 2nd Avenue line are waiting to be built in Manhattan. A further extension of the 7 line, this time to New Jersey, has been under discussion, as is the reactivation of the remainder of the Rockaway Beach line and the Staten Island Railway's North Shore branch. Someone may yet make a new proposal to build the Narrows Tunnel, extend the Concourse line to the Northeast Bronx, or construct the Utica Avenue line. The rapid transit needs of northeastern, eastern, or southeastern Queens may finally be addressed.

Will it happen? If there is a new generation of planners like Daniel Lawrence Turner, Henry M. Brinckerhoff, or William Barclay Parsons who have the vision to see the region as a whole and how the rail network needs to grow to meet its needs, then yes, it could happen. If there are elected officials like John Purroy Mitchel or George A. McAneny who share that vision, and if the voting public is willing to support the attainment of those goals, then it is even more likely. Whether that is the case, however, remains to be seen.

Appendixes

Appendix A: The 1944 Service Plan

On August 9, 1944, Board of Transportation General Superintendent Philip E. Pheifer sent a memorandum titled *Service to Be Operated When the Second Avenue Line Is Constructed*. It recommended the IND/BMT service plan for when that line was operating and the DeKalb Avenue switches were rebuilt.

IND/BMT CONNECTIONS

- Fourteen trains per hour from the Jamaica Avenue line to the Queens Boulevard line, via the Williamsburg Bridge, Chrystie Street, and the 8th Avenue line.
- Ten trains per hour from the Sea Beach line to Washington Heights via the Manhattan Bridge, Chrystie Street, and the 6th and 8th Avenue lines.

BMT/2ND AVENUE LINE CONNECTIONS

- Ten local trains per hour from the West End line to 72nd Street via the Montague Street Tunnel, Nassau Street, Chrystie Street, and 2nd Avenue.
- Eight local trains per hour from the 4th Avenue line to a northern terminal via the Manhattan Bridge, Chrystie Street, and 2nd Avenue.
- Eight local trains per hour from the Brighton Beach line to a northern terminal via the Manhattan Bridge, Chrystie Street, and 2nd Avenue.

2ND AVENUE LINE TRAINS

- Ten express trains per hour from a northern terminal to Chambers Street on the Nassau Street line.
- Ten express trains per hour from a northern terminal to Broad Street on the Nassau Street line.
- Ten express trains per hour from a northern terminal to Bergen Street on the Smith Street line via 2nd Avenue, 57th Street, 6th Avenue, and Houston and Smith Streets.

IND	BMT
D Line (Concourse express)—Bronx to Church Avenue or Coney Island	Ten Sea Beach express trains—Coney Island to Times Square
Concourse local—Bedford Park Boulevard to Hudson Terminal	Twelve West End express trains—Bay Parkway to Times Square
F line—Parsons Boulevard to Hudson Terminal	Ten Brighton Beach express trains—Brighton Beach to Times Square
A line—207th Street to Rockaway Avenue	Ten 4th Avenue local trains—95th Street to Queens Plaza
Brooklyn/Queens Crosstown line—71st Avenue to Smith–9th Street	Twelve Brighton Beach local trains—Coney Island to Queens Plaza
	Eight Myrtle Avenue line trains—Metropolitan Avenue to Broad Street
	Eight Broadway short line trains—Rockaway Parkway to Chambers Street

Appendix B: The 1947 2nd Avenue Service Plan

On December 16, 1947, the Board of Transportation released the following list showing how existing subway lines would change once the 2nd Avenue Trunk Line was built.[1] These lines would use the Chrystie Street connection and other planned links.

From	To	Via
Washington Heights[2]		
207th Street	Lefferts Boulevard	8th Avenue / Fulton Street
168th Street	Jamaica	6th Avenue / Broadway– Brooklyn / Jamaica Avenue
Concourse[3]		
205th Street	Brighton Beach	6th Avenue / Brighton
Bedford Park Boulevard	Hudson Terminal	8th Avenue
Pelham Bay Park[4]		
Pelham Bay Park	Hudson Terminal	2nd Avenue / 57th Street / 6th Avenue
	Coney Island	2nd Avenue / Montague Street Tunnel / West End
	Fort Hamilton	2nd Avenue / Montague Street Tunnel / 4th Avenue
	Grand Street	2nd Avenue
Queens Boulevard[5]		
179th Street	Lefferts Boulevard	8th Avenue / Fulton Street
	Coney Island	6th Avenue / Culver
Forest Hills		Broadway / Brighton
	City Hall	Broadway
	Church Avenue	Brooklyn–Queens Crosstown

(continued)

From	To	Via
Fort Hamilton[6]		
95th Street	57th Street	4th Avenue / Manhattan Bridge / Broadway
	Astoria	4th Avenue / Montague Tunnel / Broadway
	Pelham Bay Park	4th Avenue / 2nd Avenue / Pelham
Sea Beach[7]		
Coney Island	57th Street	Manhattan Bridge / Broadway
	149th Street	Manhattan Bridge / 2nd Avenue
West End[8]		
Coney Island	Pelham Bay Park	2nd Avenue / Montague Street Tunnel
	57th Street	Manhattan Bridge / Broadway
Culver[9]		
Coney Island	179th Street	6th Avenue / Queens Boulevard
Brighton Beach[10]		
Brighton Beach	205th Street	8th Avenue / Concourse
Coney Island	149th Street	Manhattan Bridge / 2nd Avenue
	Forest Hills	Broadway / Queens Boulevard
Canarsie[11]		
Rockaway Parkway	8th Avenue	14th Street–Canarsie
	Chambers Street	14th Street–Canarsie / Broadway–Brooklyn
Fulton Street[12]		
Lefferts Boulevard	207th Street	8th Avenue
	179th Street	8th Avenue / Queens Boulevard
Euclid Avenue	Court Street	Fulton Street

From	To	Via
Jamaica Avenue[13]		
168th Street–Jamaica	168th Street–Manhattan	8th Avenue
	8th Avenue	14th Street–Canarsie
White Plains Road[14]		
East 241st Street	New Lots Avenue	Lexington Avenue
	Flatbush Avenue	Broadway–7th Avenue

Appendix C: The Cast of Characters

Most New York City subway lines have had a range of route designations, using letters and numbers. The IND lines have always had letter designations. The BMT lines were numbered, though they switched over to letters as they were merged with the IND from the 1950s into the 1960s (e.g., the Brighton line was the No. 1 line; since the change-over, the B, D, Q, QB, QJ, and QT lines have operated along its tracks). IRT lines were known by their name only until number designation began to be introduced in the 1940s. Even so, this system did not fully take hold until the 1960s. Line names were the primary form of designation on subway maps until then.

Several lines never had letter or number designations. The 2nd, 6th, and 9th Avenue Els were just known by name; the only part of the 3rd Avenue El that had a number designation was the line segment in the Bronx that survived the demolition in the 1950s, which was known as the No. 8 line. Several letter designations are no longer used, such as the HH, K, RJ, NX, T, TT, and W lines, along with the No. 9; others, such as the P, will probably never be used.

It was for that reason that I avoided using letter and number designations except for the chapter on the Flushing line. However, just to give you an idea of what now runs there, I've prepared the chart below.

Line	Primarily served by in 2013
Archer Avenue line	E, J, Z
Astoria line	N, Q[1]
Brighton Beach line	B, Q
Broadway line	N, Q, R
Broadway–Brooklyn line	J, M, Z
Brooklyn–Queens Crosstown line	G
Chrystie Street line	B, D
Concourse line	B, D
Dyre Avenue line	5
Eastern Parkway line	2, 3, 4, 5

Line	Primarily served by in 2013
8th Avenue line	A, C, E
Far Rockaway line	A
Flushing line	7
42nd Street Shuttle	S
4th Avenue line	D, N, R
14th Street–Canarsie line	L
Franklin Avenue Shuttle	S[2]
Fulton Street line	A, C
Hillside Avenue line	F
Jamaica Avenue line	J, Z
Jerome Avenue line	4
Lexington Avenue line	4, 5, 6
Liberty Avenue line	A
Livonia Avenue line	3
Montague Street line	R
Myrtle Avenue line	M
Nassau Street line	J, Z
Nostrand Avenue line	2, 5
Pelham line	6
Queens Boulevard line	E, F, M, R
Rockaway line[3]	A, S
Rockaway Park line	A, S
Sea Beach line	N
7th Avenue–Broadway line	1, 2, 3
6th Avenue line	B, D, F, M
60th Street line	N, Q, R
63rd Street line	F
Smith Street–Culver line	F, G
Staten Island Railway	No line assigned, although the terminal station is used to designate the routing
West End line	B
White Plains Road line	2, 5

Notes

1. BUILDING (AND NOT BUILDING) NEW YORK CITY'S SUBWAY SYSTEM

1. *New York Times*, March 25, 1900.

2. *New York Times*, May 16, 1902.

3. Later the 1916 Republican candidate for president, U.S. secretary of state, and chief justice of the U.S. Supreme Court.

4. *New York Times*, June 23, 1907.

5. *New York Times*, October 14, 1906.

6. *New York Times*, April 29, 1907.

7. *Brooklyn Daily Eagle*, November 17, 1910.

8. *Brooklyn Daily Eagle*, February 14, 1910.

10. *New York Times*, January 2, 1919.

11. *New York Times*, December 16, 1919.

12. *New York Times*, October 23, 1921.

13. *A Report by the Chief Engineer Submitting for Consideration a Rapid Transit Plan Covering All Boroughs of the City of New York*, July 29, 1920.

14. *New York Times*, September 26, 1920.

15. Ibid.

16. *New York Times*, January 27, 1921.

17. *New York Times*, February 15, 1923.

18. *New York Times*, March 19, 1923.

19. *New York Times*, April 1, 1923.

20. *New York Times*, April 9, 1924.

21. *New York Times*, April 11, 1924

22. Ibid.

23. *Brooklyn Daily Eagle*, October 12, 1930.

24. *Ridgewood Times*, February 20, 1930.

25. Ibid.

26. *New York Times*, September 17, 1929.

27. *Brooklyn Daily Eagle*, February 17, 1930.

28. *The Wave*, February 20, 1930. *The Wave* began publication in 1893. It is one of New York City's oldest newspapers.

29. *New York Times*, December 28, 1933.

30. Wall mosaics at the Queens Boulevard line's 65th Street station refer to service to the Rockaways. MTA New York City Transit uses the third platform at Roosevelt Avenue–Jackson Heights as office and storage space.

31. *New York Times*, December 28, 1933.

32. *Long Island Daily Star*, April 19, 1934.

33. *New York Post*, May 21, 1936.

34. *New York Times*, June 1, 1936.

35. Letter from John H. Delaney to Rexford G. Tugwell, September 13, 1938. From the New York City Municipal Archives.

36. *Brooklyn Eagle*, June 3, 1942.

37. *Brooklyn Eagle*, June 12, 1940.

38. *Bronx Home News*, May 13, 1942.

39. *New York Times*, August 20, 1958.

40. *New York Times*, October 11, 1945.

41. *New York Times*, December 1, 1945.

42. *New York Post*, October 22, 1947.

2. SOUND TO SHORE: THE UNBUILT BROOKLYN–QUEENS CROSSTOWN LINE

1. Brooklyn wouldn't become part of New York City for another twenty years.

2. *Brooklyn Eagle*, May 1, 1878.

3. *Brooklyn Eagle*, June 4, 1878.

4. *Brooklyn Eagle*, June 3, 1878.

5. *Brooklyn Eagle*, December 9, 1889.

6. *Brooklyn Eagle*, August 3, 1886.

7. Trains running on electrical power were a new concept in 1886. Traction power was just being developed at the time.

8. *Brooklyn Eagle*, October 21, 1886.

9. Namesake of a Brooklyn high school.

10. *Brooklyn Eagle*, October 21, 1886.

11. Decades later, the support columns for this elevated line along 3rd Avenue would be used to support the Brooklyn–Queens Expressway.

12. *Brooklyn Eagle*, January 5, 1887.

13. *Brooklyn Eagle*, March 23, 1887.

14. Ibid.

15. *Brooklyn Eagle*, February 21, 1888.

16. One of the people most responsible for the major expansion of the subway system in the twentieth century.

17. *Brooklyn Eagle*, January 10, 1890.

18. *Brooklyn Eagle*, January 17, 1890.

19. *Brooklyn Eagle*, January 25, 1890.

20. *Report of the Board of Rapid Transit Commissioners for the City of New York for the Year Ending December 31, 1903*, 11–12.

21. This segment of the Brighton line is still in operation as the Franklin Avenue Shuttle.

22. The northern extension represented the start of planning for the Astoria line.

23. This line would connect with what would be the IRT in downtown Brooklyn. It would have used lower-level platforms under the Nevins Street station before connecting with the line north of the station. The lower-level outbound platform is still there.

24. In a long and distinguished career, George A. McAneny (1869–1953) served as Manhattan borough president, president of the Board of Aldermen, and New York City comptroller. He also chaired the New York State Transit Commission, the Regional Plan Association, and the 1939–40 New York World's Fair, and was New York City sanitation commissioner.

25. Bedford and Stuyvesant were separate communities in that era.

26. Rev. Cadman (1864–1936) was born in Wellington, Shropshire, England, and worked in coal mines before joining the ministry. He came to the United States and started Manhattan's Metropolitan Methodist Church in 1895. He became pastor of the Central Congregational Church in 1901, serving there until his death in 1936. He wrote a column on religion for the *New York Herald Tribune* and was a pioneer in religious broadcasting, beginning to broadcast his sermons in 1923. He was a vocal opponent of anti-Semitism and racial intolerance, and was renowned for his progressive views. Rev. Cadman was the namesake of the plaza and park in downtown Brooklyn built following the demolition of that area's elevated lines.

27. *Brooklyn Times*, March 23, 1912.

28. In 2009 dollars, $114 million, according to MeasuringWorth.com.

29. *Brooklyn Daily Eagle*, March 23, 1912.

30. *Brooklyn Daily Eagle*, March 26, 1912.

31. *Brooklyn Times*, May 28, 1912.

32. Robert F. Wagner (1877–1953) served in the New York State Assembly from 1904 to 1908 and the State Senate from 1908 to 1918. He was a New York State Supreme Court justice from 1918 to 1926. Elected to the United States Senate in 1926, he served until 1949. Among the bills he sponsored were the National Recovery Act, the National Labor Relations Act, the Social Security Act, and the Public Housing Act. His son was mayor of New York City from 1954 to 1965; his grandson served in the Koch and Giuliani administrations.

33. *Brooklyn Daily Eagle*, May 26, 1912.

34. The team wouldn't officially and only be known as the Dodgers until 1932.

35. *Brooklyn Daily Eagle*, May 28, 1912.

36. *New York Times*, December 31, 1924.

37. *Brooklyn Daily Eagle*, January 14, 1913.

38. *Brooklyn Daily Eagle*, January 18, 1913.

39. *Brooklyn Daily Eagle*, January 19, 1913

40. *Brooklyn Daily Eagle*, January 20, 1913.

41. *Brooklyn Daily Eagle*, January 30, 1913.

42. The legislation remains in place today as part of Section 20 of the New York State Rapid Transit Law. If the Metropolitan Transportation Authority wished to extend the Franklin Avenue Shuttle northward, the law would need to be amended by the New York State Legislature.

43. *Brooklyn Times*, March 5, 1914.

44. *New York Times*, August 22, 1915.

45. *Brooklyn Daily Eagle*, October 8, 1913.

46. *Brooklyn Daily Eagle*, June 30, 1914.

47. *Brooklyn Daily Eagle*, May 16, 1916.

48. The Fulton Street Elevated barely entered Manhattan, crossing the Brooklyn Bridge and making one stop at the BRT's City Hall Terminal.

49. *New York Times*, August 3, 1922.

50. *New York Times*, October 18, 1922.

51. *New York Times*, March 22, 1924.

52. Ibid.

53. *New York Times*, June 1, 1924.

54. *New York Times*, June 6, 1924.

55. *New York Times*, June 13, 1925.

56. Ibid.

57. *New York Times*, July 2, 1925.

58. *Brooklyn Daily Eagle*, February 5, 1926.

59. *Brooklyn Daily Eagle*, April 6, 1927.

60. Ibid.

61. *Brooklyn Standard Union*, July 17, 1927.

62. *Brooklyn Daily Times*, July 28, 1927.

63. Traces of the connection can be seen east and west of the Queensboro Plaza station.

64. *New York Times,* November 26, 1940.

65. *New York Times*, July 22, 1937.

66. A comment that must be a shock to anyone who takes the Q88 bus from Queens Boulevard and Woodhaven Boulevard to reach Flushing Meadows Corona Park.

67. *New York Times*, July 22, 1937.

68. *Long Island Star Journal*, December 16, 1939.

69. *New York Times,* November 26, 1940.

3. WHY THE NO. 7 LINE STOPS IN FLUSHING

1. It was not until 1948 that numbers were used to designate IRT routes.

2. *Documents of the Senate of the State of New York: One Hundred and Thirty-Seventh Session, 1914*, 509–10.

3. The Steinway Tunnels, also known as the Belmont Tunnels (after August Belmont, the chairman of the IRT), were completed in 1907, finishing a project that had begun in 1892. There was no regular service through the tunnels until the Flushing line (then known as the Queensboro Subway) began service in 1915. David Rogoff, "The Steinway Tunnels," *Electric Railroads*, April 1960.

4. It was another three years until LIRR trains operated to Pennsylvania Station in Manhattan. The LIRR ran trains on a branch line to College Point and Whitestone until 1932.

5. In 2011 dollars, $8.15, according to MeasuringWorth.com.

6. *New York Evening Telegram*, October 3, 1907.

7. *Newtown Register*, December 2, 1909.

8. The routing connecting the Astoria line and the BRT's Broadway line hadn't yet been developed. By the time that Mayor Gaynor approved the basic concept on April 9, 1912, a route had been proposed that would run over the Queensboro Bridge and into a tunnel portal in Manhattan. The 60th Street Tunnel wouldn't be proposed until later.

9. Amity Street wouldn't become part of Roosevelt Avenue until that street was extended across the Flushing River in 1927.

10. *Flushing Evening Journal*, December 12, 1912.

11. *Flushing Evening Journal*, December 14, 1912.

12. Wateredge Avenue was a street that no longer exists along the eastern waterfront of the Flushing River.

13. *Flushing Evening Journal*, December 24, 1912.

14. *Flushing Evening Journal*, January 3, 1913.

15. *Flushing Daily Times*, January 4, 1913.

16. Queens, along with the rest of the city, was divided into wards, reflecting the villages that were expanding and meshing into one borough. The First Ward represented Long Island City, Astoria, and the rest of northwest Queens; the Second Ward included Elmhurst, Maspeth, and central Queens; Flushing and the rest of northeast Queens made up the Third Ward; the communities of southern Queens made up the Fourth Ward; and the Rockaway Peninsula constituted the Fifth Ward.

17. *Brooklyn Daily Eagle*, January 14, 1913.

18. *Flushing Evening Journal*, January 6, 1913.

19. Ibid.

20. *Flushing Evening Journal*, January 7, 1913.

21. Both Fitch and Spear needed to say Myrtle Avenue, Brooklyn, to distinguish it from Flushing's Myrtle Avenue, which has long since been renamed 32nd Avenue.

22. *Flushing Evening Journal*, January 8, 1913.

23. *Flushing Evening Journal*, January 10, 1913.

24. Daniel Carter Beard (1850–1941) was one of the people responsible for the founding of the Boy Scouts of America. A middle school and a plaza in the Flushing area are named after him.

25. *Flushing Evening Journal*, January 10, 1913.

26. Ibid.

27. In 2011 dollars, $1.41 million, according to MeasuringWorth.com.

28. *Flushing Evening Journal*, January 14, 1913.

29. The Lexington Avenue line.

30. *Flushing Evening Journal*, January 14, 1913.

31. Ibid.

32. *Flushing Daily Times*, January 16, 1913.

33. *Long Island Daily Star*, January 17, 1913.

34. *Long Island Daily Star*, January 20, 1913.

35. *Flushing Evening Journal*, January 21, 1913.

36. *Flushing Daily Times*, January 23, 1913.

37. The Stewart Railroad's right of way was eventually used to build the Kissena Corridor Park and parts of other parks in Queens. It is also found in the backyards of properties in the Bellerose and Floral Park communities.

38. *Flushing Daily Times*, January 28, 1913.

39. Ibid.

40. *Flushing Daily Times*, January 29, 1913.

41. *Flushing Daily Times*, January 29, 1913.

42. *Flushing Daily Times*, January 31, 1913.

43. Ibid.

44. Ibid.

45. *Flushing Evening Journal*, February 1, 1913.

46. Ibid.

47. Ibid.

48. *Flushing Daily Times*, February 10, 1913.

49. According to the *Flushing Evening Journal*, Treadwell was rumored to have been in the employ of the LIRR.

50. In 2011 dollars, $4.45 million, according to MeasuringWorth.com.

51. *Flushing Evening Journal*, February 13, 1913.

52. Ibid.

53. *Flushing Evening Journal*, February 25, 1913.

54. *Long Island Daily Star*, March 6, 1913.

55. *Flushing Evening Journal*, March 18, 1913.

56. *Flushing Evening Journal*, March 13, 1913.

57. *Long Island Daily Star*, March 14, 1913.

58. *Brooklyn Daily Times*, March 20, 1913.

59. *New York Times*, April 6, 1913.

60. Ibid.

61. *Flushing Evening Journal*, April 3, 1913.

62. Ibid.

63. Ibid.

64. *Flushing Evening Journal*, April 5, 1913.

65. *Flushing Evening Journal*, April 8, 1913.

66. *Flushing Evening Journal*, April 5, 1913.

67. *Flushing Evening Journal*, May 15, 1913.

68. *Long Island Daily Star*, May 28, 1913.

69. *Brooklyn Eagle*, May 27, 1913.

70. *Flushing Evening Journal*, June 5, 1913.

71. Mitchel was thirty-four years old when he took office, acquiring the nickname "The Boy Mayor."

72. *New York Evening Post*, November 8, 1913.

73. Ibid.

74. The ferry ran to the Bronx. The ferry landing in the Bronx is located on the site of today's Ferry Point Park. The ferry line ceased operation with the opening of the Bronx–Whitestone Bridge.

75. *Flushing Evening Journal*, February 23, 1915.

76. *Flushing Evening Journal*, February 27, 1915.

77. *Flushing Evening Journal*, March 1, 1915.

78. *Brooklyn Daily Eagle*, March 6, 1915.

79. *Brooklyn Daily Eagle*, March 11, 1915.

80. *Flushing Evening Journal*, March 13, 1915.

81. At various times in the twentieth century, there were at least six other Myrtle Avenues in Queens besides the one that we know today.

82. *Flushing Evening Journal*, March 24, 1915.

83. *Flushing Evening Journal*, March 25, 1915.

84. Ibid.

85. *Flushing Evening Journal*, March 30, 1915.

86. *Brooklyn Daily Eagle*, March 26, 1915

87. *New York American*, April 4, 1915.

88. *New York Times*, April 2, 1915.

89. *Flushing Evening Journal*, July 17, 1915.

90. *Flushing Evening Journal*, July 19, 1915.

91. *Brooklyn Daily Eagle*, August 15, 1915.

92. *New York Times*, January 6, 1916.

93. *Brooklyn Daily Eagle*, March 29, 1916.

94. Ibid.

95. State of New York Public Service Commission for the First District, *Proposed Extension of the Corona Line Operations over Long Island Rail Road Tracks to Whitestone and Little Neck: Report of the Chief Engineer*, January 18, 1916, 6–7.

96. Bridge Street was another name for what is now Northern Boulevard.

97. *Brooklyn Daily Eagle*, May 17, 1916.

98. *Brooklyn Daily Eagle*, May 18, 1916.

99. *Brooklyn Daily Eagle*, May 20, 1916.

100. IRT trains from the Steinway Tunnels used the track network at Queensboro Plaza to run to Astoria; BRT / BMT trains used those connections to run to Willets Point. The crossover service ended in 1949 and the two northern platforms and tracks were removed later. IRT signs could be found on the Astoria line into the 1980s.

101. Not to be confused with James J. Walker, the future mayor of New York City.

102. *Flushing Evening Journal*, February 2, 1917.

103. *Brooklyn Daily Eagle*, March 15, 1917.

104. *Brooklyn Daily Eagle*, September 14, 1917.

105. *Brooklyn Daily Eagle*, October 16, 1917.

106. *Flushing Evening Journal*, October 31, 1917.

107. *Flushing Evening Journal*, November 15, 1913.

108. Ibid.

109. Ibid.

110. Ibid.

111. Mitchel then enlisted in the United States Flying Service, the precursor to the Air Force, and died in a training accident. Mitchel Field on Long Island is named for him, and there is a large memorial to him by Central Park's East 90th Street entrance.

112. *Flushing Evening Journal*, November 15, 1913.

113. *Brooklyn Daily Eagle*, November 25, 1917

114. Ibid.

115. *New York Sun*, December 2, 1917.

116. *Brooklyn Daily Eagle*, June 3, 1920.

117. *Brooklyn Daily Eagle*, June 1, 1921.

118. *New York Times*, June 12, 1921.

119. *New York Times*, April 22, 1923.

120. Now the Mets–Willets Point station, slightly to the west of the original station. The station had been moved westward to facilitate access with the 1939–40 World's Fair.

121. *New York Times*, March 14, 1927.

122. *New York Times*, March 30, 1927.

123. Ibid.

124. *Brooklyn Daily Eagle*, January 22, 1928.

125. *New York Times*, January 24, 1928.

126. *Report by the Board of Transportation on the Proposal of the Long Island Rail Road Company to Transfer the Whitestone Branch to the City of New York*, June 1928.

127. See Chapter 11.

4. THE BATTLE OF THE NORTHEAST BRONX, PART 1

1. *Bronx Home News*, September 23, 1919.

2. *New York Times*, June 30, 1912.

3. *New York Times*, December 21, 1913.

4. *Time*, April 24, 1944.

5. *Bronx Home News*, June 22, 1922.

6. See Chapter 9.

7. *Bronxboro*, December 1924.

8. *New York Times*, February 22, 1925.

9. Richard Planz, *A History of Housing in New York City* (New York: Columbia University Press, 1990), 151–53.

10. *Bronx Home News*, May 14, 1927.

11. *Bronx Home News*, September 24, 1927.

12. *Bronx Home News*, December 18, 1927.

13. The namesake of the expressway.

14. *Bronx Home News*, December 21, 1927.

15. The namesake of the Boulevard and Expressway.

16. *Bronx Home News*, January 1, 1928.

17. Ibid.

18. Ibid.

19. *Bronx Home News*, January 15, 1928.

20. *Bronx Home News*, January 22, 1928.

21. *Bronx Home News*, January 27, 1928.

22. *Bronx Home News*, February 1, 1928.

23. Ibid.

24. *Bronx Home News*, February 5, 1928.

25. Ehrhart would become the Bronx's consulting engineer and, later, a member of the City Planning Commission. He played a major role in Bronx transit planning a decade later.

26. *Bronx Home News*, February 17, 1928.

27. *Transcript of the Hearing in Reference to the Concourse Line and Direct Line Downtown*, New York Board of Transportation, February 21, 1928. Transcribed by Philip Rodman, p. 13. From the Bronx County Historical Society Archives.

28. Ibid.

29. Ibid.

30. Ibid., 14.

31. Ibid., 35.

32. *Bronx Home News*, March 6, 1928.

33. *Bronx Home News*, March 28, 1928.

34. Ibid.

35. Ibid.

36. Ibid.

37. Ibid.

38. Letter to Frederick A. Wurzbach from William Jerome Daly, August 30, 1929. From the Bronx County Historical Society Archives.

39. *Bronx Home News*, September 2, 1928.

40. Ibid.

41. The brother of Sherman Billingsley of Stork Club fame.

42. Deegan, a friend of Mayor Walker, resigned after the Chamber criticized Walker, who named Deegan tenement house commissioner, a position he served in until his death in 1932 from complications after an appendectomy.

43. *Bronx Home News*, March 29, 1929.

44. Ibid.

45. *New York Times*, January 14, 1928.

46. *Bronx Home News*, March 29, 1929.

47. *Bronx Home News*, April 5, 1929.

48. Ibid.

49. *Bronx Home News*, April 6, 1929.

50. *New York Times*, April 6, 1929.

51. *Bronx Home News*, May 4, 1929.

52. Ibid.

53. *Bronx Home News*, June 9, 1929.

54. *New York Times*, July 14, 1929.

55. This was the original terminal point for the White Plains Road line, becoming a spur when that line was extended to 241st Street. This station closed in 1952, and the spur was demolished.

56. *Bronx Home News*, September 3, 1929.

57. *Bronx Home News*, September 16, 1929.

58. *Bronx Home News*, September 17, 1929.

59. Ibid.

60. *New York Times*, September 22, 1929.

61. *New York Times*, September 22, 1929.

62. *Bronx Home News*, September 18, 1929.

63. *Bronx Home News*, October 2, 1929.

64. *Bronx Home News*, October 3, 1929.

65. The namesake of the expressway in the Bronx.

66. *Bronx Home News*, October 4, 1929.

67. *Bronx Home News*, October 20, 1929.

68. *New York Times*, November 3, 1929.

69. In 2011 dollars, $65,700, according to MeasuringWorth.com.

70. In 2011 dollars, $680 million, according to MeasuringWorth.com.

71. *Bronx Home News*, February 9, 1930.

72. Ibid.

73. Ibid.

74. *Bronx Home News*, February 11, 1930.

75. *Bronx Home News*, February 18, 1930.

76. *Bronx Home News*, February 20, 1930.

77. *New York Times*, March 2, 1930.

78. *Bronx Home News*, March 1, 1930.

79. Ibid.

80. *Bronx Home News*, September 29, 1930.

81. *Bronx Home News*, June 5, 1930.

82. *Bronx Home News*, June 12, 1930.

83. Ibid.

84. *Bronx Home News*, June 13, 1930.

85. *Bronx Home News*, November 17, 1930.

86. See Appendix B.

87. Another uncle, Isidore Straus, and his wife were among the victims when the RMS *Titanic* stuck an iceberg and sank in 1912.

88. *New York Times*, September 14, 1961.

89. *New York Times*, December 21, 1951.

90. From an unpublished memoir of Nathan Straus, Jr., pp. 46–47. Courtesy of the Straus Historical Society Inc.

91. Clarence S. Stein, "New Towns for New Age Needs," *New York Times*, October 8, 1933.

92. *New York Times*, November 5, 1932.

93. Straus, p. 50.

94. *New York Times*, November 15, 1932.

95. *Bronx Home News*, October 25, 1932.

96. *Bronx Home News*, July 1, 1933.

97. *New York Times Magazine*, March 24, 1940.

98. Mand went on to a new career with the New York Fire Department, rising to the position of First Deputy Commissioner. He died of a heart attack at a fire on Ogden Avenue. The Fire Academy's library is named for him.

99. *Bronx Home News*, October 17, 1934.

100. Letter from James J. Lyons to the Board of Estimate, May 19, 1934. From *Proceedings of the Board of Transportation for 1934*, 670–71.

101. *Bronx Home News*, January 9, 1935.

102. *Bronx Home News*, January 19, 1935.

103. *Bronx Home News*, February 13, 1935.

104. Ibid.

105. Ibid.

106. *Bronx Home News*, May 22, 1935.

107. Ibid.

108. Richard Plunz, "Reading Bronx Housing, 1890–1940," in *Building a Borough: Architecture and Planning in the Bronx, 1890–1940* (New York: Bronx Museum of the Arts, 1986), 53.

109. Ibid.

110. In 2011 dollars, $315 million, according to MeasuringWorth.com.

111. In 2011 dollars, $189 million, according to MeasuringWorth.com.

112. *Bronx Home News*, March 10, 1937.

113. *Bronx Home News*, April 7, 1937.

114. *Communication from the Board of Transportation Transmitting Resolution Adopting Route and General Route for a Rapid Transit Railway in the Borough of the Bronx*, May 25, 1937.

115. *Bronx Home News*, June 12, 1937.

116. *Bronx Home News*, June 13, 1937.

117. *Bronx Home News*, June 19, 1937.

118. Ibid.

119. *Bronx Home News*, June 19, 1937.

120. Ibid.

121. Ibid.

122. Ibid.

123. Ibid.

124. *Bronx Home News*, June 21, 1937.

125. Ibid.

126. *Bronx Home News*, June 27, 1937.

127. Ibid.

128. *Bronx Home News*, June 29, 1937.

129. Ibid.

130. *Bronx Home News*, July 9, 1937.

131. Breinlinger's was located on Boston Road by Dyre Avenue. A tavern had been on this site since colonial days. Marquis de Lafayette visited there in 1824. In the early 1900s, Henry Dickert purchased the property, calling it Dickert's Old Point Comfort Park. He expanded it to a four-acre property, including dance and banquet facilities and children's play areas. Kilian Breinlinger purchased it in 1926; his family maintained it until 1957. The structure was demolished in 1960. Bill Twomey, *The Bronx* (Bloomington, Ind.: Rooftop Publishing, 2007), 30–31.

132. *Bronx Home News*, July 10, 1937.

133. Ibid.

134. Ibid.

135. Ibid.

136. Letter from Robert Moses to Judge Edwin L. Garvin, October 5, 1937. From the Robert Moses Archive, New York Public Library, Box 97.

137. Letter from John H. Delaney to Mayor Fiorello La Guardia, December 8, 1937. From the New York City Archives.

138. *Bronx Home News*, December 10, 1937.

139. *New York Times*, June 2, 1929.

140. *Bronx Home News*, December 16, 1937.

141. Ibid.

142. *New York Times*, December 16, 1937.

143. *Bronx Home News*, December 18, 1937.

5. BUY LAND NOW, RIDE THE SUBWAY LATER

1. *New York Times*, July 15, 1928.

2. Clifford B. Harmon handled Wood, Harmon's suburban investments around New York, purchasing land in Westchester County. One piece of land, near the town of Croton-on-Hudson, was sold to the New York Central Railroad for development as a railroad yard. One condition of the deal was that the Harmon name would be associated with the facility. It became the MTA Metro-North Commuter Railroad's main storage and maintenance facility, the Croton–Harmon Yards.

3. *New York Tribune*, March 22, 1899.

4. *Brooklyn Daily Eagle*, May 13, 1900.

5. *Brooklyn Daily Eagle*, September 7, 1913.

6. *Brooklyn Daily Eagle*, June 1, 1910.

7. *Brooklyn Daily Eagle*, July 15, 1910.

8. *Brooklyn Daily Standard Union*, June 17, 1910.

9. A concept later put into practice in the New York City subway system along the Flushing line's Queens Boulevard viaduct, among other locations.

10. *Brooklyn Daily Eagle*, June 17, 1910.

11. Ibid.

12. *Brooklyn Daily Times*, June 24, 1910.

13. *Brooklyn Daily Eagle*, July 14, 1910.

14. There have been about as many proposals to extend the Nostrand Avenue line to Sheepshead Bay as there have been proposals for the Utica Avenue line.

15. *Brooklyn Daily Eagle*, September 30, 1910.

16. *Brooklyn Daily Standard Union*, May 28, 1913.

17. *Brooklyn Daily Eagle*, May 16, 1913.

18. *Brooklyn Daily Eagle*, June 13, 1913.

19. *Brooklyn Daily Eagle*, June 25, 1913.

20. *Brooklyn Daily Eagle*, July 23, 1913.

21. *Brooklyn Daily Eagle*, July 23, 1913.

22. On September 1, the *New York Times* reported that stations would be built at Utica Avenue's intersections with East New York and Remsen Avenues, Winthrop Street, Church Avenue, Avenues D, H, K and N, and Flatlands, Fillmore, and Flatbush Avenues.

23. *Brooklyn Daily Eagle*, October 27, 1915.

24. *Brooklyn Daily Eagle*, January 14, 1916.

25. *New York Sun*, April 28, 1910.

26. See Chapter 9.

27. *New York Times*, February 20, 1910.

28. *Brooklyn Daily Eagle*, September 2, 1916.

29. *New York Times*, June 26, 1918.

30. *New York Times*, May 31, 1925.

31. *Brooklyn Daily Eagle*, June 19, 1924.

32. *Brooklyn Daily Eagle*, February 18, 1926.

33. *New York Times*, July 21, 1927.

34. *Brooklyn Daily Eagle*, January 13, 1928.

35. *Brooklyn Daily Eagle*, April 7, 1929.

36. See Chapter 1.

37. *Brooklyn Daily Eagle*, October 22, 1929.

38. *Brooklyn Daily Eagle*, September 16, 1929.

39. *Brooklyn Daily Eagle*, February 14, 1930.

40. Ibid.

41. See Chapter 10.

42. Traces of the South Beach line remain; more of the North Shore line's infrastructure still exists.

43. *New York Times*, May 8, 1910.

44. Namesake of the hospital on Roosevelt Island.

45. *Brooklyn Daily Eagle*, May 25, 1900.

46. For most of its history, Staten Island was known as the borough of Richmond. It wasn't officially known as the borough of Staten Island until 1975.

47. *Brooklyn Daily Eagle*, May 11, 1900.

48. *Brooklyn Daily Eagle*, September 25, 1902.

49. Staten Island Chamber of Commerce, *Tunnel to Staten Island, Arguments Before the Public Service Commission*, June 1908.

50. *Brooklyn Daily Eagle*, December 19, 1905.

51. *Brooklyn Daily Eagle*, January 18, 1911.

52. *Brooklyn Daily Eagle*, March 17, 1916.

53. *Brooklyn Daily Eagle*, March 18, 1916.

54. *New York Times*, March 23, 1919.

55. *Brooklyn Daily Eagle*, April 24, 1919.

56. *Brooklyn Daily Eagle*, June 11, 1919.

57. *Brooklyn Daily Eagle*, October 3, 1919.

58. *Report of the Transit Construction Commission to the Board of Estimate and Apportionment*, May 11, 1920, p. 6.

59. Ibid.

60. Ibid., 8.

61. *Brooklyn Daily Eagle*, January 23, 1921.

62. *Brooklyn Daily Eagle*, September 3, 1921.

63. *Brooklyn Daily Eagle*, December 21, 1921.

64. *New York Times*, December 22, 1921.

65. *Brooklyn Daily Eagle*, January 1, 1922.

66. Jameson W. Doig, *Empire on the Hudson: Entrepreneurial Vision and Political Power at the Port of New York Authority* (New York: Columbia University Press, 2001), 81.

67. *Brooklyn Daily Eagle*, January 13, 1922.

68. *Brooklyn Daily Eagle*, May 22, 1922.

69. *Brooklyn Daily Standard Union*, April 15, 1923.

70. *Brooklyn Daily Eagle*, September 14, 1923.

71. *New York Evening Post*, July 12, 1924.

72. *New York Times*, December 4, 1924.

73. *New York Times*, February 9, 1925.

74. Ibid.

75. *New York Times*, February 10, 1925.

76. *New York Times*, April 24, 1925.

77. *Brooklyn Daily Eagle*, April 21, 1925.

78. Namesake of the bridge connecting Staten Island and New Jersey.

79. *Brooklyn Daily Eagle*, April 24, 1925.

80. Letter from John H. Delaney to the members of the Board of Estimate, September 8, 1931. From the New York City Municipal Archives.

81. *New York Times*, April 26, 1925.

82. *New York Herald Tribune*, May 6, 1925.

83. Norman Hapgood and Henry Moskowitz, *Up from the City Streets: Alfred E. Smith* (New York: Harcourt, Brace and Company, 1927), 147.

84. *New York Times*, December 1, 1925.

85. *Brooklyn Daily Eagle*, March 28, 1926.

86. *Brooklyn Daily Eagle*, October 21, 1926.

87. *Brooklyn Daily Eagle*, September 30, 1926.

88. Ibid.

89. *Brooklyn Daily Eagle*, July 29, 1928.

90. *Jersey Journal*, January 7, 1930.

91. *Brooklyn Daily Eagle*, January 7, 1930.

92. *Brooklyn Daily Eagle*, April 9, 1931.

93. *Metropolitan Transportation: A Plan for Action*, February 1968, 40.

94. *New York Times*, July 19, 1928.

95. *Brooklyn Daily Eagle*, January 28, 1931. Marie Campbell Good, *always* known in print as Mrs. William H. Good, was renowned for her interest in progressive causes and charitable activities. Her home and land on St. Mark's Avenue in Brooklyn was donated to the city and became one of the Brooklyn Children's Museum's buildings. Her father, Felix Campbell, had been a congressman and a member of the Brooklyn Board of Rapid Transit Commissioners in the nineteenth century, and was one of the original advocates of bringing rapid transit to Brooklyn.

6. ASHLAND PLACE AND THE MYSTERIES OF 76TH STREET

1. *New York Sun*, December 30, 1916.

2. *Brooklyn Daily Eagle*, December 2, 1917.

3. *New York Sun*, March 15, 1919.

4. *Brooklyn Daily Eagle*, May 29, 1919.

5. *New York Times*, July 27, 1919.

6. *New York Times*, July 4, 1920.

7. See Chapter 2.

8. *New York Times*, April 1, 1927.

9. The connection with the BMT's Culver line wouldn't be open for service until 1954.

10. Letter from John H. Delaney to Fiorello H. La Guardia, January 8, 1934. From the New York City Municipal Archives.

11. Ibid.

12. *Brooklyn Eagle*, May 14, 1935.

13. *Brooklyn Eagle*, April 8, 1936.

14. Letter from John H. Delaney to the Board of Estimate, June 15, 1937. From the New York City Municipal Archives.

15. *New York Times*, June 1, 1940.

16. Ibid.

17. *Brooklyn Eagle*, June 1, 1940.

18. Merrick Boulevard has always been the main trunk route for the surface transit system in southeastern Queens. This was the only time it had been considered part of the route for a subway line by a public transit agency.

19. New York City Transit Authority, *Preliminary Proposal for Rapid Transit: Borough of Queens*, February 1963.

20. A Hagstrom's subway map from 1939–40 shows the proposed line being built out to Cross Bay Boulevard, with stations in Queens at 75th and 85th Streets and Cross Bay Boulevard.

21. The *Eagle* ceased publication in 1955 (ironically, since that was the year of Brooklyn's greatest moment, as any baseball fan will tell you); the *Star-Journal* ceased publication in 1968; the *Press* ceased publication in 1977. Their demise (along with the end of other papers such as the *Bronx Home News*) left a void in news coverage in New York City that has never been filled.

22. The underground portion of this connection still exists.

23. *Brooklyn Eagle*, September 19, 1945.

7. TO THE CITY LIMITS AND BEYOND

1. Metro-North is the latter-day incarnation of the New York Central and New York, New Haven, and Hartford Railroads, and parts of the Erie Lackawanna Railway.

2. *Brooklyn Daily Eagle*, December 4, 1910.

3. Father of the novelist.

4. William Gibbs McAdoo, *Crowded Years: The Reminiscences of William G. McAdoo* (Boston: Houghton Mifflin, 1931), 71.

5. *The Public Be Pleased: William G. McAdoo and the Hudson Tubes*, Electric Railroad Association Newsletter, June 1964.

6. *Brooklyn Daily Eagle*, February 26, 1908.

7. *New York Times*, November 19, 1910.

8. *Brooklyn Daily Eagle*, November 19, 1910.

9. *Brooklyn Daily Eagle*, November 25, 1910.

10. *Brooklyn Daily* Eagle, November 26, 1910.

11. Ibid.

12. *Brooklyn Daily Eagle*, December 13, 1910.

13. *New York Times*, December 4, 1910.

14. *Brooklyn Daily Eagle*, December 15, 1910.

15. *The Subway Problem: An Address Delivered at the Sixth Annual Dinner under the Auspices of the Board of Trustees of Plymouth Church Brooklyn . . . January 19, 1911*, 22.

16. *New York Times*, February 29, 1920.

17. While in the cabinet, he would also marry one of President Wilson's daughters.

18. McAdoo and New York Governor Alfred E. Smith were the two presidential candidates who battled for ballot after ballot at the 1924 Democratic National Convention before a third candidate, James W. Davis, won the nomination on the 103rd ballot. In 1932, McAdoo gained a measure of revenge on Smith when he provided the votes Franklin Delano Roosevelt needed to break a deadlock and win the nomination.

19. *Rapid Transit Parkway Line for Queens Borough*, New York State Transit Commission, 1923, p. 8.

20. See Chapter 4.

21. *New York Times*, September 30, 1923.

22. *Rapid Transit Parkway Line for Queens Borough*, 14.

23. *Electric Railway Journal* 56, no. 22 (November 27, 1920). Reprinted by the New York City Subway Resources website, http://www.nycsubway.org/.

24. *New York Times*, November 18, 1920.

25. *New York Times*, May 25, 1922.

26. *Brooklyn Daily Eagle*, April 27, 1924.

27. Ibid.

28. *Second Ad Interim Report of the Westchester County Transit Commission to the Board of Supervisors of Westchester County*, December 1925, p. 16.

29. *New York Evening Post*, July 11, 1925.

30. North Jersey Transit Commission, *North Jersey Transit Problem*, January 15, 1926, pp. 22–23.

31. Ibid., 29.

32. *New York Times*, June 5, 1924.

33. *New York Times*, January 10, 1927.

34. *New York Times*, January 13, 1927.

35. *Brooklyn Daily Eagle*, March 7, 1926.

36. *Brooklyn Daily Eagle*, July 17, 1925.

37. *New York Times*, December 16, 1925.

38. *New York Times*, February 5, 1926.

39. *New York Times*, April 27, 1926.

40. *New York Times*, May 3, 1926.

41. *New York Times*, January 27, 1927.

42. *New York Times*, June 11, 1928.

43. *New York Times*, January 25, 1928.

44. See Chapter 5.

45. *Jersey Journal*, February 1, 1928.

46. *Jersey Journal*, February 6, 1928.

47. Port of New York Authority, *Tentative Report of Bridge Engineer of Hudson River Bridge at New York Between Fort Washington and Fort Lee*, February 25, 1926, pp. 13, 15.

48. *Brooklyn Daily Eagle*, May 29, 1929.

49. *New York Times*, May 7, 1928.

50. *New York Times*, April 5, 1930.

51. *New York Times*, May 16, 1930.

52. *New York Times*, March 7, 1937.

53. *New York Times*, March 10, 1931.

54. *New York Times*, March 5, 1932.

55. *New York Times*, March 1, 1937.

56. *New York Times*, June 17, 1938.

57. *New York Times*, May 23, 1957.

58. *New York Times*, January 28, 1961.

8. THE BATTLE OF THE NORTHEAST BRONX, PART 2

1. *Bronx Home News*, January 13, 1938.

2. *Bronx Home News*, February 6, 1938.

3. *New York Times*, February 7, 1938.

4. Ibid.

5. *New York Times*, February 20, 1938.

6. *Bronx Home News*, February 12, 1938.

7. *New York Times*, February 12, 1938.

8. *New York Times*, February 20, 1938.

9. *Bronx Home News*, March 1, 1938.

10. Ibid.

11. *New York Times*, April 16, 1938.

12. Ibid.

13. Letter from New York State Senator Pliny W. Williamson to Governor Herbert H. Lehman, July 9, 1938. From *The Public Papers of Governor Herbert H. Lehman* (Albany, N.Y.: Williams Press, 1942).

14. Letter from Governor Herbert H. Lehman to New York State Senator Pliny H. Williamson, July 19, 1938. From ibid.

15. Letter from Robert Moses to Judge Edwin L. Garvin, June 12, 1938. From the Robert Moses Archive at the New York Public Library, Box 97.

16. *Bronx Home News*, July 2, 1938.

17. *Bronx Home News*, July 12, 1938.

18. Ibid.

19. Letter from Robert Moses to Fiorello La Guardia, July 22, 1938. From the Robert Moses Archive at the New York Public Library, Box 97.

20. *New York Herald Tribune*, December 2, 1938.

21. *Bronx Home News*, April 1, 1938.

22. *Bronx Home News*, November 2, 1938.

23. *Bronx Home News*, November 3, 1938.

24. *Bronx Home News*, November 15, 1938.

25. Ibid.

26. *Bronx Home News*, November 17, 1938.

27. Ibid.

28. *New York Herald Tribune*, November 17, 1938.

29. Ibid.

30. *Bronx Home News*, November 17, 1938.

31. *New York Herald Tribune*, November 17, 1938.

32. Ibid.

33. Ibid.

34. *Bronx Home News*, November 17, 1938.

35. Ibid.

36. Ibid.

37. *Bronx Home News*, November 17, 1938.

38. *Brooklyn Eagle*, November 16, 1938.

39. *Bronx Home News*, November 17, 1938.

40. Which became the City Council in 1937.

41. *Bronx Home News*, November 23, 1938.

42. Ibid.

43. Ibid.

44. *Bronx Home News*, November 30, 1938.

45. Ibid.

46. *New York Times*, December 1, 1938.

47. *New York Herald Tribune*, December 1, 1938.

48. *Bronx Home News*, December 1, 1938.

49. Ibid.

50. *New York Times*, December 3, 1938.

51. *New York Times*, December 1, 1938.

52. Letter from Robert Moses to Fiorello La Guardia, December 21, 1938. From the Robert Moses Archives in the New York Public Library, Box 97.

53. *Bronx Home News*, January 1, 1939.

54. *Bronx Home News*, January 12, 1939.

55. *Bronx Home News*, January 14, 1939.

56. Ibid.

57. Ibid.

58. Ibid.

59. *Bronx Home News*, February 13, 1939.

60. *Bronx Home News*, February 16, 1939.

61. *Bronx Home News*, February 18, 1939.

62. *Bronx Home News*, February 23, 1939.

63. *Bronx Home News*, February 28, 1939.

64. See Chapter 4.

65. From the Ritchie Committee report, as published in the *Bronx Home News*, March 31, 1939.

66. *New York Times*, March 31, 1939.

67. Ibid.

68. Letter from Robert Moses to Herbert H. Lehman, March 28, 1939. From the New York City Municipal Archives.

69. *Bronx Home News*, April 7, 1939.

70. Ibid.

71. *New York Times*, June 19, 1939.

72. *Bronx Home News*, June 27, 1939.

73. *Bronx Home News*, June 28, 1939.

74. Ibid.

75. Ibid.

76. Letter from George F. Mand to Mayor Fiorello H. La Guardia, June 28, 1939. From the New York City Municipal Archives.

77. *Bronx Home News*, August 23, 1939.

78. Ibid.

79. Letter from Robert Moses to John Delaney, August 30, 1939. From the Robert Moses Archive at the New York Public Library, Box 97.

80. Letter from John H. Delaney to Robert Moses, September 1, 1939. From ibid.

81. Ibid.

82. Ibid.

83. Telegram from the Burke Avenue Property Owners and Business Men's Association to New York City Council President A. Newbold Morris, September 13, 1939. From the La Guardia and Wagner Archives at Fiorello H. La Guardia Community College.

84. *Bronx Home News*, September 15, 1939.

85. Letter from Council Member Joseph E. Kinsley to Mayor Fiorello H. La Guardia, September 21, 1939. From the New York City Municipal Archives.

86. *Bronx Home News*, October 10, 1939.

87. Ibid.

88. Telegram from the Burke Avenue Property Owners and Business Men's Association to New York City Council President A. Newbold Morris, October 26, 1939. From the La Guardia and Wagner Archives at Fiorello H. La Guardia Community College.

89. Telegram from the Emile J. Cavanaugh to A. Newbold Morris, October 26, 1939. From ibid.

90. Telegram from the Herman W. Johnston A. Newbold Morris, October 26, 1939. From ibid.

91. Letter from Paul Trapani to A. Newbold Morris, October 28, 1939. From ibid.

92. Letter from A. Newbold Morris to Paul Trapani, October 30, 1939. From ibid.

93. *Bronx Home News*, October 26, 1939.

94. *Bronx Home News*, October 31, 1939.

95. Ibid.

96. *Bronx Home News*, November 2, 1937.

97. Ibid.

98. *Mount Vernon Daily Argus*, November 2, 1939.

99. Ibid.

100. Ibid.

101. Letter from Paul Trapani to A. Newbold Morris, November 14, 1939. From the La Guardia and Wagner Archives at Fiorello H. La Guardia Community College.

102. *Bronx Home News*, November 19, 1939.

103. Telegram from Paul Trapani to A. Newbold Morris, November 24, 1939. From the La Guardia and Wagner Archives at Fiorello H. La Guardia Community College.

104. *Bronx Home News*, November 23, 1939.

105. *Bronx Home News*, November 26, 1939.

106. *Bronx Home News*, December 1, 1939.

107. *Bronx Home News*, December 12, 1939.

108. *New York Times*, January 13, 1940.

109. Letter from Herman W. Johnston to A. Newbold Morris, January 17, 1940. From the La Guardia and Wagner Archives at Fiorello H. La Guardia Community College.

110. *Report on Route No. 124 to the Board of Estimate by the New York City Board of Transportation*, February 6, 1940. From the New York City Transit Archives.

111. *Bronx Home News*, February 1, 1940.

112. Ibid.

113. Letter from Paul Trapani to Mayor Fiorello H. La Guardia, March 4, 1940. From the La Guardia and Wagner Archives at Fiorello H. La Guardia Community College.

114. *Bronx Home News*, March 8, 1940.

115. Ibid.

116. *New York Times*, March 23, 1940.

117. *Bronx Home News*, November 15, 1940.

118. *Bronx Home News*, February 4, 1941.

119. *Mount Vernon Daily Argus*, April 25, 1939.

120. *Mount Vernon Daily Argus*, May 16, 1941.

121. Ibid.

122. *North Side News*, May 16, 1941.

123. Letter from John H. Delaney to Rexford Guy Tugwell, June 17, 1941. From the New York City Municipal Archives.

124. *Bronx Home News*, November 1, 1941.

125. In 2011 dollars, $10.3 billion, according MeasuringWorth.com. See Chapter 10.

126. *Bronx Home News*, May 14, 1942.

127. *Bronx Home News*, September 3, 1942.

128. *Bronx Home News*, September 8, 1943.

129. *Bronx Home News*, December 4, 1944.

130. *North Side News*, November 20, 1943.

131. *Bronx Home News*, January 1, 1944.

9. BUILDING THE LINE THAT ALMOST NEVER WAS

1. Now St. James Place.

2. *New York Times*, December 20, 1904.

3. Brian J. Cudahy, *Under the Sidewalks of New York* (1979; Lexington, Mass.: Stephen Greene Press, 1988).

4. *Report of the Rapid Transit Railroad Commissioners*, 1904, p. 24.

5. Ibid.

6. The space left for track ramps are still visible on either side of the Nevins Street station, as is a third platform built under the existing outbound platform at that station. In effect, Nevins Street would have played the same role as a transfer station that DeKalb Avenue would for the BMT.

7. See Chapter 3.

8. *New York Times*, July 16, 1910. The extension of the H&M from 33rd Street and 6th Avenue to the Grand Central Terminal was never built.

9. The original IRT line consisted of the Lexington Avenue line south of 42nd Street, what is now the 42nd Street Shuttle, and the Broadway–7th Avenue line north of 42nd Street. By adding the northern extension of the Lexington Avenue line and the 7th Avenue line's southern extension, the PSC created a system in Manhattan that looked like an "H," and newspapers referred to it as such.

10. Office of the Transit Construction Commission, *A Report of the Chief Engineer Submitting for Consideration: A Comprehensive Rapid Transit Plan Covering All Boroughs of the City of New York*, July 29, 1920.

11. They would be put to use, but not for seven decades. Right now, they are used to allow for a connection with the 63rd Street line when needed; 2nd Avenue line trains will use them on a full-time basis when that line is put into service.

12. See Chapter 7.

13. *New York Times*, August 6, 1923.

14. The Bloomingdale family had a history of supporting transit construction. His father, Lyman, had led efforts to support the RTC plans for the East Side two decades earlier.

15. *New York Times*, December 20, 1924.

16. Ibid.

17. *New York Times*, June 12, 1925.

18. *New York Times*, January 17, 1927.

19. *New York Times*, April 6, 1929.

20. *New York Times*, August 30 and 31, 1929.

21. *New York Times*, October 6, 1929.

22. *New York Times*, January 12, 1930.

23. *New York Times*, April 5, 1931.

24. *New York Times*, May 7, 1931.

25. *First Avenue Association Bulletin*, no. 58, October 1932.

26. Stopping at the Court Street station, then part of a shuttle line running between there and Hoyt–Schermerhorn. The station closed in 1946 and later became the home of the New York Transit Museum.

27. *Bronx Home News*, September 28, 1930.

28. Most of it, anyway. Almost sixty years later, when the New York City Department of Transportation rebuilt 6th Avenue's roadway, they found that the footings of the 6th Avenue Elevated were still there. The structural columns had been removed in a way not dissimilar to cutting down a tree.

29. *Bronx Home News*, October 27, 1939.

30. *Bronx Home News*, October 28, 1939.

31. *New York Times*, February 23, 1940.

32. *New York Times*, May 29, 1942.

33. Ibid.

34. *Brooklyn Eagle*, June 6, 1940.

35. *New York Times*, June 7, 1940.

36. *New York Herald Tribune*, June 7, 1940.

37. *Long Island Daily Press*, May 29, 1942.

38. *Air and Space Magazine*, November 1, 2001. According to this article, when a Hellcat would land on an aircraft carrier, support crews would announce, "Here comes another piece of the Second Avenue El!"

39. From *The Third Rail Online*, July 2, 2001, available at http://www.thethirdrail.net/.

40. *Bronx Home News*, February 6, 1945.

41. *New York Times*, January 6, 1944.

42. See Appendix A.

43. Two years later, O'Dwyer would appoint Bingham to serve as BOT chairman.

44. A truncated version of this connection opened in 1968, connecting the lines running over the bridges with the 6th Avenue line.

45. *New York Herald Tribune*, December 16, 1947.

46. William A. Reid's career in the New York City government began during John Purroy Mitchel's administration and ended in that of Robert F. Wagner. He worked in the office of Comptroller William Prendergast in 1913 and served in a number of financial positions in the city government. He was the fiscal adviser to Fiorello H. La Guardia when he was appointed to the Board of Transportation. William O'Dwyer appointed Reid chairman of the BOT after Charles P. Gross resigned. He became deputy mayor of New York after Mayor O'Dwyer's reelection in 1949. He subsequently was the chairman of the Hudson and Manhattan Railroad and then served as the chairman of the New York City Housing Authority from 1958 through 1965. A Housing Authority development in Brooklyn is named after him.

47. *New York Times*, December 29, 1948.

48. *New York Times*, August 30, 1950.

49. *New York Times*, August 18, 1952.

50. The other stations closed for this reason during this period were City Hall, Worth Street, and 17th Street on the Lexington Avenue line and 91st Street on the Broadway–7th Avenue line.

51. *New York Times*, April 24, 1952.

52. In 2011 dollars, $12.2 million.

53. *New York Post*, January 26, 1954.

54. *New York Post*, June 3, 1954.

55. *Memorandum to the New York City Transit Authority: Demolition of Third Avenue Elevated Line South of 149th Street*, report to the TA Board by Colonel Sidney H. Bingham, July 1954.

56. *New York Times*, January 3, 1956.

57. *New York Herald Tribune*, September 23, 1955.

58. *New York Times*, September 23, 1955.

59. *New York Times*, April 24, 1956.

60. MacNeil Mitchell served in the New York State legislature for twenty-seven years. He is remembered for legislation written with Assembly Member Alfred A. Lama providing tax abatement and low-interest mortgages for developers and nonprofit organizations building middle-income co-op housing and housing with affordable rentals.

61. *New York Times*, January 18, 1957.

62. *New York Times*, March 9, 1957.

63. *New York Times*, November 26, 1957. This is the first instance I've found of plans to make any part of the subway system accessible to the elderly or disabled. Needless to say, the ramps were never built.

64. *New York Times*, January 2, 1968.

65. *New York Times*, August 13, 1968.

66. Ibid.

67. *New York Times*, May 24, 1969.

68. *New York Times*, August 15, 1968.

69. *New York Times*, March 5, 1969.

70. Ibid.

71. Ibid.

72. *New York Times*, June 5, 1969.

73. Later a member of the MTA Board.

74. *New York Times*, June 6, 1969.

75. *New York Times*, July 24, 1969.

76. Of "Hit Sign, Win Suit" at Ebbets Field fame.

77. Metropolitan Transportation Authority, *Public Hearing in the Matter of: Second Avenue Subway, Route 132A, East 34th Street to East 126th Street, Manhattan*, September 16, 1971, pp. 51–54.

78. In 2011 dollars, $134 million.

79. This was also the sixty-eighth anniversary of the opening of the original subway line.

80. *New York Times*, January 21, 1973.

81. *New York Times*, February 18, 1973.

82. Department of City Planning/Municipal Arts Society, *Humanizing Subway Entrances: Opportunity on Second Avenue*, New York, September 1974, p. 8.

83. *New York Times*, July 26, 1974.

84. *New York Times*, October 16, 1974.

85. *New York Times*, November 1, 1974.

86. *New York Times*, November 12, 1974.

87. *New York Times*, July 27, 1995.

88. *New York Times*, March 12, 1999.

89. "Public advocate" is the title of the position that has been known in the past as "president of the Board of Aldermen" and "City Council president."

90. NY1 News, May 13, 2003.

10. OTHER PLANS, OTHER LINES, OTHER ISSUES IN THE POSTWAR YEARS

1. *New York Times*, November 12, 1946.

2. Ibid.

3. *New York Times*, May 6, 1946.

4. The *Home News* itself was fading away, being slowly absorbed by the *New York Post*. In 1949 the *Home News* name would disappear.

5. *North Side News*, March 25, 1946.

6. From the text of the speech given by General Gross to the Bronx Board of Trade, reprinted in the April 1946 edition of *Bronxboro* magazine.

7. *Bronx Home News*, August 2, 1946.

8. *New York Post*, July 2, 1947.

9. *New York Post*, July 30, 1947.

10. *Long Island Star Journal*, January 28, 1946.

11. *New York Times*, May 30, 1947.

12. *New York Times*, November 1, 1947.

13. Sidney H. Bingham, born in Manhattan, began his career in transit with the IRT in 1915. He worked for the Army Railway Engineers during World War I and gained a degree in electrical engineering from Columbia University in 1922. He worked for the IRT and BOT until World War II, when he played a significant role in logistical planning before and during the Normandy invasion, gaining the rank of colonel. He returned to the BOT after the war, becoming chairman in 1950 and general manager and executive director of the TA. After his retirement in 1953, he spent the rest of his professional career working as a transit-planning consultant.

14. See Appendix B.

15. *New York Times*, March 2, 1948.

16. *New York Times*, March 30, 1948.

17. Letter from William Reid to the members of the Board of Estimate, November 30, 1948. From the New York City Municipal Archives.

18. Ibid.

19. *Long Island Daily Press*, June 24, 1948.

20. *New York Post and Home News*, December 6, 1948.

21. Ibid.

22. *New York Post and Home News*, January 25, 1949.

23. Ibid.

24. Ibid.

25. *New York Post and Home News*, March 25, 1949.

26. *New York World-Telegram*, November 5, 1949.

27. *New York Herald Tribune*, November 6, 1949.

28. *Brooklyn Eagle*, November 4, 1949.

29. *New York Herald Tribune*, November 5, 1949.

30. *New York Post*, November 6, 1949.

31. *Brooklyn Eagle*, June 22, 1949.

32. Ibid. The right-of-way underneath the line was envisioned as a parking area for beachgoers—then, as now, at a premium—but became one of the few east–west streets on the peninsula, the Rockaway Freeway.

33. *New York Times*, June 23, 1949.

34. *Brooklyn Eagle*, March 12, 1951.

35. *Brooklyn Eagle*, September 19, 1951.

36. *Brooklyn Eagle*, May 8, 1950; *New York Times*, May 9, 1950.

37. *Brooklyn Eagle*, May 31, 1950.

38. *New York Times*, May 17, 1951.

39. *New York Times*, September 11, 1951.

40. Ibid.

41. *New York Times*, September 14, 1951.

42. *Brooklyn Eagle*, September 14, 1951.

43. *New York Times*, March 4, 1952. The TBTA is now MTA Bridges and Tunnels.

44. *New York Times*, March 10, 1952.

45. *New York Herald Tribune*, October 9, 1952.

46. *New York Times*, October 27, 1952.

47. *Brooklyn Eagle*, March 18, 1953.

48. *Brooklyn Eagle*, March 21, 1953.

49. *New York Times*, March 27, 1953.

50. General Casey, born in Brooklyn, was a West Point graduate who earned a doctorate in engineering after World War I. He carried out hydropower and flood control projects in the United States and the Philippines and later played a major role in the design of the Pentagon. He was General Douglas MacArthur's chief engineer at the time of the start of the U.S. involvement in World War II. He was evacuated from the Philippines along with MacArthur and continued to serve as his chief engineer to the end of the war.

51. *New York Times*, June 2, 1953.

52. *Brooklyn Eagle*, June 17, 1953.

53. *New York Times*, July 14, 1953.

54. Ibid.

55. *New York Times*, January 6, 1955.

56. *New York Post*, December 19, 1954.

57. Charles L. Patterson, a native of Pittsburgh, was born into a railroading family. His grandfather was a vice president of the Baltimore and Ohio Railroad; his father worked for William Gibbs McAdoo at the Federal Railroad Administration during the First World War. Before coming to the New York City Transit Authority, he worked for the Pennsylvania Railroad, the Long Island Rail Road, the Lehigh Valley Railroad, the Duluth, Mesabi, and Iron Range Railroad, and the Bessamer and Lake Erie Railroad. His passing in 1962 was publicly mourned not only by elected officials and his colleagues in TA management, but by Michael J. Quill and the leadership of the Transport Work-

ers Union as well. His last place of residence was at 205 East 63rd Street, right over one of the subway lines that he would have been trying to build a few years later.

58. See Chapter 2.

59. The route that this line would have followed to the East River is unspecified, but based on other BOT plans it probably would have run under East 72nd Street.

60. *New York Times*, November 28, 1955.

61. Now WNBC-TV.

62. *Long Island Daily Press*, July 30, 1956.

63. *New York Times*, July 30, 1956.

64. *New York Times*, July 31, 1956.

65. *New York World Telegram and Sun*, July 31, 1956. The *Brooklyn Eagle* had ceased publication in 1955, and the *World Telegram and Sun* was trying to fill the void that the *Eagle* had left in providing coverage to Brooklyn.

66. *Long Island Star-Journal*, July 31, 1956.

67. *New York Times*, August 3, 1956.

68. *New York World Telegram and Sun*, August 2, 1956.

69. *New York Times*, July 17, 1957.

70. The discontinuation of service on the remainder of the Rockaway Beach line gave rise to what was then an innovation in transit service. Green Bus Lines Inc., one of several privately operated bus lines serving Queens, began service on the XQ23 bus line, which ran between Midtown Manhattan and the stations served by that LIRR line. This was the first of what would be many express bus routes in New York City.

71. *New York Times*, April 12, 1957.

72. Ibid.

73. *New York Times*, September 4, 1957.

74. *New York Times*, September 5, 1957.

75. *New York Times*, August 20, 1958.

76. *New York Times*, July 15, 1959.

77. *Long Island Star-Journal*, January 28, 1961.

78. *New York Times*, October 22, 1959.

79. *New York Times*, January 8, 1966.

80. *New York Times*, July 20, 1962.

81. Ibid.

82. *New York Times*, August 12, 1962.

83. Merrick Boulevard serves as the trunk route for a number of bus lines in southeastern Queens. This is the only proposal made by a public agency to build a subway line to run along it.

84. The Atlantic line is now known as the Far Rockaway line.

85. *New York Times*, May 3, 1963.

86. *New York Times*, July 24, 1963.

87. *New York Times*, August 4, 1963.

88. *New York Times*, December 28, 1963.

89. *New York Times*, February 24, 1964.

90. Ibid.

91. *New York Times*, December 10, 1964.

92. *New York Times*, December 16, 1964.

93. *New York Times*, January 15, 1965.

94. *New York Times*, March 8, 1966.

95. New York City Department of City Planning, *Queens–Long Island Rail Transit: A Transit Strategy for a Growing Metropolitan Corridor*, staff report prepared by Joseph McC. Leiper, January 1965, p. 21.

96. *A New Long Island Rail Road: A Report to Nelson A. Rockefeller, Governor of New York, from the Special Committee on the Long Island Rail Road*, February, 1965, p. 12.

97. *New York Times*, March 9, 1966.

11. WHAT HAPPENED TO THE REST OF THE SYSTEM?

1. Peter Derrick, *Tunneling to the Future: The Story of the Great Subway Expansion That Saved New York* (New York: New York University Press, 2001), 214.

2. Ibid.

3. *Brooklyn Daily Eagle*, October 10, 1921.

4. Clifton Hood, *722 Miles: The Building of the Subways and How They Transformed New York* (New York: Simon and Schuster, 1993), 196.

5. *New York Times*, February 8, 1925.

6. Hood, *722 Miles*, 227.

7. *New York Times*, October 6, 1921.

8. *New York Times*, October 25, 1921.

9. Charles Garrett, *The La Guardia Years* (New Brunswick: Rutgers University Press, 1961), 211–12.

10. August R. Heckscher with Phyllis Robinson, *When La Guardia Was Mayor* (New York: W.W. Norton, 1978), 377.

11. Ibid., 378.

APPENDIX B. THE 1947 2ND AVENUE SERVICE PLAN

1. *New York Herald Tribune*, December 16, 1947.

2. Current service—A and C lines.

3. Current service—B and D lines.

4. Current service—No. 6 line.

5. Current service—E, F, M, and R lines.

6. Current service—R line.

7. Current service—N line.

8. Current service—D Line.

9. Current service—F line.

10. Current service—B and Q lines.

11. Current service—L line.

12. Current service—A and C lines.

13. Current service—J and Z lines.

14. Current service—Nos. 2 and 5 lines.

APPENDIX C. THE CAST OF CHARACTERS

1. It is expected that the Q line will run along the 2nd Avenue line when it opens. Another route designation will be used for the second route on the Astoria line

2. All shuttle lines carry the S designation.

3. This is the line segment from Ozone Park to the Rockaways.

Bibliography

Brooks, Michael W. *Subway City: Riding Trains, Reading New York.* New Brunswick: Rutgers University Press, 1997.

Cudahy, Brian J. *Under the Sidewalks of New York: The Story of the World's Greatest Subway System.* Lexington, Mass.: Stephen Greene Press, 1985.

Dahl, Gerhard M. *Transit Truths.* New York: Era Publications, 1924.

Derrick, Peter. *Tunneling to the Future: The Story of the Great Subway Expansion That Saved New York.* New York: New York University Press, 2001.

Fein, Michael R., *Paving the Way: New York Road Building and the American State, 1880–1956.* Lawrence: University Press of Kansas, 2008.

Fischler, Stan. *Uptown, Downtown: A Trip Through Time on New York's Subways.* New York: Hawthorn Books, 1976.

Fogelson, Robert M. *Downtown: Its Rise and Fall, 1880–1950.* New Haven: Yale University Press, 2001.

Garrett, Charles. *The LaGuardia Years: Machine and Reform Politics in New York City.* New Brunswick: Rutgers University Press, 1961.

Harwood, Herbert H. *The New York, Westchester, and Boston Railway: J. P. Morgan's Magnificent Mistake.* Bloomington: Indiana University Press, 2008.

Heckscher, August R., and Phyllis Robinson. *When LaGuardia Was Mayor: New York's Legendary Years.* New York: W. W. Norton, 1978.

Hood, Clifton. *722 Miles: The Building of the Subways and How They Transformed New York.* New York: Simon and Schuster, 1993.

Kaplan, Lawrence, and Carol P. Kaplan. *Between Ocean and City: The Transformation of Rockaway, New York.* New York: Columbia University Press, 2003.

Kramer, Frederick A. *Building the Independent Subway: The Technology and Intense Struggle of New York City's Most Gigantic Venture.* New York: Quadrant Press, 1990.

———. *Subway to the World's Fair.* Westfield, N.J.: Bells and Whistles, 1991.

Lewinson, Edwin R. *John Purroy Mitchel: The Boy Mayor of New York.* New York: Astra Books, 1965.

Lewis, Harold MacLean. *A Concrete Plan for a Better Description of New York's Commuter Traffic from Westchester.* New York: Parsons Brinckerhoff, 1929.

Malcolm, Tom. *William Barclay Parsons: A Renaissance Man of Old New York.* New York: Parsons, Brinckerhoff, 2010.

Queens Planning Commission. *Initial Report of Queens Planning Commission.* Edited by H. J. Haarmeyer. New York: Queens Planning Commission, 1929.

———. *Report of Queens Planning Commission.* Edited by Leon M. Schoonmaker, assisted by Andrew L. Muller. New York: Tavern Printing Corporation, 1937.

Thomas, Lately. The *Mayor Who Mastered New York: The Life and Opinions of William J. Gaynor.* New York: Morrow, 1969.

Ultan, Lloyd. *The Beautiful Bronx, 1920–1950.* Westport, Conn.: Arlington House, 1979.

Walker, James Blaine. *Fifty Years of Rapid Transit, 1864–1914.* New York: Law Printing Company, 1918.

William E. Harmon and Company Inc. *South New York, Formerly Staten Island: A Booklet Relating to Property for Sale at South New York.* New York: Wood, Harmon, 1906.

———. *Wood-Harmon Magazine* (New York). August 1902–January 1918.

Willis, Walter I. *Queens Borough.* Brooklyn: Brooklyn Eagle Press, 1913.

Acknowledgments

This book is the result of a labor of love that took many years to achieve fruition. I am indebted to a number of people who helped me complete the work.

It would be wrong for me to not mention first Robert Olmsted and Stephen Dobrow. They both knew far more about the New York City transit system than I could ever aspire to learn. I wish that they were both still here for me to personally express my gratitude to them.

I owe a great deal of thanks to the faculty of York College and Queens College of the City University of New York. I gained an appreciation for doing research and learning that I never quite had before, which has served me very well since then. I particularly want to remember Peter Wengert and Edward Rogowsky at York and Carol Brown and David Gurin at Queens.

If there is one person who was indispensible to making this book a reality, it's my friend and former neighbor Peter Eisenstadt. He did more than did anyone else to give the whole project focus and push me in the right direction. I also want to thank my colleagues at MTA New York City Transit, Glenn Lunden and Jeffrey Erlitz, for their advice and kind words.

I can't say enough about the help that I've gotten from the New York Transit Museum and its Archives. Gabrielle Shubert heads one of the great research resources on New York City history—not just transit history—an institution that has been invaluable to me. I particularly want to thank Carey Stumm for all her help.

Many words of praise are also owed to the staffs of the New York, Queens, and Brooklyn Public Libraries and the Brooklyn and Bronx Historic Societies for their help, despite the ways that I've terrorized them over the past two decades or so, looking for more information. Dr. Peter Derrick of the Bronx County Historical Society has also been of major help to me.

And I must say many words of thanks to my other family, the Division of Government and Community Relations at MTA New York City Transit, for putting up with all my talk about unbuilt subway lines for such a long time. Having gotten all this out of my system in this book, I can finally talk about other things as well.

And a few more words about my dad, Jack Raskin, whose memories of the Burke Avenue line started me on my trips along New York City's unbuilt subway lines. He passed away on January 27, 2013, after ninety years and three weeks of a wonderful life that touched countless others. There's never going to be a time in my life when I won't be missing him a lot. I wish that he was still here to read this book, but I have the feeling that he's looking over my shoulder as I type these words.

Index